Resources for
Early Childhood

GARLAND REFERENCE LIBRARY
OF SOCIAL SCIENCE
(VOL. 118)

RESOURCES FOR EARLY CHILDHOOD

An Annotated Bibliography and Guide for Educators, Librarians, Health Care Professionals, and Parents

Hannah Nuba Scheffler

GARLAND PUBLISHING, INC. • NEW YORK & LONDON
1983

Library of Congress Cataloging in Publication Data

Scheffler, Hannah Nuba
    Resources for early childhood.

    (Garland reference library of social science;
v. 118)
    Includes indexes.
    1. Child development—Abstracts.   2. Child develop-
ment—Addresses, essays, lectures.   3. Child development—Bibliography.   I. Title.   II. Series.
HQ767.9.S3   1983   016.3052'3   81-48421
ISBN 0-8240-9390-9

Cover design by Laurence Walczak

Printed on acid-free, 250-year-life paper
Manufactured in the United States of America

Contents

Preface   vii

Foreword   ix

Introduction   xi

Pregnancy, Birth, and the First Year   1

Child Development   37

The Family   77

Parenting   105

Health   167

Nutrition   201

Children's Play   227

Choices in Child Care and Management of
   Child Care Settings   253

Schooling   281

Literature   329

Expressive Arts   365

Multicultural Education   407

Special Needs   427

Nonsexist Education   479

Film and Television   495

Resources for Service and Information   509

Afterword   527

Index   533

Preface

Recent years have seen an extraordinary flourishing of research in early childhood.

This volume, the first of its kind, represents a unique approach to the diverse and prolific materials in the field. *Resources for Early Childhood: An Annotated Bibliography and Guide for Educators, Librarians, Health Care Professionals, and Parents*, a selective cross-section to the literature, is designed to meet the informational needs of all concerned with the well-being of young children. Materials have been chosen on the basis of timeliness, contribution to the field, and relevance to parents and professionals. Inevitably, materials have been omitted. In fact, some deserving sources are not included because of their similarity to those selected. The intended scope is comprehensive and embodies all the major areas in early childhood, including those that meet special needs, and primarily covers the best of the last decade in the literature of early childhood.

Developed as a reference tool, the book is topically organized into sixteen chapters—each preceded by cogent essays by leaders in the field—followed by annotated, evaluative bibliographic entries. Materials have been compiled based on the resources housed at The New York Public Library Early Childhood Resource and Information Center; however, the book is national in scope, and the materials are available throughout the country. Indexes list community and education services throughout the country found in the chapter on resources.

Framed by Dr. Burton White's Foreword and Dr. Bettye Caldwell's Afterword, each chapter reflects the insights and responses of the particular chapter's essayists and compilers. The joint efforts, by editors and contributors alike, intertwined with committment and conviction in the value of this undertaking, were the vital sparks that made this long-awaited work a reality.

It is not possible to recognize and acknowledge all who directly or indirectly gave of time and energy in the preparation of a work of this scope. Special tribute, however, must be given to Marie Ellen Larcada, who kindled the idea and gave invaluable guidance throughout the stages of the book's development; to the editorial committee, Drs. Bernice Cullinan, Dorothy Strickland, Renee Queen, who were the "guiding lights" along the way; to Drs. Jeanne Chall, Burton White, Israel Scheffler, Howard Coron, who were there, right from the start; to the members of The New York Public Library Resource and Information Center's Advisory Committee for their valuable insights and suggestions; to my colleagues of The New York Public Library, outstanding among them, Barbara Rollock, Coordinator of the Office of Children's Services, who wrote the proposal that started the center.

Hannah Nuba Scheffler
Director, The New York Public Library
Early Childhood Resource and Information Center

Foreword

Since 1965 and the initiation of the Head Start program, the field of Early Childhood Education has undergone a remarkable expansion and transformation. I think it's fair to say that, prior to that time, the bulk of the activities in Early Childhood Education focused on nursery school, kindergarten, and the elementary grades and, on the whole, was regarded by the education community as a comparatively low status venture. All that changed in the years following 1965. The field as a whole, and the public, too, now assigns far more importance to a solid beginning for the developing child. Especially important in the new view are the developments of the first few years of life, which, prior to the 1960s, were regarded as having nothing to do with serious educational issues.

Accompanying the growth of interest in the early years of a child's life has been an enormous increase in the amount of published material, ranging from basic research reports, on through applied research, and ultimately to materials for the public. For example, in the years since 1965 an average of about thirty-six books on how to raise children have appeared annually. The publications of research likewise have grown in numbers to a truly formidable total. As a result, it has become difficult, if not impossible, for parents and professionals alike to deal with this enormous mass. Since many views that have been put forward conflict, or in other ways are confusing, there has developed a need for authoritative and coherent treatments of the material. Professional response to this need has been diverse. One type of response has been the creation of The New York Public Library Resource and Information Center in New York City. Other resource centers have been sponsored by state departments of education, as in Minnesota and New York, or by mental health groups.

Resources for Early Childhood: An Annotated Bibliography and Guide for Educators, Librarians, Health Care Professionals and Parents is a very special addition to the effort to help parents and professionals. The volume consists of carefully selected, high-quality treatments of many facets of the complicated and important topic of Early Childhood Education. Because of its quality and its comprehensiveness, it is therefore a rare and special contribution to the subject.

Thanks are due particularly to Hannah Nuba Scheffler for initiating this effort and for persisting in seeing it through to completion. Also, of course, gratitude is owed to the many professionals who have donated their time to this valuable project.

Burton L. White
Director, the Center for Parent Education
Newton, Massachusetts

Introduction

It is a library! . . . or is it? If you were to mount the steps and enter The New York Public Library's Early Childhood Resource and Information Center, chances are that you would be greeted by the sounds of children's voices and happy noises. Glancing to the right, your eyes would confirm what your ears had discerned, the sounds of babes in arms, barely ambulatory toddlers ensconced in a couple of play pens, and active two-, three-, or four-year-olds exploring and using the learning tools placed strategically around the room. Some children are organizing themselves spontaneously into groups of three or four to slide to the floor or to share the building blocks or are simply enjoying a one-to-one sharing experience with a book while in the lap of an accompanying parent or caregiver. Among the very young children, assorted adults meander amiably or watchfully, but all seem to be involved in the activities in the room.

I mention all this in order to place in context the contents of this resource book. Like the center, it is a working tool that grew out of contributions, suggestions, and labors of professionals and practitioners in the field of Early Childhood Education. Many of the works cited have been written or created by the very professionals who form a vital part of the center's Advisory Committee. Few library collections can boast such a strong relationship to those active in the field that The New York Library's Early Childhood Center strives to present for public information or perusal.

Each chapter of the resource book, as a consequence, is introduced by a professional who has either recommended, used, or made a contribution to the literature in the particular area of the field of Early Childhood Education under consideration. The majority of the materials cited are recent, expressing contemporary thought and theories about child rearing and child development. There are sources for practical discussion or study, geared to students in the field as well as the lay persons who are parents, day-care personnel, or others whose concerns stem from their work or living experience with preschoolers.

Among the works cited, one may find something for the expectant father, the minority parent, or teenage mother, or books that explore the shibboleths of early sexual stereotyping, or information about early giftedness or disabilities in childhood. The range of topics is remarkably broad in a compact and selected collection such as this. The volume is fitting documentation for a modern library that shares a mutuality of interests with other cultural and educational institutions in its immediate community. It not only reflects the interests of the center's community but extends beyond those boundaries.

This book reveals a library, reaching beyond its walls, involving all possible resources, people as well as books and other forms of recorded knowledge, to transmit the information its patrons most frequently request.

Barbara Rollock
Coordinator of Children's Services
The New York Public Library

Editorial Committee

Bernice Cullinan, Ph.D.
Dorothy Strickland, Ph.D.
Renee Queen, Ph.D.

Essayists

Joan Hagan Arnold, R.N., M.A.
School of Nursing, Adelphi University

Frances Weber Aronoff, Ph.D.
Music Education, New York University

Lawrence Balter, Ph.D.
Professor of Educational Psychology,
New York University
Psychoeducation Center
Child Psychologist, WABC "Talk Radio"

Beryle Banfield, Ph.D.
The Council on Interracial Books, Inc.

Vicki Breitbart, M.C., C.S.W.
Bank Street College of Education
Kingsborough Community College
Methodist Hospital

Deirdre Breslin, Ph.D.
Fordham University
New York State Division of Substance
Abuse

Bettye M. Caldwell, Ph.D.
Donaghy Professor of Education
University of Arkansas, Little Rock

Bertha D. Campbell, M.A.
Director of Child Development
and Parent Education
SUNY, State Education Department

Jeanne Chall, Ph.D.
Harvard University

Alexandria Church, M.A.
Educational Consultant

Joseph Church, Ph.D.
Brooklyn, College of the City
University of New York

Catherine Cowell, Ph.D.
New York City Dept of Health
Bureau of Nutrition

Bernice Cullinan, Ph.D.
New York University

David Elkind, Ph.D., Eliot Pearson
Department of Child Study
Tufts University

Vincent Fontana, M.D.
New York Foundling Hospital
Mayor's Task Force of Child Abuse
and Neglect

xiii

xiv

Dolores Welber
Psychoanalyst

Burton L. White, Ph.D.
The Center for Parent Education
Newton, Massachusetts

Chapter Coordinators

Vicki Breitbart
Deirdre Breslin
Ellen Brooks
Vivien P. Y. Chen
Alexandria Church
Phyllis Cohen
Shirley Cowan
Francine Cristel
Rosemary J. Diulio
Wende Doniger
Merle Froschl
Nancy Gropper
Jane Hornburger

Dolores Kazanjian
Arlene Litwack
Barbara Mates
Luberta Mays
Naomi Noyes
Clara Lluberes Ostrowski
Marguerita Rudolph
Judith Schwartz
Michael Searson
Deborah Lovitky Sheiman
Maureen Slonim
Iris R. Sutherland

Contributors

Deborah Allen
Dorothy Arkell
Gertrude Asher
Fran Barnes
Florence Baskas
Lynn Snyder Beer
June Berger
Joanne E. Bernstein
Jennifer Birckmayer
Theodora Blackman
Rima Blair
Helen Boehm
Frances S. Bolin
Mary Jane Bolin

Ann S. Bowden
Muriel Broadman
Claudine K. Brown
Jan Brown
Nancy Brussolo
Phyllis Bryce
Mary Burns
Kent Garland Burtt
Elva Pilgrim Butler
Carolyn W. Carmichael
Anjean B. Carter
Lisa Challenger
Mirina T. Chaplin
Sylvia Chavkin

Edward Chittenden
Frances Connor
Anne Cook
Eileen Cowe
Angela Cox
Lorna Davis
Joan Dithchik
Stuart Doline, D.D.S.
Amy Laura Dombro
Catherine Dorsey-Gaines
Carol Dowdy
Julia Drake
Jan Drucker
Virginia Ehrlich

Linda Elswick
Margo Ely
Barbara Engel
Joanna M. Erickson
Beth Estrine
Betty Farber
Rachel Feldman
Cecil Frey
Barbara Mayers Friedlander
Maureen Gaffney
Ellen Galinsky
Joy Garland
Joanna Gaughan
Audrey Gaul
Judith Gellman
Felicia George
Mary Joan Gerson
Sybil Gilmar
Joyce Corner Glassman
Robin Glazer
Susan M. Glazer
Lin Goetz
Ruby Goode
Ellen Gruber
Henry S. Hale
Arline Harris
Elaine Heffner
Rochelle Hendlin
Celia Henerofsky
Laurel L. Hinze
Sister Margaret Mary Holden
Alice S. Honig
Margaret Houlihan
Margaret Howe
Helen Iaankos
Lucia Jack
Ruth Jacobson
Angela Jagger
Beatrice Kelvin
Rosalie B. Kiah

Glenn Koponen
Mary Ann Lang
Lila Lasky
Debbie Lefkowitz
Gail Levine
Lucille Lindberg
Beth Linnerson
Tony Liquori
Julianne Lutz
Cathy Lyons
Elin McCoy
Carol McLoughlin
Carabelle McNeil
Jean Mandelbaum
Rosalee Mazur
Laura Merkelson
Ellen Meyers
Edwina Meyers-Lynch
Anita Miller
Mary Miller
Cynthia G. Jones Moore
Lorette Moser
Nancy Nager
Gwen Neser
Carol Nuba
Robert Nuba, M.D.
Norma Nurse
Gertrude Orion
Lillian Oxtoby
Jacqueline S. Paulson
Elizabeth Bernard Pettit
Barbara Pilon
Karen M. Quinn
Bertha Raphael
Carol Raphael
Mary Reath
Janet S. Reinbrecht
Esther Robison
Gail Robinson
Paula Rohrlick

Minerva Rosaria
Jean Roshei
Susan Rubin
Steven Ruffin
Sheila E. Sadler
Nancy Samalin
Shirley C. Samuels
Marion Alice Sanborn
Lillian Shapiro
Rochelle Shatzman
Shirley Shufer
Ann Simon
Ruby Sinckler
Dorothy Singer
Alene Smith
David Smith
Madeline Smith
Ruth Spencer
Miriam Stecher
Sr. Susan Steremberg
Virginia Scott Sterling
Sylvia Stovall
Ruth Stukalin
Rita Swedlow
Christine Takacs
Denny Taylor
Leslie Tedeschi
Laura J. Tenenbaum
Kathy Tolman
Joan Treble
Terri G. Trilling
Patricia Suarez Weiss
Robert Wilkes
Gloria Wolinsky
Evangeline Vaughan
Clara V. Velaques
Steve Yarvies
Evelyn Yee
Paula Zajan

1
Pregnancy, Birth, and the First Year

PREGNANCY AND CHILDBIRTH

Gail Sinquefield

According to Asian custom a child is credited with the age of one year on the day of its birth as a recognition of the enormous growth and development that has already taken place since conception. Although there is some controversy among experts about how much human beings are affected by the birth experience itself, many psychologists, such as Otto Rank and Arthur Janov, believe it to be the most important event in life. Thus it seems that the management of these early months of prenatal life and the circumstances surrounding birth set the stage for future potential and development of each individual.

In the United States today most women having their first baby find themselves ill prepared for such an important life event. Separation from an extended family often means lack of experience in infant care as well as an absence of supportive persons during this critical time. Educational systems have not prepared the women for pregnancy, childbirth, and parenthood, and many experience deep fears of giving birth. The traditional American way of birth still features a passive mother and non-participating father, relying on medical experts to guide them safely through this hazardous experience.

Medical experts have in fact designed impressive technology to insure safe passage of the infant through its prenatal life, birth, and early infancy. Physicians today are able to diagnose, medicate, and even operate on fetuses in utero to correct certain abnormalities. Pregnancies that were conceived in the laboratory rather than in the mother's body can be carried to term. Very small premature infants now have a much greater prognosis for survival due to neonatal intensive care units. Women with chronic illnesses such as diabetes and heart disease are often able to give birth to healthy children. Older women can determine that their babies are "normal" before deciding to continue the pregnancy.

Obstetricians in general have begun to develop practices that specialize in the treatment of "high-risk" patients. Risk factors such as age, disease, previous obstetrical problems, and genetic factors are identified early in pregnancy and become the focal point in planning prenatal and delivery management. Such technical procedures as sonography, amniocentesis, fetal activity or stress testing, and electronic fetal monitoring are utilized frequently to detect fetal abnormalities or distress. In such high-risk practices medical intervention has profoundly changed the natural course of childbirth. Women are commonly medicated or anesthetized during delivery, labor is frequently induced, and birth by Cesarean section has risen as high as 25 percent in many hospitals.

Although the application of technology to the field of obstetrics has undoubtedly improved the outcome of truly high-risk pregnancies, the routine utilization of these techniques in apparently normal, low-risk pregnancies and deliveries has become cause for question and even alarm among many professionals and parents.

Even though the public educational systems do not generally prepare young couples for childbirth and parenthood, many prospective parents today are breaking from the traditional American way of birth and seeking alternatives in which there is a shared responsibility between themselves and health care providers. Parents are beginning to see themselves as consumers of health care and are demanding a more egalitarian relationship with their physician. Childbirth education is readily available in most parts of the country, and childbirth educators usually view their role not only as educators but also as advocates for parents. Classes include both breathing and relaxation techniques to promote a "natural" childbirth and instructions on how to make the health care system more responsive to individual needs.

Due in part to a growing literature in childbirth-related subjects, many parents realize that there are alternatives in pregnancy and birth management available to them, and they actively seek out the type of care that best suits their goals. A declining birth rate in recent years also has functioned to make both professionals and hospitals more receptive to consumer influence in determining their practices surrounding childbirth. In response primarily to consumer demands, numerous hospitals, particularly smaller ones, have adopted a family-centered approach to childbirth. Such a program usually makes provision for a support person during labor and delivery, encouragement of natural childbirth, active help with breast-feeding and infant care, birthing rooms, rooming-in facilities, sibling visits, and early discharge. Even high-technology medical centers have begun to allow a father to be present in the operating room during a Cesarean birth to support his wife and to allow early contact with his newborn child.

Childbirth experts believe that the way a woman feels emotionally and physically during pregnancy and delivery and the amount of contact she has with her baby immediately after birth strongly influence her feelings about being a mother. Research by Marshall Klaus and John Kennell, both professors of pediatrics, has shown that early contact between parents and their newborn helps to establish a bonding that will favorably influence future interactions. Unfortunately, the American way of childbirth has long been insensitive to this need, and routine separation of parents and their infants has been the rule in most hospitals. Family-centered approaches such as rooming-in, which allows mother and infant to remain together in the same room for most of their hospital stay, are aimed at changing this situation.

Primarily due to the work of a French obstetrician, Dr. Frederick Leboyer, attention also has begun to focus on minimizing the traumatic aspects of the birth process that the infant may experience. Although still considered highly controversial by most American obstetricians, a gentle birth approach is requested by increasing numbers of parents. Such an approach primarily involves soft lighting at delivery and immediate skin to skin contact between mother and infant, followed by a warm tub bath for the baby. The bath is generally administered by the father and not only has the advantage of easing the transition into life outside the womb, but also provides an excellent opportunity for father-infant bonding. Thus in a Leboyer birth gentle handling and quiet observation of the newborn are substituted for the loud and often rough stimulation with which infants are traditionally greeted in American hospital delivery rooms.

For most American women the obstetrician is still the birth attendant of choice. In their search for health providers who are more responsive to their individual needs, however, many couples are turning to nurse-midwives. Certified nurse-midwives are experts in the care of normal women during pregnancy and birth, but they always work cooperatively with obstetricians should problems develop. Midwives generally provide a flexible, naturally oriented type of care with emphasis on counseling and teaching as well as providing medical management. Nurse-midwives tend to avoid routine interventions in the labor and delivery processes; however, they are trained to use appropriate technology in case of complications. Perhaps the most appreciated aspect of midwife care is the supportive presence throughout the labor and delivery processes.

Some parents have become so dissatisfied with the restrictions of American hospitals, however, that they are seeking birth settings outside the hospital. In some parts of the country home births are once again increasing in number. Nationwide organizations have formed to help such parents plan for and find qualified assistance for home births. Although a small group of obstetricians and nurse-midwives attend home deliveries, many are attended by lay midwives and others are carried out by parents with no professional help.

In 1976, the Maternity Center Association in New York City opened their Childbearing Center, a unit designed to provide safe, family-centered, low-cost maternity care outside a hospital. Following this model, numerous other such centers have opened around the country. All screen patients carefully to rule out high-risk situations and most are located within minutes of hospital backup services in case of unexpected problems. Many of these alternative birth centers are staffed by nurse-midwives who attempt to provide "homelike deliveries" without sacrificing safety features.

In reviewing childbirth options available in the United States today, two things become apparent. Both obstetrical technology and the humanistic family-centered approach to childbirth are important and well established. It remains for parents and professionals to continue to work together so that each philosophy can be utilized appropriately to give all children a safe and satisfying beginning.

BEFORE BIRTH AND THE FIRST MONTHS OF LIFE

Dorothy W. Gross

The human infant begins its development in its mother's womb in a complex and remarkable process. The first eight weeks after conception are a particularly crucial period, with the unborn child being most vulnerable to disruptions and adverse influences. For example, the first three months of pregnancy are critical for the development of the heart, eyes, and ears; after the third month the first real bone cells are formed. Also during the third month the process of sex differentiation takes place, and during the fourth month the unborn baby grows more than in any other period. (By the end of that month, it weighs about 6 ounces and measures about 6 inches.) The fetus now can turn its head, push its arms and legs about, even suck its thumb. Because of all this activity, this is the time when many mothers first experience "quickening," a term given to the exciting movement of the baby in the womb. By the fifth month a regular sleep/wake pattern has been established, and many babies have selected a favorite position. Taste buds form in the sixth month, the grasp reflex develops, the baby even opens its eyelids. In the last trimester of pregnancy, growth slows down while the baby's sensory systems develop further, particularly touch and hearing.

The most remarkable aspect of prenatal development is the way in which it reflects both the baby's own nature and biological drive and the state of the mother during pregnancy. Her age, height, and weight, her blood oxygen level; whether she smokes, drinks coffee, takes drugs, receives radiation; her nutrition and her level of stress; the existence of disease—all of these are highly significant for the baby's development. Despite the great susceptibility of the human organism to all these influences, most babies are born normal. This is because of what has been called the "self-righting" tendency, a built-in mechanism to produce normal outcomes in all but the most adverse circumstances. This interaction, between the unborn infant and its environment, is characteristic of the process of development, both physical and psychological, after birth and, indeed, throughout life. How does it work?

Within the very first weeks of life, babies demonstrate a remarkable set of capacities. They are highly sensitive to their environment and they can take in much information because the brain and the nervous system are constantly receiving and registering stimulation. They are able to react differentially to a variety of stimuli—and they have innate preferences for human voices and faces, for patterned objects, for certain colors (especially blue and red), for rhythmic movements, for sweet tastes, for warmth, for novelty. They can protect themselves from overly intense stimuli (like loud sounds, strong lights, constant jiggling) by shutting them out, pushing them away, even by falling asleep in the face of too much disturbance. They can make their needs known by crying and grimacing and wriggling. They can evoke concern, care, and feelings of affection by cuddling, clinging, and following faces with their eyes. They have a strong drive for survival and possess the reflexes to support it, like rooting for food, sucking, swallowing, grasping, blinking if an object approaches the face. As early as two weeks of age, infants can distinguish their mothers' faces from strangers', and even earlier than that, their movements are synchronized in precise time to human speech.

All babies have these basic reflexes and sensory sensitivities; they represent the human potential for physical, mental, and emotional development. Yet, all babies are different. They have distinct individual activity levels, natures, and temperaments. How each baby develops is always a function of the unique ways in which he or she interacts with his or her particular environment. That interaction creates what we may call the baby's "effective" environment, not necessarily what actually occurs. What does this really mean? Let us look at two hypothetical babies within the first three months of life and contrast their effective environments.

Erica is a big (9 pounds, 4 ounces at birth), lusty, active, intense baby. If she is uncomfortable or hungry, she yells loudly—and her parents come running. She sucks her mother's nipples in a greedy, gulping way, and when her belly feels nicely full, she relaxes into a deep sleep. When awake, she appears to be in perpetual motion, moving her arms and legs in rhythmic patterns, turning her head, beginning to reach for objects that come near, "cruising" around her crib. Often she builds up too much steam, becoming overexcited by her own activity, and then she begins to cry. At such times only the touch of her mother's hand or being held closely in an upright position is able to calm her down—but even these are not always effective, and then her loud shrieks persist either until she falls asleep exhausted or she is vigorously rocked in her carriage. When she is in a calm, alert state, she is able to examine the world around her with interest—her mobile, the bright design on her pillow, the pattern made on the wall by the sun, her father's face—and her examination is almost always active, mouthing or reaching. She tends to react to most stimuli with vigor and excitement: intense stares, frowns, loud crying, repetitive shaking of her legs, restlessness when being diapered, cocking her head at new sounds, even beginning vocalizing. Although she is persistent in pursuing satisfaction when wet, hungry, or uncomfortable, at other times she can be distracted by being rocked or being offered a toy or a pacifier. The intensity of Erica's demands and her high activity level make her, in some ways, a difficult baby for her parents—but because of her positive interest in everything and her quick responsiveness, they also find her an exciting little person to be with.

Jonathan is entirely different—relatively inactive, able to soothe himself by sucking his hands, nondemanding, regular in his patterns of eating and sleeping. He is able to go for long periods without demanding attention. Left in his crib, he is content to spend much time staring at his fingers, the wall hanging near his crib, the curtain swaying in the breeze. He responds to gentle sounds: when he hears his mother's voice or soft music on the radio, he turns his head in their direction. In addition, although he does not demand it, when his father rocks him gently back and forth in his arms, Jonathan's enjoyment is evident. Unlike Erica, he shows his displeasure in quiet ways, by turning his head away from the unwanted stimulus or simply by behaving as if it was not there. Further, too much exertion all at once does not lead to excitement and out-of-control shrieks, or even to crying, but to quiet frowns and often, to falling asleep. Also unlike Erica, whose connection to her world is through movement of her total body, Jonathan's primary mode of expression is visual and auditory. Sometimes, he is so quiet, watching the patterns of light at his window or listening to the music box next to his changing table, that his parents are uneasy. He seems almost too "good," too able to amuse himself. But they are reassured as they note his sensitivity to his environment: he is increasingly unwilling to accept substitutes for his mother when being given his bottle, and he shows a definite preference for one of his toys, a yellow teddy bear. Gentle stimulation is what he seems to enjoy, and as his parents learn how to respond to that style, they note that Jonathan's satisfaction seems to increase.

Both children are healthy suckers, but because of their different styles (Erica intense, almost greedy, Jonathan more even), their feeding experiences are very different. If, for example, the milk does not flow quite freely enough, Erica becomes almost frantic; Jonathan pauses, as if quizzical, then goes on sucking. Both children are responsive to stimuli, different ones and in different ways. Erica is often not even aware of the very stimuli that are most interesting to Jonathan—the gentle tinkle of the wind chimes, the sway of leaves in the wind. He, on his part, turns away from the vigorous bouncing that delights Erica. Both babies have the same number of loving parents (and grandparents who are nearby)—but Erica is frequently surrounded by much bustle and noise, while Jonathan lives in a quiet world where people's comings and goings are less accompanied by exclamations and sudden swoops. This is only partly because of differences in the two families. The babies themselves evoke varying responses: in Erica's case often a rush to alleviate her loud expressed frustration or pain; for Jonathan, quiet watching in order to ascertain his needs or preferences.

In other words, the effective environment for these two babies—and for all babies—is largely determined by the nature of their sensory systems and temperaments. Which aspects of the external environment they detect, how they take these in and integrate them, the style and intensity of their responses, as well as the ways in which they detect and respond to their own internal states, are critical for how they experience their environments. The same kind of *actual* experience, in an adult view, may have a very different impact on different babies and therefore have a different meaning for them. What would be experienced as respectful nonintrusiveness by Jonathan might mean neglect for Erica, while exciting interaction for her would likely be felt by him as assaultive.

What is most significant—even awe-inspiring—during the first few months of life is the way in which each infant learns to link his repeated sense impressions with his body feelings and emotional states, thereby investing those impressions with personal meaning. For example, Jonathan begins to connect the rosy night light in his room with the warm feeling in his belly, and Erica puts together the excitement of being rocked in a carriage with her subsequent collapse in tears. How do such linkages come about, since the very young infant is not cognitively advanced enough to figure them out on his own? Let us look at the process.

In the beginning, an infant does not differentiate between himself and others. He likely experiences himself as merged or continuous with the world, including his mother or caregivers. The implication of such continuity is that he cannot see them as separate people who can respond (or not) to his needs and expectations. Instead, he feels his own experience as fused with everything else in his world. Gradually, as he is indeed cared for and responded to, the baby begins to differentiate the quality of his experience, pleasurable from painful. Gradually, he comes to know that there is an agent "out there" helping to produce this experience. If he is cared for by a consistent and loving person— touched, picked up, held, fed, smiled at, looked at, sung to, talked to, rocked, in a fashion reasonably in tune with his own nature—then the newborn is helped to move from absorption in its own psychic cocoon to an eager and trusting awareness of the world outside. That awareness is the baby's first sense that he is not alone and is reliably being cared for. If the caregiver supports and protects the infant from premature separateness and independence, allowing him to lean on her, encouraging him to feel the reality of her presence, in time he will come to know that events are caused and do not simply happen. Jonathan learns that it is his mother who turns on the night light and then feeds him, following which there is that good feeling inside. Erica discovers that her father provides both the delight of the rocking (along with the upsetting loss of control) and the firm support when it becomes too much to bear.

Such discoveries, which emerge in the first months of life, are the first steps in a profoundly important journey leading toward the capacity to love another and to make one's own connections. In other words, the making of human relationships and learning to think are both dependent on early nurturance. Without that nurturance, an infant's potential capacities remain only potential. To be sensitive to one's environment, only to have that environment a nonresponsive one, leads to the atrophy of one's sensors. To be eager for stimulation and to find none, or the wrong kind, dulls the appetite for that stimulation. To cry for attention to one's needs and to have those needs unmet creates a lack of trust in the world. In other words, only inter-action with a caring adult can invest an infant's early skills and reflexes with meaning and help transform them into genuine competence. The foundation for that transformation is laid in the first weeks and months of life.

PRINCIPLES OF QUALITY
CARE IN INFANCY

Irene S. Shigaki

Whether an infant is cared for in the home by parents or in some form of family or group day care, certain guidelines for quality care apply. The particulars of the implementation of these guidelines may differ, reflecting varying settings, but the underlying principles remain the same. There are five such key principles, and these will be explored in this essay: the need for individualized care, the importance of maintaining an affectionate emotional-social climate, the significance of an interplay between consistency and variety, the value of a responsive environment, and the potential for developing competencies through daily routines.

Individualized Care

Quality care for the young child must reflect the unique characteristics of each infant. While comparisons with siblings or other children in care may provide rough developmental indices, the range of normal variability is such that one cannot expect same-age children to develop identically. Instead, there is a need for caregivers to pick up clues from the child through careful and sensitive observations, leading to the formulation of appropriate ways of tapping the child's strengths while nurturing areas requiring development.

Affectionate Emotional-Social Climate

Infants should be cared for in a warm, affectionate way that lets them know that they are special. Central to the development of such a climate is the formulation of attachment. In group care such attachment can be fostered by an individual assuming the role of the primary caregiver for each infant. Responding promptly to the cues of the child most of the time builds a relationship of trust and also contributes significantly to a positive climate. In addition for a child in care, a favorable climate stems from a caregiver who enjoys the role and who maintains open communication with the child's family. Through such communication, greater consistency between day-care and home caregiving practices can evolve.

Interaction of Consistency and Variety

A dynamic between consistency and variety in both caregiving practices and the physical environment needs to be maintained in order to provide the child with security and a sense of self-confidence through constants upon which the child can rely while introducing change conducive to growth. Specifically, the physical environment should include consistency as represented by provisions such as a designated place to eat and to sleep. Variety can be introduced into the environment through planned periodic changes in materials available and through varying outdoor ventures to the yard, to the park, to the supermarket, and elsewhere. The daily schedule should also be sensitive to the needs of the child, including consistency in scheduling time to eat, to nap, etc., and should include variety through the introduction of differing age-appropriate activities. Reflected in the thoughtful schedule is balance between such areas as indoor-outdoor play and active-quiet activities and appropriate sequencing, as exemplified by a quiet story-time period preceding nap time. Recognizing the rapid rate of growth during the first year of life, the thoughtful caregiver is continuously defining and redefining the developmentally appropriate range in which the child can operate, providing the child with the security of general expectations while allowing the child to explore greater challenges to continually increase competence.

Responsive Environment

The social and physical environment in which the infant spends much time needs to be sufficiently responsive to the cues from the child, so that the child learns that he or she is his or her own agent who can exercise some control over the environment. This includes a developmentally appropriate environment that will allow the infant to explore by using all of the sensory modalities and that will promote growth in fine and gross motor skills, self-esteem, social-interpersonal skills, language, and cognitive development. Developmentally appropriate and appealing activities and materials must be available that help children have the satisfaction of making sense of the world in which they live through the acquisition of concepts. Such materials and activities will involve the range of open-ended to closed-ended tasks. Particularly effective are versatile materials and activities appropriate for a range of abilities and ages that allow the child to interact at varying levels with her growing competence. Crucial to the process of learning is allowing the child to explore fully for as long as he finds necessary a new material, a new activity, or a new situation within the bounds of safety so that the child can begin to discover patterns and to predict outcomes.

Development of Competencies Through Routines

Infants should be cared for in a way that optimizes opportunities for learning, including social interactions in all facets of the day, especially daily routine activities. For example, feeding can promote the following: fine motor skills as one feeds oneself; sense of self-esteem at growing competence in feeding self; social-interpersonal skills as the child and caregiver interact at the table; language development as various foods are identified for the child; and cognitive development as concepts such as texture, color, and temperature are explored. Encouragement of developmentally appropriate independence in self-help areas is recommended. When the infant is able to coordinate fingers and thumb around seven or eight months of age, the baby can be given finger foods in order to become an active participant in the feeding process. Likewise, when the child is able to negotiate a cup, around eleven months, a nonbreakable child-size cup with good balance can be provided. Active involvement in these daily routines encourages the growth of competence in the child.

BIBLIOGRAPHY

Bailey, Rebecca Anne, and Elsie Carter Burton. *The Dynamic Self: Activities to Enhance Infant Development*. St. Louis: Mosby, 1981.
The authors stress the key role the infant years of birth to two-and-one-half years play in the development of a child's prerequisite learning skills. Combining traditional theories of infant development with practical activities, guidelines are provided for a free-flowing curriculum that teachers, day-care personnel, and the parents can easily adapt to their children.

Baldwin, Rahima. *Special Delivery: The Complete Guide to Informed Birth*. Millbrae, Ca.: Les Femmes Publishing, 1979.
While primarily focusing on home birth, Baldwin also covers all aspects of pregnancy and birth, stressing the responsibility of the couple in obtaining a childbirth tailored to their own needs. The volume is filled with charts, illustrations and personal experiences. Because the focus is home birth, there are very complete descriptions of the birth process, complications, and care of the newborn during the first hours and days. These surpass details found in most childbirth books. In addition to a great deal of practical information, the text also deals well with the spiritual and psychological aspects of pregnancy, birth, and parenting.

Berezin, Nancy. *The Gentle Birth Book*. New York: Simon & Schuster, 1980.
This book presents a comprehensive review of the Leboyer approach to childbirth as it is practiced in the United States.

Bing, Elizabeth. *Six Practical Lessons for an Easier Childbirth*. New York: Bantam, 1981.
The author aims to help the reader prepare and condition her body through a series of exercises for labor and childbirth the Lamaze way. Emphasis is on developing the necessary

stamina and physical strength for an easier, less painful delivery. Bing describes neuromuscular control, body-building, and breathing exercises that she relates to the various stages of labor. The couple-approach is stressed in this easy-to-read volume filled with photographs.

Bing, Elizabeth, and Libby Colman. *Having a Baby After Thirty.* New York: Bantam, 1980.

Written by a well-known childbirth educator and a psychologist who have written extensively on the subject of childbearing, the book approaches childbearing from the viewpoint of the woman over thirty and addresses her special problems and concerns. A chapter on the meaning of pregnancy for older parents focuses on the effects of the changes in lifestyle. There are also chapters on special concerns of older fathers and older mothers. The portion of the book that deals with the birth and first months stresses psychological aspects. A section on mothering and working explores various options.

Bradley, Robert A. *Husband-Coached Childbirth*, rev. ed. New York: Harper & Row, 1974.

The author, who introduced fathers into the delivery room, sets forth his method for natural childbirth. The style is simple and basic but fully explains the rationale for eliminating unnecessary interventions and medications and using relaxation techniques and concentration as tools for labor. A large part of the book is directed toward fathers who seek an active role in pregnancy and birth.

Brazelton, T. Berry. *Infants and Mothers: Differences in Development.* New York: Dell, 1972.

This volume stresses the uniqueness of each child. Month-by-month discussion of three different yet typical babies in their first year of life—the average baby, the quiet baby, the active baby—is the format followed. Insights are provided on how these three types interact with their mothers and how they affect and are affected by their home environments. The warm, narrative style makes for interesting, informative, and reassuring reading for parents, in particular, and for all caregivers.

Brazelton, T. Berry. *On Becoming a Family: The Growth of Attachment.* New York: Delacorte/Seymour Lawrence, 1981.

The author explores the issue of attachment and shows that it is not an instantaneous or automatic process. He discusses how attachment grows and the circularity of responses needed. Particular attention is paid to fathers and new babies. There is also consideration of attachment under less than ideal circumstances, as with handicapped children. It is a very supportive book for parents.

Brewer, Gail Sforza, and Tom Brewer. *What Every Pregnant Woman Should Know. The Truth About Diet and Drugs in Pregnancy.* New York: Random House, 1977.

The volume should be required reading for all women seeking healthy babies and easier childbirth. Brewer's important work on the effects of nutrition on the fetus is clearly explained and supported by scientific evidence that points to the disastrous effects of protein and calorie restrictions, limitations and the use of diuretics during pregnancy. There are also recommended diets and recipes.

Brewer, Gail Sforza, and Janice Presser Greene. *Right from the Start: Meeting the Challenges of Mothering Your Unborn and Newborn Baby.* Emmaus, Pa.: Rodale Press, 1981.

The theme of helping mothers is developed through the use of contrast—how the "standard" advice of the last fifty years came to differ markedly from the nurturing norms of preceding generations and how to avoid the pitfalls that may result from following "standard" advice. Current medical thinking fills the pages so parents can make decisions on prenatal nutrition, neonatal circumcision, and a host of other issues of the childbearing period and the first months of the infant. The appendix provides helpful hints on baby carriers through rashes and sunbathing as well as a bibliography, glossary, and a directory of useful items and services available. Health professionals can gain from the wealth of material in this instruction manual for mothers.

Brewster, Dorothy Patricia. *You Can Breastfeed Your Baby . . . Even In Special Situations.* Emmaus, Pa.: Rodale Press, 1979.

The author provides a complete guide to nursing under more unusual circumstances. She covers situations involving working mothers, chronically ill mothers and babies, through multiple births. It can be used by medical professionals or parents.

Burck, Frances Wells. *Babysense.* New York: St. Martin's Press, 1979.

This volume reflects an understanding of what it is like to be a new mother. It covers the issues of immediate concern, from breast- vs. bottle-feeding to adaptation to parenthood, but does so in an original way. The wisdom of other mothers is interspersed with advice and lists of resources. Written in short, concise sections, the book could be read by a mother in the irregular and infrequent intervals of free time that are part and parcel of having a new baby.

Caplan, Ronald M. *Pregnant Is Beautiful: The Complete Body Conditioning Program for Pregnant Women and New Mothers.* New York: Appleton-Century-Crofts, 1981.

Caplan outlines simple, medically sound methods said to assure good health and good looks before, during, and after pregnancy. Suggestions are given for establishing a healthful diet plan, exercise program, and skin care, as well as ways for coping with emotional stress and understanding labor and childbirth. A chapter on pregnancy for the older women is included.

Cedeno, Lazar, Olinda Cedeno, and Carole Monroe. *The Exercise Plus Pregnancy Program: Exercises for Before, During, and After Pregnancy.* New York: Morrow, 1980.

This small volume is designed to help the pregnant woman prepare for a healthier, easier pregnancy, childbirth, and recovery by maintaining optimum physical fitness. There is a series of twenty-five exercises for all parts of the body with special emphasis on rhythmic breathing.

Colman, Arthur, and Libby Lee Colman. *Pregnancy: The Psychological Experience.* New York: Bantam, 1978.

The focus is on changes of consciousness and emotions as well as the physiological aspects of pregnancy. Chapters are devoted to the expectant mother's experience, stages of labor and delivery, the expectant father's experience, and psychological complications of pregnancy.

Donovan, Bonnie. *The Cesarean Birth Experience: A Practical, Comprehensive, and Reassuring Guide for Parents and Professionals.* Boston: Beacon, 1977.

This is the first book written expressly for parents anticipating a Cesarean birth. The tone is factual and reassuring. There are chapters dealing with indications for Cesarean birth, emotional aspects, laboratory tests for fetal health and maturity, hospital routines, and anesthesia. A comprehensive discussion of the Cesarean birth as well as a photo essay cover the birth well. The postpartum section includes discussion of bonding, breast-feeding, what can be expected during the postpartum stay, etc. The author attempts a factual, reassuring presentation of the experience of Cesarean births as well as debunking commonly held myths and succeeds in so doing.

Elkins, Valmi Howe. *The Rights of the Pregnant Parent.* New York: Schocken, 1980.

The book's premise is based on the conviction by the author that too many women are still deprived of what is seen as a positive birth experience. A return to home birth is not advocated as the best answer. In fact, the author feels that there are advances in obstetrical care for high-risk babies and mothers, which home birth cannot provide. Advocated is prepared childbirth that permits the desired childbirth within the hospital setting, and guidelines are given for choosing doctor and hospital, finding the best possible childbirth preparation course as well as for communicating on a positive level with the hospital staff. Discussed are the growing trends toward Cesarean sections, family style birth in the hospital, and the birthroom.

Environmental Programs, Inc. *Infant Development Guide. You and Your Baby: The First Wondrous Year.* Piscataway, N.J.: Johnson & Johnson Baby Products Company, 1978.

This is a handbook for parents on the development of a young child from birth to twelve months. The text covers the infant's effect on the family and relationships; social, emotional, and physical development; and play as a means of learning. Many pictures are used to illustrate statements and developmental tasks identified in the text.

Feldman, Silvia. *Choices in Childbirth.* New York: Grosset & Dunlap, 1978.

A very objective and humane overview of alternatives in birth that are available, this book discusses pros and cons of home birth, hospitals, medications and modern obstetrical technologies; doctors vs. midwives and how to find the right birth assistant; how to choose the childbirth method best for you; breast- vs. bottle-feeding; and nutrition and exercise. The primary focus is on tailoring the birth experience to fit the couples and gives helpful information on how to decide and then how to find what has been chosen. Feldman has written an excellent and very complete source book with a very personal and warm perspective.

Fraiberg, Selma. *Every Child's Birthright: In Defense of Mothering.* New York: Basic Books, 1977.

Written for professionals and parents, this book strongly advocates motherhood and cautions against current trends to devalue this role. Research information is cited that supports the importance of attachment and bonding that occurs during the early stages of development. Implications of these findings for child-care institutions are also discussed. As with the *Magic Years* (1968), the author provides lively and interesting reading.

Fraiberg, Selma (ed.). In Collaboration with Louis Fraiberg. *Clinical Studies in Infant Mental Health: The First Year of Life.* New York: Basic Books, 1980.

The late Selma Fraiberg and her colleagues at the Child Development Project in Ann Arbor, Michigan, present a collection of papers that describe the major aspects of their work. The research is confined to babies from birth to one year of age, with a detailed analysis of the clinical methods used. It is an important book for infant mental health professionals and educators.

Gaskin, Ina May. *Spiritual Midwifery* rev. ed. Summertown, Tn.: Book Publishing Company, 1978.

Gaskin advocates the rights of women, the newborn, and the family during childbirth and the return of the major responsibility for normal childbirth to well-trained midwives. She emphasizes the spiritual dimension of birth and stresses the importance of energy flow in opening up and facilitating the birth process.

Gates, Wende Devlin, and Gail McFarland Meckel. *Newborn Beauty.* New York: Viking Press, 1980.

More than a beauty book, this book is dedicated to the looks and feelings of the pregnant woman and new mother. The discussions of pregnancy changes cover the causes and management of these changes. In addition to fashion, areas discussed are hygiene, diet, fitness, and sex. The final chapter on coping is particularly valuable to the new mother. A glossary and bibliography are included.

Gazella, Jacqueline Gibson. *Nutrition for the Childbearing Year.* Wayzata, Mn.: Woodland Publishing, 1979.

Designed to be a practical book that answers frequently asked questions about nutrition in pregnancy and lactation, this spiral-bound paperback provides six weeks' worth of menus and fifty-seven pages of recipes. These include such specialties as the "pregnant person's orange juice cocktail" (orange juice and sparkling water), and the "nine-month cocktail" (high-protein milkshake with vitamins and minerals). The chapter on selection and preparation of food focuses on the use of the basic four food groups. Two other noteworthy chapters cover nutrition during lactation and a very comprehensive discussion of the thirty-four nutrients known to be needed by the body. Written by a nurse-midwife who is also a childbirth educator, this book is intended for lay people, but professionals could also learn much by reading it.

Goldbeck, Nikki. *As You Eat, So Your Baby Grows.* Woodstock, N.Y.: Ceres Press, 1980.

This nutrition guide for the pregnant woman includes a discussion of essential nutrients, noting the common food portions that supply these nutrients, and points out the six food groupings for achieving a balanced diet. Information is up-to-date, especially the section on weight gain, recommended daily allowances, and substances to be avoided. The section on non-animal protein sources is brief but adequate. One of the highlights of this pamphlet is the extensive bibliography at the end.

Goldfarb, Johanna, and Edith Tibbets. *Breastfeeding Handbook: A Practical Reference for Physicians, Nurses and Other Health Professionals.* Hillside, N.J.: Enslow, 1980.

The authors provide a sensitive approach to breast-feeding that combines factual information on the physiology of lactation, the nutritional value of human milk, with issues involved in deciding to nurse, and answers to problems which may arise in the course of lactation. This is a valuable and comprehensive resource for the health professional and families due to the inclusion of a wide range of material. Some of the information is hard to find, such as that on relactation, induced lactation for adoptive parents, management of feeding after a Cesarian birth, premature infant care, twins, congenital anomalies as well as the nitty-gritty facts about breast pumps, pads, and milk storage for working mothers.

Hannon, Sharron. *Childbirth: A Source Book for Conception, Pregnancy, Birth and the First Weeks of Life.* New York: Evans, 1980.

This volume is important reading for any pregnant couple or couple considering parenthood. From consideration of whether to have a baby, moving through pregnancy, labor, and delivery, postpartum, and parenting—nearly every aspect of importance has been included. Part two, a particularly valuable section, presents options regarding birth and offers suggestions on shopping for them.

Hendin, David, and Joan Marks. *The Genetic Connection*. New York: New American Library (Signet), 1979.

Hendin and Marks present a comprehensive discussion of prenatal tests (such as amniocentesis), laboratory studies, family history reviews, and all the other recent genetic counseling techniques that help insure that the unborn child is physically and mentally well. Guidelines are given on how to seek genetic counseling.

Herzig, Alison C., and Jane L. Mali. *Oh, Boy! Babies!* Boston: Little, Brown, 1980.

A sensitive book, it chronicles the adventures of several school-age boys learning how to take care of babies. With pictures and humorous narration, this volume is useful for educators and parents alike, as it deals not only with preparation for parenthood, but also the more immediate problems of preparation for siblings.

Honig, Alice S., and J. Ronald Lally. *Infant Caregiving: A Design for Training*, 2nd ed. Syracuse, N.Y.: Syracuse University Press, 1981.

This handbook provides a complete design for training primary caregivers of children under three years of age. It tells how to meet infants' physical, emotional, social, and cognitive developmental needs in child care. In practical language the authors recommend activities and tell why they are important. They describe how to use settings and spaces and how to allocate time so that the tempos and rhythms of days help to optimize the infants' development. Positive learning experiences are arranged and provided for within the context of daily routines and group care activities.

Hotchner, Tracy. *Pregnancy and Childbirth: The Complete Guide for a New Life*. New York: Avon, 1979.

Hotchner has written a comprehensive guide that covers all essential aspects of childbearing—including controversial issues —in an unbiased, balanced, objective way. It provides well-researched psychological and medical information that potential parents need to make decisions throughout pregnancy, especially with regard to nutrition, choices in method of birth, dealing with doctors and hospitals, home birth, and breast-feeding.

Jimenez, Sherry Lynn Mims. *Child Bearing: A Guide for Pregnant Parents*. Englewood Cliffs, N.J.: Prentice-Hall, 1980.

The book is designed to deal with the whole process of pregnancy, birth, and early parenthood. The focus is on the adjustment needed as the pregnant family experiences the childbearing year. A practical sourcebook, it provides point-by-point explanations of the process, from prenatal nutrition to postpartum depression, including a chart that summarizes the emotional and physical sensation of each stage and phase of labor.

Kamen, Betty, and Si Kamen. *The Kamen Plan for Nutrition During Pregnancy*. New York: Appleton-Century-Crofts, 1981.

The authors, broadcast journalists specializing in nutrition education, explore the common myths about what diet can and cannot do for a woman's health during these important nine months. Menu plans are given as well as recipes for dishes such as carrot, sesame, and tofu salad, seed balls, tofu omelet, easy millet, no-bake granola, and tarator soup. Suggestions are included for seed or bean sprouting, yogurt and cottage-cheese making, and simple pickling.

Karmel, Marjorie. *Thank You, Dr. Lamaze: A Mother's Experiences in Painless Childbirth*. Philadelphia: Lippincott, 1959.

The author traces the history of the Lamaze method through an interesting first-hand account. Explained are the breathing exercises to lessen the strain of labor along with the biological reasons as to why they work. The book is a must for couples contemplating and anticipating a natural birth experience.

Kitzinger, Sheila. *The Complete Book of Pregnancy and Childbirth*. New York: Knopf, 1981.

This highly readable book is directed at those who wish to become active participants in the birth of their child. The author includes almost every topic of interest to expectant parents and encourages couples to explore the options available in childbirth.

She discusses bonding and the changing family relationships that come with the birth of a child, as well as current information on drugs, nutrition, exercise, fetal development, breast-feeding, baby care, labor and other topics. The text is well illustrated.

Klaus, Marshall H., and John H. Kennell. *Maternal-Infant Bonding*. St. Louis: Mosby, 1982.

A number of specialists describe the impact of early separation or loss on family development. There is an emphasis on caring for parents of children who are ill, have congenital malformation, or die.

La Leche League International. *The Womanly Art of Breastfeeding*. Franklin Park, Ill.: The League, 1974.

As a handbook for parents and prospective parents, the text is written simply for the layman, but also will be helpful and informative for health professionals. La Leche League has been recognized worldwide as true experts and good resource people for breastfeeding information, and much of their knowledge is detailed in this manual. Chapters include sections with prenatal information, "how to," and special circumstances (e.g., Cesarean birth, the premature baby, sore nipples). The La Leche League philosophy comes through strongly: breastfed is best!

Lawrence, Ruth A. *Breast-Feeding: A Guide for the Medical Profession*. St. Louis: Mosby, 1979.

This guide provides in-depth information on the physiology of lactation and the composition of human milk. Discussions on the clinical management of various nursing problems are based on years of work with lactating mothers. There is a particularly useful appendix that contains growth/development charts, drugs in human milk, and breast-milk bank protocols.

Leach, Penelope. *Your Baby and Child, From Birth to Age Five*. New York: Knopf, 1980.

This comprehensive volume on child care, health, and development that is laden with facts and advice for parents and educators covers the areas of everyday care and feeding of children, their play, and their physical, cognitive, emotional, and behavioral development. There is a separate chapter for each stage. An encyclopedia/index section offers quick reference in specific areas. The author's expertise in her field, as well as her deeply caring attitude toward her subject are evident on every page. The color illustrations are excellent. The content, based on the most recent, however orthodox, information in the field, is clearly written. The book is truly a classic.

Leboyer, Frederick. *Birth Without Violence*. New York: Knopf, 1975.

Leboyer writes in a poetic style and describes birth, pain, and life in the new world from the newborn's point of view. Questioning routine hospital delivery rooms for their lack of sensitivity to the newborn, the author suggests many alternatives to make the adjustment from womb to real world a more pleasant and healthy one.

Lewis, Michael, and Leonard A. Rosenblum (eds.). *The Origins of Behavior*. Vol. 1, *The Effect of the Infant on Its Caregiver*. New York: Wiley, 1974.

This volume discusses the significance of the interaction between mother and infant and the subtle contributions that each makes to the other in shaping their relationship. It emphasizes the impact of the infant as a *source* of information, regulation, and even the malevolent distortion of the caregiver's behavior. It encompasses the effect of infant defect on caregivers from a variety of viewpoints, using both humans and monkeys as subjects, while also examining in normal infants data drawn from many fields, including morphology, physiology, and behavior.

Lichtendorf, Susan, and Phyllis Gillis. *The New Pregnancy: The Active Woman's Guide to Work, Legal Rights, Health Care, Travel, Sports, Dress, Sex, and Emotional Well-Being*. New York: Random House, 1979.

The authors have prepared a volume of complete, authoritative information on legal rights on the job; pros and cons of medical intervention from amniocentesis to induced labor;

effects of cigarettes, alcohol, and drugs on pregnancy; sports participation; and travel. They wrote especially for the 1.5 million pregnant women in the work force.

Luke, Barbara. *Maternal Nutrition.* Boston: Little, Brown, 1980.

The purpose of this book is to provide a comprehensive overview of the field of maternal nutrition. It furnishes in-depth descriptions of the most common nutritional problems in obstetrics as well as suggestions for clinical management. Although written primarily for experienced practitioners, the book does contain a glossary with definitions that will be helpful to students.

McLaughlin, Clara J. *Black Parents' Handbook: A Guide to Healthy Pregnancy, Birth, and Child Care.* New York: Harcourt Brace Jovanovich, 1975.

Real-life experiences are the basis for this practical, readable handbook. The goal is to highlight the enjoyment of parenthood by black parents with children from conception to age six. A practical, readable, child-rearing guide.

Mahler, Margaret S., Fred Pine, and Anni Bergman. *The Psychological Birth of the Human Infant: Symbiosis and Individuation.* New York: Basic Books, 1975.

A landmark in the study of child development, this book describes the process of becoming an individual as a child evolves throughout the first three years of life. The study, containing both theoretical and case material, is based on direct observation of normal mothers and their children within a research setting. There is invaluable insight into the vicissitudes of child behavior during the early years, particularly the "terrible twos." Although this volume is a technical one, used by psychoanalysts, child therapists, and educators, it is recommended for the layman and parent.

Marilus, Esther. *Natural Childbirth the Swiss Way.* Englewood Cliffs, N.J.: Prentice-Hall, 1979.

Marilus introduces the Swiss method that takes the best of the Lamaze, Grantly Dick-Read, and other successful systems of natural childbirth and combines them with a prenatal exercise program. The method is a new approach that is unknown to most obstetricians in the United States. The book's first section details a physical fitness program for the mother-to-be, including exercises for varicose veins and preparation for nursing. The second section describes coping techniques for labor and delivery, including detailed chapters on controlled breathing and perfecting the push. The final section on recovery covers recovery-room exercises and postpartum followup. All of the exercises are easy to follow, and the text is easy to read, with many illustrations and photos.

Marzollo, Jean, compiler. *9 Months, 1 Day, 1 Year: A Guide to Pregnancy, Birth, and Babycare.* New York: Harper & Row, 1976.

This compendium of parents' thoughts, feelings, experiences, and practical advice on pregnancy, childbirth, and baby care for the first year is very readable, informative, and reassuring, especially for first-time parents. Differences in parents' attitudes and ways they coped make it clear that there is no one right way. The appendix on infant paraphernalia is particularly useful.

Maternity Center Association. *A Baby Is Born.* New York: Grosset & Dunlap, 1975.

Drawings, black and white photographs, and diagrams are used to tell the story of a baby from conception through birth. The photographs of the Dickinson-Belskie sculptures are particularly helpful in explaining the miracle of conception, fetal development, and the process of labor and birth. There is minimal text in this book, which seems fitting and appropriate because its story is universal. The photographs of breech birth are especially interesting and unique. This book is equally suitable for children and adults and is a good teaching aid for professionals.

Meyer, Linda D. *The Cesarean (R)Evolution: A Handbook for Parents and Childbirth Educators.* Washington, D.C.: Charles Franklin Press, 1979.

In this paperback on Cesarean birth for the lay public the author advocates controversial megadoses of vitamins for pregnancy and postpartum depression. Useful information includes the patient's rights and a state-by-state list of Cesarean support groups.

Nilsson, Lennart. *A Child Is Born*, rev. ed. New York: Delacorte, 1977.

With exceptionally beautiful and detailed photographs, the author tells the story of the developing fetus from conception to birth. Originally published in 1965, this book has been translated into twelve languages and has sold over 1 million copies. As well as advice for expectant parents, this revised edition also includes remarkable photographs of birth.

Noble, Elizabeth. *Essential Exercises for the Childbearing Year: A Guide to Health and Comfort Before and After Your Baby Is Born.* Boston: Houghton Mifflin, 1976.

The author, a physical therapist specializing in obstetrics and gynecology, presents women with a self-help guide that focuses on prevention of problems and the promotion of health and well-being. The emphasis is on simplicity and on developing self-confidence in all women, not just those capable of gymnastic feats. Coordination, relaxation, and control of muscle groups is stressed rather than extreme physical fitness or exertion. The muscles of the pelvic floor and the abdomen receive special attention. The illustrations accompanying the text are a helpful adjunct to the detailed explanations.

Noble, Elizabeth. *Having Twins: A Parent's Guide to Pregnancy, Birth and Early Childhood.* Boston: Houghton Mifflin, 1980.

Statistically, one in about fifty people is a twin, yet the phenomenon of multiple birth is still seen as an unusual occurrence. The author provides detailed information on current medical research as well as practical suggestions for prenatal care and meeting the special needs and demands of twins. Helpful ideas from experienced parents are given, covering the feeding, dressing, and raising of twins as well as how to join or start a local Mothers of Twins Club. It is a useful guide not only for couples who know they are going to be the parents of twins, but also for childbirth educators and other professionals.

North, A. Frederick. *Infant Care*, rev. ed. Washington, D.C.: U.S. Department of Health and Human Services, Administration for Children, Youth, and Families, 1980.

This booklet, one of the most popular of government publications, has been completely rewritten six times, always reflecting the latest thinking of experts in the field. It continues to be a valuable guide for parents who want to learn the basic facts about the best ways to raise a healthy child.

Oakley, Ann. *Women Confined: Toward a Sociology of Childbirth*. New York: Schocken, 1980.

Oakley focuses on women's emotional responses to the experience of childbirth and examines the tie between the social, psychological, and medical factors in the management and context of childbirth. An academic sociologist, she discusses literature, research, and practice in the reproductive field from the cultural perspective on maternity.

Parfitt, Rebecca Rowe. *The Birth Primer: A Source Book of Traditional and Alternative Methods in Labor and Delivery*. New York: New American Library, 1980.

This is a guide to birth options available to parents, including the Lamaze, Bing, Dick-Read, and Leboyer methods. It summarizes procedures used in medicated births and has detailed discussions of medical procedures, such as the use of forceps and episiotomies. It examines the role of midwives, fathers, and doctors as well as the respective advantages of birth at hospital, home, and birthing centers. Historical origins are described, and personal experiences included. It is a well-documented, detailed source book.

Pizer, Hank, and Christine O'Brien Palinski. *Coping with a Miscarriage: Why It Happens and How to Deal with Its Impact on You and Your Family*. New York: New American Library, 1980.

The authors have written a comforting book that provides down-to-earth information about the possible causes of a miscarriage, warning signals, and current approaches to prevention. The physiological and psychological effects of a miscarriage are discussed as well as the impact of the experience on all family members. It is an informative guide that deals with the subject sensitively.

Princeton Center for Infancy and Early Childhood. *The First Twelve Months of Life.* New York: Grosset & Dunlap, 1973.

The maturation of an infant during the first year of life is presented. The text is divided by month and includes developmental milestones and special accomplishments that may occur during that period. The stress is on the importance of parent-infant interaction and the environment, allowing for, and emphasizing, the uniqueness of each parent and every infant.

Simkin, Diana. *The Complete Pregnancy Exercise Book.* New York: New American Library, 1980.

Written by an experienced exercise teacher who is also a Lamaze childbirth educator, the volume is intended for pregnant women who are interested in keeping fit during pregnancy, regardless of their previous experience with exercise programs. The exercises are meticulously described so that they can be learned even by women who will not have the assistance of an instructor. A unique feature is that the exercises not only are explained and their rationale delineated, but also the author notes how the exercises should feel when being done correctly. There is an abundance of photographs: in some cases as many as four pictures accompany one exercise description. The author includes postnatal exercise routines, suggestions for establishing an exercise habit, as well as information on common pregnancy problems and concerns. A positive attitude pervading this book should help increase the self-confidence of pregnant women who read it.

Stone, L. Joseph, Henrietta T. Smith, and Lois B. Murphy (eds.). *The Competent Infant: Research and Commentary,* 3 vols. New York: Basic Books, 1974.

This excellent resource for students, professionals, and researchers in child development is based on findings of the 1960s. The editors have chosen more than 200 articles stressing insights, methods, and interpretations. In addition, introductory comments provide cogent perception of the work covered.

Todd, Linda. *Labor and Birth. A Guide for You.* Minneapolis: The International Childbirth Education Association, 1980.

This publication presents the events of conception, pregnancy, labor, and birth in a concise, outline form that is complemented by illustrations depicting multiethnic families. The tone of the book is honest, straightforward, and warm. Adjustments after birth, the special needs of single parents, the role of the father, and the question of placing the baby for adoption are all addressed.

Tronick, Edward, and Lauren Adamson. *Babies as People: New Findings On Our Social Beginnings.* New York: Macmillan, 1980.

Taken from behavioral research, informative insights are provided. By helping parents understand the child's internal mechanisms, the book points out ways to provide the best possible environment for the baby.

Uzgiris, Ina C., and J. McVicker Hunt. *Assessment in Infancy: Ordinal Scales of Psychological Development.* Urbana: University of Illinois Press, 1975.

The authors' approach to the assessment of psychological development in infancy is based on Piaget's writings on infant intelligence. They discuss the scales they have devised and give instructions for administering them.

Weissbourd, Bernice, and Judith Musick (eds.). *Infants: Their Social Environments.* Washington, D.C.: National Association for the Education of Young Children, 1981.

Leading authorities in infant development and care offer research-based insights on children under the age of three on such topics as infant competence, group care, disabilities, mothers' and fathers' interactions with their infants, and public policy. Teachers, medical personnel, mental health workers, researchers, parents, and policy makers will find a wealth of new information about what we know about babies and their families.

White, Karol. _What To Do When You Think You Can't Have a Baby._ _Based on the Clinical Experience of More than Thirty Infertility Specialists._ Garden City, N.Y.: Doubleday, Inc., 1981.

In the past two decades notable advances have been made in the evaluation and management of infertility. In layman's terms, the author talks about these breakthrough findings, diagnostic tests, and follow-up procedures. A comforting encouraging book, it clearly states what a childless couple might gain from the most recent medical information available. Specific procedures such as microsurgery and hormone therapy are discussed as well as test-tube babies and artificial insemination.

Williams, Phyllis S. _Nourishing Your Unborn Child._ New York: Avon, 1975.

This is a basic nutrition guide for expectant mothers in which the nutritional facts and principles have been skillfully woven in with fetal development, changing maternal physiology of childbearing, and postpartum adjustments. A chapter deals with potential internal and external environmental hazards and how to "reasonably avoid, change or lessen one vulnerability." Two-thirds of the book applies the principles through suggested menus and recipes. A special consideration has been given to parents who may have a less than perfect baby in spite of carefully trying to provide an optimum prenatal environment. Although the author has written for the mother-to-be, there is much valuable and common-sense information of benefit to the tradition-bound health-care provider.

2
Child
Development

CHILD DEVELOPMENT THROUGH AGE FIVE

Joseph Church and Alexandria Church

Psychological development goes on lifelong. We are never too old to arrive at new insights, new perspectives, new ways of comprehending the world and our own situation in it. But it is in the early years that development takes place most rapidly and dramatically. The contrasts between the social and mental functioning of a five-year-old and of a newborn baby are spectacular. Note, though, that we are not talking about a contrast between something and nothing. The neonate is a long way from being a nothing. One of the impressive discoveries of the past twenty-five years has been learning just how complicated a creature a little seven- or eight-pound bundle can be.

It is still widely believed, for example, that babies, like kittens and puppies, cannot see at birth. In fact, neonates can see very well. About the only things lacking in their visual sense are awareness of color and ability to focus. They can track a slowly moving object with their eyes. They seem to be especially responsive to the pattern of a human face. Their hearing is likewise good. They can detect slight variations in speech sounds, as between "puh" and "buh." They are particularly sensitive to the human voice, and within three days after birth babies can tell the difference between their mother's voice and that of an unfamiliar female.

Newborn babies move their arms and legs in rhythm with the cadences of adult speech. This so-called synchrony is thought to be vital to the establishment of good parent-child relations. Both the parents and the child must learn to intermesh and coordinate their behavior; in other words, they must learn to "dance" well together. The response to adult speech is also an

example of the kind of empathy of which babies are capable
from birth.

One puzzle has only recently been solved. Some observers
have reported that newborn babies turn to look in the direction
of a sound, whereas others have claimed that this behavior does
not appear until somewhere between ages two and four months.
The answer seems to be that newborns, under favorable testing
conditions, do indeed orient visually to a sound source. However, this behavior becomes less reliable during the next couple
of months and reappears in full force only around age four
months.

Newborns are also sensitive to pain and show clear likes and
dislikes for various flavors and odors. They recognize the
mother's smell as well as her voice. They do not yet smile in
response to a human face or voice, but when at peace with the
world, they may show what is called a "pleasure smile."

Newborn babies are capable of learning. When repeatedly
exposed to the same stimulus, they stop responding. However,
if the stimulus is changed only slightly, they immediately show
renewed interest, as in the "puh"-"buh" contrast mentioned
above. Newborn babies have little control over their own bodies,
but when they are given a chance to use their limited capacities
to make something happen, they learn how to do it. For instance,
babies learn to turn their heads in the correct direction to
produce a squirt of milk from a nipple. In experimental situations they learn to vary the speed and force of their sucking, to
control the light level in the room, or to keep a picture projected
on the wall in focus.

An area of dispute is whether newborn babies imitate adults'
facial contortions—lip pursing, sticking out the tongue, eye-
brow raising. The weight of evidence, we believe, shows that
such early imitation does occur. The resistance to this fact
seems to come from some psychologists' belief that imitation
requires complicated cognitive processes, as though the baby
first had to analyze what the adult was doing, then figure out
that the adult wanted him or her to do likewise, and then
discover how to control his or her own facial features to reproduce what the adult was doing. In fact, there is a much simpler
explanation. It is called empathy, which refers to the fact that

we rather often respond automatically by mimicking in action or feeling the events around us. We see someone fall, and we feel a jolt of pain. We watch the pole vaulter strain to get over the bar, and we find ourselves straining right along with him or her. We have spoken of synchrony as a form of empathy. Newborn babies also cry empathetically—if one baby cries, the whole nursery joins in. Empathy has many ramifications, but it is a neglected area of investigation.

At the other extreme of our five-year gap, we have a child who moves around freely in space, running and galloping and climbing, and maybe even riding a two-wheeler, who can draw quite elaborate pictures, use basic tools, and talk, perhaps endlessly. The five-year-old has already grown a full set of baby teeth and is now beginning to shed them in anticipation of the permanent teeth that are on their way.

An important change has taken place by age five. From infancy on, children become aware of themselves as psychological beings and of other people who are also psychological beings. Young children are egocentric. They assume that the world as it appears and feels to them must be the same for everybody else. It is a slow and frustrating process for children—and their families—to learn that different people can view the identical situation in quite different lights, that each has different stores of information, values, tastes, and interests and different goals, power, and abilities. Establishing communication means first establishing a common frame of reference so that one does not talk either at cross-purposes or into the void.

In sum, five-year-olds have become budding common-sense psychologists. Not so very long ago, the study of children's thinking was directed largely at the child's understanding of physical phenomena, such as the child's perception of what happens to something when it is out of sight, and logical thinking, as in learning to turn the TV knob to control the volume. Now we have become aware of the significance of social cognition in children's development, that is, children's awareness of their own and other people's inner states. Children do not perceive very deeply into their own and other people's workings, but they know at least intuitively that they and other people have knowledge, ideas, purposes, feelings, memories, traits, awarenesses, abilities, and varying degrees of self-control. They know about love and hatred and jealousy and envy. They are frequently baffled by other people's behavior. For example, five-year-olds find it hard to understand why all-powerful adults do not indulge themselves totally, staying up all night to watch television and gorging themselves on candy and ice cream; they are at a loss to understand their parents' fallings out; they cannot conceive of the authority relationships that exist in the workplace—but they are quite adept in their everyday commerce with parents, siblings, and playmates. Five-year-olds have a sense of identity, a far cry from what they will know as adults, but enough to make them aware of their own naughtiness or goodness, competences and limitations, likableness or unattractiveness, daringness or timidity.

Let us leave the children in action for a moment and mention some theories and issues about development. There are numerous theories of how people come to be what they are. Some theorists emphasize emotional development (affect) and drives, as represented by Sigmund Freud and his follower Erik Erikson. Others emphasize the intellect, thinking and knowing (cognition), as represented by Jean Piaget and Heinz Werner. Others emphasize the acquisition of habits of behavior through conditioning, with no regard to either feelings or thought (behaviorism), as represented by B. F. Skinner. And still others emphasize the theory of social learning, such as Albert Bandura. Social learning is an offshoot of behaviorism but departs from it in that it allows for learning without reinforcement or reward and includes the concepts of modeling and identification. It is impossible in these few pages to elaborate on the views of these theorists. For a summary, we suggest Stone and Church, *Childhood and Adolescence*, listed in the bibliography. For those who wish a more detailed discussion of any one theorist, the bibliography provides a number of suggested books.

We want, however, to stress social learning theory because it has given us the important notion of modeling: If you want your children to grow up right, then set them a good example. Parents who smoke are teaching their children to smoke. Parents who scream have children who scream back. Parents who behave generously and sensitively have children who are inclined to be altruistic and to share.

Although theorists tend to carve a person into components— emotions, drives, intellect, and all the rest—it should be obvious that all such partitionings of people are arbitrary and to some degree false. What we are really talking about when we discuss development is children's concern with the environment and with themselves, about how things appear to them and what kind of sense they make for them, what they think and feel about and how.

If we accept that what the child reacts to initially is the physiognomies and demand qualities of objects and situations, then we can understand that feelings are always an important ingredient of so-called intellectual functioning. It turns out, for instance, that a number of children fear being sucked down the bathtub drain. The parent may not even suspect this until one day the child announces, "I wouldn't fit, would I?" Indeed, a capacity for emotional involvement is at the very heart of intellectual development. In effect, intellectual development means translating emotional reactions into ideas, giving them shape and order and meaning. In the same way, intellectual development brings with it new capacities for feeling. At an advanced level, we may be able to deal with the coolly rational, but even here we are usually guided by an aesthetic sense of fitness.

Let us look briefly at an ever recurring theme in child development, the relative contributions of nature (genes) and nurture (the environment) to what we become. Our position is simple. We are all biological organisms, but our very biology makes us responsive to all the environmental influences that make us human. That is, our biological makeup contains all our human potentialities, but it is our experience that determines which potentialities get realized and which are left untouched. Among the topics involved in discussions of nature and nurture are psychological sex differences, group and individual differences in intellectual ability, the origins of mental health or mental illness. Unfortunately, space does not allow us to treat these crucial issues in detail. But to ask whether these differences are genetically or environmentally determined is pointless. The only meaningful question is what kinds of environmental arrangements are most conducive to what forms of psychological functioning. We hope it is obvious, for example, that "intelligence" comes in a great variety of shapes, sizes, and colors.

Since different facets of development will be described in other essays, we have chosen to concentrate on language, a major component in our common humanity, with special attention to its beginnings. Language is so much part of our lives that we are likely to take it wholly for granted except when it fails us: "I've lost the word for it," or "I can't figure out how to phrase it." But language cannot be taken for granted. It is a remarkable achievement of the species as a whole, one that is still evolving and taking new shapes as people strive to make sense of their lives. It is an equally remarkable achievement of the individual child, who in a matter of a year and a half or so makes the transition from being a speechless infant to a rather sophisticated manipulator of linguistic materials. Receptive language (understanding what is said) occurs much earlier, usually by ten months and, in some cases, long before; and receptive language has been preceded by babbling, cooing, crowing, gurgling, and a variety of vocal sounds.

The child's early one-word utterances are called holophrases, meaning that the child is trying to compress an entire sentence into a single word. Thus, "Up" means "I want to be picked up"; "Out" signifies "I want to go out." By noting the context and the child's manner, one can discern what the child is trying to convey. The child is insatiably word hungry and seeks the names of things as though compiling a catalogue of the environment. "Whadda?" is one of the themes of toddlerhood. As suggested by "Up" and "Out," children use parts of speech other than nouns. They also use a fair number of interjections (hi, bye-bye, ouch); verbs (go, carry, eat); and adverbs (up, out, again, back). In general, the toddler is liberal with imperatives, commands, and demands, sometimes, in all likelihood, in imitation of the way the child is addressed. The child's unabated hunger for words suggests the sense of power over reality that language seems to provide.

Learning to talk, however, is more than the child's acquiring a stock of words. It is no great trick to learn that such and such a sound pattern "stands for" thus and such a phenomenon. But even here there are subtleties. Some words do not connect up with anything perceptible. How does the child learn to understand a word like "forget"? Children do, and quite early in their linguistic careers. The problem that stumps everybody is simply this: every normal child says perfectly sensible things that he or she has never heard said. That is, children acquire and use the raw materials of language in ways that we have not yet fathomed. By some mysterious process they learn the rules by which we assemble words into meaningful utterances, the rules of grammar and syntax.

We are skipping over many subtleties in favor of some basic issues. We ignore the child's saying things that are not so, whether out of ignorance, out of playfulness, or out of a desire to deceive, as when toddlers deny a misdeed with a vigorous, head-shaking "No!" We skim over children's utterances of self-awareness, as in a two-year-old's plea to her mother, "Pick me up, please. I want to cry in the mirror." Or such aspects of children's self-awareness as pride—again a two-year-old's comments to his mother for having used the "potty": "Sometimes I wet my diaper and sometimes you are not proud of me. Now you are proud of me. And I am proud of myself, too." We omit children's punning, use of metaphor, figurative language, sarcasm, irony, parody, invective, and flattery, all of which usually emerge a little later.

The problem of how children learn the rules of utterance making is so intractable that some people, nativists such as Noam Chomsky and his followers, have solved it by saying that children do not—learn the rules, that is. Instead, the rules are part of children's biological equipment.

Such an assertion leads to a lot of back-and-forth argument that goes nowhere but does raise some interesting points. For instance, not all languages have the same rules of grammar. Does this point to differing biological structures in the speakers of different languages? In French, for example, possessive pronouns agree not only in gender and number with the thing possessed, but also in number with the possessor (but plural possessives obliterate gender differences, complicating things further). One cannot tell from *sa plume* whether the pen is owned by a male or a female. By contrast, the English "her friend" tells us that the possessor is a she, but it does not tell us whether the friend is male or female. Of course, in French there are only two genders compared with the English three or as many as twenty in some languages.

Nativists have an ingenious answer for this: languages may differ in their surface structures, but they all have in common a single, universal deep structure. The basic grammatical distinctions of parts of speech (nouns, verbs, adjectives, etc.), gender, number, and tense are found in all languages. It is simply that they are manifested in different ways in different languages. This may or may not be so. No one has ever surveyed all known languages to find out if they all make the same grammatical distinctions, and even what we know is subject to debate.

A psychologically more interesting objection to the nativists' theory of built-in grammar comes from the way grammar emerges in the speech of young children. When children begin to string words together, they at first do so with no regard to grammar. But as their speech develops, two interesting phenomena arise. One is the misplaced rule, as in "He pick it ups" or "I walk homed." The other is what is called overregularization: the application of a regular form to an irregular word, as in "I have two foots" or "He runned all the way." Note that children first use irregular forms correctly, as in "I brought my teddy bear." When the regular forms start to take hold, all sorts of strange hybrids begin to appear, not only "foots" but "feets," "ranned," as well as "runned," and "bringed," "brang," "branged," and "broughted."

In recent years psychologists have traced out in considerable detail the way children's language flowers from one-word sentences to elaborate, grammatically correct and intellectually sophisticated (which does not necessarily mean factually true or logical) exchanges of feelings and ideas.

It appears that the basic mechanism in acquiring the rules for composing sensible utterances is our old friend modeling.

Modeling is akin to imitation, but it differs in that what is absorbed is not particular acts but whole styles of acting. Thus, children become able not only to repeat things they have heard said, but also to construct utterances quite unlike anything they have ever been exposed to.

What is left out of these accounts is a special characteristic of language and a function that it makes possible. This characteristic is symbolic realism (or word or linguistic realism), which means that words (and other symbols, like national flags and religious emblems) are not experienced as mere stand-ins for a more basic reality but have a vital, intrinsic reality of their own. Thus, what a word "means" is not some nonlinguistic phenomenon to which it points but qualities and feeling tones that reside in the word itself, that can create realities so potent that they transcend the concrete immediacies of here and now. Humankind has for centuries used words to create nonexistent entities, from demons to ghosts to fairies to Santa Claus. People use words to create worlds. Toddlers begin this lifelong process by thinking out loud to an adult, engaging in dialogues that enable the child to formulate, catalogue, and systematize experiences. In sum, symbolic realism permits us to dominate and reshape reality, seriously or whimsically, and this provides the motivation to learn language. With language, we give form to our own identities.

It is symbolic realism that underlies our pleasure in playing with words, as in joking. Arrangements of words can turn our stomachs, move us to rage, shatter our self-esteem. It is symbolic realism that permits us to become emotionally involved in fiction, responding erotically to love scenes, trembling with fear as the good guys blunder into an ambush, exulting in the hero's triumph, and gloating at the villain's ignominious downfall. It is symbolic realism that can infuse a neutral reality with blazing emotion and disguise emotional realities in bland abstractions. Military strategists talk about how best to wage nuclear war, omitting any mention of the human horrors that are the basic truths of thermonuclear catastrophe.

It does not matter that people's symbolic ordering of self and world may be cockeyed, shot through with misinformation, superstitions, delusions, inconsistencies, and illogic; it is a basic need for human beings to find a pattern in their lives, and language is the medium of choice.

The child's growing language skills are reflected in everything he or she does. In addition, though, these language skills open new realms of activity, making possible the learning, thinking, and social interchange that will come to occupy an ever increasing part of their still narrow existence.

This does not mean that all our knowledge and beliefs must be verbalizable. Long before we can talk, we form attitudes, attachments, and expectations that may influence our behavior throughout life. Erik Erikson has given us the notion of "basic trust," which is a phenomenon of infancy. Roughly, it translates into an attitude of optimism, a sense that the world is benign and predictable and manageable. Trusting babies feel good about themselves and view the world as satisfying. The opposite of Erikson's first stage of emotional crisis is "basic mistrust," or pessimism. Mistrusting babies view themselves as helpless and the world as a treacherous, uncertain place loaded with emotional booby traps. Basic mistrust carried to its extreme is paranoia. Basic trust is an expression of attachment, the powerful emotional bonds that normally develop between parent and child.

A fallacy that has had to be dispelled is that attachment is mostly automatic: group parents and child into a family, and love will bloom. Something more is needed. How babies are treated by their parents is in some measure a product of the baby's own qualities, actual or perceived. The baby has to have the right stimulus qualities to evoke those special feelings and actions in their parents. Parents, in turn, must be sensitive to those infantile qualities that call forth the right feelings and behaviors toward their babies. For example, if the baby resists being held, or seems indifferent to being fed, or does not stare at the face of the adult who is giving the feeding, or does not reach up to clasp the breast or bottle, parents may feel rejected and lose much of their initial enthusiasm. If the parents hold the baby awkwardly or timidly, if they, in turn, do not study the baby's features, if they fail to fondle and cuddle the baby, or if they do not croon and murmur and babble the loving nonsense that parents are traditionally inspired to produce, the baby may lose interest. Attachment is a two-way street and takes place out of the increasingly complicated reciprocal exchanges that go on between parent and child—touching, playing, hugging, kissing, singing, cooing, crooning, and, eventually, having conversations.

Attachment may be complicated in a number of ways, as when there is enforced separation between mother and child right after birth. In some maternity wards, premature babies are still kept in extreme isolation for prolonged periods, and this does not help the bonding process at all. Or the baby may need special medical treatment at birth, and parents may need a great deal of extra help coming to loving terms with a baby born flawed or deformed.

Out of attachment grows identification. We come to feel at one with the familiar people, places, foodstuffs, smells, utensils, music, speech sounds, rituals, and behavior patterns. They are part of us and we of them. We *belong*. What begins as identification with one's own family gradually expands to an identification with the larger culture whose ways are expressed and embodied in the family's own ways. Young children come to take for granted our society's assumptions, beliefs, values, and ways of doing things. Never mind that later in adolescence we may fervently repudiate and rebel against the same cultural givens. We begin by incorporating them into our own sense of identity. Indeed, the fervor with which we rebel against society's values may be a measure of how deeply we have absorbed them.

Identification with the family and its settings and patterns is emotionally stabilizing for the baby and fosters good communication and the necessary control that we know as discipline. The child wants most awfully to please a well-loved parent, and any expression of displeasure can have an electric effect. (In fact, young children also need a certain amount of external regulation if they are to feel safe, control their impulses, and grow into social responsibility. However, here we shall not go into this.)

The cozy togetherness of the family has another side, what we shall call stranger anxiety. This behavior is first noticeable between ages five and nine months. At the approach of an unfamiliar person, the baby is likely to scream, bury its face in the parent's neck, clutch at the parent, and put as much psychic distance as possible between stranger and self. Places, speech, sounds, smells, foodstuffs, and other things that do not match the image of the familiar are perceived as fearsome, repulsive, and perhaps even dangerous.

Stranger anxiety is of both practical and theoretical interest. On the practical side, we have the hurt feelings of loving grandparents, aunts and uncles, who cannot understand why the baby should reject their advances and who may secretly suspect, however irrationally, that the parents have taught the baby to dislike them.

On the theoretical side, stranger anxiety is interesting, first, because it tells us that the baby, out of repeated exposure, has built up a stable mental framework of the familiar against which strangeness shows up by contrast. Then there is the theoretical question of why some babies show stranger anxiety and others do not. It appears that those babies who have been exposed to only a limited variety of caretakers are likely to show stranger anxiety, while those who have been close to a diversity of people are less likely to. Thus, kibbutz children, who are reared in groups by a variety of caretakers, rarely show stranger anxiety. Notice, though, that we are talking about diversity within a fairly limited range, since very few children have close contact with people representing all the variety to be found in humankind.

A further question is, When do we outgrow stranger anxiety? The answer in many cases seems to be never. Many of us are guilty of ethnocentrism, an unquestioning acceptance of our own society's ways of doing things as the only truly human way. This acceptance may be so deep that it seems perverse, depraved, and even subhuman for people from alien backgrounds to perceive, value, and act differently from the way we do. Ethnocentrism can be viewed as an extension of both egocentrism and stranger anxiety. It may lead to fear or distrust of foreigners, racial prejudice, bigotry, and prejudice against the handicapped. Prejudice, it seems, has some of its roots in the cradle.

For Piaget, the ages between two and seven represent the preoperational stage of cognitive development. This stage is characterized by both new capabilities and those that have not yet appeared. On the positive side, the preoperational stage is marked by the child's blossoming capacity for the symbolic thinking we have been talking about. Basic to symbolic functioning is deferred imitation, the ability to perceive an event, store it away, and then reproduce it later in word or action. Other forms of symbolic thinking are dramatic play, the re-enactment of scenes from everyday life, and drawing as the depiction of past experience. On the negative side, there are limitations in the preoperational stage, such as egocentrism, which certainly does not end with this stage but which is much more profound at the beginning of the period than at the end. Other limitations are the inability of the child to take account of more than one feature of a situation at a time, that is, the inability to conserve, and the child's primitive idea of cause and effect. For example, children may mistake coincidence for causation, so that if a parent arrives home from work just as the sun is setting, one (either event) will be seen as causing the other.

For Erikson, the chief issue of toddlerhood is the development of autonomy, the sense of being in charge of one's own life, making one's own decisions and carrying them through. The contrast of shame and doubt imply withdrawal from taking charge and strong negative feelings toward one's own body and functioning.

Two words define the toddler's battle cry for autonomy, "Me!" and "No!" "Me!" means that I want to do it myself, without even helpful interference. "No!" accompanies one of the visible manifestations of the drive to autonomy, negativism. Negativism does not, however, need verbal expression. The child may go rigid or limp; he or she may kick, bite, scratch, run away, or throw a temper tantrum. Strong adult reactions to negativism seem to act as reinforcers, increasing its frequency, whereas nonreinforcement, ignoring the display, lessens its occurrence.

It is important to notice, too, that many times the child's seeming negativism is in fact nothing more than play acting, trying out how it feels to say no, and a parent who continues unperturbed to dress the child or tuck it into bed finds the child cooperative through a refrain of verbal resistance. In general, if toddlers have ample opportunity to explore and practice things on their own, balanced by the support they sometimes need and by a few necessary restrictions, they emerge from this period with a sound sense of their own abilities and the readiness to undertake new activities of the preschool years in the development of what Erikson calls initiative.

Just as children's self-respect depends on the world's respect for them, their esteem for others is contingent on their own self-esteem. Hostility, viciousness, and evil seem to originate in one's own sense of worthlessness, and whether one is caught in a vicious circle of hatred or a benign circle of love, one cannot escape the circularity of development.

We take it for granted that children strive relentlessly toward maturity and that parents enthusiastically cheer them on. Sometimes yes, sometimes no. Young children are prone to fits of growth ambivalence, where they are not quite sure whether they are ready to tackle the next task—feeding oneself, using the toilet, moving from crib to bed, going to school—or to give up the precious privileges of babyhood. Parents, too, have their bouts of growth ambivalence. Frequently when the child makes progress, the parent greets the event both with applause and with the lament that "I'm losing my baby!" Of course, parents want their children to grow up—but not too fast and not just *now*. When we combine the growth ambivalence of children with that of parents, we end up with a condition of dual ambivalence. This makes for a complicated pattern of reaching out, backing off, urging on, holding back, and all-round uncertainty that may last until the child reaches adulthood and has to cope with the dual ambivalence in his or her own household.

What we have been trying to say in these few pages (and we realize that much has been omitted) is that the dramatic physical, social, emotional, and intellectual development of the first five years takes place within a family that nourishes the child in mind and body but that also imparts, for better or for worse, an entire cultural outlook. The five-year-old does not know, and may never know, the history of his or her culture, but he or she has been profoundly shaped by that history. The youngster may have been made trustful, bright, open to experience and people, avid to learn, or may already be crippled by petty-minded rigidities, fears, and superstitions. The first five years do not fix our characters in permanent patterns, but they can make a very big difference.

BIBLIOGRAPHY

Ames, Louise Bates, Frances L. Ilg, and Carol Chase Haber. *Your One Year Old: The Fun-Loving Fussy 12-to-24-Month-Old*. New York: Delacorte, 1982.

A down-to-earth guide devoted exclusively to one-year-olds, this is only one volume in a series dealing with children from ages one to six. Each volume provides techniques that parents can use through the various stages of a child's development. In each the reader will find an extensive index and a valuable listing of age-appropriate toys and books.

Anastasi, Anne. *Psychological Testing*, 4th ed. New York: Macmillan, 1976.

A widely read text on the issue of testing, it provides a comprehensive view of psychological tests and testing problems, including a discussion of intelligence and the principles of test construction.

Aries, Phillipe. *Centuries of Childhood: A Social History of Family Life*. New York: Random House, 1965.

The author traces the evolution of the family and how children have been perceived and treated over the last few centuries. It is a good discussion of the discovery of childhood as a distinct phase of life.

Bandura, Albert (ed.). *Psychological Modeling: Conflicting Theories*. New York: Lieber-Atherton, 1971.

This extensive review of the major theories of learning by modeling highlights the most important work done in this area. Such questions are debated as the role of reinforcement in observational learning, relative effectiveness of models presented in live action or pictorial presentations or through verbal description, what types of models are most influential, what is the scope of modeling.

Bandura, Albert. *Social Learning Theory.* Englewood Cliffs, N.J.: Prentice-Hall, 1977.

The author explains social learning. The theory is derived from Skinner, but Bandura has added such important concepts as modeling, learning without reinforcement, and cognitive mediation.

Bemporad, Jules R. (ed.). *Child Development in Normality and Psychopathology.* New York: Brunner/Mazel, 1980.

This volume attempts to survey four basic areas: theories of development; stages of development (infancy through adolescence); factors that may affect development such as autism, mental retardation, chronic illness, learning disabilities, and psychosis, to name a few; and methods of diagnostic evaluation. The target audience is clearly professionals, and the attempt is made to explore a variety of theories and approaches, as opposed to espousing any single mode. It is a good reference source, but the writing is uneven. Certainly, the last two sections represent a greater contribution to the field of child development than the material that precedes them. Of particular note is the chapter dealing with the special concerns raised in the therapeutic relationship that is established with a dying child.

Bettelheim, Bruno. *Children of the Dream.* New York: Macmillan, 1969.

This book is an informative and clear description of child-rearing practices on the kibbutzim in Israel. It is the author's opinion that insights gained through his observations of kibbutz life have significance for working with children in the United States who come from deprived circumstances.

Brazelton, T. Berry. *Toddlers and Parents: A Declaration of Independence.* New York: Delacorte, 1974.

The subtitle, *A Declaration of Independence*, is the focus. The author explores the themes of the turbulent toddler period, a time of critical struggle for both child and parents, the ambivalence between autonomy and dependence, and the importance of a sound resolution for the future development of the child.

Bronfenbrenner, Urie. *Two Worlds of Childhood, U.S. and U.S.S.R.* New York: Simon & Schuster, 1972.

This study provides insights into child-care development through incisive comparisons between American and Soviet education.

Cable, Mary. *The Little Darlings.* New York: Scribner, 1972.

Cable has written a highly readable, thoroughly researched history of childhood in America. From the Puritan view that the child was born evil, the author traces the changing climate of child care—"from birch rod to lollipop." Along the way, she provides a lively history of the changes in attitudes toward sex education, clothing, toilet training, discipline, etc.

Cazden, Courtney (ed.). *Language in Early Childhood Education,* rev. ed. Washington, D.C.: National Association for the Education of Young Children, 1981.

This well-known anthology of articles and research studies about language development in the preschool years has been revised by the editor. Examples of topics included are language development in school and at home, the teachers' role in helping young children develop linguistic competence, curriculum, language and learning to read. There is a valuable annotated bibliography.

Chukovsky, Kornei. *From Two to Five.* Berkeley: University of California Press, 1963.

Of particular interest is this Russian psychologist's view of the preschool child. Rich in anecdotes, this book makes a unique contribution to our appreciation of the language of children during this period and is revealing of the child's thought processes and imagination. Chukovsky shares with his readers his observations of children's mental dexterity in learning to speak, their linguistic creativity, and their predilection for poetry. The cultural contrasts are striking and intriguing.

Church, Joseph. *Language and the Discovery of Reality.* New York: Vintage Books, 1961. (Also translated into German.)

The author describes how children acquire language, the kinds of behavior that language makes possible, and the reality to which language gives children access. The book is highly readable, richly informative, and filled with real-life observations of children in the process of beginning to understand speech and to speak.

Church, Joseph. *Understanding Your Child From Birth to Three.* New York: Pocket Books, 1980.

A simply, well-written view of good child-rearing practices, this book has often been used as a text for paraprofessionals and other child-care workers. The first seven chapters deal with such practical issues as parents' and children's fears, sleeping, feeding, discipline, and early sexuality. The remaining chapters focus on language and general cognitive development, individual differences, and the child as a social being. Toward the beginning of the chapter on intellectual development is one of the best (and briefest) descriptions of the intertwining between intellect and emotion.

Church, Joseph (ed.). *Three Babies: Biographies of Cognitive Development.* Westport, Ct.: Greenwood Press, 1978.

This is a record by three mothers of their babies from birth to just over two years, using guidelines provided by Church, but also recording anything of interest. The author has successfully woven into the anecdotal descriptions a set of comprehensive notes that allow the serious students of infant behavior to make links between the real-life material and laboratory data on children and theoretical views about growth and development. Although the title indicates an emphasis on cognitive development, it is clear from the content and the editor's comments that the emotional life of these youngsters cannot be separated from their cognitive growth. This volume is one of the few observational records so rich in depth and scope. Parents and professionals will find it illuminating reading.

Cohen, Dorothy H., and Virginia Stern. *Observing and Recording the Behavior of Young Children.* New York: Teachers College Press, 1978.

The second, enlarged edition of a widely used book, as the first (published in 1959), describes methods of studying children in a variety of settings to help teachers understand the behavior of preschoolers and children in the primary grades.

Cohen, Stewart. *Social and Personality Development in Childhood*. New York: Macmillan, 1976.

The basic issues of childhood social and personal development are examined, including theories, origins of social development, and specific topics such as aggression, achievement, morality, and sex roles.

Dennis, Wayne. *Children of the Crèche*. Englewood Cliffs, N.J.: Prentice-Hall, 1973.

The author demonstrates the devastating psychological effects of institution rearing based on a study conducted in Lebanon over a ten-year period. Improvement was shown in boys who were moved at age six to a more stimulating environment and in children adopted into private families.

De Villiers, Jill G., and Peter A. De Villiers. *Language Acquisition*. Cambridge: Harvard University Press, 1978.

This clearly written summary account of how children acquire language deals with such questions as kinds of experience needed to support language acquisition, critical periods for language acquisition, is there a genetic predisposition for speech, language in developmentally disabled children.

Dobzhansky, Theodosius. *Genetic Diversity and Human Equality*. New York: Basic Books, 1973.

The subtitle of this book is *The Facts and Fallacies in the Explosive Genetics and Education Controversy*. The author, acknowledged as one of the world's greatest geneticists, attempts to rectify the host of misconceptions and mischaracterizations about the nature both of heredity and intellect. The volume is vital for policy makers, scientists, and the concerned citizen.

Elkind, David. *Children and Adolescents: Interpretive Essays on Jean Piaget*, 3rd ed. New York: Oxford University Press, 1981.

Elkind provides a clear and informative introduction to Piaget and his work. The book is introduced by the author's personal recollection of Piaget. The implications of Piaget's work for the education of children pervades the volume's nine essays.

Elkind, David. *The Child and Society: Essays in Applied Child Development.* New York: Oxford University Press, 1979.

In his collection of twenty-two essays the author attempts to analyze child development in relation to contemporary social, cultural, education, and religious influences. He also tries to bridge theory, research, and practice.

Erikson, Erik H. *Childhood and Society,* 2nd ed. New York: Norton, 1964.

Child development is presented from a modified psychoanalytic perspective. Erikson presents his theory of psychosocial development from infancy to old age. He describes his "eight ages of man," each of which represents a psychosocial conflict that must be resolved positively for good ego development, healthful functioning, and progression to the next stage or "age."

Flavell, John. *Cognitive Development.* Englewood Cliffs, N.J.: Prentice-Hall, 1977.

Flavell has written a very readable, personal approach to human cognitive development, emphasizing the work of Piaget. The three chapters devoted to infancy, early and middle childhood, and adolescence are the core of the book. Taken as a whole, they describe the child's growing understanding of the social and physical world. Chapters on perception, communication, and memory complete the book. The book is for both professionals and parents.

Flavell, John, and Lee Ross (eds.). *Social Cognitive Development: Frontiers and Possible Futures.* Cambridge, Eng.: Cambridge University Press, 1981.

In this description of social cognitive development the editors bring to bear the implications of their own theoretical positions and research findings. The volume is one of the first books on the subject.

Fraiberg, Selma H. *The Magic Years.* New York: Scribner, 1968.

Writing from a psychoanalytic perspective, Fraiberg translates theory into practical suggestions for child rearing. Especially prominent are reflections of Anna Freud's writings on ego psychology. The book is organized into three major sections: the first eighteen months, eighteen months to three years, and age three to six. It is a classic and vivid portrayal of child life. Anyone seriously engaged in the study of early childhood should be familiar with this book.

Freud, Anna. *Normality and Pathology in Childhood: Assessments of Development.* New York: International Universities Press, 1965. This book has become a classic in the field of child development. While the text is in part technical, with a section on child analysis, the author's observations of child behavior and her understanding of the child's "world view" as this changes throughout development make this book valuable reading for the parent, educator, or professional. The author's well-known concept of developmental lines, first set forth here, is particularly recommended. Anna Freud writes with respect for the child's uniqueness and with consideration of individual differences and the environment in her assessment of normality and pathology.

Furth, Hans G. *Piaget for Teachers.* Englewood Cliffs, N.J.: Prentice-Hall, 1970.

Furth clarifies Piaget's theories of intellectual development as they relate to learning in the early years and notes the implications for nurturing intelligence at different stages by appropriate experience. The author presents school situations that stimulate thinking—and it is thinking, not rote learning that matters!

Furth, Hans G. *The World of Grown-Ups: Children's Conceptions of Society.* New York: Elsevier, 1980.

Based on many interviews with British children, the book plots the course of thinking of children from ages five to eleven, illustrating the development from the playful imagery of preschoolers to the more logical thinking of adolescents. The author furnishes an insightful description of children's society experiences, capturing the child's own perspective as it gradually approximates adult thought.

Ginsburg, Herbert, and Sylvia Opper. *Piaget's Theory of Intellectual Development*, 2nd ed. Englewood Cliffs, N.J.: Prentice-Hall, 1979.

This book represents a clear outline of Piaget's basic ideas, his early research and theory, and a discussion of the implications of his work. The authors give a detailed treatment of the sensorimotor stage of cognitive development as well as other stages of intellectual development.

Gordon, Ira J. *Baby Learning Through Baby Play: A Parent's Guide for the First Two Years*. New York: St. Martin's Press, 1970.

This very useful guide to games and interactions for infants and toddlers for parents, paraprofessionals, and teachers can be used for building day-care programs for these age groups.

Gordon, Ira J., et al. *Child Learning Through Child Play: Learning Activities for Two and Three-Year-Olds*. New York: St. Martin's Press, 1972.

The author supplements his "baby" play guide with this volume. It is a low-key approach to games and activities that develop the intellectual and physical capabilities of two- and three-year-olds. Although the content is aimed primarily at parents, it can be used for building a day-care program for the age group.

Gruber, Howard E., and J. Jacques Voneche (eds.). *The Essential Piaget*. New York: Basic Books, 1977.

This is an interpretive reference and guide to the work of Piaget. Piaget, himself, described this substantial volume as "the best and most complete." He also stated that "in reading the explanatory texts, I came to understand better what I had wanted to do." Taking the overwhelming mass of Piaget's work, the editors clearly examine much of Piaget's work, spanning a period of about seventy years. It is a most complete work on Piaget that clarifies Piaget's aims, ideas, and underlying themes.

Guillaume, Paul. *Imitation in Children*. Chicago: University of Chicago Press, 1971.

Guillaume sets forth a theoretical discussion of imitative

learning in very young children, including in his comprehensive treatment the role of memory, perception, mental images.

Hale, G. K., and M. Lewis (eds.). *Attention and Cognitive Development*. New York: Plenum, 1979.

This volume offers a broad perspective on the concept of attention—an integral aspect of theories on perception, thought, and feeling—that is becoming increasingly prominent in the study of cognitive development. Several chapters are concerned with the role of attention in such cognitive processes as visual scanning, stimulus identification, perception and memory, problem solving, and the lateralization of function. Attention is also explored as a factor in the child's everyday functioning. Chapters are devoted to the role of attention in the school classroom and television watching, as well as to attentional factors associated with individual differences in children's functioning. Individual differences discussed include hyperactivity, learning disabilities, cognitive styles, and infant mental handicaps.

Hymes, James L., Jr. *The Child Under Six*. Englewood Cliffs, N.J.: Prentice-Hall, 1963.

Hymes focuses on the feeling, thinking, and behavior of the child from birth to six. Although the discussion is directed to parents, it can be an important resource for all who work with young children. Emphasis is given to guiding the child toward individuality. Establishing relationships of love and respect are also stressed.

Irwin, D. Michelle, and M. Margaret Bushnell. *Observational Strategies for Child Study*. New York: Holt, Rinehart and Winston, 1980.

The authors have written a very clear presentation of the why and how of observing children. Actual examples of such techniques as anecdotal records, running records, case studies, time sampling, checklists, rating scales, are provided. Each technique is explained in terms of use, advantages, and disadvantages. The data gathered is analyzed, and suggestions are offered for using the data. There are summaries of each approach as well as listings of further reading. It is a very useful, practical book.

Isaacs, Susan. *The Nursery Years: The Mind of the Child from Birth to Six Years*. New York: Schocken, 1968 (originally published in 1929).

This is a classic work by a British educator-psychoanalyst. In contrast to the prescriptions for habit training that was prevalent in the literature when this book was first written, the author was concerned with the child's point of view and with understanding children's fears, hostility, jealousies, and the like.

Isaacs, Susan. *Social Development in Young Children*. New York: Schocken, 1972 (first published in 1933).

Isaacs meticulously recorded observations dealing with the social and sexual aspects of the child's primary egocentric attitude: hostility and aggression, friendliness, and cooperation. Psychoanalytically inclined, she explored in detail the deeper sources of love and hate concerned with sexuality.

Kamin, Leon J. *The Science and Politics of IQ*. New York: Halstead Press, 1974.

Kamin critically examines the relationship between race and intelligence and analyzes the social and political implications.

Kaplan, Louise. *Oneness and Separateness*. New York: Simon & Schuster, 1978.

This volume is a lyrically written account of the inner emotions and experiences of the infant through the first three years. Emphasis is on the struggle to become an independent and separate human being. The author shows how every parent or caregiver can effectively respond to the push-pull feelings of the child. Much of the work is based on the theories of Margaret S. Mahler.

Kliman, Gilbert W., and Albert Rosenfeld. *Responsible Parenthood: The Child's Psyche Through the Six-Year Pregnancy*. New York: Holt, Rinehart and Winston, 1980.

The book examines the effects of societal and parental attitudes and the child's genetic inheritance on his personality and development until the age of six. In clear, concise language, it discusses how a child develops psychologically. Early danger signals that lead to emotional disturbance are described. The three-pronged message is that emotional disturbance begins before the birth of the child, it involves everyone who comes into contact with children, and it can be prevented with more knowledge about early development.

Kohlberg, Lawrence. *The Philosophy of Moral Development: Moral Stages and the Idea of Justice.* New York: Harper & Row, 1981.

The author attempts to deal empirically with a definition of human morality. This volume is based on his experiences in the classroom as well as his collection of articles on the subject written for academic journals. Kohlberg has tried to compress a highly complex issue that philosophers have struggled with throughout the ages into six development stages, from the first that deals with morality as a way of avoiding punishment to the sixth and highest stage that deals with morality as understanding the difference between what is just and legal and the dignity of civil disobedience. The author makes a valiant and noteworthy effort, which is not altogether successful and sometimes simplistic, to explicate a subject of enormous scope and intricacy. The volume should be of interest to educators who have had to work with secondary sources on the author's work until now.

Krogman, Willard M. *Child Growth.* Ann Arbor: University of Michigan Press, 1972.

Krogman examines motor growth, language, and personal-social development. He discusses pathology due to genetic inheritance and poor nutrition. A short book, it reads easily and is full of information.

Lerner, Richard. *Concepts and Theories of Human Development.* Reading, Mass.: Addison-Wesley, 1976.

In this excellent survey of the technical issues of theory building and research, such major issues as the nature-nurture controversy, research and social implications, and theories of development are covered.

Lewis, Michael (ed.). *The Origins of Intelligence: Infancy and Early Childhood.* New York: Plenum, 1976.

The volume examines infant intelligence from a wide variety of perspectives: biological, social, cognitive, affective, historical, and sociopolitical. It offers a complete picture of the findings and conclusions of each of the major schools of thought in the field in thirteen articles that touch on almost every critical aspect of infant intelligence.

Lewis, Michael, and Jeanne Brooks-Gunn. *Social Cognition and the Acquisition of Self.* New York: Plenum, 1979.

The authors review the results of recent studies in self-recognition, postulating that development is both an active process involving plans, intentions, and feelings and a process influenced by biological imperatives and social controls. They also offer a theory of social cognition. Chapters focus on the development of self in early life; the role of self, affect, and cognition; and the uses of a concept of self to explain such diverse topics as empathy, friendship, and sex-role identification.

Lewis, Michael, and Leonard Rosenblum (eds.). *The Development of Affect: The Genesis of Behavior*, Vol. 1. New York: Plenum, 1978.

This volume surveys advances in methodology and theory that have promoted understanding of the meaning and development of affect. Essential information is presented on the use of measurements of facial expression, ANS responsivity, and other techniques for the measurement of affect; the relationship of affect to cognition and the maturation of self; individual differences in affect development; and affective dysfunction, especially as it appears in infants with Down's syndrome. Taken as a whole, these distinctive perspectives provide a synoptic view of both our present and potential knowledge of the nature of affect and its functions in human life.

Lewis, Michael, and Leonard Rosenblum (eds.). *Friendship and Peer Relations. The Origins of Behavior*, Vol. 4. New York: Wiley, 1975.

The focus is on the infant's social behavior that does not directly involve the relationship with its caregiver. Peer relations and the establishment of friendships represent an appropriate arena within which to consider the infant's social relationships in a broader perspective than that traditionally provided by studies of infant-adult interaction. The eleven chapters, together with the editors' introduction and overview, constitute a comprehensive assessment of early peer relations.

Lewis, Michael, and Leonard Rosenblum (eds.). *The Origins of Fear. The Origins of Behavior*, Vol. 2. New York: Wiley, 1974.

This volume examines the expression and development of fear in human infants in various settings and considers pertinent aspects of parallel phenomena in the behavior of animals. The book considers the origins of fear in individual organisms as well as within specified phylogenetic and ontogenetic groupings.

Liedloff, Jean. *The Continuum Concept*. New York: Warner Books, 1979.

Anthropological comparisons of cultures and child-rearing practices are used to develop the continuum concept in family living. The author stresses the importance of physical contact between family members.

Maccoby, Eleanor E. *Social Development: Psychological Growth and the Parent-Child Relationship*. New York: Harcourt Brace Jovanovich, 1980.

This summary and analysis of the role of the family in children's social development includes a historical overview, with separate chapters on attachment, impulse control, aggression, self-concepts, sex typing, moral development, and child-rearing practices. The content spans infancy through middle childhood. The approaches include the cognitive-developmental, the Freudian, and the behavioristic, although the author's bias is for the first. A summary of research and theory is presented for each topic.

Maccoby, Eleanor E., and Carol N. Jacklin. *The Psychology of Sex Differences*. Stanford, Ca.: Stanford University Press, 1974.

In a comprehensive survey of research in the areas of intellect and achievement, social behavior, and the origins of psychological sex differences, the authors make the complexity of the issues very clear. An extensive annotated bibliography is included.

Maier, Henry W. *Three Theories of Child Development*, 3rd ed. New York: Harper & Row, 1978.

Maier presents a discussion of the psychoanalytic theory of Erik H. Erikson, the cognitive theory of Jean Piaget, and the learning theory of Robert R. Sears. He compares the three theories and notes their implications for applied child development.

Mussen, Paul, and Nancy Eisenberg-Berg. *Roots of Caring, Sharing, and Helping: The Development of Prosocial Behavior in Children.* San Francisco: Freeman, 1977.

The text explores important questions relating to child development, such as how the cultural environment helps or hinders children's tendencies to help others and which child-rearing practices and parental attitudes foster caring in children. Special attention is paid to the development of altruism, generosity, and personal consideration. The authors, who believe that such behavior is learned, show how it develops and how it can be modeled and enhanced.

Mussen, Paul H., John J. Conger, and J. Kagan. *Child Development and Personality.* 5th ed. New York: Harper & Row, 1979 (originally published in 1956).

The fifth edition remains encyclopedic in its coverage of research but provides little in terms of the descriptive behavior of children. It is divided into five parts, chronological in sequence, except for Part 3, which devotes itself to language and cognitive development. There is a heavy emphasis on Piaget's theories. The book is primarily for the professional.

Nelson, Keith (ed.). *Children's Language*, Vols. 1, 2. New York: Gardner Press, 1978, Vol. 1; 1979, Vol. 2.

Both volumes are a good summary of recent research on children's language development. Volume 2 also deals with teaching language to apes.

Neubauer, Peter (ed.). *The Process of Child Development.* New York: New American Library, 1976.

This "reader" anthology, edited by a prominent child analyst, contains a fine representative sampling from the literature of child development. This book is divided into four sections—on developmental concepts, cognitive development, clinical issues, and special issues. A general introduction as well as introductory sections for each section assist the reader in obtaining a conceptual overview of the material. Authors such as Anna Freud, Margaret Mahler, and Jean Piaget are represented. The book is particularly recommended for child educators as well as parents who wish to increase their understanding of the developing child's capacities, stages, and view of life.

Phillips, John L., Jr. *Piaget's Theory: A Primer.* San Francisco: Freeman, 1981.

As the title suggests, Phillips, in simple language, summarizes Piaget's theory of cognitive development. His text is a nontechnical presentation of the material, suitable for laypeople and professionals. An innovative "introsummary" serves as both an introduction to lay concepts and a summary that helps the readers to review and integrate the ideas as they make their way through the book. The author writes with cognizance of the difficulty of the material, both of its contents and the original language and provides encouragement to the reader in terms of approaching and understanding the material. It is an interesting book, useful to the parent who wants to gain a better understanding of his or her child's development as well as for educators and health professionals.

Piaget, Jean. *The Origins of Intelligence in Children.* New York: International Universities Press, 1966 (originally published in 1952).

Piaget's classic presentation of the six sequential stages of the sensorimotor period is abundantly illustrated with observations of his own children.

Piaget, Jean. *Success and Understanding.* Cambridge: Harvard University Press, 1978.

Piaget casts new light on the processes involved in the growth of children's comprehension and validates the saying of early childhood teachers, "Children learn by doing." In an earlier companion volume, *The Grasp of Consciousness,* Piaget demonstrated the act of becoming conscious of an action, such as walking on all fours, serves to transform the scheme into a concept. In this book he illustrates children's success in solving a variety of physical puzzles by being able to anticipate actions and results. The text is an excellent exposition of the relations between thought and action. It is not for the beginning student of Piaget.

Pulaski, Mary Ann Spencer. *Understanding Piaget,* rev. ed. New York: Harper & Row, 1980.

A clear, readable, nontechnical interpretation of the research and thinking of Jean Piaget, this work is especially suitable for teachers and anyone who works with children in understanding Piaget's view of children's cognitive development. The author helps the reader understand clearly how Piaget believes children perceive the world around them at different ages, why they ask questions and interpret information in ways that often seem strange to adults, and thus what to expect of them.

Pulaski, Mary Ann Spencer. *Your Baby's Mind and How It Grows: Piaget's Theory for Parents.* New York: Harper & Row, 1978.

The author tries to make clear to parents the stages of cognitive growth described by Piaget, whose theories may not be easy for the average parent to understand. Sections on toys and games will help the reader to follow up on explanations of baby behaviors at each successive stage.

Redl, Fritz, and David Wineman. *Children Who Hate: The Disorganization and Breakdown of Behavior Controls.* New York: Free Press, 1965.

This study of why children's behavior breaks down and what can be done to prevent it probes behavior of children whose extreme aggressiveness requires clinical treatment. The authors suggest methods to parents and teachers for handling less troubled children.

Rickman, John (ed.). *General Selections from the Works of Sigmund Freud.* Garden City, N.Y.: Doubleday, 1957.

Included are Freud's selected works from 1910 to 1923, covering such topics as the origin and development of psychoanalysis, the ego and the id, repression, and beyond the pleasure principle. Someone interested in the main theses expounded by Freud would find the volume helpful.

Rubin, Zick. *Children's Friendships*. Cambridge: Harvard University Press, 1980.

In this readable exploration of the development, variety, and consequences of children's friendships, combining research and anecdotes, the author shows how children's friendships change with increasing sophistication and deals with popularity and unpopularity, cliques, the role of adults in facilitating or hindering social skills, and other pertinent topics. The pages are filled with examples from real-life conversations between and among children.

Samuels, Shirley C. *Enhancing Self-Concept in Early Childhood*. New York: Human Sciences Press, 1977.

Samuels critically summarizes the major theories relating to the development of self-esteem and integrates the practical and theoretical aspects of self-concept development. The book is intended to help the teacher and parent with the normal child and to recognize when further help is necessary. The author includes practical activities, books, and experiences that can be provided to enhance children's self-concepts.

Scharf, Peter (ed.). *Readings in Moral Education*. Minneapolis: Winston Press, 1978.

The contents are divided into five parts: the philosophy and psychology of moral education, classroom moral education, teacher as moral educator, an integrated approach to moral education, and criticism and controversy. The distinction between moral education and the values-clarification approach is made. The authors of the articles include Peter Scharf, Lawrence Kohlberg, Edwin Fenton, and John Broughton. Although the selections are directed mostly at older children and adults, there are a number of pieces that focus on the moral judgment and the moral education of young children.

Schorsch, Anita. *Images of Childhood: An Illustrated Social History*. New York: Mayflower Books, 1979.

This fine, basic informal history of what it was like to be a child in the past few centuries shows how changing attitudes toward children have been reflected in the visual arts. The author has chosen fascinating illustrations to complement her well-written commentary on the child at play, at work, in the family, at school, and on the concept of the good and bad child.

Sidel, Ruth. *Women and Child Care in China: A Firsthand Report.* New York: Penguin, 1973.

The changing traditional attitudes toward child rearing in China are described, and the practices in Chinese nurseries are compared with those in Israeli kibbutzim and Russian nurseries.

Skinner, B. F. *About Behaviorism.* New York: Knopf, 1974.

Skinner attempts to account for human behavior through the principles of operant conditioning, a controversial philosophy that has aroused both admiration and opprobrium. Skinner is the best-known spokesman for this view of human nature.

Spitzer, Dean R. *Concept Formation and Learning in Early Childhood.* Columbus, Oh.: Merrill, 1977.

Spitzer has written a simple but comprehensive description of the different theories of how children form concepts, allowing them increasingly to organize their many experiences. Although the author deals with most of the well-known cognitive theorists and with complicated material, he does so in a way that is accessible to nonprofessionals as well as to preservice educators. The book has two parts: the first deals with theories of concept formation, and the second provides a compilation of activities that can be used to enrich the early experiences of young children.

Spock, Benjamin. *Baby and Child Care.* New York: Pocket Books, 1981.

Spock's book, first published in 1946, continues to be a classic for millions of parents. It describes the day-by-day development of the child and includes the behavioral problems and physical disorders that are common to children.

Stone, L. Joseph, and Joseph Church. *Childhood and Adolescence,* 4th ed. New York: Random House, 1979.

This distinguished and widely used text in child development is known for its unique ability to combine the most up-to-date scientific thinking with vivid depictions of the living child. Now in its fourth edition, it has influenced several generations (since it was first published in 1957) of psychologists, educators, social workers, health practitioners, theologians, and parents. Its organization is excellent. In addition, each chapter is followed by a summary, references, and suggested readings. The references and suggested readings are then combined at the end of the book into a general bibliography. There is also a glossary of technical terms, and a combined subject/author index.

Stone, Lawrence. *The Family, Sex and Marriage in England 1500–1800*. New York: Harper & Row, 1977.

This scholarly, superbly written, and brilliantly argued book charts the evolution of family life from the pattern of the extended family in the Middle Ages to the nuclear family that emerged in the late eighteenth century. It offers a clear and provocative analysis of why and how that evolution took place. The chapters on changes in child rearing over the centuries are filled with fascinating examples.

Szasz, Suzanne. *The Unspoken Language of Children*. New York: Norton, 1980.

A well-done integration of words and photographs demonstrates the importance of nonverbal communication. The main focus is on children's feelings expressed through their nonverbal messages. The need for adult awareness of body language as a mode of communication is stressed. The volume's 192 photographs, with comprehensive explanations, capture such moods as joy, triumph, contentment, anger, and jealousy, through body expression.

Tanner, John M. *Education and Physical Growth*, 2nd ed. New York: International Universities Press, 1979.

Tanner furnishes an easily read account of physical development from birth to maturity. He summarizes basic principles of growth and factors that affect growth. He also discusses developmental versus chronological age, brain development, critical periods, and the influence of heredity. The information is given in clear, nontechnical terms.

Tronick, Edward, and Lauren Adamson. *Babies as People: New Findings on Our Social Beginnings.* New York: Macmillan, 1980.

The authors contend that newborn babies are *able* to respond socially. But, they also show how this ability is dependent on our ability to discern babies' movements and special ways of communicating and how to respond to these in order to help babies develop their own uniqueness. The discussion is based on research, especially that having to do with the intertwining of baby and adult relationship as the basis for social development. The book is written for parents as well as infant health-care specialists.

Vygotsky, Lev Semenovich. *Thought and Language.* New York and Cambridge: Wiley and M.I.T. Press, 1962 (original Russian edition, 1934).

Vygotsky deals with the relationship between language and thinking. Unlike theorists such as Piaget, he assigns primacy to language in cognitive development. His main thesis is that language dominates thought.

Vygotsky, Lev Semenovich. [Edited by Michael Cole, V. John-Steiner, S. Scribner, and E. Souberman.] *Mind in Society: The Development of Higher Psychological Processes.* Cambridge: Harvard University Press, 1978.

The editors have presented a unique selection of Vygotsky's important essays. In these essays Vygotsky argues that the mind cannot be understood in isolation from the surrounding society. He applies this theoretical framework to the development of perception, attention, memory, language, and play, and he examines its implications for education.

Walsh, Huber M. *Introducing the Young Child to the Social World.* New York: Macmillan, 1980.

Although human beings have the potential for acting in prosocial behavior, the author suggests that it must be learned. The book is designed to help parents and educators understand how prosocial behavior develops, the processes underlying that development, and how ways can be formed to encourage that development.

Warren, Rita M. *Caring: Supporting Children's Growth*. Washington, D.C.: National Association for the Education of Young Children, 1977.

This small pamphlet that deals sensitively with how children come to accept themselves and others is especially helpful to parents and teachers.

Weeks, Thelma E. *Born to Talk*. Rowley, Mass.: Newbury House, 1979.

This book is unique. Unlike many books that focus largely on the acquisition of language structure, it is concerned with how children learn to use language as a tool to accomplish things. It stresses the social and functional aspects of language development. Writing in clear, nontechnical language, the author discusses the communicative and noncommunicative functions of language, the acquisition of conversational skills, language play and games, and nonverbal communication. She includes many examples of young children's language behavior and provides valuable information that has implications for early childhood teachers and paraprofessionals. The content and style are appropriate for parents as well as professionals.

Weininger, Otto. *Out of the Minds of Babes: The Strength of Children's Feelings*. Springfield, Ill.: Thomas, 1981.

The author explores why children feel the way they do and parents' roles in children's emotional reactions. The intensity of children's thoughts and emotions is examined, and the effect on development outlined and explained. The chapters describe reactions to a variety of situations based on the child's various developmental stages.

Werner, H. *Developmental Processes: Heinz Werner's Selected Writings*, Vols. 1, 2. Edited by Sybil S. Barten and Margery B. Franklin. New York: International Universities Press, 1978.

These volumes are the work of a noted developmental theorist who contributed such principles as the orthogenetic principle that contends that development proceeds from a state of relative globality and lack of differentiation to a state of increasing differentiation and articulation. He also gave us other polarities of development, such as egocentrism vs relativism, from lability to stability. Werner's theories are easily observable in children's development. The volumes are written primarily for professionals.

Williams, Frederick, Robert Hopper, and Diana S. Natalicio. *The Sounds of Children*. Englewood Cliffs, N.J.: Prentice-Hall, 1977.

The authors provide an excellent introduction to current view of language, how it is acquired, how it varies depending on situation, region or social group, and how the attitudes teachers develop about children's language influence learning. The content is particularly relevant for those who work with native Spanish- and Black-English-speaking children. There are recordings of each example of children's speech used in the text. The book is of value to speech and language students, parents, paraprofessionals, and teachers.

Zigler, Edward F., and Irving L. Child. *Socialization and Personality Development*. Reading, Mass.: Addison-Wesley, 1973.

The authors present an exhaustive and integrated discussion of theories, disciplines, and major areas on children's social development in this comprehensive source book.

3
The
Family

THE IMPORTANCE OF THE FAMILY

Marjorie W. Kelly

The influences of the family on its members are complex and lingering. The young child's first sustained experience of the world usually occurs within this intimate group where, as Leichter stresses, "virtually the entire range of human experience can take place" (1975, p. 1). For very young children the family is indeed the world in microcosm, and their experiences as a part of this system are a compelling influence on the ways they will grow and realize their potential.

Family interactions form a framework that shapes the development of self-image and the physical, emotional, intellectual, and social capabilities. Family forces may encourage and stimulate the individual's budding capabilities or discourage, thwart, and misdirect them. Either way, living in a family provides the child with lasting first impressions of self and others and how self and others interrelate. Time and events may radically modify these first impressions and inclinations. They remain, however, as a "baseline" against which new ideas are interpreted and evaluated. Self-esteem, perceptions of physical and mental capabilities, imagination, expectations of others, skills, talents, hopes, fears, and the ability to take risks and effectively tap one's own resources to love, work, and play are all shaped and fashioned in the family.

What exactly a family is defies simple definition. To understand and then maximize the positive effects of family living, it is important to differentiate between family as a form and family functioning. *Form* simply indicates who is in the intimate group. *Functioning* emphasizes the processes that determine what it is like to live in a particular family.

Many forms of family exist in the United States—nuclear, extended, single-parent, blended, and communal. There is no proof that one form is intrinsically superior to any other. Each seems to have distinct strengths and weaknesses. We need to consider family processes—how the group meets the needs of its members and finds mutually satisfactory answers to existential problems—if we want to understand and improve the quality of family life. Satir, in her book *Peoplemaking* (1972), believes family processes form patterns of functioning that range from "nurturing" to "troubled." Ability to nurture depends on four interrelated factors: (1) level of self-esteem of family members; (2) quality of communication; (3) realism, reasonableness, and flexibility of the family's basic rules of operation; and (4) the quality of "links" or relationships to neighbors, friends, school, work, community, and the larger society. People in nurturing families are able to meet life's challenges with some degree of realism, optimism, and success. They take risks, learn from mistakes, and keep growing.

Thinking about families in terms of their ability to nurture places the emphasis on living, learning, and growing not on static forms or standard sociological variables such as ethnicity, race, or religion. It reminds us of the continuous give-and-take that typifies the strong family as it accommodates and supports daily life, acknowledging cycles of activity and rest, group involvement and withdrawal into privacy, work and play, laughter and tears. This emphasis recalls John Dewey's assertion that education is, after all, using life experiences for learning and growth.

The family is, in fact, the first "educator" of the child. Viewing the family as educator also emphasizes process rather than form, that is, what is happening within families and between families and other groups in society. Leichter (1975) sees the family as an "arena" where numerous educational encounters take place between all members. The teaching and learning runs the gamut from planned and formal to spontaneous and informal. Adults educate children and are also educated by them and by each other. Children learn from each other. Moreover, children learn to learn and develop educative style within the family. Values, attitudes, and skills developed here affect the ways the children respond to school and the larger world as they use family experiences to "mediate" or interpret new experiences.

The family is indeed the first educator. What happens there continues to influence how we manage at school, at work, and in relationships with others as we seek to create new families of our own for the nurture of ourselves and our children.

References

Leichter, H. J. *Family as Educator*. New York: Teachers College Press, 1975.

Satir, V. *Peoplemaking*. Palo Alto, Ca.: Science and Behavior Books, 1972.

THE FAMILY: AN OVERVIEW

Nina Lief, M.D.

"The family is the backbone of the nation." This statement and similar ones have been made often and are accepted without question. One, however, needs to stop and think what is meant by "family."

In the early part of the twentieth century the accepted family structure was portrayed to consist of a loving hardworking father providing for his wife and three or four children; a mother, always at home, supervising her children's care, often with the help of grandparents, aunts, and uncles living under the same roof or close by. This early family has been discussed glibly and perhaps romanticized too much. But, this extended family, romanticized or not, is hard to find today and is now the exception rather than the accepted family structure.

The Nuclear Family

With World War II innumerable families were dislocated from their places of origin. Thus the "nuclear" family became accepted as representative of the family. The "nuclear" unit was identified as a mother and father with one or two children stripped of the support of the extended family and often living far from them. However, the unit was still a two-parent family.

The Single-Parent Family

Today the family in increasing numbers has been stripped further; there are one-parent families consisting usually of a mother, sometimes only a father, with one or more children.

In some quarters there is a small outcry against these changes in the nature of the family unit, particularly from agencies required to give aid to these families. However, in general, there is complacence. Some even approve the demise of the old family structure, welcoming the possibility of living freer lives without so many family ties; others prefer to remain unmarried— with changing partners and children by different partners. Some prefer to choose a "family" from unrelated people and live in communes; these communes then serve as substitute families.

Observing the many changes taking place in the family, one cannot help but consider the functions of the family and ponder how these changes affect our society.

Functions of the Family—Then and Now

Historically, one of the primary functions of a family has been to accumulate property and pass along the wealth to succeeding generations. Wealth was preserved by families so that the family could care for itself. Philanthropies were carried on by families. Today the government is more involved in the care of the family's welfare needs.

Another function of the family was as the conservator of the culture and the means of conveying it from generation to generation. However, homogenization by the communication media has brought a tendency to uniformity rather than uniqueness.

But the main function of the family, throughout time, is the care of children, for they are the real backbone of society and the hope of the future. This role, too, is being jeopardized. The mother who used to stay home may no longer be able to do that. She, too, has to go to work. According to Urie Bronfenbrenner (1976), a third of all working mothers have children under age three and a half of all working mothers have children under age six. Who, then, is assuming the role of the family? Who is taking care of these children? There are reported to be 1.8 million latch-key children in the United States. With so many mothers going out to work there are fewer adults at home to take care of children. Obviously, these children are getting little care.

Why Mothers Have Joined the Work Force

The economic reasons for so many mothers becoming full- or part-time members of the labor market are not difficult to understand. The high cost of living makes it impossible for many families to subsist on the father's income alone. For some families it is not a question of subsistence that forces mothers to work but societal pressure to sustain a level of material standards for which they feel they must compete.

On the other hand, there are those mothers who may not *need* to earn but feel that because they have professional talents they must express them; and, if the drive to do so does not come from within, society puts pressure on them—for a profession has more status than simply being a mother. If a woman is asked, "What do you do?" and replies, "I am a mother," the response is, "Oh, you're only a mother" or "What else do you really do?" But, if she is an interior decorator, computer expert, beautician—that's fine. These occupations have status and she is valuable; she is doing something "worthwhile."

Similar pressures come from our welfare institutions who have to get people off the welfare rolls. Even mothers of very young children are encouraged to train for work outside the home, while someone else is paid to take care of their children during working hours. Then, of course, there is the notion that anyone can take care of children. To be a mother is not a *real* job. This is an attitude that causes much concern.

Parenting as a Career

It takes talent, dedication, and understanding to rear a child in our complex world. It is a *real* career, but as such it is not appreciated by our society. At present, child rearing is a profession that is undertrained, underpaid, and understaffed. It is an important job that takes understanding and training. It does not have to be only a mother's job—fathers can do it too. Certainly, it can be done in partnership; but whether done singly or in partnership, it is very important that it should be done—and done well.

Day Care

A limited attempt to fill the gap left in child care by the absence of the mother is being made through day-care facilities. Many are excellent, but in many cases, not properly staffed or financed. According to Selma Fraiberg (1977), much of our child care is just warehousing young children. We are aware that uncared-for children become uncaring parents who, in turn, repeat the cycle—even to the point of being abusing parents.

Preserving the Family

It is, therefore, apparent that if at all possible there is a need to have mothers stay home to care for their own children until the children are preschool age. Not only should mothers be encouraged to do this, but they should also be provided with parent training in order to understand child development and make the time spent with their young children productive and pleasant for parent and child. Instead of remunerating other people to take care of her child while she goes to work or takes some kind of occupational training, the mother is trained in child rearing and being remunerated for staying home and caring for her own child. This can be a practical way to increase the size of the force of competent personnel for child care and can allow mothers who want to stay with their children the opportunity to do so. According to Selma Fraiberg (1977), programs involving parents as child caregivers are more economical and satisfactory than those paying strangers to provide child care.

By this means the most important function of the family would be preserved in a way consistent with social change. Being a parent would truly become a worthwhile profession. As Joseph Pisani of New York said at the first conference in New York State on Parenting: "Good parenting may be the one link that will put our society together" (1977). Therefore, let us try by supporting parenting and reviving the family so it can continue its primary function of child care. To be sure, the present is a time calling for revision of our family structure. It must be a revision, though, whereby the needs of the developing child are considered the most important so that the family can again resume this part of its role but with the added advantage of enhancing the child's development by the family's knowledge and understanding of good parenting.

References

Bronfenbrenner, U. Who cares for Americans' children? In V. Vaughan and T. Brazelton (eds.), *The Family.* Chicago: Year Book Medical Publications, 1976.

Fraiberg, S. *Every Child's Birthright.* New York: Scribner, 1977.

Galinsky, E., and W. Hooker. *The New Extended Family: Day Care That Works.* Boston: Houghton Mifflin, 1977.

Lief, N. *The First Year of Life: A Curriculum for Parenting Education.* M. E. Fahs (ed.). New York: Sadlier Press, 1979.

Pisani, Joseph. Paper presented at the New York State Conference on Parenting, 1977.

CHILD ABUSE

Vincent J. Fontana, M.D.

The maltreated child for too long has been hidden in a corner of a dark closet among our national skeletons; now this skeleton is out in the open. Efforts to enlighten the medical profession in the past decade have brought the problem out of its virtual blackout. The picture is an ugly one. Maltreatment is extensive, and it is increasing. We can ask ourselves, "Who are the maltreated children?" They are the children who are being pushed around, thrown down stairs, dropped out of windows, burned with cigarette butts, scalded in boiling water, manhandled, beaten, tortured, victims of bizarre accidents, battered to death, sexually abused, and starved. They are also life-starved and love-starved, flagrantly or insidiously neglected, growing up without a sense of self-esteem and becoming future child abusers themselves.

Throughout the country efforts have been made to protect the abused or battered child by the enactment of child-abuse laws. Every state of the nation has such legislation. Fundamentally, these laws are only the first step in the protection of the abused and neglected child. It is what happens after the reporting that is of the utmost importance. A multidisciplinary network of protection needs to be developed in each community to implement the good intention of the legislation.

Treating a maltreated child is totally inadequate unless coupled with a simultaneous concern for the parents. They must be given the benefit of the therapeutic programs directed toward rehabilitation and preventive measures that will help eliminate the psychological and social environmental factors that foster the battering-parent syndrome. If these parents are to be given any real help, they must be made to recognize their own intrinsic worth and potential as human beings. This can only be accomplished by a recognition that there are two victims of this disease: the child and the parent. Effectiveness of any intervention to break the cycle of parental violence from generation to generation can only be achieved through cooperative efforts of all child-caring professionals and paraprofessionals.

Let us not forget that the fragility of the American family is being further threatened by the increasing incidence of child maltreatment. We must recognize the pressures on the systems of the family and work toward change that will preserve and strengthen rather than destroy and weaken family life.

BIBLIOGRAPHY

Atlas, Stephen L. *Single Parenting: A Practical Resource Guide.* Englewood Cliffs, N.J.: Prentice-Hall, 1981.

The guide is a positive, healthy, and creative approach to single parenthood written by one who understands. The author discusses all types of single parents. Practical advice based on personal experience and insights is shared. There are helpful suggestions for a person new to single parenthood as well as for those looking for ways of enhancing single-parent family life.

Berman, Claire. *Making It as a Stepparent: New Roles, New Rules.* Garden City, N.Y.: Doubleday, 1980.

Berman has written one of the best books available for parents involved in stepfamily situations. Anecdotal and professional opinions are combined in an extremely helpful and informative manner. The author helps stepparents to feel that they are not alone and not to blame. This well-written, sensitive volume is highly recommended.

Berman, Eleanor. *The New-Fashioned Parent: How to Make Your Family Style Work.* Englewood Cliffs, N.J.: Prentice-Hall, 1980.

Family patterns are in flux, with the increase in divorces, working mothers, and expanding roles of fathers, but the upbeat message in this book is that the family works for most parents and children. A historical overview indicates the evolution of changing roles within the persistent value of providing the best we can for children. Throughout the author provides a supportive approach.

Bernard, Jessie. *Self-Portrait of a Family.* Boston: Beacon, 1978.

Written by a renowned sociologist, the book is a highly personalized account of a single parent's struggles to keep up with the changes in herself, her three children, and the larger society around them. A reassuring feature of the book is the clear demonstration that even "professional" parents often say the wrong things to their children, and everyone survives. The author presents a fascinating combination of family and societal analyses that is important for professional and parent alike.

Brazelton, T. Berry. *On Becoming a Family: The Growth of Attachment.* New York: Delacorte/Seymour Lawrence, 1981.

If prospective parents plan to read only one book pertaining to their anticipated blessed event, this should be the one they choose! It is a delightful and sensitively written book in which Brazelton's warmth and understanding make each page a joy to read. The author discusses a wide variety of aspects of parenthood with knowledge and empathy. In addition, he enables readers to become comfortable with their reactions to the responsibilities of parenthood through the use of numerous "case histories."

Brazelton, T. Berry. *Toddlers and Parents: A Declaration of Independence.* New York: Delacorte, 1974.

Brazelton presents a realistic profile of a few families shaping the lives of their toddlers. At the end of each profile, he interjects personal opinion, explanations, and ideas in italics to "converse" with the reader. It is an excellent book for parents of toddlers.

Burgess, Ann Wolbert, A. Nicholas Groth, Lynda Lytle Holmstrom, and Suzanne M. Sgroi. *Sexual Assault of Children and Adolescents.* Lexington, Mass.: Lexington Books, 1978.

Designed as a handbook to guide those whose work brings them into contact with either victims or offenders, this book examines sexual abuse through three major themes: the human dimension, community program planning, and interagency cooperation.

Clemes, Harris, and Reynold Bean. *Self-Esteem: The Key to Your Child's Well-Being.* New York: Putnam, 1981.

Therapists Clemes and Bean have developed a unique program that fosters the development of self-esteem in children. Through clear explanations and suggested activities, parents may acquire concrete methods to improve family relationships.

The book is a sensitive and outstanding approach to understanding the needs of children.

Comer, James P., and Alvin F. Poussaint. *Black Child Care*. New York: Pocket Books, 1980.

The stated purpose of this volume is to provide guidance on how to bring up a healthy black child in America. Departing from the traditional premise of American child development literature, which employs white middle-class families and child behavior as the norm, the authors' premise is that growing up in an often antagonistic or at least indifferent environment poses special problems for black parents and their children, from family planning through infancy, preschool, puberty, and adolescence. The authors utilize a question-and-answer format to respond to problems raised by black parents.

Despert, J. Louise. *Children of Divorce*. Garden City, N.Y.: Doubleday, 1962.

A classic in the field, this sensitive, well-written book is intended for parents experiencing marital discord, separation, or divorce. It is easy to read, yet thought-provoking, and discusses every possible family circumstance, both pre- and post-divorce. The central theme is always the child(ren)—how to understand their emotional needs, feelings, and fears and how to safeguard them from the damage of divorce. Louise Despert, the late child psychologist, was optimistic about children's capacities to understand, cope, and adjust to the divorce situation.

Dodson, Fitzhugh. *How to Grandparent*. New York: Harper & Row, 1981.

Dodson, in his excellent, well-written how-to book, discusses the unique role of grandparents, especially in the context of the changing nuclear family. This book has a strong point of view in that it feels that the extended family offers many advantages over the nuclear family.

Dolan, Edward F., Jr. *Child Abuse*. New York: Watts, 1980.

The purpose of this book is to encourage the reader to become concerned about the growing problem of child abuse and to motivate the reader to help stop it. Chapters deal with a history of child abuse, sexually abused children, incest, and child pornography and programs for action.

Dreikurs, Rudolf. *Children: The Challenge.* New York: Hawthorn Books, 1964.

Almost twenty years after publication, this theory of Adlerian family life is being appreciated by a second generation of parents. It is a philosophical approach implementing concepts of cooperation, responsibility, logical consequences, and mutual respect in the interdependent relationships of parents and children. Examples of situations given in text deal with young children, but the principles apply as well to older students.

Fernandez, Happy Craven. *The Child Advocacy Handbook.* New York: Pilgrim Press, 1980.

The book's main focus is on teaching how to become a child advocate, be one a parent, grandparent, educator, community service worker, or just a caring citizen. The author gives practical ways how to go about trying to change things and cites examples of how this has been done in other communities. There are names and addresses of national organizations, many of which have state and local chapters that can supply ideas, materials, and training assistance to interested parties.

Galper, Miriam. *Joint Custody and Co-Parenting Handbook.* Philadelphia: Running Press, 1980.

One of the few books available that focuses on the ever growing popularity of joint custody arrangements, it is comprehensive in scope and supplies "solid" information about the how-to's of this arrangement. It is filled with anecdotal material, largely from the author's own experiences. At times, the book takes on a somewhat defensive tone. A nice feature is the chapter describing adjustment from the child's point of view.

Gardner, Richard. *The Boys' and Girls' Book About Divorce.* New York: Aronson, 1971.

Written in a simple narrative style appropriate for children, the book represents children's thoughts and fantasies about the experience of separation and divorce. Gardner identifies the emotions and fantasies that are problematic to children in these situations and offers meaningful explanations.

Gardner, Richard. *The Parents Book About Divorce.* New York: Bantam, 1979.

This is an important guide for parents who are interested in easing the impact of their divorce on their children. It is a good companion to the author's *The Boys' and Girls' Book About Divorce.*

Goldstein, Joseph, Anna Freud, and Albert J. Solmit. *Before the Best Interests of the Child.* New York: Free Press, 1980.

Written after the companion piece *Beyond the Best Interests of the Child,* which deals with children already involved in the legal system or placement, this book examines the rationale for state intervention in the parent-child relationships. The authors believe that the ideal for child development is an intact family with "reciprocal affection between the child and two, or at least one, caretaking adult." Yet they acknowledge that at times the child's well-being, safety, or his life may be at stake and measures must be taken. This book identifies the criteria for determining when the child's interests would better be served outside the family and what kinds of intervention would be most effective.

Goode, Ruth. *A Book for Grandmothers.* New York: McGraw-Hill, 1977.

This self-help book is full of practical advice for the grandmother and her relationship with her children and grandchildren in the context of the changing family structure. Down-to-earth issues are talked about, such as the grandmother's role when there is a divorce. This is a simply written book that is fun to read.

Grollman, Earl. *Talking About Divorce and Separation: A Dialogue Between Parent and Child.* Boston: Beacon, 1975.

There are useful suggestions for parents of the younger child. Advice is given on how to help children understand that they are not to blame for the divorce, what divorce means, and why it happened to their parents. Parents are helped to learn how to be responsive to a child's special needs and feelings. It is a warm and sensitive approach to the problem from the child's perspective.

Halperin, Michael. *Helping Maltreated Children: School and Community Involvement.* St. Louis: Mosby, 1979.

Designed as a starting kit for people concerned with education's obligation to maltreated children, this book addresses the teacher, administrator, school board member, parents, and neighborhood groups, all of whom view the school as an integral part of community life. It gives a brief overview of the problem and addresses the role that educators can play in preventing and remedying child maltreatment.

Halpern, Howard. *Cutting Loose: An Adult Guide to Coming to Terms with Your Parents.* New York: Bantam, 1978.

Through Halpern's many examples of how adults' parents still may manipulate them, with or without their consent, the reader comes to recognize many of the pitfalls all parents face. The book is helpful in releasing one from the bonds of childhood that can prevent full development of one's own adulthood with its concurrent responsibilities and privileges.

Hope, Karol, and Nancy Young (eds.). *Momma: The Source Book for Single Mothers.* New York: New American Library, 1976.

"You are not alone" is the basic message of this sourcebook that covers all aspects of life for single mothers. It is helpful for those who have just become single parents as well as for the seasoned veteran. Being in this role requires all the support, confidence, and practical help one can muster; *Momma* gives all of that and more.

Howard, Jane. *Families.* New York: Simon & Schuster, 1978.

The author makes a case that families are as much a part of human makeup as is language. "The trouble we take to arrange ourselves in some semblance or other of families is one of the most imperishable habits of the human race." Howard visits many families, from her own in Marshall County, Illinois, to a commune in Tennessee, and participates in their daily routines and social rituals. Through her experiences, she finds ten qualities common to "good families," whether these families are composed of blood relations or acquaintances.

Justice, Blair, and Rita Justice. *The Abusing Family*. New York: Human Sciences Press, 1976.

The Justices are concerned with the physical abuse of children, its causes, treatment, and prevention. They use the transactional analysis approach to treating families caught in this cycle. The subjects covered include life crisis, group therapy techniques, and innovative interventions in the abusing family.

Justice, Blair, and Rita Justice. *The Broken Taboo: Sex in the Family*. New York: Human Sciences Press, 1979.

A follow-up to *The Abusing Family*, this book continues to focus on parents and children and is based on the authors' own study of actual cases. Given are the cues that incest is going on, what to do about it, as well as guidelines on how to prevent incestuous behavior.

Kahn, Alfred J., and Shelia B. Kamerman. *Not for the Poor Alone*. New York: Harper & Row, 1977.

The text is a product of the authors' eight-century study of social services here and abroad. Kahn and Kamerman explore a variety of family services such as health visiting in England, day care in Sweden, and housing for the young and single in Holland and France. Each presentation discusses differences and similarities with related activities in this country and makes insightful recommendations for American social policy makers, program planners, and administrators or operators of family-support programs.

Kempe, Ruth S., and C. Henry Kempe. *Child Abuse*. Cambridge: Harvard University Press, 1978.

The authors report the results of their extensive research into the causes and treatment of child abuse. They discuss the kinds of social and family situations that are likely to trigger abuse and offer guidelines for prevention and treatment.

Keniston, Kenneth, and the Carnegie Council on Children. *All Our Children: The American Family Under Pressure*. New York: Harcourt Brace Jovanovich, 1978.

The myth of the self-sufficient family is disputed. Instead, Keniston and his colleagues in the Carnegie Council on Children argue that when raising children parents must compete with an overload of social, economic, political, and technological factors —everything from television to schools to food additives. The final chapters advocate specific social policies and political agenda to be implemented in order "to solve the problems of children and families in our society."

Korbin, Jill E. (ed.). *Child Abuse and Neglect: Cross-Cultural Perspectives.* Berkeley: University of California Press, 1981.

Korbin explores child abuse and neglect from a cross-cultural, particularly a non-Western, perspective. Culturally appropriate definitions and factors in the cultural milieu that can contribute to, or prevent, the occurrence of child abuse and neglect are the focus.

Kornhaber, Arthur, and Kenneth Woodward. *Grandparents-Grandchildren: The Vital Connection.* Garden City, N.Y.: Doubleday, 1981.

This is an important book that discusses the links between family generations—in particular, between child and grandparent. Although the authors stress the emotional differences and difficulties of children trying to relate to their grandparents, they also emphasize the many positive aspects of this relationship on the emotional and personality development of the grandchildren. It is a warm and sensitive book that should appeal to educators, parents, grandparents, and professionals.

Lewis, M., and L. Rosenblum (eds.). *The Child and Its Family: The Genesis of Behavior,* Vol. 2. New York: Plenum, 1979.

The Child and Its Family examines social development in children as it is affected by complex environmental influences— especially the family, but also friends, teachers, acquaintances, peers, and the culture at large. The book begins by considering the total impact of the society within which the infant develops —the effects of societal demands and the role of the family in the emerging socialization and development of the infant. The influence of specific members of the child's family are then examined, including the roles of parents as well as older and younger siblings. Such extrafamilial influences on the child's social responsiveness as people and objects with which the child interacts are explored. Finally, the book examines the social character of nonhuman primates, the development of adaptive behavior in these species, and the applications of this knowledge to the study of human social development.

Livingston, Carol. *"Why Was I Adopted?"* Secaucus, N.J.: Lyle Stuart, 1980.

In this well-written, vividly illustrated volume, the author helps an adoptive parent answer the questions that a young child asks about adoption.

Lorimer, Anne, and Philip Feldman. *Re-Marriage: A Guide for Singles, Couples, and Families.* Philadelphia: Running Press, 1980.

An excellent source book, *Re-marriage* is honest, straightforward, and helpful for all families involved in building a new family out of two. It is comprehensive and unafraid to examine sticky issues, such as sex, money, and grandparents. An important message of the book is that open communication before the marriage smooths the way for an easier adjustment afterward.

Maddox, Brenda. *The Half-Parent: Living with Other People's Children.* New York: Signet, 1975.

Maddox presents a personal yet scholarly look at the experience of being a stepparent, written in a sensitive, warm, and at times humorous manner. She examines the myths of stepparenting and helps relieve some of the guilt stepparents often feel when the family does not easily live "happily ever after." One of the best books on the subject, it is highly recommended for professional and parent alike.

Martin, Harold P. (ed.). *The Abused Child: A Multidisciplinary Approach in Developmental Issues and Treatment.* Cambridge, Ma.: Ballinger, 1976.

This volume is a collection of research data on abused children, clinical impressions gained from years of work with such children, and descriptions of treatment programs to try to obviate the effects of the abusive environment on maltreated children. The programs were developed at the National Center on Child Abuse and Neglect, Children's Bureau, Administration for Children, Youth, and Families.

Martin, J. P. (ed.). *Violence and the Family.* New York: Wiley, 1978.

Martin examines family violence from a variety of perspectives, some of which describe and analyze the forms it takes, while others consider practical issues of policy, social action, and the training of social workers to deal with the problem.

Miller, Maureen. *Family Communication: Keeping Connected in A Time of Change.* Ramsey, N.J.: Paulist Press, 1980.

The family of today comes in changing varieties. The author offers guidelines for communication problems that may occur in any family, traditional or not. Basic principles are given for communication skills, including examples and dialogues designed to actively involve the reader. This book, written simply, is a valuable guide, meant to help families get along together.

Minuchin, Salvador. *Families and Family Therapy.* Cambridge: Harvard University Press, 1974.

In the family literature, this book is one of the more comprehensive ones. It covers a wide range of family situations through clinical vignettes, analyses of why families develop problems, and discussions of therapists' techniques. Although the book is geared to novice family therapists, it can be appreciated by a wider audience because of its clear language.

Napier, Y. Augustus, and Carl Whitaker. *The Family Crucible.* New York: Harper & Row, 1978.

This extremely readable and valuable book describes the course of family therapy as illustrated by one family's experience. Using examples of the process of treatment and the issues that were resolved, the authors then expand upon general family therapy themes. This book is an excellent learning experience for therapists, educators, and individuals wanting to learn more about family dynamics and treatment. It is written with humor and compassion.

Noble, June, and William Noble. *How to Live with Other People's Children.* New York: Dutton, 1979.

The authors, themselves stepparents, have done an admirable job of compiling practical information and advice about many difficult situations that arise when one lives with someone else's children, either because of marriage, living together, temporary foster care, and the like. They include areas that often are overlooked in other sources, such as financial obligations, wills, step-grandparenting, to name a few. A drawback of the book is the nature of the clinical material, which tends to be too idealistic and rational in an often highly charged emotional situation.

O'Neil, Onora (ed.). *Having Children: Philosophical and Legal Reflection on Parenthood.* New York: Oxford University Press, 1979.

Thirty-two essays explore the questions of genetic counseling, parental rights, children's rights, abortion, child neglect, and the division of responsibilities between mothers and fathers in the area of child care. There are also selections of court opinions, reviews of current legal decisions, and an annotated table of court cases dealing with parenthood as well as a chapter on what grown children owe their parents. Introductions to each selection are provided.

Petrillo, Madeline, and Sirgay Sanger. *Emotional Care of Hospitalized Children: An Environmental Approach.* New York: Harper & Row, 1980.

The authors, a nurse and a psychiatrist, provide a guide to deal with the common problems of children who become hospitalized. They review the specific developmental needs of children at different ages; analyze different types of families; examine child, parent, and staff interactions; and discuss preparations for hospital procedures and how to do them in terms of the different types of procedures. This volume is an excellent resource for professionals, child-care workers, and parents.

Polansky, Norman A., Mary Ann Chalmers, Elizabeth Buttenwieser, and David P. Williams. *Damaged Parents: An Anatomy of Child Neglect.* Chicago: University of Chicago Press, 1981.

The authors present a comprehensive study of the problem of child neglect, a problem even more widespread than child abuse. Even the operational definition of neglect is not simple because the question at issue is most complicated, although less dramatic than outright abuse. When the level of care is marginal at best, there is parental failure, and children must be protected, even if it means removal. A national effort to control child neglect is advocated—not only for humanitarian considerations, but also as a matter of national self-interest.

Postman, Neil. *The Disappearance of Childhood.* New York: Dell, 1981.

A knowledgeable commentator on media points toward effects on young people. The author documents his thesis—that the period called childhood is disappearing—with vivid examples from books, films, television, clothing, and many others. The book is well written and most timely.

Riley, Sue Spayth. *How to Generate Values in Young Children: Integrity, Honesty, Individuality, Self-Confidence, and Wisdom.* Los Angeles: New South, 1979.

There is no quick and simple formula parents can use for teaching values to young children, but if parents are willing to see that in order to achieve a strong sense of right or wrong children must be allowed to choose, decide, and evaluate as much as possible, then the process of ethical education is well established. It is an important book for all concerned with early education.

Ross, Heather L., and Isabel V. Sawhill. *Time of Transition: The Growth of Families Headed by Women.* New York: Urban Institute, 1975.

The authors deal with the phenomenon of the female-headed, single-parent family. They analyze what factors have contributed to the rapid growth of female-headed families, as well as examining the impact on the income of the families. Concrete suggestions for public policy direction are offered.

Salk, Lee. *What Every Child Would Like Parents to Know About Divorce.* New York: Harper & Row, 1978.

Salk speaks to both the parent and child with insight and compassion. Suggestions are offered on how to avoid problems as well as how to make the child an integral part of the process of divorce in order to reassure and comfort him or her.

Sanford, Linda Tschirhart. *The Silent Children: A Parent's Guide to the Prevention of Child Sexual Abuse.* Garden City, N.Y.: Doubleday, 1980.

This book is about prevention. The author feels strongly that if parents are informed they will be able to help their children recognize and avoid circumstances that may precipitate abuse.

Sinberg, Janet. *Divorce Is a Grown-up Problem.* New York: Avon, 1978.

Through simple words and delightful illustrations, Sinberg lets a child tell how he feels about his parents' divorce: his confusion, anger, hopes, and fears. Fortunately for him and his readers, his parents are very understanding and knowledgeable about ways to help children through difficult times like this. This is a lap book, meant to be read by parents to their children, and one that is particularly well liked by young children. The Preface for Parents is informative and well written, offering parents many good hints about how to react to their children during what may often be a particularly stressful time.

Skolnick, Arlene, and Jerome Skolnick. *Family in Transition: Rethinking Marriage, Sexuality, and Childrearing and Family Organization,* 3rd ed. Boston: Little, Brown, 1980.

As described in the title, this book discusses the trends and changes in modern family organization. It also focuses on transitions in parenting due to the role changes of parents with implications for child rearing. It is a comprehensive textbook that poses important questions regarding the family, such as whether the family has a future because of all the challenges presented by societal changes. The book is well written and clear and should be of interest to all.

Smart, Laura S., and Mollie S. Smart. *Families: Developing Relationships.* New York: Macmillan, 1980.

This family textbook is comprehensive and clear, especially in its beginning discussions of all aspects of the development of a family, family structure and communication styles. The issues are not explored in depth. The style is dry and simply written. It is a good beginning book for students in family-life courses and for parents.

Sorosky, Arthur D., and Annette Baran. *The Adoption Triangle: The Effects of the Sealed Record on Adoptees, Birth Parents, and Adoptive Parents.* Garden City, N.Y.: Doubleday, 1978.

In this comprehensive study of the relationship between the adoptee, the adoptive parents, and the biological parents when the true identity of the biological parents has been revealed, a compelling argument is presented for reform of legal issues involving adoption.

Stenson, Janet Sinberg. *Now I Have a Stepparent and It's Kind of Confusing.* New York: Avon, 1979.

A sequel to *Divorce Is a Grown-up Problem* (see Sinberg, Janet), this book contains many of the fine features of its predecessor, particularly the illustrations, the articulateness of the storyteller, and the knowledgeable preface. Again, it is written in the first person, a child's reflections on his mother's remarriage, simply and warmly told. However, a possible drawback of the book is how easy the transition into a new, blended family sounds. Unless forewarned, parents and children might expect their own efforts to make new families go as smoothly, and they might be unnecessarily disappointed and confused.

Straus, Murray A., Richard J. Gelles, and Suzanne K. Steinmetz. *Behind Closed Doors: Violence in the American Family.* Garden City, N.Y.: Doubleday, 1980.

This book is a part of the Family Violence Research Program conducted at the University of New Hampshire. The authors have avoided overly technical terms in order to reach the general public as well as professionals. Some of the goals were to examine the extent of violence in the American family, the variety of forms of violence, what violence means to the participants, and how to understand the problem for possible prevention.

Stuart, Irving R., and Lawrence E. Abt (eds.). *Children of Separation and Divorce: Management and Treatment.* New York: Van Nostrand Reinhold, 1981.

The authors furnish an outstanding complement to the title's previous edition, *Children of Divorce.* This book focuses upon the management and treatment of the social, emotional, and legal consequences of divorce. Experts explore gay parenthood, the school's role in helping children cope, the psychiatric aspects of custody, and single fatherhood. Clear explanations and concise evaluations of the latest methods of treatment provide readers with invaluable means of coping with these problems.

Visher, Emily, and John Visher. *Step-Families: A Guide to Working with Stepparents and Stepchildren.* New York: Brunner/Mazel, 1979.

Professionals consider this book to be one of the best resource books in the field; they find it comprehensive, well written, and sensitive. It is useful also for parents involved in stepfamily situations, for it clarifies some of the human reactions to the inherent difficulties in this arrangement and shows how professional help can aid in alleviating some of the pain involved.

Wallerstein, Judith S., and Joan Berlin Kelly. *Surviving the Breakup: How Children and Parents Cope with Divorce.* New York: Basic Books, 1980.

This very important book describes what the authors learned about how divorce affects parents and children from their landmark study of sixty families during divorce and over the following five-year period. They concentrate particularly on the children, using quotes and specific, concrete family situations to show, very movingly, how children actually cope with the breakup and how their everyday lives are affected. Their findings alter many conventional ideas about the experience of the family of divorce.

Weiss, Robert S. *Going It Alone: The Family Life and Social Situation of the Single Parent.* New York: Basic Books, 1979.

This extremely valuable book discusses in detail all the aspects of being a single parent—the problems of raising children, organizing the household, and developing a personal life. Weiss quotes single parents and children in single-parent families. His commentary on the problems is well-written and compassionate. One of the most useful and interesting points the book makes is that there can be advantages to growing up in a single-parent family.

Wishard, Laurie, and William R. Wishard. *Adoption; The Grafted Tree.* New York: Avon, 1981.

All who are involved in the adoption process—the natural parent, the adoptive parent, and the adopted person—will find this an excellent guide. Concrete information is provided. The book can be fully utilized in the decision-making process of adoption.

4
Parenting

AN OVERVIEW

Eugene B. Friedman, M.D.

Any overview of "parenting" must first attempt to assign a label to this elusive noun. Even the most modern dictionary offers no such listing in its roster of words; instead, the word "parent," defined as "from which others are derived, source" will have to suffice. We must always remember that parenting is not and never will be subject to definition.

All parents are different, as are their offspring, in regard to temperament, health, intellectual capacity, development, and ability to deal with stress. Therefore, the role of parents is incapable of being scripted. There is always a dynamic interplay between parent and child that is constantly being modified by inherent and extrinsic influences; hence, equilibrium is almost impossible to establish.

Some children are more difficult than others to raise because they are colicky, fretful, subject to vomiting and temper tantrum episodes, even though these may well represent variants of normal. Each individual in a household automatically lives in an environment totally different than that of the other members simply by virtue of age or position. Parents grow and mature just as their children do and at various stages may interact differently in that they have changing social and financial pressures with which to cope, as well as more or less time to spend with each child. As no two objects can occupy the same space simultaneously, so each child in the family unit will be exposed to parental attitudes and pressures that vary. Those resultant changes will surely alter the character of children—sometimes to their betterment, other times to their detriment.

Parents come to their improvisational source role with dissimilar degrees of preparation—be it experience, education, values and interests, self-concepts, and most importantly with their past family interaction. Some parents are able to ward off group pressures and artificial standards, while others cannot and succumb to placing unfair demands on their children. As all parents were once children themselves, they too have been bent and shaped by the forces of nature and nurture.

Along with the positive aspects of having responsibility for the welfare of a child or children, the parent may have an accompanying dramatic change of lifestyle with which to cope. New avenues of enjoyment become available to the parent along with new demands caused by the child's temperament. Thus, to become an effective parent, one must allow the child to enter one's life without feeling that the child is a "crimp." The parent must at the same time be unafraid to communicate clearly, simply, and guiltlessly his or her attitudes, feelings, and demands to the child. Bad behavior and intentional disregard for the feelings of others is to be met with disapproval, while consideration is to be met with appreciation. If the parent is basically consistent in what is asked of the child, then he is allowed to make "mistakes," as these will be discarded by the child and not hinder development.

All children need love, which is to be differentiated from unlimited love. Unlimited love implies acceptance of poor behavior at the expense of the feelings of others and will act as a deterrent to the child's adaptive mechanisms. All children surely are one of a kind but just as surely are one of many, and each must learn to function according to the social contract. Those parents who set limits will be better able to impart to their children the benefit of their own personalities, styles, and experiences. It is within the province of the parent to inculcate and cultivate those qualities they themselves use to stabilize their own relationships with members of society. If they do this, the child will automatically feel loved and wanted as he will acquire the concept of self-esteem. If the parent is able to have fun, is able to enjoy the movement of the child through space and time, then the parent can be absolutely certain that the child is reaping a harvest of plenty.

The parent should also know that since parenting is an art, there are many people of different backgrounds and viewpoints who have multiple insights to offer us in respect to child development, guidance, and education. Parents must know that each child passes through the various developmental stages at different times and velocities and may even decelerate before moving on to the next phase. The child may need help in distinguishing correct standards from false ones in the confusing welter of new ideas and values that bombard each person in everyday life. As the child usually will choose role models from adults, it is imperative to stress interpersonal relationships as an aid in overcoming detours to communication. This may enhance the adult's ability to deal with the child even in the most trying situations. Only with good role models can the child develop character, responsibility, and knowledge of himself.

A child is forced to develop, refine, and hone all kinds of skills in the early years of life. If the parent-child bond is not more than temporarily disrupted, then the child should be able to develop judgmental, motor, communication, listening, and social skills. If the child feels that love has been irretrievably lost, he too will be lost. As the child realizes that love will be given, but must also be earned, he or she will master the demands of parents and society and will gain self-competence and self-confidence. So equipped, the child will be able to direct inner drives to the good of society.

Unfortunately, this is not always the case as we have witnessed the emergence of drug abuse, battered-child syndrome and juvenile delinquency to the forefront of society.

Many who have turned to drugs have felt isolated from their families and society and employ narcotics as an escape valve from their confused, unfriendly world. It is the parent's responsibility that children understand the consequences involved in drug use. Also, the parent must be willing to combat denial and openly discuss the family problems that may have contributed to the child's abuse. The drug-abuse problem is always a domestic one. It is during this crucial time that all lines of communication must be kept open or else the youngster will surely fall off this dangerous precipice to oblivion. The parent must call on all human and nonhuman resources to aid in the trying period and must remember to be firm and fair to the abuser.

Another problem of parent-child dysfunction is the battered-child syndrome. Unbelievably, it has only been recognized during the past generation, an example of how society may close its eyes to a glaring injustice. In this syndrome the parent has not developed sufficiently to handle the responsibilities of parenthood in regard to the baby's feeding, sleeping, or crying problems and in other variables that occur subsequently. Instead, the child is expected, even commanded, to act in an age-inappropriate manner, which leads to the neglect, beating, starvation, or verbal abuse of the child. Battered-child syndrome transcends all class, ethnic, and religious systems and demonstrates that abusive parents were themselves deprived of proper parenting. Abusive parents are confused. Although they may love the child, unrealistic expectations force them to lose control of their emotions. Early institution of therapy is of the essence to establish or reestablish the parent-child bond before the physical and/or emotional destruction of the child ensues.

Another problem of recent vintage that has brought with it changed concepts of parenting is that of the startling changes in the family life of the Western world. In many families there has been an interchange of roles between mother and father; there has been an accelerating divorce rate; there has been increasing mobility of society as a whole with a resulting decrease in contact with immediate relatives and friends.

The problems of "displaced" or "newly placed" families, of working mothers, single fathers and single mothers, stepparents and stepsiblings have cut through society like a sharp knife, leaving in their wake the problem of depression in young children. Almost unrecognized as a clinical entity until recently, as it was often masked by other forms of behavior such as irritability, delinquency, or overaggressiveness, parents and health professionals have become increasingly aware of its prevalence. The depressed child may lack trust, feel worthless, angry, or hopeless and may sometimes feel guilty for the family situation. A parent may be oblivious to the problem of other family members if he or she has made an easy adjustment to a changed situation. Anticipatory guidance prior to such a move should be sought by the family to prevent such situations from occurring.

Parenting also has a different meaning to the working mother who constitutes almost 50 percent of all mothers. It is reassuring to note that no evidence of harmful short-term or long-term effects has been documented as resulting from maternal employment. Instead, what has been demonstrated is that quality rather than quantity of love has emerged triumphant and that the parent-child bond has not been severed. The working mother may find herself in a guilt-ridden anxious state as she worries about the upshot of separation on her child or children (especially the preschooler). It is hoped that some or all of this stress is overcome before the mother begins employment through the use of adaptive mechanisms by other family members.

The single-parent home is another growing entity in American life, constituting a staggering 20 percent of United States households. When a person becomes a single head of a family, he or she assumes tremendous responsibility conventionally shared with the spouse. These responsibilities can become overwhelming, especially if associated with the trauma of death or divorce. All resources must be made available to the single head of household as he or she is in a position of increased parenting demand at the same time as he or she is in a position of increased vulnerability to stress. The parent who feels isolated, fearful and guilty must seek help.

The reconstituted family, where the members are forced to adjust to new interactions and old loyalties is also on the rise. This situation exerts tremendous push and pull on all members of the new unit, which in turn may give rise to misunderstandings, anger, and guilt. A power struggle ensues that leads to an armed camp. Again, we are fortunate to have resources available to help reestablish parent-child bonds.

Communication becomes a central element in all these situations. The child and parent must be able to express themselves and be listened to if any meaningful progress is to be made.

No discussion of parenting is complete without mention of sex education. Many parents have abdicated their responsibility in this regard even to the preschool child. Proper sex education begins in early infancy with loving body and eye contact. As things progress and the child asks questions in regard to sex, the parent should respond in as a relaxed, candid, simple manner as he or she can muster. Although there may be some parental anxiety about discussing sexuality, most parents can surmount this obstacle if they are comfortable in their parent-child relationship.

The parent's job is to help the child understand his or her own body in a physical, emotional, and social context. The parent assists the child in overcoming any fears, anxieties, and false information that may be held in regard to his or her sexuality. With the aid of parents, the child will be able to develop a good rapport with boys and girls and will be able to develop social responsibility and ethical values in regard to sexuality and, indeed, in all behavior.

In summary, if parents are willing to give of themselves while at the same time adopting an attitude of patience, respecting the child's own ability to solve problems and empathizing with the child, then parenting will be a very pleasurable experience.

COPING WITH PRACTICAL ISSUES IN CHILD REARING

Eda J. LeShan

All human beings are saints and sinners, angels and devils. The younger you are, the harder it is to control uncivilized behavior; that is why there are adults around—to teach, to help children gain control, so that they will not do anything to other people that you would not want them to do to you. It is not a question of being good or bad; it is being human and little.

Being shy, afraid of the dark, jealous, selfish, inclined to hit and bite, inclined to take what you want when you want it are all normal parts of being a person and growing up. If, as parents, we could go back to our own childhoods and reassess how we felt about ourselves, then the exact technique used at the "right" moment will not really matter that much at all. It is our basic love and understanding that gets transmitted to the child, even when we get angry or make "mistakes." With this in mind, I discuss some of the issues in matters of the practical routines of parenthood. But, remember, these are not just "routines." They are some of the most important moments when exchanges of affection and learning about oneself can take place.

Fears

Almost every child of two, three, four, and five years of age will have fears. Some fear animals, others fear the dark, ocean currents, ghosts, swaying curtains, and so on. Some children have nightmares and fantasies. Some fears are real; others, imaginary. They reflect the child's growing sense of vulnerability. When we say to the fearful child, "Why are you afraid?

113

There's nothing to be afraid of," the message that may get across is that there is something wrong with the child because he or she has these fears. When my own young child was having nightmares, I behaved terribly and kept saying, "There's nothing in the dark here; you're perfectly safe." Finally she put me in my place by saying, "I'm afraid of *my* dark." That stopped me because I understood that she was frightened by what was inside, in her dark, in her fantasy.

If a parent can give children an awareness that at their age those inside fears are sometimes overwhelming and those imaginary terrors do not change reality, the message does get through. "I'm not different, I'm not a coward, I'm not a baby, but I am afraid, and that's O.K." As children grow and develop greater understanding of the world, their emotional reactions are influenced, enabling them to deal with some fears and, at the same time, generating others.

Parents should avoid transmitting their own adult irrational fears to their offspring in ways that are disturbing. Instead, if parents have irrational fears, children are comforted to hear about them and to talk with parents about them. In this way children can feel more "normal" about their own feelings. They can also see how irrational fears can be handled through humor, closeness to someone else, and honest communication.

Some fears serve healthful functions and keep the child safe—fear of speeding cars, dangerous tools, hot stoves, fire, and the like. On the other hand, parents should encourage some level of willingness on the part of their children to try themselves out, even at the risk of minor hurts, so that they can develop a general sense of competence and confidence. Most of us want children who are neither reckless nor overwhelmed by terrors but who can eventually exercise good judgment. As parents we can only do our best to achieve the best balance.

Toilet Training

In the past one of the "bug-a-boos" of child rearing was toilet training, but today parents in general seem to be taking a more relaxed attitude. Parents should recognize that some babies have a physiological inner rhythm that makes them very regular. They get hungry at a certain time, move their bowels at a certain time, etc. Depending on their rhythm, their physical maturation, and their sensitivity to being wet or soiled, children complete their toilet training at different ages. The average period seems to be between eighteen to twenty-four months, but the child's behavior is a better indicator than the calendar. Too much pressure and emphasis may cause anxiety and delay. Ignoring the process totally, in the belief that it will happen naturally, can also have unfortunate results.

Most important is that the child find toilet training a natural, pleasant experience, and that it does not escalate into a battle between a determined parent and a baby who is simply not ready for this step. Praising the child who succeeds produces feelings of satisfaction. Excessive joy and rewards can place too much emphasis on the process.

Once the child is toilet trained, there are bound to be slips or regression in times of stress, or excitement, or involvement in play, or when a new baby appears on the scene. These will pass. Remember, the child is striving toward autonomy and wants to please those he or she loves, but, once again, a lot depends on the baby's digestive system and the manner in which parents approach the whole process.

Death

About age three or four many children learn about death—often through the death of a pet or a grandparent. (It is not until the school years that most children acquire a sense of their own mortality.) When it is a parent who dies, the underlying theme of young children's questions will be, "Will I be left alone?" "What will happen to me?" At this time, children need reassurance that there are many people who love them, they will not be alone, and they will be taken care of.

Truthfulness and sharing in the grief is essential if the child is not to be left with hidden anxieties and fears and misconceptions. If, for example, a beloved grandparent dies and the child asks if Mommy or Daddy will die too, the answer is that we all die eventually but not for a long time so let us bake some cookies or play ball or some other activity.

Remember, too, the concreteness of young children's thinking. When one says that grandma went to "heaven," the child may think that it is a street like the one he lives on. This is confusing enough, but when a child is told that death is like a continuing sleep, the child may become terrified of going to bed.

The matter of death today is also complicated by children's exposure to all kinds of killing on TV—both on regular programs and in the news. And so, at the same time, there is a casualness about the meaning of death, a lack of sense of the sacredness of life because death is around us in so many terrible ways.

To repeat, it is important to be truthful with children, but to the extent that they can understand and manage. The enormity and complexity of death is such that when children cope with their fears of it, one realizes how strong young children can be. How many adults can deal with death—their own or others?

Sibling Rivalry

It is hard for a young child to share parents, the two people loved and needed most in the world, when a new baby arrives on the scene. The child is sacrificing what is most important to him or her, and that is to be the big "I" in the center of the universe.

Some jealousy is bound to occur and will be expressed in a number of ways: outright or surreptitious assaults on the new arrival, a number of suggestions about how to get rid of it and get back to the good old days, or regression to infantile behavior. After all, if you have to be a baby to get all that attention, then I'll be a baby!

Jealousy can be minimized if the parents are sensitive to their older child's feelings. First, it is important to tell the child at the right time that a new baby is coming. Involve the child in preparations for the baby, in moderation. When the baby arrives, the older sibling can participate in its care—to the extent that he or she is able.

Too many parents overromanticize the event of a new baby. Losing the "only-child" status to a new arrival is especially difficult for children between three and six years of age. Most important is to make sure that the older child has some of the parents' time all to himself or herself for outings or just "comfortable togetherness" and for the many questions about the new baby. Try, if possible, not to sacrifice too many of the older child's routines, such as the bedtime story or other bedtime rituals.

Treated with understanding and sensitivity, however worn out the parents may be, siblings can grow up to be loving friends and relations.

Temper Tantrums

Most children have tantrums, usually between the ages of fifteen and thirty-six months. Some are more prone to them than others. It may be that the parents have an excitable nature and the child simply models it. The outbursts may result from encountering frustrations as the child strives to master something in another step toward autonomy. Children may have difficulty communicating their needs or wants because their language is still limited and the adult is not sensitive at that particular moment to the nonverbal cues. Unless they occur too frequently or are overly severe and long-lasting, tantrums are a normal part of growing up. And there is not much an adult can do about them since the child is too busy having the tantrum to be accessible to help.

Screaming back simply leads to a screaming match. Physical punishment is totally inappropriate. Away from home, the best way to handle a tantrum is to remove the child from the scene. At home, tantrums that are ignored and therefore go unrewarded usually subside.

Spoiling and Discipline

It is very hard to spoil a young baby. Fulfilling an infant's needs is vital in establishing strong attachment and the basic trust that is the necessary foundation for the discipline needed at a later time. In fact, the danger lies in failing to satisfy a baby's basic needs, thus leading to further needs on the child's part. On the other hand, some parents are so confused, anxious, or filled with guilt that they run to attend a baby whether the child needs attention or not. Thus, the wrong need may be getting gratified, and this may later emerge as what we see as "spoiled behavior."

As a baby's mobility increases in toddlerhood and the preschool years, discipline becomes one of the parents' tasks. And, as a parent, it helps if you are "grown-up." Many parents vacillate between indulgence and overindulgence or fear that they may be starving children's creative powers by disciplining their offspring's behavior or setting limits. How grown-up are we? Can we stand a little discomfort in order to let our children know that we are there to protect them? The truth is that children who are allowed to do whatever they want are cordially disliked by everyone and scared to death themselves; the abdication of responsibility that produces such results is not love! Of course, children should be creative and imaginative, have a chance to explore the world, and struggle for independence. That is part of growth. But children must also feel protected and cared for; they cannot be permitted to do things that are hazardous or antisocial; they cannot be expected to control their immature, childish impulses—that's where true "grown-ups" come in.

When imposing limits or exercising discipline, these should be firm, definite, and brief. A sharp "No!" as the toddler reaches for a forbidden object or physically restraining a child firmly but soothingly is more effective with young children than "reasoning" with toddlers or young preschoolers endlessly, discussing why one must not hit or bite another child, or how nice and good it is to share things with other children, or whatever.

Physical punishment should rarely be used, if ever. Parents' main instrument of control is love for the child. At the heart of discipline is human relations, how we get along with one another in the world, and how we respect one another as human beings. This is a value we want to have our children learn and exercise. And, if we want them to learn it, we, as adults, must abide by it ourselves.

PARENTS' CONCERNS

Lawrence Balter

The popularity of books, magazine, and newspaper columns as well as radio and television programs devoted to the subject of childrearing indicates that there is a strong and growing need on the part of parents to seek assistance for their child-raising activities. In addition to the media, continuing education programs in many of our schools and universities offer programs in child-rearing practices as do organizations such as The New York Public Library Resource and Information Center. Self-interest groups have developed so-called *networks* for parents. Parents Without Partners and Mothers of Twins Clubs are representatives of this trend. Contemporary parents have many concerns about bringing up their children for which they seek authoritative advice.

Parenthood can be considered to be a developmental stage. Although we are more accustomed to applying the concept to children, parenthood brings with it particular developmental tasks. One must serve as a protector and guardian of a virtually helpless creature at great emotional, financial, and physical costs to the parental investor. Because of the stressful nature of this stage along with the reemergence of old psychological struggles, it is possible for parents to undergo personality alterations and changes in their self-concepts. This can be a positive experience for some while for others it may be an exceedingly difficult phase of life. To the extent that one's parental role is enhanced by a responsive and thriving infant, one's self-image as a parent is enriched. If the experience is predominantly frustrating, self-esteem is diminished and there may be an unfavorable change in personality.

119

For parenthood to be a fruitful and growth-inducing experience for both the adult and the child, attention must be turned to the preparation that one receives for this important phase. Parenthood consists of roles for which there is no formal preparation. There are no certificates attesting to quality control or skill attainment. To become a parent, one needs only the biological capability. The psychological capability is obtained from the "informal" curriculum of the family, for better or for worse. Valuable traditions are passed from one generation to another in this way. However, new techniques are not introduced, and the weeding out of the ineffective or harmful behavior is absent. Parents are trained in their early childhoods when they are immature and highly impressionable. The result is that many adults harbor childishly exaggerated ideas of the parental role. The reality of parenthood can be awesome if there is little else available to serve as a guide to child rearing. A child may be unconsciously regarded as an extension of oneself, or as a devoted supplier of admiration and love, or perhaps as an object testifying to one's importance. In such instances the child, of course, will be a blameless victim of parental confusion, ambivalence, or guilt. The random, circumscribed, and idiosyncratic ways in which parents have evolved into parenthood accounts for much ineffective activity, agony, and an urgently felt need for a helping hand.

Parents need to concern themselves with goals. Closely related to the issue of preparation for parenthood is the fact that aims are rarely made explicit and operational goals are almost nonexistent. Lofty goals may be stated concerning our progeny: independent, self-confident, leadership quality, warm, humane, moral, intelligent, gifted, talented, etc. Frequently, little is done to develop short-term goals that can facilitate the attainment of those ideal qualities. In fact, short- and long-term goals are often paradoxical. Consider the all-too-common situation of soothing a fretful toddler by taking the child into the parents' bed and then a year later the parents' wishing to break the child of the habit of coming into their bed every night because he or she is now too old for such nocturnal entertainment. The establishment and implementation of short-range solutions that are consonant with the achievement of long-term goals is more easily said than done!

Parents ought to concern themselves with their own survival and well-being. Parents have the last word on sanctions and prohibitions for their children. The responsibility can become burdensome. Self-protective measures must be taken by parents if they are to sustain their roles as protectors and guides for their children. Time away from the child, assistance from relatives, friends, or employees, outside interests, and so on, can each have a prophylactic function. At the same time, however, there is also the matter of appropriateness and timing from the point of view of the child's emotional readiness and well-being. A very delicate balance must be maintained between self-interest and self-sacrifice. This implies that one avoids a prolonged separation at the time of a child's heightened attachment and fear of losing the parent. Furthermore, new fathers or mothers may feel stressed due to unrealistic expectations that they have imposed on themselves or their children. If one accurately gauges a child's comprehension and ability, a good deal of frustration may be eliminated. In this regard, parents must learn to appreciate a child's view of the world. Common to young children are such attributes as egocentrism, short attention span, low frustration tolerance, idiosyncratic judgment, and poor time concept, to mention a few. An acceptance of these characteristics lessens the need for fruitless competitions. It should quickly be added that one can accept and understand a child's outlook without necessarily *condoning* it. Power and control seem to be the major areas of conflict between parents and children.

The concerns parents have regarding their children are numerous and familiar. Probably the most popular concern is termed *discipline*. This usually boils down to "How do I get my daughter (son) to do what I say?" Discipline also tends to be defined as a synonym for punishment. Much of the preceding discussion has suggested that concerns must be understood in the context of a complex, intimate, and emotionally charged interpersonal relationship. Discipline might better be thought about with reference to its root word—disciple. When we give up thinking in extremes such as spoiling the child versus blind obedience, we will possibly find that the discipline rubric is not quite fitting. Among the common concerns of parents are also technical ones, such as toilet training and weaning. There are situational issues, such as sibling rivalry, reaction to a move or a death in the family, school entry, and separations. Developmentally appropriate reactions are often experienced as problems by parents—for instance, excessive clinging at one year, negativism in toddlerhood, transitory phobias, and stuttering, nightmares, and the like. These are examples of problematic behaviors that do not reflect pathology but may give rise to concern in parents. Security blankets and imaginary companions are oddities that parents occasionally react to with anxiety. It is important to distinguish a concern that is due to a psychological problem in a child from a personal preference of the parents or an imposed problem due to a relative's or friend's disapproval of the behavior. Thumbsucking and masturbation are two examples of the latter point. The common child-rearing problems have remained fairly constant over the past several decades, with a few notable exceptions, that is, single parenthood, working mothers, and the father's role in child care.

Several sources of valuable help are available to parents. There is no paucity of written and recorded material that can help parents to become more conversant with the needs, abilities, and limitations of children at different ages. Moreover, parent discussion groups can be excellent sources of information, companionship, and relevant time-away periods. Finally, an activity that can be enormously valuable is that of recalling how your developmental stages were dealt with by your parents when you were a child. Whether or not to employ the family's informal curriculum should be decided upon by conscious reflection rather than by unwitting repetition.

BIBLIOGRAPHY

(See also Bibliography for Chapter 3, "The Family.")

Arnold, Eugene L. (ed.). *Helping Parents Help Their Children.* New York: Brunner/Mazel, 1978.

This is an excellent book for the professional and educator who is giving guidance to parents, including the abusive parent and the parent of handicapped children. A wide range of parent issues are discussed. The book is comprehensive and sophisticated in its concepts and language. Because of its practical orientation, it is very appropriate for parents.

Auerbach, Stevanne. *The Whole Child: A Source Book.* New York: Putnam, 1981.

A lively format makes locating a specific piece of information easy. An overview of essential information on child rearing, the first section covers the decision to have a child, the impact on husband-wife relationships, methods of childbirth, and baby care. The second part ranges over a wide spectrum of subjects— from diet to day care, working mothers, cultural awareness, sexism, religion, birthday parties, to psychological services, to mention only a sampling of the topics included.

Badinter, Elisabeth. *Mother Love: Myth and Reality.* New York: Macmillan, 1981.

The author concludes, in this history of child care in France, that the notion of mother love is nothing more than a byproduct of our culture and maternal instinct only a myth. Not to be taken for granted, mother love is shown to be not an innate, dependable impulse, but a special gift to the fortunate child who receives it. In fact, it also cannot be taken for granted that loving, maternal behavior is more specifically female than male. Many a father is better in the nurturing role than the mother, and certainly today women do not have an exclusive prerogative for child care. The author strongly suggests that men and women be given equality in the responsibilities and pleasure of raising children.

Barber, Virginia, and Merrill Maguire Skaggs. *The Mother Person.* New York: Schocken, 1977.

Barber and Skaggs explore the myths and realities of motherhood, always attempting to portray as honest a picture as possible. They advise about how to deal with parents and in-laws, how to cope with one's own conflicting feelings (boredom and joy), and how to handle problems with siblings and other mothers.

Barkin, Carol, and Elizabeth James. *The Complete Babysitters' Handbook.* New York: Simon & Schuster, 1980.

Written for concerned parents and baby-sitters, the handbook offers practical suggestions on all aspects of baby-sitting. It covers child-care advice, play suggestions, as well as first-aid information. Included are work sheets designed to help baby-sitters carry out their duties in a professional manner.

Barron, Cheryl, and Cathy Scherze. *Great Parties for Young Children.* New York: Walker, 1981.

There are party ideas for children aged one to nine. Included are complete plans for twelve "super" special parties, with briefer suggestions for another thirty. Numerous games and activities, ideas for decorations, favors, invitations, and special menus are all included. There is even a chapter pointing up do's and don'ts for parties with handicapped children.

Bartz, Wayne R., and Richard A. Roson. *Surviving with Kids: A Lifeline for Overwhelmed Parents.* San Luis Obispo, Ca.: Impact Publishers, 1978.

The authors spell out thirty psychological principles in clear lay language explaining effective methods of rewarding in order to change behavior. As a handbook for parents, the volume is filled with practical examples, many in a cartoon format, showing empathy for both parent and child.

Becker, Wesley C. *Parents Are Teachers: A Child Management Program.* Champaign, Ill.: Research Press, 1971.

Becker provides descriptions of basic principles of behavior modification and offers practical applications to a variety of common daily situations in the home environment. His book is a very useful resource tool that is relevant to parents, caretakers, and educators. Special education teachers and counselors will find it a particularly valuable means of promoting parent involvement and consistency between home and school.

Berends, Polly Berrien. *Whole Child—Whole Parent.* New York: Harper & Row, 1975.

Berends has written a spiritual approach to parenthood with love as a central theme. She integrates scripture readings, poetry, and popular quotations with practical ideas from coping with pregnancy to toys parents can make. There are lists of books and discovery activities to correspond with a child's developmental level, and there is an excellent mail-order reference section.

Berenstein, Stan, and Jan Berenstein. *How to Teach Your Child About Sex . . . Without Making a Perfect Fool of Yourself.* New York: McCall, 1970.

A tongue-in-cheek style enables the authors to capture some of the uneasy feelings of parents as they try to provide honest answers to their children's questions and concerns about sex.

Berger, Eugenia Hepworth. *Parents as Partners in Education: The School and Home Working Together.* St. Louis: Mosby, 1981.

The author presents practical ideas for organizing and implementing parental involvement as well as programs designed to foster interaction between home and school. Parents and teachers will find it a valuable, comprehensive resource.

Bernard, Jessie. *The Future of Motherhood.* New York: Penguin, 1975.

Bernard reviews recent sociological and anthropological research in order to construct a picture of motherhood today. Her perspective is clearly feminist—soundly based on a wide-ranging and thorough study of the literature. Her prognosis for the future of motherhood is both illuminating and thought-provoking.

Bode, Janet. *Kids Having Kids: The Unwed Teenage Parent.* New York: Watts, 1980.

Sensitively aimed at aiding and guiding teenagers growing up in today's confusing society, the book opens with an overview of the topic in cultural and historical terms. Areas covered include the special health risks connected with teenage pregnancy, abortion, adoption, being a single parent. The author focuses on actual experiences of young women and gives the reader an understanding of the issues through straightforward language.

Boston Women's Health Book Collective, Inc. *Ourselves and Our Children.* New York: Random House, 1978.

The Boston Women's Health Book Collective has produced another book like its first, *Our Bodies, Ourselves.* This time the subject is parenthood. The book covers every aspect of parenthood from deciding whether to have a child, to adopting, to the grown children's departure. Most notable in the book are the quotations from parents, each of which recalls those maddening or funny or illuminating moments that happen when parents are with children. The quotations are frequently capped with self-discoveries and insights. Also useful are the bibliography and list of resources for parents.

Braga, Joseph, and Laurie Braga. *Children and Adults: Activities for Growing Together.* Englewood Cliffs, N.J.: Prentice-Hall, 1976.

This resource book successfully converts everyday tasks into learning activities for children (birth through age six). It encompasses the development of growth-oriented relationships and a healthy self-concept. A varied progression of activities is prescribed in clear, concise, easy-to-follow steps.

Briggs, Dorothy C. *Your Child's Self-Esteem.* Garden City, N.Y.: Doubleday, 1970.

The philosophy espoused is that having a positive self-image is a critical personality-forming characteristic. Guidelines are provided for helping a child become more self-confident and thus become a happier, more cooperative person.

Buscaglia, Leo F. *Love*. Thorofare, N.J.: Slack, 1972.

Buscaglia has written an essay on the process of education helping children to discover their own individual uniqueness and the importance of developing this uniqueness. He quotes many humanist psychologists, such as Rogers, Maslow, and Otto, and authors, such as Thoreau and Wilder. *Love* is a must reading for all who influence the early years of children, particularly parents.

Bush, Richard. *A Parent's Guide to Child Therapy*. New York: Delacorte, 1980.

This comprehensive overview of children's mental health services is written in a clear, jargon-free style. The range of childhood behaviors is considered, and guidelines are given for behavior that suggests help may be needed. The author, a practicing child psychologist, clarifies the approaches of different mental health professionals, the major schools of psychotherapy, and reviews some controversial subjects, such as psychological testing and drug management. Practical information is included to help parents find the right kind of help. The book should be equally useful to teachers and any professional working with children and their families.

Cahoon, Owen, W., Alvin H. Price, and A. Lynn Scoresby. *Parents and The Achieving Child*. Provo, Ut.: Brigham Young University Press, 1979.

There are suggestions for parents willing to spend time in understanding, and working at helping the young child grow into an achiever. Discussion of each parent's role in a child's life and the importance of each area of development is matched with suggested activities to help parents implement a home instruction plan for an individual child's needs. Excellent suggestions are made for making day-to-day living easier and rewarding for both parent and child.

Calderone, Mary S., and Eric W. Johnson. *The Family Book About Sexuality*. New York: Harper & Row, 1981.

Sexual issues as they concern every member of the family receive a comprehensive review.

Campbell, Donald Ross. *How To Really Love Your Child*. Wheaton, Ill.: Victor Books, 1981.

A psychiatrist delineates in plain language for parents and child caretakers three practical approaches that will help a child feel loved and find emotional wholeness: the necessity of physical touch, positive eye contact, and how to give focused attention. This is a small how-to book filled with the author's deep personal insight, spiritual values, and a great sensitivity both to children and parents.

Capaldi, Frederick P., and Barbara McRae. *Step-Families: A Co-operative Responsibility*. New York: Watts, 1979.

Parenting in a step relationship still causes special problems. The authors see as the main contributing factor a lack of a model. They construct such a model and offer effective ways for planning communicating with all family members working together to achieve a well-functioning stepfamily.

Caplan, Frank (ed.), *The Parenting Advisor*. The Princeton Center for Infancy. Garden City, N.Y.: Doubleday, 1978.

In this comprehensive guide for parents a multitude of present-day child-rearing practices are covered, including nutrition, personality development, childbirth, and illness. It is a practical, easily understood reference book.

Cerf, Christopher (ed.). *Kids Day In and Day Out: A Parents' Manual*. New York: Simon & Schuster, 1979.

Ideas and insights relating to children, suggestions about birthday parties, toilet training, sex education, parental privacy, strategies for positive parenthood are a sampling of the diverse topics touched upon by many well-known figures, both in and out of the field of "child education." The book is filled with good advice given with a sense of humor.

Chess, Stella, Alexander Thomas, and Herbert G. Birch, *Your Child Is a Person: A Psychological Approach to Parenthood Without Guilt*. New York: Penguin, 1978.

This common-sense, deceptively simple book focuses on the constant interplay between the child's temperament and the environment as the important factor in shaping personality. It deals with the years from birth through first grade and with such topics as the arrival of a new baby, the "later bloomer," feeding without fuss, graduating to a cup, bedtime, toilet training, coping with new situations, setting limits, etc. Much of the material is derived from a ten-year longitudinal research study of 231 children. The writing is lucid and jargon-free.

Child Study Association of America. *What to Tell Your Child About Sex*. New York: Pocket Books, 1975.

The simply written question-and-answer format enables parents to play their crucial roles as the primary sex educators of their children. The book deals not only with the process of reproduction but also with sexuality and related areas of knowledge. It also helps parents come to terms with themselves as sexual human beings. Although there are many books on this subject, this is still at the top of the list.

Chodorow, Nancy. *The Reproduction of Mothering. Psychoanalysis and the Sociology of Gender*. Berkeley: University of California Press, 1978.

This book is for those interested in an analysis of the role of the mother. Written as a psychoanalytic and sociological treatise, the book argues for the increased involvement of fathers in caring for infants and toddlers.

Church, Joseph. *Understanding Your Child from Birth to Three*. New York: Pocket Books, 1980.

In the first seven chapters Church deals with such practical issues as parents' fears, children's fears, the baby as a social being, sleep, feeding, elimination, scheduling, discipline, sex differences, and early sexuality. The author, a well-known developmental psychologist, sees the parent not as a slave to the child or to "the expert" but as a partner in the process of socialization. He offers no blueprint but does provide something more important—a clear, readable and sound guide to child understanding that will, in turn, help the parent deal with the practical issues of raising a child. This book is recommended to child-care workers as well as parents.

Cline, Victor B. *How to Make Your Child a Winner: Ten Keys to Rearing Successful Children.* New York: Walker, 1980.

A psychologist, family therapist, and father of nine offers practical and effective techniques for laying the groundwork of success in handling the everyday problems that are crucial in building a child's self-esteem and sense of responsibility. For every parent who wants to raise happy, confident, and competent children, this is the ultimate parenting book. Cline runs the gamut from laziness to lying, from going with the wrong friends to making TV your friend.

Close, Sylvia. *The Toddler and the New Baby.* London: Routledge & Kegan Paul, 1980.

As the title implies, this volume focuses on a specific time in a child's development. Parents will find many suggestions for preventing difficulties if they will consult this book when anticipating the child's arrival. Readers will find the British author's language and point of view practical and charming.

Church, Joseph (ed.). *Three Babies: Biographies of Cognitive Development.* Westport, CT.: Greenwood Press, 1978.

This is a biographical record of the growth and development of three babies, as kept by their mothers over the first two years of their lives and somewhat beyond. Although the focus is cognitive development, cognition cannot be separated from other facets of growth. Therefore, the book contains examples of real babies and real parents dealing with such practical issues as temper tantrums, bedtime, toilet training, crying (real and sham), discipline, eating, fears and fear reactions, food preferences, jealousy of new baby, negativism, manipulation of things and people, preferred playthings and toys, sex typing, etc. There is one excellent index that cross-references topics among the three case studies. A superb source of information from real life, the book contains insightful but unobtrusive comments by the editor.

Clemes, Harris, and Reynold Bean. *Self-Esteem: The Key to Your Child's Well-Being.* New York: Putnam, 1981.

Parents and other caregivers are told how to foster high self-esteem in their children while at the same time improving their own. The authors present a program of practical suggestions designed to show the way children develop into secure, healthy adults if self-esteem is nurtured from the start.

Coles, Robert, and Jane Hallowell Coles. *Women of Crisis: Lives of Struggle and Hope.* New York: Delacorte, 1978.

Women of Crisis is unique in presenting beautifully edited oral histories of women taped at different points in their lives. Although not all of the poignant case studies in this book are about mothers, those that are reveal how ideas of motherhood change from childhood, into adolescence, and then through the ever-changing realities of being a mother.

Colman, Arthur, and Libby Colman. *Earth Father, Sky Father: The Changing Concept of Fathering.* Englewood Cliffs; N.J.: Prentice-Hall, 1981.

Traditionally, father's primary family role has been that of the provider who meets the needs that money can buy. Even in today's changing society, the nurturing father still feels that he is "mothering" not "fathering." The authors expose the changing concept of fathering and present fathering models that provide new images of what fatherhood can be all about in today's society.

Comfort, Alex, and Jane Comfort. *The Facts of Love: Living, Loving & Growing.* New York: Crown, 1979.

Although this book is written for children over eleven years of age, some younger children and their parents may also find it useful. Beautiful illustrations and a well-written text present very specific information but also raise many questions about attitudes and values. The authors are explicit about their beliefs: don't exploit others, and never run the risk of producing an unwanted child.

Curtis, Jean. *Working Mothers.* New York: Simon & Schuster, 1977.

Basing her conclusions on interviews with over 200 men, women and children, the author addresses the problems of working mothers and the impact on family life. Brisk and down-to-earth guidelines are given for the best times to return to work, finding child care, coping, and handling new adult relationships. Curtis speaks to all women in the work force, regardless of the nature of their position. She shows how one can be successful as a parent, wife, and working person all at the same time.

Daley, Eliot A. *Father Feelings.* New York: Morrow, 1978.

This is a personal account of a year and a half of the author's life as a father. It is unusual in two respects: most firsthand books on parenthood are written by women and cover the early years of motherhood. Not only is this book about fatherhood, but it is about being the father of elementary-school-age and teenage children. Lively, funny, and genuine—this book will help parents understand and appreciate themselves and their children.

Daniels, Pamela, and Kathy Weingarten. *Sooner or Later: The Timing of Parenthood in Adult Lives.* New York: Norton, 1982.

Through a systematic comparative study, the authors explore the question of how people decide to become parents. Chapters deal with the impact of the new member on the rest of the family, the tension in women's lives between family and career, and parenthood the second time around. Addressed to both men and women, this is a thoughtful book that permits readers to find their own answers for their own situation.

Delli Quadri, Lyn, and Kati Breckenridge. *Mother Care: Helping Yourself Through the Emotional and Physical Transition of New Motherhood.* Los Angeles: Tarcher, 1978.

Drawing on their own professional as well as personal experiences, backed by current research, the authors suggest attitudes and techniques effective in helping the new parent during this initial period of adjustment. Chapters deal with myths of motherhood, physical transitions, postpartum energy crisis, getting back into shape, sharing responsibilities and redefining roles. A special chapter gives a brief description of some special complications that may occur and offers guidelines for handling difficulties.

Dodson, Fitzhugh. *How to Parent*. New York: New American Library, 1973.

Writing in an informal, conversational style, Dodson focuses on developing a strong and healthy self-concept in children by using the science of parenting. Parenting is defined as "using, with tender loving care, all the information science has accumulated about child psychology in order to raise happy and intelligent human beings." The book deals with infancy through age five. Its appendices include information about toys and play equipment for different ages and stages, free and inexpensive toys, children's books and records, and a book list. It is rather "dated" since the father's role is seen generally as one of playmate; thus, the "parenting" is left solely to the mother.

Dreikurs, Rudolph. *Coping with Children's Misbehavior*. New York: Dutton, 1972.

In this virtual encyclopedia of common childhood misbehaviors and how to deal with them, the author explains how to discover which of four possible purposes the misbehavior is serving, how to help the child to see its purpose, and how to encourage the child toward more constructive behavior. It is a practical book with clear, concise theory and a wealth of practical examples.

Entwisle, Doris R., and Susan G. Doering. *The First Birth: A Family Turning Point*. Baltimore: Johns Hopkins University Press, 1981.

The authors, social scientists, inquire into the sociological and psychological aspects of a family's first birth, concentrating on how pregnancy and earlier life styles may affect the couple's reaction to this new experience. The book covers many topics, including perception of the birth event, depression, effects of Cesarean delivery, parents' reactions according to baby's sex, resumption of sexual activity, role conflict, and husband participation. It is a comprehensive text that explores the social forces impinging on new parents and how these pressures can be dealt with.

Evans, Judith, and Ellen Ilfeld. *Good Beginnings: Parenting in the Early Years.* Ypsilanti, Mich.: High/Scope Press, 1982.

"What does being a parent mean?" "How will it fit in with the rest of your life?" "What do you expect for and from your family?" In today's complicated world of family circumstances, there is no right answer to these questions. The authors say, "You need to become your own expert on your own child." In this book parents are challenged to develop their individual parenting skills while they observe, care for, and enjoy their growing child. There is a wealth of information about seven stages of child development—Heads Up, Looker, Creeper-Crawler, Cruiser, Walker, Doer, and Tester—to help parents observe their child's intellectual and emotional development. The authors' relaxed, easy-to-read style combined with the book's charming photographs and attractive, large-print format promise to make the volume an invaluable resource for parents and caregivers of infants and young children.

Ewy, Donna, and Rodger, Ewy. *Guide to Parenting: You and Your Newborn.* New York: Dutton, 1981.

Addressing the first six weeks of age, this volume is a helpful guide for new parents. Discussed are such crucial issues as family bonding, changing parental roles, and the shared parenting experience. There is sound information on daily infant care, health, and nutrition as well as choosing a pediatrician and selecting the right nursery equipment.

Fabe, Marilyn, and Norma Wikler. *Up Against the Clock: Career Women Speak on the Choice to Have Children.* New York: Random House, 1979

Want to remain childless, adopt, become a single mother, or combine motherhood and a career? The authors wrote this book to help undecided women make up their minds by offering tools and techniques for decision making. Main issues are examined, including possible social stigmas, psychological risks, potential consequences for the child, and feelings and attitudes toward children. New choices are outlined for today's woman, who often has no precedents to follow.

Faber, Adele, and Elaine Mazlish. *How to Talk So Kids Will Listen, and Listen So Kids Will Talk*. New York: Rawson Wade, 1980.

This approach to children is based on Haim Ginott's theories. The book appears to be a sequel to the authors' first volume, *Liberated Parents—Liberated Children*, in which the authors put into practice what they had learned from Ginott's workshops. *How to Talk* . . . teaches communication skills with children in a format that is lively and entertaining, using cartoons, exercises, and role-playing situations.

Faber, Adele, and Elaine Mazlish. *Liberated Parents—Liberated Children*. New York: Avon, 1975.

The authors offer practical suggestions of applications of Haim Ginott's philosophies of parenting. The reader is constantly reminded that nurturing children is an art, not an exact science. They stress that the importance of parents accepting their own limitations as human beings.

Fassler, Joan. *Helping Children Cope*. New York: Free Press, 1978.

A child psychologist suggests the use of children's literature to help children cope with the difficult situations, the fears and anxieties they meet as they develop. She has reviewed the literature and makes specific suggestions in regard to such topics as death, illness, hospitalization, separation, divorce, adoption, birth of a sibling, imprisonment of a parent, natural disasters, etc. There are also suggests as to questions for adults to help initiate discussion between adults and children.

Fisher, Seymour, and Rhoda Fisher. *What We REALLY Know About Child Rearing: Science in Support of Effective Parenting*. New York: Basic Books, 1976.

The Fishers, a husband-wife team of psychologists, have assembled extensive research on many aspects of raising children and adolescents (e.g., emotional security, sex, school, discipline, divorce, etc.). By combining such information with their own clinical experience, they have put together valuable information for parents and educators. Their style is clear and readable.

Freud, Sigmund. *The Sexual Enlightenment of Children.* New York: Macmillan, 1963.

In this paperback volume one finds a selection of Freud's writing on child sexuality spanning the years from 1909 to 1922. These papers are a landmark in our understanding of child development, heralding the notion that children from their earliest years are capable of sexual arousal and of interest in these matters. While the clinical material—most specifically, the notion that sexual feelings and curiosity gone awry in childhood form the basis of adult neurotic disturbances—has since been augmented by more recent developments in theory, the writings are of great value in helping the reader develop a realistic understanding of the child's conceptualizations of sex. The collection is recommended for counselors, child health professionals, and interested parents.

Friedland, Ronnie, and Carol Kort (eds.). *The Mothers' Book: Shared Experiences.* Boston: Houghton Mifflin, 1981.

This book is like an in-print support group. It includes short, personal essays written by mothers. They cover every aspect of new motherhood: pregnancy; birth; staying home; going back to work; sexuality; the only child; becoming a single, step, foster, or adoptive mother. Included are sections on children with special needs, dealing with the death of a child as well as being a teenage mother.

Furman, Erna. *A Child's Parent Dies: Studies in Childhood Bereavement.* New Haven: Yale University Press, 1974.

Furman's psychoanalytical analyses of twenty-three case studies of children who lost a parent seek to understand the impact of bereavement on the young and to offer concrete suggestions for helping children cope with their loss. The book won the 1978 Heinz Hartmann Award for the thoroughness and sensitivity of its discussion from both the chronological age and the developmental stage of the child. It includes an extensive discussion of relevant literature.

Galinsky, Ellen. *Between Generations: The Six Stages of Parenthood.* New York: Times Books, 1981.

The author theorizes that parents have stages of expectations of how their children will develop and behave. She describes six stages in the parent-child relationships. Her theory is, of course, based on the stage theory of writers such as Piaget. The book is interesting primarily because of the interviews with over 200 parents. The theoretical underpinnings for the stages are under-developed, but the quotations are revealing.

Ginott, Haim G. *Between Parent and Child. New Solutions to Old Problems.* New York: Avon, 1973.

Ginott provides specific information on the ways parents can deal with their children's day-by-day problems. The goal is better communication between parents and children. The areas that are covered are sex education, discipline, fears and anxie-ties. Ginott helps one to understand when there is a need for professional support. Although dated in its sexist connotations, the book is highly recommended.

Glover, John A. *A Parent's Guide to Intelligence Testing: How to Help Your Children's Intellectual Development.* Chicago: Nelson-Hall, 1979.

The volume is designed to demonstrate to parents how they can develop the kind of communication with children that will foster and achieve their potential. Glover explains the impact of television and peer pressure. He shows how and why such skills as block design, coding, and picture arrangement are meas-ured in intelligence testing and gives guidelines for helping children become more adept at these skills. There is a section on how to recognize and nurture creative abilities in young children.

Gordon, Sol, and Irving Dickman. *Schools and Parents—Partners in Sex Education.* Pub. No. 581. New York: Public Affairs Com-mittee, 1980.

This pamphlet presents a brief, general overview of sex edu-cation for parents and teachers.

Gordon, Sol, and Judith Gordon. *Did the Sun Shine Before You Were Born?* Charlottesville, Va.: Ed-U-Press, 1977.

Parents and preschool children will enjoy the clear discussion of the question "Where do babies come from?" and will be interested in the information about other kinds of families.

Gordon, Thomas. *Parent Effectiveness Training.* New York: Wyden, 1971.

Parents will learn more effective ways of talking with their children in this communication skills text. Gordon's theory defines roadblocks to communication, language of acceptance, and confrontation skills, all necessary to effective problem solving. In *toto*, the book is an excellent explanation of interpersonal communication skills applicable to all relationships.

Gregg, Elizabeth, and Judith Knotts. *Growing Wisdom, Growing Wonder: Helping Your Child Learn from Birth Through Five Years.* New York: Macmillan, 1980.

Based on the theories of Piaget, Montessori, Dewey, White, and Brazelton, this book is filled with creative ideas for parents to use in interacting with their child from birth to five years of age. Individual chapters deal with topics such as color, shape, texture, sound, smell, temperature, language, and food. Each chapter is divided into developmental stages. Additionally, there are guidelines for use with the special-needs child.

Grollman, Earl A. *Talking About Death: A Dialogue Between Parent and Child.* Boston: Beacon, 1976.

This is an excellent book for everyone—parents, teachers, therapists, and even children. In story fashion, the author, in a dialogue, explains death to children. In the process, he presents the language to use with children. He also offers consolation and empathy to the adult who must present this harsh reality. There is a good listing of parent resources.

Guerney, Louise F. *Parenting: A Skills Training Manual.* State College, Pa.: Institute for the Development of Emotional and Life Skills, 1980.

Developed especially for group parent-training sessions, the text is on a fairly low reading level, yet it covers a wide range of skills vital to good parenting. There are work sheets to augment each section, which could help in assessing the mastery of each topic, as well as a means for less verbal group members to react to concepts covered in each session. The book is further enhanced by many simple, yet typical examples of parent-child interactions. Perhaps the best sections are those dealing with what parents can expect of children, showing understanding and setting rules, limits, and consequences. The material seems sure to spark lively discussions in a parent-group setting.

Hale, Nathan Cabot. *Birth of a Family: The New Role of the Father in Childbirth.* Garden City, N.Y.: Doubleday, 1979.

This is a book about childbirth from the father's point of view. According to the author, of all human instincts, the one of fatherhood is less understood and more taken for granted by Western culture than any of the other human qualities. The goal of the author is to help men find that natural tendency. Discussed are some of the methods of natural childbirth helpful to both parents, the new relationship between husband and wife during pregnancy and the birth process, as well as the new relationship with doctor, midwife, nurse, and hospital.

Hall, Francine S., and T. Douglas. *Two-Career Couple.* Reading, Mass.: Addison-Wesley, 1979.

In this timely book the authors discuss not only the relationship of a two-career couple, but also touch on the impact on the family of the arrival of a child. Practical suggestions for child care within the family are given.

Heater, Sandra Harvey. *Teaching Preschool Reading.* Provo, Ut.: Brigham Young University Press, 1980.

Basing her text on the teachings of Marie Montessori, who saw a love of reading as the heritage of every child, the author offers helpful guidelines to parents for an understanding of what prereading is and how reading readiness can be achieved by young children. Included is a chapter addressed to kindergarten and primary school teachers with activity suggestions to be used in the classroom.

Heffner, Elaine. *Mothering: The Emotional Experience of Motherhood After Freud and Feminism.* Garden City, N.Y.: Doubleday, 1978.

Heffner discusses normal feelings aroused in mothers during interactions with children and the ways in which these feelings influence maternal response. She encourages mothers

to have confidence in their own expertise based on their observations and knowledge of their children. This book speaks to
the mother as a person and validates her needs and feelings.

Hersh, Stephen P. *The Executive Parent.* New York: Sovereign
    Books, 1979.

Addressed to those who combine parenting and a demanding
career, this volume will help working parents to cope with
everyday as well as more serious problems and shows how to
cope with the psychosocial pressures that confront the executive
parent.

Honig, Alice S. *Parent Involvement in Early Childhood Education.* Wash-
    ington, D.C.: National Association for the Education of
    Young Children, 1975.

The author reviews model early childhood programs and
suggests methods for expanding parent participation and skills.
This overview of successful programs across the country highlights the importance of including parents as an integral part of
child-care services during the preschool years.

Hooks, William, et al. (eds.). *The Pleasure of Their Company: How to
    Have More Fun with Your Children.* Radnor, Pa.: Chilton, 1981.

Addressing parents, relatives, teachers, and other caregivers,
this joyful book suggests ways to foster a positive child-adult
relationship in the context of the humanist philosophy and
development of the Bank Street College of Education and its
interactive approach to educating young children. It deals with
such matters as vacations and travel, mealtimes, music, dramatic
play, special days and holidays, decision making, choosing books,
daily activities, routines, and a myriad of other practical topics.

Jones, Sandy. *To Love a Baby.* Boston: Houghton Mifflin, 1981.

Combining theory and practice, the author presents a warm
and sensitive guide to effective baby care. Chapters deal with
topics such as the body language of nursing, meeting your
baby's motion needs, steps to establishing trust, and the gifts
your growing baby brings you. Included is a comprehensive
section of readings that support the chapters with the latest
research in early childhood development.

Kaplan, Louise. *Oneness and Separateness: From Infant to Individual.* New York: Simon & Schuster, 1978.

The author has written very clearly about attachment and separation in the mother-child relationship. She discusses in detail the stages through which the child passes from oneness with the mother into self-hood. Additional discussion suggests how the parent or any other adult caregiver can most effectively respond to these maturational changes.

Kappelman, Murray, and Paul Ackerman. *Parents After Thirty: A Guide to Making the Right Decision, Having a Healthy Pregnancy and Normal Baby, and Raising a Well-adjusted Child When You Are over Thirty Years Old.* New York: Rawson Wade, 1980.

The authors address common concerns of older prospective and present parents with a question-answer format, breezy informative style, and bibliographies at the conclusion of each chapter. In an attempt to be nonjudgmental, Kappelman and Ackerman tend to "fence sit," but the information will help readers analyze their decisions and support their actions.

Kelly, Marguerite, and Elia, Parsons. *The Mother's Almanac.* Garden City, N.Y.: Doubleday, 1975.

This delightful book, written by mothers for mothers, is designed to teach parents how to raise happy children. It includes practical suggestions and guidelines on every aspect of parenting from pregnancy through raising children from infancy until about age six. There are some particularly helpful sections on finding the right preschool, starting a baby-sitting co-op, teaching values through activities rather than lectures, and developing imagination, creativity, and independence in a child.

Kitzinger, Sheila. *Women as Mothers.* New York: Random House, 1978.

Motherhood is seen from a cross-cultural, historical perspective. The author, a social anthropologist and a mother of five, examines what having a child means to a woman. She has written a timely book that sensitively discusses what is involved with making a conscious decision as to whether or not to have children.

Klein, Carole. *How It Feels to Be a Child.* New York: Harper & Row, 1977.

The book is concerned chiefly with understanding the basic human emotions of fear, anger, guilt, etc., as they are experienced by the child. It deals simply with common childhood myths and manners of experiencing these emotions. It also confronts the myth of the happy child—i.e., the illusion that childhood is a carefree time and is not filled with all the complexities of human development. It is a good resource for parents and educators.

Kliman, Gilbert. *Psychological Emergencies of Childhood.* New York: Grune & Stratton, 1968.

This is a classic book in the field of child psychotherapy, but one that has benefit for parents and educators as well. In a clear, sensitive, and straightforward manner, Kliman describes how traumatic events, such as death, illness, divorce, and national disasters affect children's adjustment and emotional development. He offers important advice as to ways of minimizing the damage in such situations, and guidelines about seeking professional help. It is highly recommended.

Knight, Bryan M. *Enjoying Single Parenthood.* New York: Van Nostrand Reinhold, 1981.

The author, a single father, sensitively addresses the special concerns of single parents. He offers guidelines designed to help overcome the feelings of guilt, depression or loneliness that can be by-products of trying to cope alone. These suggestions include charts that help the reader assess his own feelings toward self-discovery. The book is most helpful to the new single parent.

Knight, Michael E., Terry Lynne Graham, Rose A. Juliano, et al. *Teaching Children to Love Themselves: A Handbook for Parents and Teachers of Young Children.* Englewood Cliffs, N.J.: Prentice-Hall, 1982.

Parents and classroom teachers will find a wide variety of activities designed to foster healthy self-concepts and to involve children actively in their own education. There are specific suggestions for creating a positive learning environment at school and at home as well as suggestions for home and school working together in a unified approach.

Knox, Laura. *Parents Are People, Too.* Englewood Cliffs, N.J.: Prentice-Hall, 1981.

In her humanistic approach to bringing up children, the author manages to take parents' as well as children's needs into account. Written in a warm, informal style, the book helps parents deal with everyday situations in a way that encourages them to empathize with their children's point of view.

Kohl, Herbert. *Growing with Your Children.* Boston: Little, Brown, 1979.

In this excellent book the author uses personal experiences from his own childhood, his family, and his teaching career to explore five basic themes: discipline and self-discipline; intellectual, emotional, and physical strength; respect and self-image; being fair in an unfair world; learning to enjoy your children. As its title suggests, the book encourages growth and exploration on the part of parents as a way of developing those traits in children. It is an enjoyable volume, written in simple language.

Krementz, Jill. *How It Feels When a Parent Dies.* New York: Knopf, 1981.

A score of children aged seven to fifteen speak openly of their feelings upon a parent's death. They reveal their fears, anxieties, ways of dealing with grief, schoolmates' reactions, and the struggle to remember—and to forget. Krementz has written a personal, deeply moving book to help and comfort children and adults facing that terrible experience.

Kuzma, Kay. *Teaching Your Own Pre-School Children.* Garden City, N.Y.: Doubleday 1980.

In Kuzma's diary of her experiences with her three children during their first home preschool year readers will find a great variety of ideas that can assist any parent in providing a pre-school-nursery school experience at home. The activities presented require little, if any, special equipment. Interested parents are helped to capitalize on the curiosity of young children, which is the most important ingredient in learning and language development.

Lamb, Michael E. (ed.). *The Role of the Father in Child Development.* New York: Wiley, 1976.

This collection of contributions by various specialists in infant development provides an overview of the nature of father-child interaction. Included is discussion of the question of whether there are similarities in this relationship among cultures and from species to species. Important questions are raised.

Lamme, Linda, et al. *Raising Readers: A Guide to Sharing Literature with Young Children.* A project of the National Council of Teachers of English. New York: Walker, 1980.

Advice is given for parents on ways to insure that their children will grow up loving books and reading and that reading will become an integral part of their lives. The four specialists in children's literature whose ideas and suggestions comprise this book offer practical information on how to select books for children and how to share them. Beyond that, they describe ways in which, by making reading a part of family life, parents can foster lifetime reading habits beginning at a very early age. Activities suggested by books are outlined, and there is an annotated list of highly recommended titles for childhood reading.

Lansky, Vicki. *Vicki Lansky's Best Practical Parenting Tips.* Deephaven, Minn.: Meadowbrook Press, 1980.

This small, easily read book includes over 1,000 practical tips for parents. The varied topics—feeding, sibling problems, coping with twins, planning trips, play activities, organizing children's rooms, storing toys—touch the lives of many children and parents. Parents with specific questions will thumb through this often.

Lazarre, Jane. *The Mother Knot.* New York: Dell, 1977.

Lazarre documents her own passage into motherhood. From the wealth of detail, the reader becomes aware in a much deeper sense than in any of the other literature of how one's self-concept changes in the early years of parenthood. The author describes how her sense of identity retreated "into a protective shell tied in a knot." This book is strong, harshly angry at times, yet also profoundly loving and always honest.

Leach, Penelope. *Your Baby and Child from Birth to Age Five*. New York: Knopf, 1978.

An authoritative, illustrated guide to child care and development, the book is divided into five stages of child development, from newborn to preschool, and within each stage deals with play, sleep, bathing, feeding, crying, comforting, learning, loving, and spoiling. The author, a doctor of psychology specializing in child development, offers detailed and specific advice imbued with sensitivity to the child's feelings and needs.

Learning Technology, Inc. *How to Talk with Children About Sex*. New York: Wiley, 1973.

This programmed instruction guide leads parents step by step through the process of developing "a constructive approach to children's questions about sex." Some parents may like this approach; others will find it cold and artificial. Emphasis throughout the book is on facts rather than values or attitudes.

Lepman, Jella (ed.). *How Children See Our World*. New York: Equinox Books, 1975.

The volume is a lovely edition of poems, prose, and short stories written by children from all over the world. It touches on poignant expressions of emotions regarding the central issues of children's lives. Some of the issues are parents, divorce, and work. It is very touching and very helpful for anyone who would like to be sensitized and open to children.

Lerman, Saf. *Parent Awareness Training: Positive Parenting for the 1980s*. New York: A & W Publishers, 1980.

Lerman, who conducts workshops for parents, bases the text on the experiences and concerns that parents brought to her sessions. The subject matter is presented as a series of parent-child anecdotes in which the problem or situation is described and positive responses are suggested. The anecdotal structure makes for interesting reading, but the organizational structure is somewhat elusive.

LeShan, Eda J. *The Conspiracy Against Childhood.* New York: Atheneum, 1967.

A leading educator presents a passionate plea to permit children to enjoy and benefit from being children and going through the stages of childhood that are so vital to their health and growth. By the frantic pressures we are putting on young children—be it to read earlier, to assume a pseudo maturity, to surround them with "things" instead of ourselves, to reinforce achievement at the expense of learning by trial and error— we risk raising people with shallow feelings and an underdeveloped sense of responsibility and sensible moral values. The main message is "Let's return childhood to children."

LeShan, Eda J. *In Search of Myself and Other Children.* New York: Evans, 1976.

The volume is probably the most personal and poignant book the author has written. In evoking her own childhood, she shows how the ability to rear children is deeply rooted in love. All the problems that we encounter as we struggle to help our children grow into decent human beings are part of our common humanity, and although we have learned a good deal about children and how they develop, no book or expert is enough if we cannot recall the feelings of our own childhood and how our image was mirrored back to us by those around us.

LeShan, Eda. *Learning to Say Good-bye: When a Parent Dies.* New York: Macmillan, 1976.

Although written for children, this is a family book and important for parents. The author describes the feelings and grief one suffers when a parent dies. No attempt is made to gloss over difficult areas. The author feels that children should see and share grief and have the privilege of expressing their sadness in their own way. A good bibliography is included.

LeShan, Eda J. *Natural Parenthood: Raising Your Child Without a Script.* New York: New American Libraries, 1970.

The author advocates a return to parental self-confidence in raising children. The plethora of "experts" telling parents what to do and what to say, often "word for word" have made too many feel guilty and afraid to raise children "from the heart."

The book describes such issues as the spoiled child, spanking, running away, eating problems, night fears, death and the young child, sibling rivalry. The author's discussions are not moralistic, nor do they offer "the solution."

LeShan, Eda. *On "How Do Your Children Grow?"* New York: Warner, 1972.

The book is based on two television series hosted by LeShan over National Educational Television. The format of the TV series and of the book is an open dialogue among parents and the author about raising children who are developmentally sound and decent human beings in a complex and confusing society. The topics covered include the ability to read children's behavior, spoiling babies, sibling rivalry, sleeping, divorce, death, verbalizing fears, children's search for approval, imaginary playmates, sex education, and a host of other issues commonly encountered. The format allows parents to tell each other about similar problems and how they have dealt with them, removing the terrible isolation many parents feel. The author clarifies issues, suggests alternatives, provides examples, but does not preach or moralize. Once again, this very human, humane person offers parents the comfort of knowing that there is no one answer or simple formulas but that there are ways to help children grow and retain adult sanity.

LeShan, Eda. *What's Going to Happen to Me? When Parents Separate or Divorce.* New York: School Book Service, 1978.

In her usual warm, empathic, and knowledgeable way, LeShan deals sensitively and realistically with the harsh reality of divorce both for children and their parents. She advocates the open expression of feelings so that mutual understanding is given a chance to occur, and even in time, perhaps, acceptance. Dark, hidden feelings, the author emphasizes, are inimical to understanding and growth.

Levine, James A. *Who Will Raise the Children? New Options for Fathers (and Mothers).* Philadelphia: Lippincott, 1976.

Levine looks at those men who have chosen to be nurturing fathers. He details their decisions to do so and their lives with their children. He also discusses in a thought-provoking and illuminating way some of the issues in fatherhood, such as men and custody, being a single adoptive parent, and being a "house-husband."

Lévy, Janine. *You and Your Toddler: Sharing the Developing Years.* New York: Pantheon, 1980.

This book focuses upon the exciting period when a child begins walking and actively engaging her or his world. It is meant as a companion work to the author's popular and valuable book, *The Baby Exercise Book.* Three chapters deserve special mention for addressing important need areas for parents searching for ways to share and enhance this unique period of development—the chapters on growing up in an urban environment, day-care centers, and the special needs of handicapped children. The photographs that profusely illustrate the simple text complement the author's joyful prose.

Lewis, Michael, and Linda Michalson. *Children's Emotions and Moods.* New York: Plenum, 1983.

The authors present a theory of emotional development and a methodology to measure individual children's emotional development and potential psychopathology. The text is of special interest to those concerned with the emotional development of children in the first three years.

Lowndes, Marion. *A Manual for Baby-Sitters.* Boston: Little, Brown, 1974.

The manual offers general and specific advice on how to take care of children in a baby-sitting situation. Included is a "twelve essentials for baby-sitters chart" with guidelines from activities to accident prevention. It is helpful to baby-sitters as well as the parents who make use of the services.

Lynn, David L. *The Father: His Role in Child Development.* Monterey, Ca.: Brooks/Cole, 1974.

Lynn presents a synthesis of current research and theories on the father's impact on the child in all areas of development. He includes discussion on the historical role of fathers and the absence of fathers.

McBride, Angela Barron. *The Growth and Development of Mothers.* New York: Harper & Row, 1975.

By writing of her own experience, McBride has touched upon many of the issues that new mothers face. In compelling terms, she describes the contradictions and complexities of motherhood—for example, the simultaneous desire for our children to be individuals but at the same time to live out our fantasies and reflect our best side. This book is a useful analysis of the early years of motherhood.

Mack, Alison. *Toilet Learning.* Boston: Little, Brown, 1978.

Mack addresses parents and children in two separate parts and considers toilet learning as one more learning experience in the child's growing-up process. The emphasis is on helping parents become "nonstressed" and children self-motivated. The section for children is illustrated in picture-book fashion.

Marion, Marian. *Guidance of Young Children.* St. Louis: Mosby, 1981.

The text is addressed primarily to students and teachers but also is worthwhile for parents and other adults who seek to assist young children develop in healthy ways. The emphasis is on how to plan for short- and long-range goals. For example, sharing is not automatic for young children. How does a teacher guide young children to acquire this behavior? What knowledge of child development must the teacher have? What are the effects of direct or indirect guidance? Theoretical approaches to child guidance are discussed, drawing on the work of the behaviorists, Adlerians, and Rogerians.

Markun, Patricia Moloney (ed.). *Parenting.* Washington, D.C.: Association for Childhood Education International, 1973.

A series of eleven papers presents a variety of parenting issues—parenting perspectives from other nations, redefining family roles, TV, and a parenting high school program for future parents. The book represents a departure from the traditional parent education concept with its implication of a right and wrong way to be a parent.

Maxim, George W. *The Very Young: Guiding Children from Infancy Through the Early Years.* Belmont, Ca.: Wadsworth, 1980.

The focus is on decision making. The field of early childhood education has grown and enlarged so rapidly that those who work with young children need to have the most comprehensive means to make informed decisions. The text, therefore, covers almost all possible areas from the social-emotional development of children through their cognitive development to creative development and parental involvement. The chapter entitled "Physical and Motor Development: Patterns of Fitness, Coordination and Control" is a noteworthy feature, for the subject is often lightly considered in other early childhood education texts. Cartoons are used, perhaps to make the subject matter "easier" to understand.

Mayle, Peter. *Where Did I Come From?* Secaucus, N.J.: Lyle Stuart, 1973.

Cartoonlike illustrations and light-hearted text appeal to many parents, but some find the approach offensive. Four-to-eight-year-olds will study it seriously.

Miller, Susan Mary. *Bringing Learning Home: How Parents Can Play a More Active and Effective Role in Their Children's Education.* New York: Harper & Row, 1981.

The author urges parents not to stand by helplessly if they see their children educated in ways with which they do not agree. A parent, by working with the teacher, can make sure that the child's education is a creative and need-fulfilling experience. The author points out ways to motivate the child by sharing, guiding, and reaching out into the community. She has written a book designed to give parents the confidence needed to play an active part in the education of their children.

Miller, William Hansford. *Systematic Parent Training: Procedures, Cases, and Issues.* Champaign, Ill.: Research Press, 1975.

This manual is intended as a training text for professionals in the field of child mental health. Its fullest use will be possible for those readers who have some familiarity with social learning principles and procedures. An attempt has been made to provide a coherent, stepwise framework for intervention procedures, and guidelines are based on demonstrated clinical utility.

Mills, Gretchen C., et al. *Discussing Death: A Guide to Death Education.* Homewood, Ill.: ETC Publications, 1976.

Based on research that indicates children are vitally interested in learning about death, this book provides sequential learnings aimed at providing the cultural, social, biological, and personal basis for integrating the meaning of death into a philosophy of life, according to the child's developmental level. It talks about difficulty for teachers to deal with the topic because of the variety of religious and cultural beliefs and values about death. It is an excellent and comprehensive volume for educators involved in confronting and implementing a program of death education.

Missildine, W. Hugh. *Your Inner Child of the Past.* New York: Simon & Schuster, 1963.

The author's purpose is to help parents make peace with their "inner child" and free energies for adult living. By describing and illustrating with case histories various child-parent relationships and their results, Missildine helps the adult to recall the forgotten child of the past. Suggestions for the prevention of pathogenic attitudes in the next generation are explored in the last chapter, and helpful implications are examined.

Montanari, A. J., and Arthur Henley. *The Difficult Child.* New York: Stein & Day, 1979.

The authors offer some answers to difficult questions of how to deal with children's unpleasant behaviors. They forthrightly discuss socially unacceptable situations. Their book is an excellent straightforward approach to problems encountered by most parents at some time in their children's growth.

Montessori, Maria. *Dr. Montessori's Own Handbook.* New York: Schocken, 1965.

The handbook was first published fifty years ago as a response to America's parents and teachers who wanted information on her approach used in Italy after she opened her first school for slum children in 1907. The materials she outlines for use with young children may be outdated, but the respect for the dignity of purpose in young children as they learn is as important today as it was in 1907. *Dr. Montessori's Own Handbook* gives vital information on liberty for the child and the organization of work. The insights on the true role of the teacher of young children are perhaps the best ever written.

Mueser, Anne Marie, and George E. Verrilli. *Welcome Baby: A Guide to the First Six Weeks.* New York: St. Martin's Press, 1982.

Written for both father and mother, this is a helpful guide that tries to answer most questions new parents have. It is suggested that parents find out in advance if the hospital where the birth will occur is family-centered and will permit contact with the new baby from the start. There is a useful guide to assess a baby's condition at birth. Colic, pros and cons of circumcision, cradle cap, navel care, pacifiers, pets in the house, sibling rivalry are just a few of the topics discussed with sensitivity and a common-sense approach.

Neser, Gwen, and Janna Gaughan. *Infantoddler Parenting: Activities for Child with Adult.* Elberon, N.J.: Uni-Ed Associates, 1980.

The authors provide practical and down-to-earth suggestions that focus on the adult's role in fostering the child's development. The book represents the culmination of a five-year research project that originated in the Education Department at Monmouth College. Puppet lessons, finger plays, creative dramatics are just a few activities presented. It is a valuable resource for all caregivers.

Nicholson, Luree, and Laura Torbet. *How to Fight Fair with Your Kids . . . and Win!* New York: Harcourt Brace Jovanovich, 1980.

The authors have written a realistic book that offers new ways of family communication.

Oakley, Ann. *Becoming a Mother.* New York: Schocken, 1980.

Through extensive interviews, the reader gleans viewpoints of varied attitudes toward pregnancy, birth, the experience of motherhood including the bleakness and the rosy hue. New mothers who read this will be better prepared to face the realities without guilt about any negative responses. Ways to cope are included in the autobiographical histories.

Osofsky, Howard J., and Joy D. Osofsky. *Answers for New Parents: Adjusting to Your New Role.* New York: Walker, 1980.

A doctor, who is a psychiatrist and a professor of obstetrics and gynecology, and his wife, a professor of psychology, both of whom are on the research staff at the Menninger Foundation, offer straightforward answers to more than 150 concerns shared by all prospective parents. Fears about the baby's normalcy, the new roles parenthood brings, issues of sexuality during and after pregnancy, and many more questions—acknowledged or unacknowledged—are all dealt with in a blend of scientific information (completely jargon-free) and informed common sense. A wide range of readers will find the book useful.

Patterson, Gerald R., and Elizabeth M. Gullion. *Living with Children: New Methods for Parents and Teachers.* Champaign, Ill.: Research Press, 1968.

Based on a social learning approach, this book can help parents to change the behavior of their children. Following a short introduction, the entire book consists of incomplete statements about behavior or specific situations involving children and parents. The reader completes the sentence by selecting a word from the bottom of the page. It is suggested that the parent discuss the sentences with another person in order to develop a course of behavior for the child. This book will be appealing to persons who believe that behavior can be taught and learned through reinforcement.

Peairs, Lillian, and Richard H. Peairs. *What Every Child Needs.* New York: Harper & Row, 1974.

The text is specifically addressed to parents who find it hard to confront the stresses of child rearing and do not have consultation services available. An educator and a psychologist provide concrete examples and practical suggestions for coping with such stresses and strains as bedtime problems, eating, toilet training, thumbsucking, discipline, etc. They reduce abstractions into real situations that parents meet daily and help parents meet these with confidence.

Pearce, Joseph Chilton. *Magical Child.* New York: Bantam, 1980.
This book is written for parents, teachers, and all adults who
need further understanding of the world of the child. It explains
the differences in thinking and orientation of a child from those
of an adult. It elucidates the importance for the child of play and
the development of a sense of self. It is an excellent book for a
more attuned understanding of the child's world.

Peck, Ellen, and William Granzig. *The Parent Test: How to Measure
and Develop Your Talent for Parenthood.* New York: Putnam,
1978.

In a guidebook designed to measure and improve the readers'
parenting potential, the authors question the reader's reasons
and expectations in wanting to become a parent. A scoring
process and evaluation of that score offer opportunities to examine values. Alternatives to parenthood are explored. It is
excellent for young adults who are considering starting a family.

Pizzo, Peggy Daly, and Judy Manning. *How Babies Learn to Talk.*
Washington, D.C.: Georgia Appalachian Outreach Project of
the Day Care and Child Development Council of America,
1974.

Simple cartoonlike drawings by Manning are the feature of
every page on which Pizzo, with Ilse Mattick's help as consultant,
spells out, step by step, just how children grow in ability to
speak. The volume is helpful to any parent who wants to know
what is "normal" in a child's speech development. The Research
Notes are concise, simple, and valuable.

Rapoport, Rhona, Robert N. Rapoport, and Ziona Strelitz. *Fathers,
Mothers and Society: Perspectives on Parenting.* New York: Random
House, 1980.

Basing their text on a selective review of the state of knowledge of the needs of parents, the authors discuss social expectations of parenting, diversity of modern parental situations,
prenatal parenting, parental issues in child development, grand-
parenting, and new directions in parenting. This is a companion
volume to their 1977 volume (see below).

Rapoport, Rhona, Robert N. Rapoport, and Ziona Strelitz. *Fathers, Mothers, and Society: Toward New Alliances.* New York: Basic Books, 1977.

The Rapoports have been leading researchers on the dual-career family in Great Britain. Their book is an excellent, comprehensive survey of all of the research on parenthood, not only in England but in the United States and many other nations as well. The family is not seen as an isolated entity. The attention given to the impact of the family on society and of society on the family is one of the distinguishing features of this work.

Redl, Fritz, and David Wineman. *When We Deal with Children: Selected Writings.* New York: Free Press, 1966.

These are the selected writings of a widely known and acclaimed professional about his life's work in the group care of disturbed children. As stated in the preface, Redl has selected from his writings, lectures, and speeches those with enough concrete examples of daily events in the lives of children he has worked with so as to achieve not only a range of the disciplines involved but also to retain some of the flavor of the daily struggle with child behavior in the raw. Like his other books, such as *Children Who Hate, Controls from Within,* and *The Aggressive Child,* Redl's work with children of different ages enlightens our understanding, challenges our thinking, and helps us deal with both children's feelings and our own.

Reschly, B. *Supporting the Changing Family: A Guide to the Parent-to-Parent Model.* Ypsilanti, Mich.: High/Scope Press, 1979.

The High/Scope Parent-to-Parent Model set forth in this guide provides a complete training program and delivery system through which a community can develop a low-cost and self-sustaining program to support parents. The book will be useful for persons interested in developing or adapting a parenting program. Chapters include a description of the program's philosophy, strategies to use in home visits with families, staff selection, staff training, and effective program administration. The concluding chapter answers some often asked questions about parent programs. An appendix describes child behavior at six stages during the period from birth to three years. Five dimensions are included—sense of self, physical changes, relationships, understanding the world, and communication.

Rice, F. Phillip. *A Working Mother's Guide to Child Development.* Englewood Cliffs, N.J.: Prentice-Hall, 1979.

In this practical, reassuring, and informative book for working mothers or those considering work, the author's attitude toward the working mother is supportive and instructive throughout. Rice maintains that it is not the amount of time the mother is available, but how she performs her mothering and her many other functions that will determine the impact of her job on her family. He organizes his material into three main categories: child development, child-care arrangements, and the family. His research and case material enliven the text. This author, free of sex-role bias, has fashioned a gift for the working mother!

Rudolph, Marguerita. *Should the Children Know? Encounters with Death in the Lives of Children.* New York: Schocken, 1980.

For parents and teachers, this is a sensitive and knowledgeable book about helping children to deal with death. The author draws on her own professional and personal experience and demonstrates convincingly that even the youngest children observe and struggle with and grasp different facets of the reality of death. She does not relate her suggestions to developmental stages in children's understanding of death. However, because it is a book filled with wisdom and understanding, it is a valuable contribution that deserves to be pondered. There is an excellent annotated bibliography.

Saunders, Rubie. *The Franklin Watts Concise Guide to Baby-Sitting.* New York: Watts, 1972.

The author points out that baby-sitting is a big responsibility and knowing what to do will make the job easier. It is suggested that, if at all possible, a would-be baby-sitter take a course in child care. The book gives specific advice on finding jobs, on establishing rates, as well as on other practical problems involved in baby-sitting. Discussed is first aid, feeding time, changing baby, safety precautions along with a sample schedule and a checklist of do's and don'ts for easy reference.

Schachter, Frances Fuchs, *Everyday Mother Talk to Toddlers: Early Intervention*. New York: Academic Press, 1979.

Schachter describes a study of communication patterns between highly educated black and white mothers and their toddlers and compares them with communication patterns of inner-city mothers and their toddlers. Results indicate the importance of a responsive communication strategy that contributes to a toddler's learning potential. The chapter entitled "Talking with Young Children" can be helpful to parents and those working with toddlers. The chapters that cite various studies are perhaps best for developmental researchers.

Schaefer, Charles, and Howard Millman. *How to Help Children with Common Problems*. New York: Van Nostrand Reinhold, 1981.

The authors, both child psychologists, have written an excellent resource book for parents, presenting information in clear, nontechnical language. They identify normal childhood problems as opposed to those that may require professional help. Of great value are the sections on preventive techniques that all parents may benefit from reading and putting into practice in order to promote less problematic transitions within childhood.

Schiff, Harriet Sarnoff. *The Bereaved Parent*. New York: Penguin, 1978.

This is a beautiful and profoundly moving book written by a parent after the death of her son. Schiff speaks not only of the suffering engendered by grief, but also describes in practical terms how one can eventually go about rebuilding one's life. The volume is reassuring by virtue of its honesty and depth.

Segal, Julius, and Herbert Yahraes. *A Child's Journey: Forces That Shape the Lives of Our Young*. New York: McGraw-Hill, 1978.

Although this is a nonfiction book, it reads like a detective thriller. Citing the latest research studies in the field of child development, the authors reveal that social science has much to say about many troublesome problems: divorce, child abuse, foster care, peer influences, inadequate parents, etc. This volume can be a valuable source book for both the professional and the concerned parent.

Serebriakoff, Victor, and Steven Langer. *Test Your Child's I.Q.* New York: McKay, 1977.

Included is a complete standardized I.Q. test for children seven to seventeen designed specifically for parents to use as a guide rather than a firm evaluation.

Sharp, Evelyn. *Thinking Is Child's Play.* New York: Avon, 1970.

Part One is largely theoretical in its discussion of current research about children's thinking. Part Two, the larger section of the book, lists games that encourage children to think for themselves and do things for themselves. The description of each game and how to play it is illustrated, along with comments as to what the parent should observe and understand.

Siegel, Ernest, Rita Siegel, and Paul Siegel. *Help for the Lonely Child: Strengthening Social Perception.* New York: Dutton, 1978.

This is a book for parents and educators concerned about children who are lonely. It includes guidelines for identifying factors that bring about and sustain loneliness and acquiring skills that will alleviate these situations. Readers will find recommended sources of remediation as well as a bibliography.

Sills, Barbara, and Jeannie Henry. *The Mother to Mother Baby Care Book.* Los Angeles: Camaro, 1980.

Although the authors welcome the concept of shared parenting, they feel that economic and social realities still make the mother the chief caregiver. Here is a very readable, down-to-earth book. It deals with much the same topics one finds in other good child-care books, but it goes beyond by giving specific suggestions on solving everyday problems. There is a helpful chapter on baby-sitters and day care for working mothers. There is a comprehensive resource list. A unique feature is the section of suggestions for naming the new baby.

Silver, Gerald A., and Myrna Silver. *Weekend Fathers: For Divorced Fathers, Second Wives and Grandparents—Solutions to the Problems of Child Custody, Child Support, Alimony and Property Settlements.* Los Angeles: Stratford Press, 1981.

Divorced fathers are seen as an ill-treated minority. This book is as much about men's rights as it is about being more than merely tolerated "weekend" fathers. An outgrowth of their own experiences as a divorced father and a caring second wife, the authors give specific suggestions designed to help overcome the unbalanced treatment traditionally given to the divorced father.

Stein, Lincoln David. *Family Games.* New York: Macmillan, 1979.

Even the most reluctant family member will find pleasure in this lively collection of games for all occasions. Easy-to-follow rules and explanations will furnish all ages with many hours of entertainment.

Stein, Sara Bennett. *Open Family Series: For Parents and Children Together.* New York: Walker, 1974 and 1979.

This series of eight volumes written for both children and parents is concerned with real-life situations and provides suggestions to parents and children on how to cope with their feelings when dealing with them. The text is presented in two type sizes—a large type face for young children and a smaller one for adults and older children. The discussion is amply supplemented by photographs. The titles are as follows:

About Dying (1974)—a sensitive treatment of death.

About Handicaps (1974)—a man with a hook for a hand makes it easy for child to reveal his or her fears.

A Hospital Story (1974)—a reassuring description of hospital procedures; in this case, a tonsillectomy.

Making Babies (1974)—answers children's questions about birth.

About Phobias (1979)—explores the onset of sudden fears, even of the familiar.

The Adopted One (1979)—the joys (and occasional storms) of an adopted family.

On Divorce (1979)—an occasional quarrel between parents need not spell disaster for a family.

That New Baby (1979)—the difficult adjustment to an age-old problem.

Steinberg, David. *Fatherjournal: Five Years of Awakening to Fatherhood.* Albion, Ca.: Times Change Press, 1977.

The journal is notable as one of the few fully developed pictures of early fatherhood. Many of the feelings that Steinberg describes are those that have been historically attributed to women, raising the question of whether it is the extent of the involvement with parenthood rather than the biological sex of the parent that shapes one's response. *Fatherjournal* is a book that will reaffirm the normalcy of our feelings as parents, regardless if we are "new" or "old" parents, and make us remember or appreciate this time of life. It is a touching volume.

Stern, Daniel. *The First Relationship: Infant and Mother.* Cambridge: Harvard University Press, 1977.

Based on observations of social interactions between caregivers and infants, this book describes the social interactive process during the first six months of life, culminating in the emergence of the infant as a social human being. The text reflects new understanding of the infant's partnership role in social learning. It is very readable and of interest to professionals and new parents.

Stimpson, Catherine R., and Ethel S. Person (eds.). *Women: Sex and Sexuality.* Chicago: University of Chicago Press, 1981.

This is a collection of scholarly articles of high quality. Particularly relevant to the needs of parents and teachers are the articles by Petchesky, "Reproductive Freedom: Beyond a Women's Right to Choose"; by Liefer, "Pregnancy"; and by Contratto, "Maternal Sexuality and Asexual Motherhood."

Stone, Jeannette Galambos. *A Guide to Discipline,* rev. ed. Washington, D.C.: National Association for the Education of Young Children, 1978.

The revised edition of a pamphlet first written in 1969 is still a classic on how to deal with children's difficult behavior. Clearly written, it explores the issue from the point of view of adults, environment, and children and offers suggestions that are constructive. The author offers examples of skilled ways of talking to children in various situations as guides for teachers. It is a valuable booklet.

Theroux, Rosemary T., and Josephine F. Tingley. *The Care of Twin Children*. Chicago: Center for the Study of Multiple Births, 1978.

In a field where there is very little written for parents, this book is a useful reference even though some of the material is outdated. However, it is valuable in emphasizing the emotional needs of twins, particularly their need for individuality.

Thevenin, Tine. *The Family Bed: An Age-Old Concept in Child Rearing*. Franklin Park, Ill.: La Leche League International, 1976.

Thevenin discusses her own philosophy on raising a family as well as others' opinions and experiences. The message to parents is to follow your instincts regarding decision making and not to succumb to social pressures to conform. The author discusses sleeping habits from early man to present day, pointing out how natural it was, until recently, for families to sleep together. Children and parents, she claims, were happier and more secure with the "family bed."

Thomas, Alexander and Stella Chess. *Temperament and Development*. New York: Brunner/Mazel, 1977.

The authors discuss the results and implications of a twenty-year longitudinal study. The study demonstrated the significance of temperament as it interacted with significant features of the environment for the normal and deviant psychological development of the different groups of children participating. The book is for parents, pediatricians, teachers, and mental health professionals.

Warrell, Susan E. *Helping Young Children Grow: A Humanistic Approach to Parenting and Teaching*. Englewood Cliffs, N.J.: Prentice-Hall, 1980.

The author emphasizes that the values parents and teachers stress in the home and in the classroom have a considerable impact on how children see themselves and the world around them. Chapters cover topics such as developing genuine relationships, responsibility, and self-direction; feelings; how to implement a humanistic classroom program; and parent involvement at home and in school. Included is a student assessment log designed to assist in measuring the child's progress and growth.

Warren, Rita M. *Caring: Supporting Children's Growth.* Washington, D.C.: National Association for the Education of Young Children, 1977.

How do we promote self-esteem in young children? What can you do to help a child understand death, divorce, or other harsh realities? The author offers supportive ways in which parents and teachers can help children grow emotionally.

Weiss, Joan Solomon. *Your Second Child.* New York: Summit Books, 1981.

Weiss offers sensible, down-to-earth advice for second-time parents blending the theoretical and practical. She discusses the physiological and psychological aspects of a second pregnancy and childbirth and presents a detailed look at the impact of a second child on the sibling as well as the rest of the family.

Wells, Hal M. *The Sensuous Child: Your Child's Birthright to Healthy Sexual Development.* New York: Stein & Day, 1978.

The author has written a very practical and sound book on children's interest and involvement in sexual play, sexual feelings, masturbation, parental attitudes, and other sex attitudes and the way adults deal with these matters. It is a warmly and compassionately written book that draws on years of professional experience. It puts the reader at ease.

Westin, Jeane. *The Coming Parent Revolution.* Chicago: Rand McNally, 1981.

Westin addresses today's harried two-parent families who are reaching out for reassurance and self-confidence. She explores the reasons behind the parents' lack of trust in their own ability and offers guidelines that will allow them to take charge and return to the idea that strength comes from within the family itself—and not from the outside professional.

Whelan, Elizabeth M. *A Baby? . . . Maybe: A Guide to Making the Most Fateful Decision of Your Life.* Indianapolis: Bobbs-Merrill, 1980.

The information and insights offered will serve as a guide for making responsible and satisfying decisions about having babies, considering a second child, or adopting a child.

White, Burton L. *The First Three Years of Life.* Englewood Cliffs, N.J.: Prentice-Hall, 1975.

A reliable and useful guide to certain important aspects of child rearing, this book details the physical, emotional and intellectual growth of the child between birth and three years of age. Seven phases of development are described, each including do's and don'ts to enhance the acquisition of social and intellectual skills necessary for good subsequent development. White also deals with selected topics including toys, equipment, crying, and creative discipline. The ideas and activities are primarily for parents, though they are useful to anyone interested in making childhood a rich and pleasurable experience for both the child and the adult.

White, Burton L. *A Parent's Guide to the First Three Years.* Englewood Cliffs, N.J.: Prentice-Hall, 1980.

Written as a companion volume to *The First Three Years of Life,* this book focuses on the role of the parent in response to the progress of the child. While White continues to be adamant about mothers staying home with babies, he concedes other arrangements are sometimes necessary and gives his preferences. He deals with specific concerns in an easy-to-follow format and includes a valuable section devoted to play and toys.

White, Burton L., Barbara T. Kaban, and Jane S. Attanucci. *The Origins of Human Competence: The Final Report of the Harvard Preschool Project.* Lexington, Ma.: Lexington Books, 1979.

The volume, the result of thirteen years of research directed by White, centers on the interrelationships among child-rearing practices, early experiences, and child development in the first three years. Suggestions to educators and parents are designed to help children reach their top social, intellectual and linguistic abilities.

White, James D. *Talking with a Child*. New York: Macmillan, 1976.

The author poses essential questions: When should we interfere in children's arguments? When do we stay out? How do we interpret a child's statement and the messages behind it? He explains how to use words to get at what is really bothering the child and how to listen "actively" and to ask nonaccusatory questions. The book is interesting reading on how to improve the ability to communicate with children.

White, Sheldon, and Barbara Notkin White. *Childhood: Pathways of Discovery*. New York: Harper & Row, 1980.

Although it repeats many familiar discussions of child development, this book is worth reading if only because of its excellent section on going to school. This piece is helpful for both parents and educators in illustrating the joys and pitfalls of this complex emotional event.

Wilt, Joy. *An Uncomplicated Guide to Becoming a Super-Parent*. Waco, Tx.: Work Books, 1977.

The author presents a light, informative look at age-old myths about preparenting and parent-child relationships. Rights and responsibilities are put in perspective, helping the reader examine values and priorities. The author explains how to create the "super" homes, churches, school, parents, etc., that are expected of today's parents. Chapter summaries provide concrete areas for developing constructive parent-child relationships.

Wolfsohn, Reeta Bochner. *Successful Children's Parties*. New York: Arco, 1979.

Author-tested, the ideas presented are practical suggestions for planning and giving a smoothly run children's party. Step-by-step instructions are given, from preparty planning to completion. A special chapter deals with avoiding common party problems with a helpful list of do's and don'ts included.

Young, Leontine. *Life Among the Giants: A Child's-Eye View of the Grown-Up World.* New York: McGraw-Hill, 1966.

In this child's-eye view of the world of the adult, the author attempts to remind adults—parents and teachers—what it was like to be a child in order to help understand the child they live or work with.

Zimbardo, Philip G., and Shirley Radl. *A Parent's Guide to the Shy Child: Overcoming and Preventing Shyness from Infancy to Adulthood.* New York: McGraw-Hill, 1981.

Theoretical, yet practical, this is a comprehensive guide for parents as well as professionals who encounter shyness. The authors point out that parents may help or inadvertently make matters worse. The guidelines given are designed to help children overcome their shyness. The role of the school and of the child's classroom experience is also explored as a factor in the life of a shy child.

5
Health

THE FAMILY, THE CHILD, AND GOOD HEALTH

Jane A. Fox and Joan H. Arnold

Health encompasses everything about humankind and the environment. Health means being connected, related, integrated —whole. Health is a state of feeling good about oneself, believing in oneself, and feeling a sense of self-worth. Health is joy and experiencing love and commitment to and from those significant others in our lives. Health is sharing (giving and receiving) —and working together, feeling satisfied with our labors. Health is being able to grieve our losses. Health is laughter, tears, and "knowing" smiles. Health is flexibility and resiliency, defending oneself and caring about others. Health is communicating effectively, growing, changing, and evolving. Health is dependence, independence, and interdependence. Health is a life process. Health potential lies within us and is related to everything outside of us. Families foster and promote health through love, trust, and support and by providing freedom to develop as a unique individual.

The young child learns health beliefs, values, and practices from the family. The child learns to be a consumer of health care. He or she learns self-care, to identify personal needs, to make decisions, and to solve problems. Growth, development, learning, and interacting are affected by and affect the health potential of the young child. This mutual interaction occurs in an on-going fashion as the child moves through life.

Each society communicates its value of the young child through the support it renders parents and its commitment to services for children. Indicators of these attitudes and values are also found in portrayals of the child to society, e.g., through media, in writings, and by artistic recordings. Human service agencies communicate their commitment through goals, use of power and interest in protecting and maintaining the health of children, and support of families. They provide those services that optimize the health potential of all children. Funding can make an agency powerful or powerless in achieving its goals.

In order to examine the difference between the actual and the achievable health potential in children, we use vital statistics to measure the status of child health. These data provide a baseline to identify needs and establish programs. These measures lead one to question the commitment and effectiveness of available services. United States immunization levels, nationwide, are far below what is acceptable. Infant mortality continues to rank below many other industrialized nations in the world indicating a lower level of general health status as a nation. Furthermore, specific populations defined by ethnicity and economics in this country are at a much higher risk for infant mortality and other health problems. After the first year of life, the leading cause of death among children is accidents. Through educational programs and family awareness many such deaths can be prevented. Another alarming factor affecting child health in the United States is the increasing incidence of abuse/neglect/family violence. Among the other trends of family and societal crises in are the lack of parent-infant bonding and attachment, the rising numbers of runaway and latch-key children, suicide and substance abuse in childhood. Basic services for health protection and guidance are insufficient. Consistent services to promote and maximize the health potential of the young child in the United States have not been realized.

Health promotion begins at conception. Parents are encouraged to adopt specific health behaviors to produce healthy newborns. "Well child care" is used frequently to define health-care visits during childhood. Such health visits benefit both parents and child. Three objectives are met through well child care: (1) prevention of disease, (2) early detection and treatment of disease, and (3) health education of the parents.

An infant should receive all primary immunizations for diphtheria, pertussis (whooping cough), tetanus, and polio during the first year of life. Boosters are given at one and a half years of age and again prior to school entrance. Measle, mumps and rubella vaccines are given at fifteen months of age. These vaccines are believed to provide long-term immunity. They have minimal risks, while the diseases can cause permanent damage or even death. Well child-care visits offer an excellent opportunity for health education. Parents learn about nutrition, accident prevention, general hygiene, and dental health. Preventive measures are utilized to promote wellness and reduce the risk of disease. Breast- and bottle-fed infants often receive vitamin and iron supplements. When the water supply has inadequate fluoride, prophylactic fluoride treatments are administered to all children, beginning at two months of age.

Well child care provides an opportunity for early detection and treatment of disease. This is done through taking the child's health history, physical examination, and specific screening tests —e.g., height, weight, head circumference, blood pressure, vision (especially for amblyopia), speech, hearing, lead screen, tine test for tuberculosis, developmental and psychological screening, blood and urine testing. Populations at risk are screened for specific diseases (e.g., Tay-Sachs, sickle cell prep).

Periodic visits with a health-care practitioner are beneficial to the parents. They receive support and reassurance. It is a time when parents should ask questions and voice their concerns about growth and development. Discussions about child rearing often alleviate parental anxiety and promote greater understanding of the child and the parent-child relationship.

Advocacy is critical in promoting the health potential of the child. The local community is an advocate for the family and the family an advocate for the child. Parents can be active learners about the health-care system. Health-care providers must be diligent teachers and advocates to all health-care consumers. The goal of advocacy is ultimately for the child to obtain knowledge and become an informed consumer of health care and an advocate of self. Advocacy involves both informing by gaining health knowledge and supporting healthful decision making.

There are various health-care providers and many forms of health-care delivery. Delivery systems may include fee for service (private), prepaid group practice, Department of Health clinics, hospital-based pediatric ambulatory care or family care, local neighborhood health centers, and emergency rooms (for acute illness). Providers of primary health care may include: nurses (pediatric nurse practitioner, family nurse practitioner, nurse-midwife, school nurse practitioner, nurse clinician, clinical specialist, public health nurse), medical doctors (pediatrician, family-care physician), chiropractors, osteopaths, or physician's assistants.

Choosing the best health-care practitioner involves considering many factors, such as availability, accessibility, financial considerations, affiliations with acute-care centers, use of referrals, openness to consultations with others, rapport with child, family-focused orientation, time and attention provided for parental concerns.

We need to protect, nurture and support the health of our children so that their potential to grow, develop, and evolve to build a healthier world is realized. The child is our future.

THE DELIVERY OF GOOD HEALTH: A PEDIATRICIAN'S POINT OF VIEW

Frederick Snyder, M.D.

Medical inquiry, which has progressed from anecdotal accounts toward reproducible experimental laboratory and clinical models, both in physical and psychiatric medicine, has given humankind the opportunity to help define as well as defend itself from the complexities of its own organism. As example, the ability to use live attenuated virus has given medicine the capability of eradicating many childhood illnesses that in the past damaged or killed countless youngsters. Increased delineation of the immune system and chromosomal patterns, each with its relation to disease and inheritance, has given medicine the insight and tools both to define and treat previously mysterious and unmanageable illnesses. In addition, new understanding of biochemical pathways and neurophysiology in recent years has given a broader scope to the understanding and treatment of psychiatric illness. And yet, our care of children has not necessarily kept pace with, nor have we been faithful to, our accrued knowledge and increased technology.

Why should this be? Not because the implementation of this knowledge cannot be accomplished. The knowledge is neither abstract nor uncommunicable. Not because the technological aspects are necessarily so sophisticated. But, because medical care over the years has been subject to the vagaries of changing lifestyles as well as economic and political factors. Thus, the focus is not always directed toward the best that can be given, but frequently toward the most expedient, the most economical, or the most faddish elements that hold sway in a changing social order. As such, the health care rendered our children could be viewed as a reflection of the health of our society.

Nonetheless, polemics will not help accomplish better health care. As parents, educators, and physicians, we must address ourselves to improving as well as making the best use of the existing health-care delivery system. Essential to this should be a basic honesty by both the professionals providing care as well as the patients and/or their parents who receive care. Implied in this concept of honesty is a harmonious agreement between the patients' expectations regarding the appropriate use of the health-care system and the physicians' expectations. There should also be mutual trust based on more than good will. It should be based upon self-examination, realization of motivations, and an understanding of the foibles inherent in dealing with areas where answers are not always apparent or available. Thus, if the physician, parent, child, or educator can approach the prevention of, or attack on, illness with adequate scientific knowledge and with a sense of his or her own limitations unfettered by intellectual or emotional prejudice or superstition, perhaps the promise that one sees in new discoveries will reach fulfillment. However, when expectations do not occur or match exactly, or when there is not mutual honesty, then there can be frustration and, with it, recrimination that can result in a further decline in medical rapport and ultimately management.

Although by necessity the social-political-economic climate must influence the health-care delivery system, each of us must fight its intrusion on the essence of medical care, the physician-patient relationship. In addition, we cannot turn back the clock to simpler times. To ignore the good that aggressive medical management has accomplished in neonatal care, childhood illnesses, infectious diseases, cancer, and cardiac therapy as well as mental illness and preventive medicine would be hypocritical.

However, in pediatric medicine there is a special situation. Honesty with regard to reasonable expectations, mutual trust, and responsible anticipatory guidance often has to take place with an intermediary—not the patient. Although the time frame should be of short duration, since the physician, educator, and parent each has an obligation to involve the child as early as possible in his or her own health care, often this is not readily accomplished. When the child is not involved early enough, whether because of professional failures or parental needs, we cannot reach the full potential both medically and psychologically that medicine can offer our children.

In brief, the delivery of health care to a patient by a practicing professional should be simplicity itself. Each participant in the delivery should be doing his or her best to understand the other and to arrive at a common goal of providing the best quality of life within the situation. The implementation of this care would be by the realistic use of all that society has accomplished to date. Finally, the results of care would be viewed as a natural consequence of people of good will working together within the limitations of human knowledge toward a common goal, with no recriminations for untoward or disappointing results.

If these events were in fact so, the questions concerning appropriateness of hospitalization and institutionalization would be academic. Preventive medicine, in the best sense, would surely take place, and cost effectiveness would not be germane in the discussion of providing fine medical care.

Unfortunately, this is not always the case at the present time, and it may never develop into a viable reality. Until it does, it would seem the duty of all health professionals, especially those caring for children, to adopt a working philosophy that embodies an honest appraisal of self coupled with the aggressive use of the latest information, tempered by reason and an appreciation for accomplishments and insights of the past. With this, all those working with children should be able to continue their attack on diseases of childhood and adolescents while providing a sound role model for their patients to emulate.

GOOD HEALTH AND YOUNG CHILDREN

Maureen B. Slonim

Child health is not an isolated topic. Just as a child should be viewed as part of his or her family system and environment, a child's health is an inseparable part of his or her overall physical and emotional development. Therefore, in seeking information on the subject of child health, the reader is encouraged to explore the books listed in this volume under child development and nutrition. An understanding of normal child development is basic to the understanding of child health.

Fortunately, there is an increasing emphasis on health maintenance and preventive medicine rather than the traditional "medical model" of the past. There is a growing trend for pediatricians and family physicians to interrelate with parents and children as "partners" rather than merely as recipients of medical services. Pediatrics is no longer a medical specialty that just treats the acute illnesses peculiar to childhood. Pediatricians and family physicians are now being trained in health promotion, child development, parent counseling, preventive and early interventive practices.

Child health is no longer the exclusive concern of the medical community. More and more children are becoming involved in day care and early childhood education programs. Public Law 94-142, the Education for All Handicapped Children's Act, mandates the department of education in each state to identify and evaluate children from birth who might require special education and other related services. Therefore, physicians working with children must learn to function as members of a team with other health professionals and with education professionals as well.

A new direction in child health is slowly evolving. The selection of books in this chapter is intended to reflect the participatory role of the well-informed parent. Thus, in addition to health per se, books on consumerism, self-help, selection of the right doctor, physical fitness, cultural influences, environmental health, and child health policy are included. Health should no longer be considered as the absence of illness. More appropriate today is this definition issued by the American Academy of Pediatrics: "Good health is a dynamic state of physical, mental, and social well-being, which is influenced by many environmental and hereditary factors over which an individual exercises varying degrees of control. It is a constantly changing entity, and acquisition of good health should never be left to chance."

BIBLIOGRAPHY

Akmakjian, Hiag. *The Natural Way to Raise a Healthy Child.* New York: Praeger, 1975.

The author's central thesis is that the dependable emotional availability of parents is the key to the child's mental health. By way of preventive medicine, psychological insights are offered to parents and caregivers, as well as practical suggestions for daily child care.

Alfano, Michael C. (ed.). *Changing Perspectives in Nutrition and Caries Research.* New York: Medcom, 1979.

In this monograph published by the American Academy of Pedodontics for specialists in children's dentistry, there are a dozen articles by some of the leading researchers in the field. Written for specialists, the papers do contain a limited amount of scientific jargon. However, several sections are especially recommended for educators and the general public. These are "Developing the Perfect Snack," "Dietary Counseling," and "Resistance to Caries: The Case for Heredity."

American Medical Association. *Handbook of First Aid and Emergency Care.* New York: Random House, 1980.

This comprehensive and up-to-date guide to first aid and emergency medicine is easy to use and fully illustrated. The emphasis is on medical information that pertains to children.

American Academy of Pediatrics. *You and Your Pediatrician: Common Childhood Problems.* Evanston, Ill.: 1977.

This compact booklet is intended to be kept and updated by each parent. It suggests ways to handle or prevent forty common childhood ailments—from allergy to whooping cough. There are valuable practical aids for parents, such as how and when to phone the pediatrician and how to take a temperature. There is space for emergency numbers, immunization record, and pediatrician instructions.

American Health Foundation. *The Book of Health: A Complete Guide to Making Health Last a Lifetime.* Ernest L. Wynder, ed. New York: Watts, 1981.

As titled, this is a guide for the preservation and maintenance of physical well-being and a guide to a lifestyle that supports good health. Much of the practical advice is directed toward children's health issues, such as diet, safety hazards from appliances, noise pollution, traffic accidents, unsafe toys, car restraints, and the effects of parental drinking and smoking. Emphasis is on prevention and understanding the function and capability of one's own body.

Arenal, Jay M., and Miriam Bacher. *Child Safety Is No Accident.* New York: Hawthorn Books, 1978.

The authors have compiled an easy-to-use guide for both the prevention and treatment of childhood accidents. For parents and professionals, stress is placed on the causes of accidents, how to anticipate them, and how to avoid them.

Austin, Glenn, Julia Stone Oliver, and John C. Richards. *The Parents' Medical Manual.* Englewood Cliffs., N.J.: Prentice-Hall, 1978.

The material presented is based on a survey of what over 500 physicians and parents wanted in a medical manual for the health care of children. The result is an easy-to-read guide to help parents understand, prevent, and manage ailments ranging from earaches and colds to viruses and worm infections.

Behrstock, Barry, and Richard Trubo. *The Parent's When-Not-to Worry Book: Straight Talk About All Those Myths You've Learned from Your Parents, Friends—and Even Doctors.* New York: Harper & Row, 1981.

In this collection of common myths about children and health issues a professor of pediatrics does provide "straight talk" about them, authoritatively examining and refuting the myths— for example, colds are spread by sneezing or coughing; teething causes fever; baby bottles must be sterilized; vitamins provide energy; feed a fever and starve a cold. There are chapters on the newborn, exercise and sports, nutrition, and environmental hazards. Throughout the content is enjoyable and informative. Although particularly recommended for new parents to help separate fact from fiction, the volume is of interest to all, including health professionals.

Belsky, Marwin, and Leonard Gross. *Beyond the Medical Mystique: How to Choose and Use Your Doctor.* New York: Arbor House, 1979.

The authors stress competence and compassion in selection of a good doctor. They suggest methods of locating the right physician and means for evaluating if that physician is right for you. Discussion of the physician's philosophy (does he use a conservative versus aggressive approach to health care, preventive versus crisis treatment of illness) and background (age, sex, cultural heritage) can all affect the patient's perception of the physician. A point of particular importance to parents of a special-needs child is made: make certain your child isn't just a medical challenge or interesting case to your doctor. A medical syndrome is only part of a total child.

Berlin, Irving Norman (ed.). *Bibliography of Child Psychiatry and Child Mental Health.* New York: Human Sciences Press, 1976.

An official publication of the Academy of Child Psychiatry, this comprehensive bibliography is designed to be used in the training of child psychiatrists and mental health professionals. It includes a selected list of training films.

Bershad, Carole, and Deborah Bernick. *Bodyworks: The Children's Guide to Food and Physical Fitness.* New York: Random House, 1981.

Previously published as *From the Inside Out*, this book was written as part of an elementary curriculum package for the Newton, Mass., schools. Appealingly illustrated by Heidi Johanna Selig, this large paperback has health information designed to attract young minds, such as "Food Choices" and "Listening to Your Body."

Better Homes & Garden's New Baby Book. New York: Bantam, 1981.

A distinguished panel of medical authors (nurses, doctors, and nutritionists) compiled this complete guide to child care for children from birth to six years of age. They also included material on prenatal care. Their objective is raising a happy, healthy child, and they advise parents on how to do so. The reader will find many helpful charts throughout.

Boston Children's Medical Center and Richard I. Feinbloom. *Child Health Encyclopedia, A Comprehensive Guide for Parents.* Consumers Union edition. New York: Dell, 1978.

As its title promises, this volume is a complete resource in the area of child health. It is divided into three main sections, covering basic health care, safety, and specific childhood diseases and conditions. The latter section is particularly handy as a reference for parents. This book advocates that parents and laymen be the "hands-on" health maintainers of children. This is a down-to-earth, useful book.

Brazelton, T. Berry, *Doctor and Child.* New York: Delta, 1978.

Brazelton, a practicing pediatrician, offers advice on the most common problems of early childhood. He includes information on such topics as the selection of a pediatrician and preparing a child for a hospital stay. It is a guide for parents and professionals alike.

Bursztajn, Harold, Richard I. Feinbloom, Robert M. Hamm, and Archie Brodsky. *Medical Choices, Medical Chances: How Patients, Families and Physicians Can Cope with Uncertainty.* New York: Delacorte, 1981.

This book will assist parents in becoming informed consumers of health care for themselves and their children. The novel approach to medical decision-making, the Probabilistic Paradigm, is written as an episodic tale. Fictional Doctor S is committed to helping parents and their families make their own choices and work out their own medical destinies. At the same time, as a physician, he sees himself as having knowledge and skill to contribute and comfort and caring to offer. Part IV (Family Decisions) shows how a family can make medical decisions with guidance and support to create their own ways of coping with illness, death, and birth.

Chinn, Peggy L. *Child Health Maintenance: Concepts in Family-Centered Care.* St. Louis: Mosby, 1974.

Practically the Bible of pediatric nurse practitioners, this volume is clearly written, comprehensive, and well illustrated. It should be an equally valuable reference for allied health and education professionals and for medically sophisticated parents. Unit IV, Infancy and Early Childhood, is especially relevant. Emphasis is on health maintenance rather than on illness.

Clark, Ann L. (ed.). *Culture and Childrearing.* Philadelphia: Davis, 1981.

Though published as a nursing text, the volume is actually a primer on culture, health, and childrearing that is valuable to all readers. There is an in-depth examination of the cultural heritage of American Indian, black Americans, Filipino Americans, Japanese Americans, Chinese Americans, Mexican Americans, Puerto Ricans, and Vietnamese. It is a unique look at the relationship of anthropology to child health customs.

Cody, Thane, R., *Your Child's Ears, Nose and Throat: A Parent's Medical Guide.* New York: Macmillan, 1974.

This book written by a doctor is an invaluable source of information for parents about the site of frequent childhood illnesses. The author clearly and simply describes the anatomy and physiology (function) of these organs, what can go wrong with them, and what to do in such cases. He provides helpful answers to questions such as, What are the signs and symptoms of problems? Could there be side effects to the usual medications? Is a doctor really necessary? What type of treatment is usual? What complications might develop?

Cohen, Matthew M., *The Family Doctor's Answer Book: A Total Guide to Your Child's Health.* New York: Appleton-Century-Crofts, 1980.

Cohen offers brief, understandable, to-the-point information for parents to help their children and their children's doctor. His intention is to aid parents achieve the maximum benefit from doctors and other health professionals who help care for their children. Cohen attempts to meet the many parental concerns surrounding routine child care, common illnesses, and rearing problems.

Colen, B. D. *Born at Risk.* New York: St. Martin's Press, 1981.

Colen takes the reader inside the intensive-care nursery of a leading hospital focusing on a typical twenty-four hours—the emergency deliveries, the split-second decisions, the surgeries performed on infants born at risk. Presented in narrative form with some changes in the chronological order in which the events happened, this is a work of nonfiction that combines medical facts with human drama.

DeCaro, Matthew V. *The Gray's Anatomy Coloring Book.* Philadelphia: Running Press, 1980.

Here is a chance for parents and children to learn about the human body and have some fun at the same time. These are elegant black-and-white drawings (from that famous medical text) reproduced in a form suitable for coloring and for being imaginative as well. The concise text is informative and complements the anatomical illustrations, at the same time suggesting some fantasies.

Diagram Group. *Child's Body: A Parent's Manual.* New York: Bantam, 1979.

The manual is a clear, concise, guide to a child's body. There are over 1,000 drawings, diagrams, and charts that make the intricate workings of the child's body easy to understand. It contains a large glossary of terms, chapters on feeding, first aid, and play. There is almost everything a parent should know about a child's growth, care, and development, beginning with the child in utero to adolescence.

Diem, Lisellot. *Children Learn Physical Skills.* Vol. 1, *Birth to Three Years.* Vol. 2, *Four to Six Years.* Trans. from German. Reston, Va.: American Alliance for Health, Physical Education, Recreation and Dance, Vol. 1, 1974; Vol. 2, 1978.

Diem is an internationally recognized teacher and lecturer on activities to enhance children's growth and development.

The two volumes are full of information and suggestions for parents and others who work with young children. Every page of text has an appropriate illustration of the material on the facing page.

Eden, Alvin N. *Handbook for New Parents*. New York: Berkeley, 1977.

A pediatrician tells new parents how to "take the worry out of caring for your new baby so you can keep the joy in." In his comprehensive source book of baby care (both health and developmental), Eden offers advice in general discussion as well as a question-and-answer section. He helps to demystify medical terms for the reader.

Fahey, Thomas D. *Good Time Fitness for Kids: A Guide for Parents, Coaches and Counselors*. Piscataway, N.J.: New Century, 1979.

Fahey presents a down-to-earth approach to athletics and recreational activities for children of all ages. His book provides a program designed to help each child, athletic or not, reach his or her full athletic potential. Motor development, transition years (puberty, adolescence), preventing injuries, developing an active lifestyle and endurance, and how to select the right sport are a sampling of the areas developed.

Farber, B. A. (ed.). *Stress and Burnout in the Human Service Professions*. New York: Pergamon Press, 1982.

This book, addressed to human service professionals, focuses upon the causes, symptoms, treatment, and prevention of "burnout." Burnout is jargon for the exhaustion, depression, and diminution of caring attendant upon assuming constant responsibility for the needs of dependent persons. It is a malady prevalent among young parents. Some of the articles suggest practical remedies for this condition.

Fassler, Joan. *Helping Children Cope*. New York: Free Press, 1978.

Stress-producing situations for children are examined. Fassler presents a review of professional literature, a discussion of children's reactions to stress-producing situations, and a discussion of relevant children's literature that can help to reduce anxiety. The chapter on hospitalization and illness can assist parents, teachers, and physicians in helping children to cope with health-care experiences.

Fox, Jane A. *Primary Health Care of the Young.* New York: McGraw-Hill, 1981.

In this comprehensive reference text, with over fifty contributors, the health maintenance and health promotion from infancy through young adulthood is described. Common health problems and concerns are discussed in detail. Emphasis is on health and promotion of health within the family. It is an excellent book for health professionals, parents, and educators.

Friedman, Stanford, and Robert Holkelman. *Behavioral Pediatrics and Psychological Aspects of Child Health Care.* New York: McGraw-Hill, 1980.

Though meant to be used as a clinical text, this book is useful for any professional concerned with the health care of children. The subject coverage is extensive. There are excellent readings on medical disorders, school-related problems, sleep, and behavioral disturbances. Extensive references are included.

Gadow, Kenneth D. *Children on Medication: A Primer for School Personnel.* Reston, Va.: Council for Exceptional Children, 1979.

In this primer Gadow has presented everything that a teacher might want to know about the use of drugs with children. The stated purpose of the book is to answer questions that teachers have frequently raised about what types of drugs are used in specific disorders, how they are supposed to help children, what possible adverse effects might arise, and how teachers should react in various situations encountered with children on medication. The text is augmented by five appendixes, three of which provide lists of psychotropic and antiepileptic drugs arranged according to their generic and trade names. The reference list has more than 300 entries. A glossary of frequently encountered terms is also included.

Garfield, Sydney. *Teeth, Teeth, Teeth.* New York: Simon & Schuster, 1969.

Writing for the reader who wants to know a little about *everything* pertaining to teeth, Garfield begins with the history of dentistry, proceeds through the teeth of sea creatures, rambles through the various human dental specialties, and ends with "the future." Some sections are better than others, but the sections on children's dentistry (pedodontia) and orthodontic unfortunately, are only fair.

Gellert, Elizabeth (ed). *Psychosocial Aspects of Pediatric Care.* New York: Grune & Stratton, Inc. 1978.

Gellert has assembled an excellent collection of original documents concerning specific problems that are noted in the early years of a child's life. Topics such as hospitalization, chronic illness, life-threatening illness, play programs, psychological testing, to name a few, are included. Although the bibliographies at the end of each chapter vary in terms of comprehension, they are excellent sources for continued research. The book is of primary value to a professional audience.

Graedon, Joe, and Teresa Graedon. *The People's Pharmacy-2.* New York: Avon, 1980.

A sequel to Number 1, this guidebook is for consumers on over-the-counter medicines. It provides a wealth of information and advice to parents for themselves and their children. Here is "everything you've always wanted to know" about drugs, drug/food interactions, and vitamins, in language a nonpharmacist can understand. Especially helpful is the chapter on drugs and children, which discusses cold remedies for children, dangers in the drugstore, dosages, swabbing sore throats at home, baffling bellyaches, and similar concerns. The chapter on saving money in the pharmacy yields self-care information for the whole family. It is a valuable reference for the family's health bookshelf.

Green, Martin I. *A Sigh of Relief: The First Aid Handbook for Childhood Emergencies.* New York: Bantam, 1977.

This is not just another book on first aid; it is a well-compiled array of instructions presented in a most useful format. It contains explicit illustrations, uses color effectively, and is arranged in a handy tab-index system. Parents can easily follow the fast, simple instructions for every childhood illness and injury, aided by the hundreds of step-by-step illustrations. There is also good information on drug identification, toy safety, infant equipment, home safety, and much more.

Grotberg, Edith (ed.). *200 Years of Children*. Pub. No. (OHD) 77-30103. Washington, D.C.: U.S. Department of Health, Education, and Welfare, 1977.

This book is intended for those interested in learning more about the major events, trends, and patterns of the past 200 years that have affected children of the United States. The discussion examines policies and provision of services, such as the conditions of life, the changes in life, the trends in consideration of children's needs in health, education, and welfare, the growing interest in children's recreation and literature, and children's rights. The chapters on child health and child development are especially pertinent.

Haessler, Herbert, and Raymond Harris. *Bodyworkbook: Medical Tests You Can Do in Your Home*. New York: Avon, 1980.

Here is a how-to guide to track your family's health safely and inexpensively in the privacy of your own home. It contains a section with all the tables and charts to start a complete history and personal health record for family members. The book provides information on children's health, safety, immunizations, detection of illnesses in infants and children, as well as a checklist for learning disabilities.

Harrison, Dorothy, H. *Health and Safety for Young Children: Child Involvement in Personal Health*. New York: Macmillan, 1974.

Harrison supplies the basic health information for administrators and teachers to use in the early childhood classroom. Stressing the teachers role in child health, guidelines are given for helping each child develop an awareness of the importance of mental and physical health. Chapters on dealing with illness and emergencies in the classroom, personal hygiene and grooming, community resources and activities on health care for the children make this a valuable source book.

Hendin, David, and Joan Marks. *The Genetic Connection*. New York: Signet, 1981.

Written for future parents and for parents who seek definitive answers to birth problems caused by genetic disorders, this volume contains vital data on preventive medicine. There is a state-by-state listing of genetic counseling and treatment centers, a bibliography, and where to get information about specific genetic diseases.

Horowitz, Alice M. (ed). *Preventing Tooth Decay: A Guide for Implementing Self-Applied Fluorides in School Settings*. NIH Publication No. 82-1196. Bethesda, Md.: National Institute of Health, 1981.

Based on the best available research findings, this publication provides the information needed to improve the oral health of all children. Guidelines are given for starting decay prevention programs in schools, day-care centers, and preschools. Included are suggestions for films and posters for community use.

Howe, James. *The Hospital Book*. New York: Crown, 1981.

This publication will make children and their caretakers familiar with the many, new situations young people may experience as hospital patients. Howe's thorough text is presented in a clear, firm, and supportive style. The realistic black-and-white photographs by Mal Warshaw are very effective.

Howell, Mary. *Healing at Home: A Guide to Health Care for Children*. Boston: Beacon, 1979.

This is a thoughtful and refreshing approach to caring for children at home written by a parent/psychologist/pediatrician. She provides the reader with facts and confidence for deciding when it is safe *not* to call the doctor. She seeks to help parents gain a sense of competence and assurance about caring for their children at home.

Huggins, Hal A. *Why Raise Ugly Kids?: Fulfill Your Child's Health and Happiness Potential*. Westport, Ct.: Arlington House, 1981.

Huggins has written a book as unconventional as the title. He has blended long-ignored but tried-and-true principles of folk medicine, misunderstood child-rearing practices of so-called primitive peoples, and the findings of the latest in space-age science into an informative text presented simply, enthusiastically, and with folksy good humor. This dentist-author emphasizes health practices affecting facial structure and appearance.

Johnson, G. Timothy. *What You Should Know About Health Care Before You Call a Doctor.* New York: McGraw-Hill, 1979.

In his book Johnson discusses the whys of needing a doctor and the ways of finding a good one. He suggests how to evaluate a physician's credentials on the basis of background, training, research-teaching experience, and hospital affiliation. A chapter presented in dictionary format explains common health-related problems. This book's goal is getting quality medical care through informed consumerism.

Kliman, Gilbert. *Psychological Emergencies of Childhood.* New York: Grune & Stratton, 1971.

This book deals not only with the fantasies and feelings of several childhood traumas, but also has the important focus of prevention. In childhood stress points of death and marital separation, the author spells out where additional support is necessary as well as where treatment by a professional might be indicated. Also mentioned are minor emergencies and separations, such as moving, first days of school, leaving for camp, etc. The author also touches on overstimulating experiences and national crises. This is a helpful book for anyone wishing to become more sensitive to appropriate action for children experiencing both major and minor traumas.

LeMaitre, George. *How to Choose a Good Doctor.* Andover, Ma.: Andover Publishing Group, 1980.

LeMaitre looks at the primary-care physician in the role of coordinator of patient's health services. Guidelines are given for locating a primary-care physician suited to the patient's needs. Determinants of credentials, such as education, specialty board certification, hospital privileges, specialty society membership, and experience, are discussed. This book helps the patient-consumer initiate a positive experience in seeking quality medical care.

Lorin, Martin I. *The Parent's Book of Physical Fitness for Children from Infancy Through Adolescence.* New York: American Book-Stratford Press, 1978.

A pediatrician details a program of regular exercise and proper diet to ensure a child's health, well-being and physical fitness. He attempts to separate fact from fad concerning nutrition and exercise. He has written for "ordinary parents" in easy-to-understand terms and provides them with practical suggestions, rules, formulas, and examples.

McCollum, Audrey T. *The Chronically Ill Child: A Guide for Parents and Professionals.* New Haven: Yale University Press, 1981.

This humane and sensitive book gives practical advice and support to parents and caretakers of chronically ill children.

McCollum, Audrey T. *Coping with Prolonged Health Impairment in Your Child.* Boston: Little, Brown, 1975.

Writing for families of children with acute or chronic illness or disability, the author explores the social, intellectual, and emotional meaning of the impairment for the developing child and the family. The challenges that must be faced differ, depending on the developmental level of the maturing child, and this book aims to help the child and family master the developmental tasks at hand. The book guides parents in anticipating needs and planning solutions. Valuable suggestions for working with professionals are included. The liberal use of anecdotes based on actual experiences with families who have coped successfully is effective. This is a valuable book for parents and professionals who work with disabled children. The book predates the Education for All Handicapped Act, and the sections regarding schooling and educational programs are out of date. However, it is still a valuable resource.

McIntire, Matilda. *Handbook on Accident Prevention: Injury Control for Children & Youth.* New York: Harper & Row, 1980.

The author discusses such topics as toy safety, falls, poisons, bicycle accidents, and burns. Special advice on safety for handicapped children is included. The appendix lists associations promoting child safety.

Mc Keown, Joseph. *Everybody's Tooth Book.* Santa Cruz, Ca.: Happy Valley Apple Press, 1973.

This book concerned with preventive dentistry is written for the lay person by a former public health service dentist. Material covered includes tooth anatomy, preventive paraphernalia/technique and information pertaining to a child's dentition. Especially valuable is the section describing the proper flossing and brushing techniques. Excellent illustrations facilitate the learning process. Extremely low-key in its presentation, the book is an appropriate primer of dental preventive knowledge.

Manela, Roger, and Armand Lauffer. *Health Needs of Children.* Beverly Hills: Sage Publications, 1981.

The authors outline major health issues confronting low-income families and their children. In nontechnical descriptions, this "human service guide" tells how to locate children with health problems, how to recognize health problems, and how to help the children obtain the services they need. Professionals in the delivery of services to children will find the book useful.

Marsh, Frank H. *The Emerging Rights of Children in Treatment for Mental and Catastrophic Illnesses.* Washington, D.C.: University Press of America, 1980.

Marsh reviews the treatment of children by the health-care system. He examines children's rights as they relate to mental and physical illness and discusses moral, ethical, and legal aspects of rights and treatment.

Marshall, Lyn. *Yoga for Your Children.* New York: Schocken, 1979.

This colorfully illustrated paperback makes even nonyoga mothers interested in trying these exercises. Yoga is presented as a form of body movement that is an alternative to the usual sports and physical education and it's fun! It is recommended to start with children about age four or five, for that is when their attention span is enlarging.

May, Lawrence. *Getting the Most Out of Your Doctor.* New York: Basic Books, 1977.

May is an advocate of the primary-care physician (family practitioner, general practitioner, pediatrician) for quality medical evaluation and health maintenance. He focuses on the complexity of the medical world and the need for the patient to have a primary-care physician to interpret and focus medical data to and from specialists. A good primary-care physician takes on the role of medical advocate and coordinator for his or her patient. Additionally, a chapter entitled "Understanding The Patient Process" helps prepare and organize the patient-consumer for successful, informed visits to the doctor.

Moffet, Hugh L. *Pediatric Infectious Diseases: A Problem Oriented Approach*, 2nd ed. New York: Harper & Row, 1981.

Moffet emphasizes the advances made in child health care between 1975 and 1980. Syndromes are defined, and differential diagnosis of possible causes are discussed. Since there is a problem-oriented approach, the book is best suited to the needs of the health-care practitioner.

Moss, Arthur. *The Essentials of Pediatrics.* Philadelphia: Lippincott, 1980.

The fundamentals of child health care are briefly reviewed in this volume. An outline format allows for a compact overview of pediatric medicine. Because of the presentation, the material is not comprehensively discussed, nor are the less common areas of disease covered. However, this book can be helpful to a wide range of educated readers.

Moss, Stephen J. *Your Child's Teeth: A Parent's Guide to Making and Keeping Them Perfect.* Boston: Houghton Mifflin, 1979.

This reference text written for laymen by a leading pedodontist follows the development of a child's dentition from conception through orthodontics. Especially good is the section entitled "Keys to Defensive Dentistry," which deals with the proven preventive measures necessary to keep teeth decay-free.

Norwood, Christopher. *At Highest Risk: Environmental Hazards to Young and Unborn Children.* New York: McGraw-Hill, 1980.

A reputable health/science writer alerts parents and future parents to the often invisible hazards that might have grave future health implications for children.

Ong, Beale H. *530 Vital Questions Every Mother Asks About Her Child's Health: And a Noted Pediatrician's Quick, Authoritative Advice.* New York: Wideview Books, 1979.

This book is everything one would expect from the title. It is recommended as a reassuring source of advice to parents on frequently asked (and unasked) questions about their child's health, growth, and development; safety; education; emotions; and problems.

Pantell, Robert H., James F. Fries, and Donald M. Vickery. *Taking Care of Your Child: A Parent's Guide to Medical Care.* Reading, Ma.: Addison-Wesley, 1977.

The authors furnish practical information and decision-making charts for the most common childhood problems—from earaches and poison ivy to smashed fingers and measles. The charts are easy to read and follow and can aid parents in deciding when a doctor needs to be consulted. This book suggests ways for parents to be wise and informed consumers of pediatric care and also examines both sides of controversial health issues.

Parent's Magazine. *Mother's Encyclopedia and Everyday Guide to Family Health*, rev. ed. New York: Dell, 1981.

Sound, straightforward information and advice on the most pressing topics of family living, childhood health, and normal child development and child care are presented in the over 1,500 entries. Featured are special sections on prevention of accidents and poisonings, dealing with emotional problems, proper nutrition and vitamins, answering children's questions, and a guide for baby-sitters. The text is amply illustrated, and there is an extensive index.

Petrillo, Madeline. *Emotional Care of Hospitalized Children*, 2nd ed. New York: Harper & Row, 1980.

This volume stresses the need to humanize the hospital experience for children and adolescents. The author discusses prehospital preparation and children's coping styles and suggests guidelines for working with children of different ages. The text is targeted to the health-care practitioner.

Pomerance, Herbert. *Growth Standards in Children*. New York: Harper & Row, 1979.

Close to 4,000 infants and children were studied over twenty-one years in order to develop new standards for growth. Representative tables for weight, height, head circumference, and chest circumference are included. There is also information on the appearance of teeth and on blood pressure levels.

Pomeranz, Virginia E., and Dodi Schultz. *The Mother's and Father's Medical Encyclopedia*. New York: New American Library, 1978.

This is a guide for handling all health and illness problems that parents are likely to encounter from infancy to college. Problems are listed in alphabetical order and cross-referenced. This book can help parents increase their general medical knowledge, understand medical terms, select the right doctor, and handle emergencies.

Pringle, Sheila, and Brenda E. Ramsey. *Promoting the Health of Children: A Guide for Caretakers and Health Care Professionals*. St. Louis: Mosby, 1981.

The reader will find valuable information on assessing, maintaining, and promoting the health status of children. The material covers five stages of childhood development: infancy, toddlerhood, preschool, school age, and adolescence. Landmarks of growth and development are presented in a simple columnar format, along with anticipatory guidance principles. Developed as a textbook primarily for nurses, the guide should also be of interest and value to allied professionals and parents seeking in-depth information.

Prudden, Suzy, and Jeffrey Susman. *See How They Run: Suzy Prudden's Running Book for Kids*. New York: Grosset & Dunlap, 1979.

Running and jogging have become so popular that it is natural to have among the many books written for adults, one for kids. With advice ranging from the kind and cost of shoes to food for health, this is a useful book. Photographs complement the text and make the instructions for the warm-up exercises easy to follow. There is a jogging chart in which one can record one's daily workout.

Reinisch, Edith H., and Ralph E. Minear, Jr. *Health of the Preschool Child.* New York: Wiley, 1978.

Topics include preschool health programs, nutrition, care of the ill child, behavioral problems, accident prevention, first aid, legal consideration, learning how to observe symptoms, knowing what to do. This well-organized book contains reproductions of record forms, a glossary of medical terms, and a guide to sources of selected publications and films.

Riley, Marie, Kate R. Barrett, Thomas J. Martinel, and Mary Ann Robertson. *Children and Youth in Action.* Washington, D.C.: U.S. Department of Health and Human Services, 1980.

This booklet written by professional physical educators who are knowledgeable about children and motor development contains a tremendous amount of information in a concise and readable form. The authors discuss physical fitness and motor skills and offer many suggestions for adults to use with children. The chapter "Growing Up with Physical Activity" treats age ranges differently, starting with birth and continuing through the teen years. Sex stereotyping, safety, and youth sports are also considered.

Rimstidt, Suzie. *Speak Up for Your Child's Health.* Indianapolis: Program Prepare, Developmental Training Center, Indiana University, 1981.

This sensitive, articulate account of one mother's (a teacher) experiences with the medical care system and her developmentally delayed son is not the usual bitter, accusatory account, but rather an attempt to understand the medical mystique. The result is an extremely helpful compilation of advocacy advice for parents in selecting a physician and dealing effectively as a partner in coordinating their child's health care needs. The excellent bibliography lists books and magazines readily available to parents.

Ryan, James H. *Pablum, Parents, and Pandemonium: Glimpses of a Pediatrician's World.* New York: Crowell, 1975.

Ryan's description of a pediatrician's world is often funny, often sad, but always good reading. He describes four types of pediatricians: godlike, grandma, lackadaisical, and the perfect blend. This book covers a broad variety of important issues such as genetic counseling, child abuse, sudden infant death syndrome (SIDS), the drug problem, and the dilemma over the quality of life. Ryan also discusses the subject of unnecessary surgery in children, hospital rules and regulations, and fee-splitting. This is definitely not your ordinary encounter with a pediatrician.

Schnert, Keith W., and Howard Eisenberg. *How to Be Your Own Doctor (Sometimes)*, rev. ed. New York: Grossett & Dunlap, 1981.

This self-care guide is based on a computer-age "course for the activated patient" for the 1980s. It contains a great deal of information on child health, suggests concise record-keeping methods, and provides additional readings on issues of concern.

Shiller, Jack G. *Childhood Illnesses and Childhood Injury*. New York: Stein & Day, 1978.

Originally published as two separate books, this one-volume edition is a practical guide for parents, clearly written and well-illustrated, by a pediatrician. It teaches parents how to recognize and treat common childhood ailments at home. The content is well organized, with easy reference according to symptoms.

Silver, George A. *Child Health: America's Future*. Germantown, Md.: Aspen Systems, 1978.

Silver presents a harsh look at this country's commitment (or lack of) to health-care services for children. He compares community (public) health services and policy in this country to European models. Silver, a former Undersecretary of HEW, suggests policy recommendations for state and federal agencies to improve the health of this country's most valuable resource— its children. It is must reading for those concerned and interested in public health policy.

Smith, Lendon. *The Children's Doctor*. Englewood Cliffs, N.J.: Prentice-Hall, 1978.

Smith offers excellent common-sense advice to mothers on how to attain the best access to a pediatrician. Information is given on how to organize phone calls to the doctor, how to make the doctor feel needed, and how to motivate the pediatrician to work for the parent. Parents will find the book easy, enjoyable reading.

Smith, Lendon. *The Encyclopedia of Baby and Child Care.* Englewood Cliffs, N.J.: Prentice-Hall, 1972.

Although published in 1972, this book remains an inclusive reference guide to the health care of children. It is helpful to parents in interpreting medical jargon. A significant feature is the material on medicines, allergies, and immunizations. An easy-to-use, alphabetized, cross-referenced encyclopedia, it is a handy book, recommended for any household with children.

Smith, Vernon (ed.). *Visual Handicaps in Children.* Philadelphia: Lippincott, 1979.

In this comprehensive review of visual handicaps, Smith covers such topics as diagnosis, screening, incidence, management, and the effects of visual impairment during early childhood.

Spock, Benjamin. *Baby and Child Care.* New York: Simon & Schuster, 1981.

Here in an updated paperback is advice on child health by the best-known pediatrician in the United States. He continues to give practical advice on feeding, clothing and equipment, child development, toilet training, discipline, illness, and first aid. In this valuable handbook, as in the many previous editions, parents will find support and reassurance.

Stoppard, Miriam. *Dr. Miriam Stoppard's Book of Baby Care.* New York: Atheneum, 1977.

Stoppard has written a guide to having and caring for a baby from conception to three years of age. The author, a medical doctor and mother of four children, effectively combines medical knowledge and firsthand experience. All aspects of pregnancy, feeding, childhood illnesses, and behavior problems are covered. The text is complemented by engaging photographs.

Stout, Glenn, R., Jr. *The First Month of Life: A Parent's Guide to Care of the Newborn*. New York: Signet, 1981.

This answer-filled guide to those panicky questions about the brand-new baby, written by a pediatrician, is easy to read and provides reassuring, practical advice for new parents. It contains information on feeding, auto safety, and other health concerns.

Sweeney, Edward A. (ed.). *The Food that Stays: An Update on Nutrition, Diet, Sugar and Caries*. New York: Medcom, 1977.

This monograph published by the American Academy of Pedodontics consists of fourteen articles by leading dental researchers concerned with nutrition and dental health. Although written with the health professional in mind, the entire monograph is easy to read and is recommended for educators and laymen. Especially well conceived and written are the sections entitled "Epidemiology of Oral Disease," "Nursing-Bottle-Mouth Syndrome," "Sugar: The Whole Story," "Dietary Analysis, Interpretation and Counseling," "Sugar: Thoughts and Management," and "Balanced Prevention."

U.S. Department of Health and Human Services/Public Health Service. *Better Health for Our Children: A National Strategy. The Report of the Select Panel for the Promotion of Child Health to States, Congress and the Secretary of Health and Human Services*. Washington: D.C.: U.S. Government Printing Office, 1981.

Vol. 1, *Major Findings and Recommendations*.

Vol. 2, *Analysis and Recommendations for Selected Federal Programs*.

Vol. 3, *A Statistical Profile*.

These recommendations from a "blue-ribbon" panel reflect a hardheaded analysis of serious unmet needs in child and maternal health, a recognition of past successes and future opportunities for effectively meeting these needs, careful consideration of the weaknesses and strengths of current federal programs and policies, and a sober and pragmatic assessment of the capacity of our institutions to provide parents, professionals, and others working to improve child health with the scientific, financial, and organizational support they need.

Vickery, Donald M., and James Fries. *Take Care of Yourself: A Consumer's Guide to Medical Care*, rev. ed. Reading, Mass.: Addison-Wesley, 1981.

The guide is recommended as a supplement and complement to a first aid manual in the home. The physician authors suggest ways to avoid unnecessary trips to the doctor's office to save time and money, how to keep family records, and recommended readings. They have included a special section on childhood diseases and emergencies.

Wei, Stephen H. Y. (ed.). *Pediatric Basics*. No. 30. Fremont, Mich.: Gerber Products, 1981.

This easy-to-read pamphlet on dental care for children contains a minimum of dental jargon. Its three articles—"Nutrition, Diet, Fluoride and Dental Health," "Infant Dental Care," and "Oral Facial Development and Oral Habits"—are succinct and well done. The monograph is highly recommended for parents of children zero to five years of age.

Weinfeld, Nanci Rogovin. *Helpful Hints and Tricks For New Moms and Dads (And Not So New)*. Chicago: Rand McNally, 1981.

This loose-leaf booklet is crammed with facts about feeding, sitters, good health habits, safety, and travel with young children. Hundreds of ideas are collected here for parents. The section on safety is especially valuable.

Zamm, Alfred V., with Robert Gannon. *Why Your House May Endanger Your Health*. New York: Simon & Schuster, 1980.

This is a guide for consumers on how to control their environment and improve their health without medication or a visit to the doctor. Case histories document scientific findings to make this readable book a priority for every consumer, every concerned parent. There is good information for parents who are concerned about a healthy environment at home for their children.

6
Nutrition

FEEDING INFANTS AND YOUNG CHILDREN

Catherine Cowell

Within hours after birth, milk—breast or formula—is fed to the newborn infant. This initial feeding contact is the first time a mother and infant begin to establish a positive maternal-child relationship. During feeding the mother's skin contact, cuddling, and cooing are important stimuli communicated to her infant. These feeding experiences form the foundation to which the infant associates food and eating. With each subsequent feeding, these cues are reinforced. The more positive the cues, the more pleasant and enjoyable the experience for both mother and baby.

Foods offered and how they are offered can significantly affect the infant's enjoyment of eating. The mother or primary caretaker should have support and information to help make prudent decisions regarding the feeding of her baby.

The first food is milk. Breast milk contains the ideal amount of nutrients needed by the baby. Some advantages of breast-feeding are the following: (1) it is *convenient and practical*, (2) it is bacteriologically safe and clean, (3) its nutritive composition is best suited for baby, (4) it offers immunological protection, (5) it helps promote sound eating habits, and (6) it helps to stimulate positive maternal-infant interactions.

If a mother is unable or chooses not to breast-feed, then in consultation with a pediatrician, an appropriate formula should be selected. There are many types of commercial formula available. The one chosen should be based on what's best for the individual infant. Consideration should be given to calories, nutrients, and compatibility with the infant's digestive system. Some mothers may choose to make their own formula. Whether commercial or homemade, these formulas should be properly prepared. Careful washing of hands and all equipment, such as bottles, can, and nipples, is a must. Proper storage and immediate refrigeration will prevent spoilage.

During the early months of life, the infant requires frequent feedings because of the small size of the stomach. The usual pattern is 4 to 6 ounces of formula every four or five hours; however, each infant is an individual so the amount and number of feedings must be regulated for each baby.

Water is also essential for the baby. Nursed infants should be given a teaspoon of cooled, boiled water, two to three times a day. Nothing should be added to stimulate the baby to drink the water. Bottle-fed infants receive adequate water through their formula. Additional water need not be given until the introduction of solid foods.

Introducing Solid Foods

Pediatric specialists recommend that solid foods be introduced around six months of age. There are no advantages to feeding solids earlier. At six months eating skills have developed to the point where the infant can chew. Up-and-down tongue and jaw movements and control of head muscles are important developmental stages in the acquisition of eating skills.

One of the first solid foods introduced is iron-fortified cereal —rice, oats, and barley. This is followed by strained or blended fruit. Only a small amount of cooked fruit, such as apples, peaches, pears, or plums, should be offered. The amount offered can be increased as the baby's appetite develops. No more than one fruit should be introduced per week. Using this time schedule allows the baby to become accustomed to a new food and will aid in detecting any reaction to a particular food.

Cooked and strained vegetables can be introduced in the same pattern as fruits. Carrots, squash, pumpkin, and sweet potatoes are among the appropriate vegetables to select. No fat or spices should be added to the strained vegetables. Natural preparation of a variety of vegetables provides for the enjoyment of the flavors while avoiding an excess of calories.

Strained meat, poultry, and fish are next on the growing list of foods for baby. Plain cooked meat that is scraped or strained should be introduced at weekly intervals.

As the infant approaches the latter part of the first year, cooked egg yolk can be served. During this period the coarser textured foods (chopped, minced, or pureed) can begin to replace strained and blended foods. Dried bread or toast are useful for the teething infant.

Around the twelfth month of age the baby's eating should begin to approximate that of the other family members. The texture of the food and the feeding time should coincide with the rest of the family. What each family member communicates verbally and nonverbally about food can make an impression on the baby. Eating behaviors can be picked up and imitated. Turning up one's nose at a bowl of spinach or saying "I don't like carrots" are behaviors that can influence what the baby will or will not eat.

Food and the Toddler

A regular schedule of feeding should help the young child grow with each new food experience. The family should be supportive of the toddler's self-feeding and be aware of changes in appetite and tastes. This is the time when a child becomes more independent and displays individuality. Family members can be helpful by remembering to (1) offer small portions of food, (2) make available additional servings of food, if needed, (3) plan nourishing in-between feedings spaced so as not to interfere with meals, (4) serve tasty, attractive foods appropriate for the age of the child, (5) use age-appropriate eating and drinking utensils that promote the development of eating skills, (6) encourage a relaxed, social environment at mealtime, (7) accept accidents of food spilling and be willing to be supportive, and (8) avoid using food and eating as a reward.

The family setting should be a positive reinforcement for building sound eating habits. Mealtime should be pleasant and relaxed. Family members should share in planning menus, making food choices, and food preparation.

Meal Planning

Meals planned should consist of a variety of nourishing foods of contrasting textures, colors, and flavors. Some soft foods, like cottage cheese, can be served with chewy, crisp foods, such as an apple. This combination of foods can be a way of encouraging a young child to chew vigorously while enjoying the sound of food.

Difficult-to-chew foods should be cut into bite-size pieces. Family members should facilitate in making food easy to handle and eat. This avoids the child's becoming frustrated and losing appetite.

Young children tend to reject strongly flavored foods and strongly spiced or highly seasoned foods should be avoided. When family preference is for highly spiced foods, a portion of food should be removed for the child before it is seasoned.

One major aim of feeding a child is to help develop sound eating habits for life. A variety of nourishing, well-prepared items offered in a relaxed and friendly climate will foster pleasant associations with food and eating. The young child will eagerly look forward to eating with the family at mealtime.

Prolonged poor nutrition during the early years can have serious effects and often lead to irreversible damage. Lack of the ability to concentrate, poor reading skills, and poor performance deficits are some observable symptoms of prolonged under-nutrition. If early nutrition intervention with adequate amounts of food to supply the necessary calories and essential nutrients does not occur, then these symptoms will persist from child-hood to adolescence into adulthood. Children who are poorly nourished do less well in school and on behavioral tests than those who are better nourished.

Children in the Kitchen

The one place in an apartment or house where young children and adults can have fun is cooking and sharing in the kitchen!

The kitchen should be a place where a young child can become fascinated with all the action around planning, growing, preparing, and serving family meals. Suggestions for stimulating the child's interest include (1) a window box with seeds for growing herbs and vegetables, (2) a hanging wire basket storing cloves of garlic, (3) a pegboard with cooking spoons, forks, and other equipment, and (4) a jar with raisins and other dried fruits for snacking.

Positive adult-child cooking experiences grow out of a cooperative effort. Getting food ready to eat can be done without using a stove or without cooking utensils too difficult to be handled by a young child. Begin by showing the child how to wash fruit or use a spoon for mixing. Then as the child grows and learns, tasks appropriate to his or her age and developmental level can be added. Just as with eating, those cooking experiences that are pleasant will be remembered for a long, long time.

CHILDREN AND NUTRITION:
AN INTRODUCTION TO A BIBLIOGRAPHY

Deborah Lovitky Sheiman and Maureen Slonim

At one time the word "nutrition" conjured images of technical charts about food values and calories. However, in recent years the American public has become increasingly conscious of the food they eat. This new awareness has caused the subject of nutrition to become a growing source of concern to parents. Books discussing childhood nutrition and special diets are being published at an ever-increasing rate. Many of these books are well-documented scientific works. Others promote fad diets or health cure-alls. Any parent or caregiver selecting a book on nutrition for children should be careful to read with a discerning eye.

A parent or caregiver seeking information on infant and childhood nutrition should recognize that food and feeding patterns are intricately entwined in a child's emotional development. Feeding is often the first and most frequent interaction between mother and infant. Therefore, it is not surprising that feeding concerns and problems are the most common categories of questions mothers ask pediatricians and nurses. The child's feeding and nutrition should be considered in a framework of the family's eating habits. Additionally, sociocultural values, such as the family's religious beliefs, can directly affect the food and food habits of the child.

A parent can contribute to the formation of the child's good eating habits by remembering that a child is an individual. A child will eat if hungry. Some children require more food than others. They may be more active or in a growth spurt. Do not urge a child to eat! Let the child eat naturally. Most children like food and will eat enough to maintain health. No child or adult likes every food. However, within the nutritional food groups (cereals and grains, fruits and vegetables, meats, and dairy), there is usually some food in each group that the child will find palatable.

Many parents worry that their child is not eating enough and therefore dispense daily vitamins or megavitamins. Many of the popular books on nutrition endorse this practice. Before handing over a candy-flavored, animal-shaped vitamin to a child, consider the following: All the vitamins required for daily survival are available in our everyday food supply. Many of the food products we eat are enriched with extra vitamins. Feeding a child one vitamin tablet that releases 100 percent of the RDA requirements, plus serving a child three meals a day, can produce a dosage of certain vitamins on the borderline to toxicity.

There are two types of vitamins: water-soluble and fat-soluble. Vitamin B complex and C are water-soluble. Vitamins A, D, E, and K are fat-soluble. Excess of any water-soluble vitamin is released through the body's process of urination. In contrast, fat-soluble vitamins are stored in the body and a potential danger of toxicity through overdosage can evolve. Supplementation of vitamins should only be considered where dietary habits are not adequate for proper nutrition and only if recommended by the child's pediatrician.

The authors of many books on nutrition adhere to the belief that children should eliminate sugar from their diets. The blame for everything from hyperactivity to obesity has been placed on the child's consumption of sugar. From the moment after birth on, a child will prefer a sweet food to any other taste. There is no conclusive evidence that exposure to sweets at an early age increases or decreases this preference.

Obesity can be blamed on sugar consumption to the extent that sugar is high in calories and can be overconsumed. However, overconsumption of calories, no matter what the source, will cause a child to be overweight. The use of honey in excess will cause the same obesity as the use of sugar in excess.

A popular theory on hyperactivity suggests that sugar and food additives can cause learning disabilities and other mental and physical health disturbances in children. Advocates of this theory advise parents to eliminate sugar and food additives from the diets of their children; however, scientific replication studies have not been able to confirm this theory. Additionally, popular diets requiring the elimination of foods have not been tested over the long term. This means that the effect that such a diet may have on your child in future years cannot be predicted. Parents and child caregivers should be aware that, as of the present time, the American Academy of Pediatrics has not endorsed elimination diets. Medical supervision is necessary for any special diet for your child.

Sugar, along with other cariogenic substances, can affect the development of dental caries. Sugar taken in at mealtime is diluted by other food sources. Therefore, sugar ingested with a meal will generally have a less harmful effect on teeth than sugar ingested between meals. Sugar in a sticky form, which is left in the mouth for a long time, is more deleterious than sugar in other forms. Bubble gum is a prime example. Cavity prevention suggests that it is important to consider not only the sugar content, but also the way and the time that the food is consumed.

The following annotated bibliography includes recent books published on childhood and infant nutrition. Always remember that many food fads exist and that many food faddists write books promoting their particular beliefs. Just because a book is about nutrition, or has an introduction written by a physician, does not insure that the content is "nutritionally sound."

There are additional reputable sources of nutrition information. Many are in pamphlet form and free. Refer to the section of this bibliography on *Resources on Nutrition* for a listing. Excellent nutrition information can also be found as a chapter in books about health or about child development.

The following annotated bibliography was developed with one thought in mind—familiarity and knowledge of the science of nutrition can help to develop optimal health for America's children.

BIBLIOGRAPHY

Amary, Issam B. *Effective Meal Planning and Food Preparation for the Mentally Retarded/Developmentally Disabled: Comprehensive and Innovative Teaching Methods.* Springfield, Ill.: Thomas, 1979.

This book is a teaching tool for use with special-needs persons. Basic information on meal planning, kitchen safety, and food preparation provides mentally retarded and developmentally disabled individuals with the skills needed to be self-sufficient or help in the kitchen.

Applegate, Kay. *The Little Book of Baby Foods.* Santa Fe, N.M.: Lightning Tree, 1978.

The author details the preparation of baby foods from formulas to cereals to meat substitutes. This basic paperback is aimed at the inexperienced mother. It is printed in English and Spanish.

Austin, Ethel, and Virginia Beal. *Robert's Nutrition Work with Children,* 4th ed. Chicago: University of Chicago Press, 1978.

This book focuses on the assessment of nutrition in relationship to physical and chronological growth. Guidelines for schools to follow in preparation of nutrition education curricula are specified. Techniques to better children's nutritional status at each developmental level are included. This book is recommended for the general public as well as professionals.

Brody, Jane E. *Jane Brody's Nutrition Book: A Lifetime Guide to Good Eating for Better Health and Weight Control.* New York: Norton, 1981.

This comprehensive guidebook on nutrition information for the entire family includes important guidelines on nutrition in pregnancy and childhood. It provides documented clarification on food myths, misconceptions, and fads (e.g., "Natural" doesn't necessarily mean good). There are hundreds of anecdotes, recipes, and helpful do's and don'ts. It is an outstanding book containing, but not limited to, pediatric nutrition.

Caplan, Frank (ed.). *The Parenting Advisor.* The Princeton Center for Infancy. Garden City, N.Y.: Doubleday, 1978.

This book is included because of its excellent and extensive chapter on infant nutrition by Dr. Myron Winick, director of the Institute for Human Nutrition at Columbia University. He discusses, in a practical way, the relationship of nutrition to infant development. Useful information is given on appetite and diet, including feeding schedules and baby foods. After reading this book, parents will better understand their child's needs and development.

Castle, Sue. *The Complete New Guide to Preparing Baby Foods at Home.* Garden City, N.Y.: Doubleday, 1981.

If one must recommend only one book on home preparation of baby food, this is it! The author describes a clever, inexpensive combination of equipment—blender plus ice cube trays are the only prerequisites. She provides a wealth of nutrition information, recipes, consumer advice, and helpful hints, such as foods for traveling, how to read labels, and how to can and store foods. The appendix lists the nutritive values of various foods.

Collipp, Platon, J. *Childhood Obesity.* Acton, Mass.: Publishing Sciences Group, 1975.

Collipp has written an advanced and well-balanced discussion of the factors involved in childhood obesity. Obesity accompanying special needs (the Klinefelter syndrome) is differentiated from simple obesity. The book is for the health-care and/or nutrition professional interested in theoretical and clinical data.

Ellis, Audrey. *The Kid-Slimming Book.* Chicago: Regnery, 1976.

Written for parents to help their children overcome obesity or tendencies toward being overweight, this book is also of interest to anyone concerned with feeding children, regardless of weight. It is organized into three parts—reasons for overweight, remedies, and recipes. Ellis states that over half of obese adults have a history of childhood obesity.

Endres, Jeanette B. and Robert E. Rockwell. *Food Nutrition, and the Young Child.* St. Louis: Mosby, 1980.

Basic concepts of nutrition are explained along with the food needs of young children from birth to age five. Mental and physical development of the child is discussed. Caregivers and food service personnel will also find food-related activities that can be incorporated into the preschool curriculum.

Energy Through Nutritive Basics (GRUB). Rowland Heights, Ca.: Food Services Department, Rowland Unified School District, n.d.

The preschool/kindergarten guide of this (K–6) sequentialized curriculum is the first of seven. Each of the seven guides are divided into five major areas: food choices, factors influencing food choices, food-related competencies, consumer competencies and food handling. The sample lesson plans within each of the major areas are accompanied by suggested student experiences, student activity sheets for evaluation and/or reinforcement, recipes, and recommended resources.

Feingold, Helene, and Ben Feingold. *The Feingold Cookbook for Hyperactive Children and Others with Problems Associated with Food Additives and Other Salicylates.* New York: Random House, 1979.

Feingold has made popular the controversial theory that hyperactivity and other behavioral and physiological problems in young children are caused by the intake of artificial food additives and salicylates. This book is a response to the many parents who have found it difficult to cook for a child on this highly restricted diet. Sample menus are presented.

Ferreira, Nancy J. *The Mother-Child Cookbook.* Menlo Park, Ca.: Pacific Coast Publishers, 1969.

There are excellent recipes and plans for involving children from two to four years of age. These plans can be broadened for older children to teach basic skills in the preparation and cooking of foods. Recipes for outdoor cooking are included.

Fomon, Samuel J. *Infant Nutrition*, 2nd ed. Philadelphia: Saunders, 1974.

Although entitled *Infant Nutrition*, this book includes information on the nutrition of children from birth through age three. It is a practical resource on nutritional problems and issues. Some of the more interesting chapters cover the topics of milk and formulas, nutritional aspects of dental caries, and food allergies as well as obesity and failure to thrive. It is targeted to the professional in the field of nutrition, but is valuable reading for the lay person as well.

Goldsmith, Robert. *Nutrition and Learning.* Bloomington, Ind.: Phi Delta Kappa, 1980.

The relationship of nutrition to cognitive and motor development is examined in this small volume from the respected Phi Delta Kappa Educational Foundation. Specific nutritionally related learning problems are discussed. Positive preventive nutrition education is considered from the viewpoint of the schools.

Goodwin, Mary T., and Gerry Pollen. *Creative Food Experiences for Children.* Washington, D.C.: Center for Science in the Public Interest, 1980.

This book helps parents, teachers, and nutritionists involve children in the preparation of whole foods and other food-related experiences. Its thoughtful organization enables the user to connect these experiences with other educational goals, such as language skills, mathematical skills, arts and crafts as well as social awareness.

Heslin, Jo-Ann, Annette B. Natow, and Barbara C. Raven. *No-Nonsense Nutrition for Your Baby's First Year.* Boston: CBI, 1978.

The title tells it all—a highly practical book with a "no-nonsense" approach to the topic. It is truly a complete handbook with chapters on breast and formula feeding, introducing new foods, home preparation, the vegetarian baby, vitamin and mineral supplements, allergies, and feeding problems.

Hofmann, Lieselotte. *The Great American Nutrition Hassle.* Palo Alto, Ca.: Mayfield, 1978.

Contemporary attitudes toward nutrition are examined. Attention is given to current issues such as fast-food meals and baby formulas. The uses and abuses of diets and vitamins are investigated. The politics and policy of food are integrated effectively.

Jelliffe, Derrick, and E. F. Jelliffe. *Human Milk in the Modern World: Psychosocial Nutritional and Economic Significance.* New York: Oxford University Press, 1978.

Nutrition, anthropology, and sociology come together in this volume. Trends and influences of breast-feeding are discussed. World consequences of early weaning and maternal nutrition are examined. Names and addresses of groups and publications interested in breast-feeding are included.

Kitzinger, Sheila. *The Experience of Breastfeeding.* New York: Penguin, 1980.

This book is by a childbirth educator and social anthropologist. It is not a how-to book but a fascinating overview of breast-feeding. Kitzinger is an obvious proponent of nursing. Throughout she identifies the importance of the whole family relationship. There is an extensive review of the literature, presented in a scholarly manner and intermingled with child development knowledge. The text distinguishes between "nutritional" and "comfort" suckling.

Krause, Marie, and Kathleen L. Mahan. *Food Nutrition and Diet Therapy,* 6th ed. Philadelphia: Saunders, 1979.

The authors have compiled a current, concise, and complete reference. Nutrition throughout the life cycle is discussed with primary consideration given to pregnancy, infancy, and childhood through adolescence. There is an excellent chapter on the nutritional management of health problems during infancy and childhood. Although the text is geared to the professional, it does contain valuable information for all readers.

La Leche League International. *Womanly Art of Breastfeeding,* 29th ed. Franklin Park, Ill.: The League, 1980.

This book, first published in 1958, is considered a "classic," if not the Bible, of breast-feeding advice and support. It stresses the role of the father and provides guidance for the nursing mother in special circumstances, such as Cesarean birth, premature birth, and illness of the infant. It is well illustrated, and there is an annotated bibliography.

Lanksy, Vicki. *Feed Me! I'm Yours.* New York: Bantam, 1981.

This popular, easy-to-read book is available only in paperback. The author's approach is positive, innovative, and fun. Included are recipes, new ideas on home preparation of baby food, and helpful hints on making mealtime enjoyable for both mother and baby. It is a good alternative to the more commonly found, traditional books on childhood nutrition.

Lansky, Vicki. *The Taming of the C.A.N.D.Y. Monster.* Wayzata, Mn.: Meadowbrook, 1978.

C.A.N.D.Y. stands for Continuously Advertised, Nutritionally Deficient Yummies! Lansky presents kid-tempting, well-balanced recipes in a very readable, humorous format. All recipes are designed to lessen your child's intake of sugar, salt, and additives. This author gives practical nutritional alternatives to "junk food." Good grocery shopping hints are also provided.

Larenzen, Evelyn. *Dietary Guidelines.* Houston: Gulf Publishing, 1978.

A vast resource of technical nutrition data is found in this volume. Normal and therapeutic diet information was compiled for use as nutritional guidelines at Texas Children's Hospital. A noteworthy feature is the chapter on diets for infants. Ingredient and composition analysis of infant formulas are given. Sound scientific information on diet is presented in this excellent book.

Lawrence, Ruth. *Breast-Feeding: A Guide for the Medical Profession.* St. Louis: Mosby, 1980.

The author examines topics such as dietary influence during lactation, the effect of maternal intake of drugs on breast milk, and the pros and cons of breast-feeding. Special consideration is given to the subject of weaning. This book is intended for the medical profession. However, it does furnish useful information for the lay reader.

MacKeith, Ronald, and Christopher Wood. *Infant Feeding and Feeding Difficulties*, 5th ed. New York: Churchill Livingstone, 1977.

This technical book aimed at the health-care professional

provides detailed information on the physiology of infant nutrition. There is a comprehensive discussion on feeding normal infants and those with feeding disorders. The authors treat the topic in a clear, concise, and scientific manner.

Maynard, Leslie-Jane. *When Your Child Is Overweight*. St. Meirnard Ind.: Abbey Press, 1980.

Practical advice is offered to parents of overweight children. Suggestions on overcoming the unescapable obstacles and impasses of children's weight control are discussed. Also included are myths about obesity and grocery shopping tips.

Mayo Clinic Diet Manual: A Handbook of Dietary Practices, 5th ed. Mayo Clinic Dietetic Staff. Philadelphia: Saunders, 1981.

The dietary management information in this manual is for the well-informed parent or clinician who is planning a special diet for the allergic child or child with health and/or metabolic problems. Specific information is given on tailoring diets to the needs of the individual. There is a resource-filled chapter on pregnancy and lactation that includes special considerations of the adolescent and diabetic mother-to-be.

McWilliams, Margaret. *Nutrition for the Growing Years*, 3rd ed. New York: Wiley, 1980.

McWilliams considers nutrition from a theoretical yet practical standpoint. A chapter is devoted to sound scientific discussion of the interrelationship of nutrition to cognitive development. The role of childhood diet in preventative and maintenance health care is examined. Attention is given to the effects of adequate and inadequate nutrition on the developmental stages of infancy and childhood.

Merritt, Doris, (ed.) *Infant Nutrition*. Stroudsburg, Pa.: Halsted Press, 1976.

Merritt has assembled a composite of classic studies in infant nutrition that are mainly concerned with normal infant dietary requirements. Topics covered include modified whole milk, proteins, carbohydrates, fats, minerals, water, vitamins, bases for feeding, hunger, and appetite. The book is a technical text aimed at the nutrition professional.

Mitchell, Helen, Henderika, Rynbergen, Linnea Anderson, and Marjorie Dibble. *Nutrition in Health and Disease*, 16th ed. Philadelphia: Lippincott, 1976.

In this classic on the science of nutrition there are chapters on nutrition counseling, meal management, mental retardation in relationship to nutrition, and foods for the infants with inborn metabolic error. The text is geared to the nutrition professional.

Morris, Linda. *The First Babyfood Cookbook*. New York: Grosset & Dunlap, 1980.

Morris offers advice on preparing a quick baby-food meal as well as adapting table food. Recipes include such "exotic" dishes as spinach souffle and osso buco. The author properly cautions parents, never feed baby a food for the first time without checking with the pediatrician.

National Cancer Institute. *A Resource for Parents of Children with Cancer*. Bethesda, Md.: Office of Cancer Communications, the Institute, 1979.

This outstanding book is available free to the public. Not only does it provide basic nutrition information for cancer patients, practical suggestions for avoiding and handling feeding problems, seven different special diets, but it does so in an extremely well-designed format. The illustrations are beautiful. A large wall chart is included, and many pages incorporate movable attractions for children. This invaluable resource is largely the result of parental contributions and involvement.

Nutrition. N.Y. State College of Agriculture and Life Sciences and U.S. Department of Agriculture. Ithaca, N.Y.: Cornell University, 1978.

This inexpensive series presents basic information for parents on infant nutrition. Sample titles are "Milk: Your Baby's First Food," "Make Your Own Baby Food," and "The What, When and How Much of Baby Food." The language is simple, and the message is depicted visually as well. The series is recommended as a reference source for any library. To receive these materials, write to Media Services, B-10 Martha Van Renseller Hall, N.Y.

State College of Human Ecology, Cornell University, Ithaca, N.Y. 14853.

Palmer, Sushma, and Dhirlye Ekvall. *Pediatric Nutrition in Development Disorders.* Springfield, Ill.: Thomas, 1978.

The reader will find a profusion of clinical and research data on metabolic and nutritional disabilities in children in this book. Attention is given to preventive practices as well as intervention strategies. This book is an excellent resource for parents and professionals working with nutritionally handicapped children.

Payne, Alma. *The Baby Food Book: A Guide for Preparing Fresh Nutritious Foods for the Very Young.* Boston: Little, Brown, 1977.

The author has included a veritable "gold mine" of practical advice on all aspects of home preparation of baby foods. She even suggests which baby foods one should buy, not make, and why (e.g., because of the nitrate controversy). Emphasis is on natural foods and cooking, and there are vegetarian recipes. The book dispels the myth that feeding solids early encourages sleeping through the night. The excellent section on necessary equipment even goes into the appropriate uses of aluminum foil, wax paper, and plastic wrap.

Pearlman, Ruth. *Feeding Your Baby the Safe and Healthy Way.* New York: Random House, 1971.

The author has divided this brief, readable book into two parts—Food and Lore and Cooking for Baby. She stresses ways to avoid preservatives and additives while suggesting appealing and wholesome menus and snacks. Included are sections on breast/bottle feeding, introduction of solid foods, and feeding problems associated with illnesses. Pearlman presents clear, easy-to-follow advice on home preparation of baby food as well as "junior" dinners. She explains what equipment is needed (for home preparation) and why.

Peavy, Linda S., and Andrea L. Paginkopf. *Grow Healthy Kids!: A Parents Guide to Sound Nutrition from Birth through Teens.* New York: Grosset & Dunlap, 1980.

A complete reference guide, this paperback presents useful

ideas for encouraging sound eating habits in children. It deals with common concerns of mothers—breast vs. bottle feeding, effect(s) of diet on hyperactivity and other behavior problems, preventing iron deficiency anemia, obesity, and feeding a child with allergies. Helpful information on nutrition exchanges for specific diets, along with calorie tables, height and weight charts, and bibliography are included.

Pennington, Jean, and Helen Nichols Church. *Bowes and Church's Food Values of Portions Commonly Used*, 13th ed. Philadelphia: Lippincott, 1980.

This is a quick resource for nutrient data. A cross-sampling of foods consumed by the general public is included. Listings describe the nutritive value of items from fast foods to baby formulas. Numerous tables and charts are presented. It is a handy, accurate reference guide.

Pinkwater, Jill. *The Natural Snack Cookbook: 151 Good Things to Eat*. New York: School Book Service, 1975.

The author presents easy-to-make recipes in a simple step-by-step format. All cooking terms are explained, and many are illustrated. The reader will learn of the need for essential vitamins and minerals in one's diet and how they work to nourish the human body.

Pipes, Peggy. *Nutrition in Infancy and Childhood*. St. Louis: Mosby, 1977.

This comprehensive guide to all aspects of child nutrition has language that is somewhat technical yet easy to read. Nutrition is discussed in relation to growth and development, feeding behaviors, and related problems. Information on vegetarian diets is included. Contributing authors provide practical experiences along with nutrition information. Nutritionists frequently recommend the volume as a "best-all-around" source.

Powers, Hugh, and James Presley. *Food Power: Nutrition and Your Child's Behavior*. New York: St. Martin's Press, 1978.

In this self-help guide for parents on improving child health and happiness through nutrition, the author begins with the controversial premise that behavioral and learning problems are the result of improper eating habits. The remedy for these problems is discussed in terms of curative nutrients. There is an excellent table of foods high in essential vitamins and minerals. Sample, wholesome menus are provided.

Richert, Barbara. *Getting Your Kids to Eat Right: A Daily Program for Giving Your Children the Vitamins and Nutrients They Need in the Foods They Love.* New York: Cornerstone Library, 1981.

Dedicated to the development of good, well-balanced eating habits, this book offers advice on curing the junk-food habit, shopping wisely, growing your own food, reading labels, and selecting fast foods with nutrition in mind. Even special-occasion foods can be prepared nutritiously with the innovative suggestions of the author. The bibliography stresses natural foods.

Roth, J. *Cooking for Your Hyperactive Child.* Chicago: Contemporary Books, 1977.

Meal-planning suggestions for additive-free diets are provided. The major premise of this book is that additive-free cooking and diet can lessen or eliminate a child's behavioral difficulties. As with other books of this nature, parents must be cautioned that scientific studies have not supported this theory.

Saville, Florence Rogers. *REAL Food for Your Baby.* New York: Simon & Schuster, 1973.

There are suggestions for easy ways to prepare nutritious infant meals, and to freeze and heat baby foods while cooking meals for the rest of the family. The author offers mothers practical advice on handling the "no-vegetable" stage, snack preparation, shopping hints, menu planning, and economical food planning. Recipes are for single-serving portions and have catchy titles such as "toddler cole slaw" (to combat the no-vegetable stage) and "very special baby sausage." It is a welcome addition to the library of "do it yourselfers."

Scarpa, Joannis, and Helen Keifer. *Sourcebook on Food and Nutrition,* 2nd ed. Chicago: Marquis Academic Media, 1980.

In this excellent resource publication the subjects covered include food fads, special diets, product labeling, vitamin myths, and food additives. A chapter is dedicated to the relationship of nutrition to the life cycle. Discussion of nutrition in fetal development and infancy is incorporated. The critical review of elimination diets should be read by any parent considering such therapy for their child.

Shanklin, Douglas, and Jay Hodin. *Maternal Nutrition and Child Health*. Springfield, Ill.: Thomas, 1979.

This is a technical compilation of nutrition information. Chapters examine prenatal nutrition, birth weight and development, and the nutritional aspects of infancy and early childhood. An important discussion of the effects of food intake on brain function is included. Target audience for this book is the health-care professional.

Slattery, Jill, Gayle Angus Pearson, Carolyn Talley Torre. *Maternal and Child Nutrition*. New York: Appleton-Century-Crofts, 1979.

This excellent reference covers nutrition during pregnancy to nutrition in adolescence and issues such as skim milk versus whole milk for the toddler and formula versus milk during late infancy are discussed. Attention is given to nutritional dysfunction and common food-related problems.

Sloan, Sara. *Children Cook Naturally*. Atlanta: Sara Sloan Nutra Program, 1980.

Through its use of plays, skits, songs, and children's drawings, accompanying the many recipes and background information, this book promotes and encourages children to eat and cook a variety of foods. These food experiences deal with everyday and holiday food encounters as well as with foods popular in other cultures. The final section takes the next and needed step of integrating this food and nutrition information with that of exercise and fitness behavior—behaviors that may, in combination, enhance long-term health.

Spock, Benjamin, and Miriam Lowenberg. *Feeding Your Baby and Child*. Boston: Little, Brown, 1955.

Dr. Spock discusses diet during infancy and childhood. He provides information on the introduction of solid foods, formulas, and vitamin supplements. Dietary aspects of caring for a sick child are considered. The format of this early Spock publication is similar to that in his well-known *Baby and Child Care*.

Stevens, Laura, and Rosemary Stoner. *How to Improve Your Child's Behavior Through Diet*. Garden City, N.Y.: Doubleday, 1979.

The authors look at diet, not from the standpoint of adequate nutrition, but from that of optimal nutrition. They briefly discuss how and what food can affect behavior. A large portion of the book is devoted to interesting and appealing recipes. There is also shopping information about natural foods.

Stommel-Fugeman, Margaret, and Leslie Ellis. *Nutrition Guide to Brand Name Baby Foods*. Jacksonville, Fl.: Heritage House, 1977.

This concise consumer reference guide for commercial baby foods and formulas has nutrition and ingredient charts for strained and junior foods. The material is helpful to parents in sorting out foods with empty calories from those with high nutritious value and thus facilitates baby-food selection.

Smith, Lendon H. *Feed Your Kids Right*. New York: McGraw-Hill, 1980.

Pediatrician Smith is well known to many parents as the Children's Doctor from his frequent appearances on television. He approaches his book with the philosophy that proper nutrition can prevent or forestall illness and help to maintain optimal health. This book contains a complete reference to the vitamins and minerals necessary for child growth and development.

Smith, Lendon, H. *Foods for Healthy Kids*. New York: McGraw-Hill, 1981.

In his own style, Dr. Smith advises parents on the prevention, treatment, and cure of physical and behavioral problems that have relevance to diet—sleep disturbances, allergies, mood swings, and hyperactivity. Each recipe lists the amounts of protein, calcium, vitamins, etc. Resource lists are included for free and inexpensive information and materials. There is a useful bibliography on this subject matter.

Stare, Fredrick J., and Elizabeth M. Whelan. _Eat OK—Feel OK! Food Facts and Your Health_, North Quincy, Mass.: Christopher, 1978.

The authors critically assess what they call the American philosophy of "eat, drink, and supplement." Their focus is on modern food processing, food safety, the relationship of food and disease, weight control, the folly of fads, and life-cycle and life-style nutritional needs. If you concur with the authors that moderation and variety are the keys to sensible eating and that today's fads are obsolete tomorrow, you will enjoy the easy-to-digest scientific facts they offer for improving health and diet.

Stevens, Laura, George Stevens, and Rosemary Stoner. _How to Feed Your Hyperactive Child_. Garden City, N.Y.: Doubleday, 1977.

This is a cookbook dedicated to parents with children on special diets. Over 400 additive and salicylate-free recipes are included. Taste appeal, appearance, nutrition, and economy are considered in each recipe. Suggestions are given on how to explain diet treatment programs to your child. Helpful hints are included on helping the child through the anxiety and frustration of food elimination.

Suitar, Carol, and Merrily Hunter. _Nutrition: Principles and Application in Health Promotion_. Philadelphia: Lippincott, 1980.

The authors have contributed a unique text to the nutrition field in that in their consideration of the development of eating habits they examine such topics as the roles of religion, culture, and behavior. In their discussion of nutrition they note the interrelationship of diet modification and physiological change. This clinical text has useful information for both the nutrition professional and lay individual.

Thomas, Linda. _Caring and Cooking for the Allergic Child_. New York: Sterling, 1980.

In this excellent resource book for the mother of a child with malabsorption syndrome or allergies, Thomas offers advice on which recipes can be used for allergic children and how to adapt recipes for these children. Even baby-food recipes are included. There is a list of brand-name foods compatible with restricted diets. The information on product substitution will assist the meal planner.

U.S. Department of Health and Human Services, Head Start Bureau. *Nutrition Education for Young Children*. Washington, D.C.: U.S. Government Printing Office, 1976.

Developed for the teacher and parent, this booklet focuses on helping children to develop good eating habits. Classroom and/or home activities allow children to be active participants in the learning process. There is an excellent reference section that suggests books, slides, and films on nutrition. The appendix gives additional nutrition-oriented projects for parent or teacher and child to try.

Vonde, Dee, and Jo Beck. *Food Adventures for Children*. Redondo Beach, Ca.: Plycon Press, 1980.

In this cookbook for parents and teachers to use with children two and one-half to five years old the emphasis is on the exploration and interest of nutritious food. Each cooking-related activity helps create a positive successful experience for the child. Guidelines for establishing appropriate expectations are given. A chapter also focuses on the developmental learning skills that can be developed during "cooking activity."

Wanamaker, Nancy. *More than Graham Crackers: Nutrition Education and Food Preparation with Young Children*. Washington, D.C.: National Association for the Education of Young Children, 1979.

The author has written an excellent book for parents and teachers to use in nutrition education. The four food groups (milk, meat, fruits and vegetables, bread and cereal) are taught through active kitchen experience. Additional learning activities, including poems, finger plays, stories, and games, reinforce sound nutritional concepts. There is an excellent chapter on nutrition education resources. This book is highly recommended.

Winick, Myron. *A Parent's Guide to Good Nutrition: Growing Up Healthy*. New York: Morrow, 1982.

The reader will find practical advice on nutrition from conception on in this concise handbook. Among the topics covered are suggestions for the mother's diet during pregnancy, a discussion of breast- and bottle feeding, and when to introduce solid food to the infant. The author stresses the establishment of sound eating patterns from the start. The volume is recommended to all parents.

Winick, Myron. *Society's Child: Nutrition in Children, Diet and Disorders.* Nutley, N.J.: Roche Laboratories, 1980.

Winick views nutrition from a sensible, well-balanced diet approach. In this publication he dispels the many myths of megavitamin therapy and points out the potential dangers. Arguments pertaining to possible hazards of salt, sugar, fat, and food additives are critically examined. This publication is recommended for its scientific treatment of current issues.

Wolff, Jurgen and Dewey Lipe. *Help for the Overweight Child.* New York: Stein and Day, 1978.

This is a handy book to help parents change the improper eating habits of their overweight children. The authors stress the role of proper nutrition. Important chapters examine the causes and penalties of being overweight and the psychology of weight loss. Techniques are suggested to motivate both parent and child.

Yntema, Sharon. *The Vegetarian Baby: A Sensible Guide for Parents.* Ithaca, N.Y.: McBooks Press, 1980.

In her guide the author includes a cross-cultural review of babies on vegetarian diets. Advice to other interested parents is based on her personal experiences as well as interviews with parents of similar interests. Emphasis is on the first two years of life, and the text is well-grounded in sound developmental principles. Included is a question-and-answer section and annotated reviews of cookbooks for babies.

7
Children's Play

THE NATURE AND FUNCTION OF PLAY

David Elkind

The importance of play in early childhood education can, perhaps, best be approached from a historical perspective. With the writings of philosophers such as Rousseau and educators such as Pestalozzi and Froebel, the uniqueness of childhood as a distinct stage of life gradually came to be recognized. In the Puritan period the task of parenting and of education was to bring children to righteousness. In this context, children's play, was regarded as evidence of original sin and of the devil's work.

The work of Charles Darwin, brought a new image of the way in which childhood was unique. From a Darwinian point of view, childhood is a stage of life from which adult life evolves. Looked at in this way, then, play was the characteristic activity of young children. Children played in order to prepare themselves for adult life. Children play at war and at keeping house for the same reason kittens pounce upon a ball; they are rehearsing in play that which they will once have to engage in earnest.

These two conceptions of play have both played a part in educational theory and practice. For example, when "progressive" education was a major theme in our schools, play was regarded as a healthy avenue of personal expression. In the current "back-to-basics" movement play, including the arts, is looked upon as trivial and at variance with the basic aims of schooling.

Clearly, then, in the educational arena, play has become a symbol of opposing educational philosophies. Those who advocate a child-centered orientation, what Dewey called "unfolding from within," consider play essential to healthy development.

On the other hand, those who advocate an adult-centered approach, what Dewey called "enforcement from without," argue that play has little useful function and takes away from the time and energy children need to devote to their studies.

As long as we look at play in these symbolic terms, heavily freighted with value and ideological baggage, it is hard to see play as a form of human behavior that has to be evaluated on its own terms. But it is just this perspective that must be taken if we wish to have an unbiased assessment of the role of play in human development. Such a perspective is provided by the writings of Jean Piaget.

From a Piagetian point of view, play always involves a transformation of reality such as to satisfy some personal need or motive. This view differs from the evolutionary perspective in that it sees play as essential to the development of the individual rather than to the evolution of the species. Likewise, this view differs from the religious perspective in the sense that the motives generating play are looked at as individual and adaptive rather than as symbolic.

Accordingly for Piaget, play does not represent either the evolutionary process or the religious point of view; it represents one facet of individual growth and development. In addition, Piaget argues not only that play is a transformation of reality, but also the nature of the transformations will change as the child matures and his or her intellectual abilities change. Infants, for example, engage in sensorimotor play, young children in symbolic play, and older children, adolescents, and adults in games with rules.

Play, then, has to be seen from an individual developmental perspective. What role, one might ask, does play have in individual development, what function does it serve? The answer, or so it seems to me, is that play is first and foremost a stress release valve. Stress is the reaction of the individual to extraordinary demands for adaptation. Our built-in systems for reacting with "fight or flight" are often not appropriate in today's society. Hence, we are often tense but without a socially acceptable outlet for response. Play, by allowing us to transform reality, allows us to discharge stress responses in the socially approved avenues of play.

The important point about play in childhood is that play serves the same function for children as it does for adults. Children, particularly today, are under a great deal of stress. Many have been witness to the separation and divorce of their parents and have been exposed to the irrational violence, to the untender, unloving sexuality, and to the almost incomprehensible horrors of war presented on television. All of this together with the usual experiences of early childhood, the demands for self-care, for politeness, and, increasingly at ever-younger ages, for academic achievement are all stressors for children.

Play—whether sensorimotor, symbolic, or games with rules —is a way children have for coping with stress. When children are running, riding their bikes, teetering on a teeter totter, swinging on a swing, they are, in part, discharging stress-related tensions. Similarly, when children are playing "house," or "store," or "superheroes," they are dealing in symbolic ways with stressful issues of power and control. Thus, when they begin to play games with rules, children can deal indirectly with the competitive pressures endemic to growing up in America.

In justifying children's play, therefore, we do not have to argue that it is the way in which children learn (play is the child's work). Play is not work, and it is not learning. It does permit learning and work to go on. Children need to play for the same reason adults do—to deal with the stress and tensions of life. If we acknowledge that the executive, or the administrator, or the workman performs better if work is balanced by recreation, why should we not acknowledge that the same holds true for children.

Play helps to distract adults from their personal concerns and to view the world of others in more objective terms. Stress always turns us inward because it is, by definition, a response to a threat to the self. Anything that helps to reduce stress also helps to free us from preoccupations with the self and to get on with what has to be done. The same is true for children. Play helps children to pay less attention to personal concerns and to proceed with the enormous task of learning to be social.

A danger should be noted. Play can be transformed into work. When winning or losing at a game, for example, is regarded as life or self-threatening, then play is no longer a transformation of reality; it is reality. When a player is so invested in a game that losing makes him or her depressed, then it is no longer a game—it is a stressful situation. The real danger of competitive sports for children is that it can change a healthy domain of play into another domain of work.

To conclude, in this essay I have argued that play is neither an evolutionary remnant nor a religious symbol. Rather play is, first and foremost, an individual's way of dealing with the stress of life. By transforming reality play makes unmanageable situations manageable at the same time that it provides socially acceptable outlets for stress. Children, no less than adults, are under stress, particularly today. Accordingly, children need to play for the same reason adults do—to enable them to go on with the difficult task of adapting to an ever more complex and bewildering society.

PLAY: A TIMELY IMPERATIVE

Claudette B. Lefebvre

Play is a universal imperative. Play phenomena cut across all cultural milieus and throughout the ages has occupied individual and disciplinary thought, inquiry, and commentary. In recent eras there has been a resurgence of interest in the study and conceptualization of play. The perceived value of play is readily attested to by its proclamation as a universal and inalienable right of childhood by the United Nations and by the issuance of numerous national mandates to provide and enhance play opportunities for society's members. General recognition of play as a significant element in individual growth and development and a potent force for socialization and enculturation has stimulated interest in the role of play in human development.

Play is seen as a predominant activity of biological maturity and as a prime modality for learning about the self and the environment. Play provides an inexhaustible source of opportunities for self-directed exploration, manipulation, and achievement of competence and mastery of skills across the sensory, motor, communicative, cognitive, and social domains. It becomes increasingly apparent, however, that play is phenomena uniquely relevant to the entire life span.

While play is a uniquely individual experience, it is simultaneously expressive and reflective of collective behaviors within a given culture at any specific point in time. Play is a vehicle for socialization, enhancement of interpersonal communication, and enculturation of the individual into the mainstream of society. Study of play across diverse cultures suggest that play is generally intimately enmeshed in the nature of the family and community, folklore and religion. As societies move toward a technological orientation, however, the experiencing of play may become increasingly segregated with regard to time, developmental stage, and even locale.

These are but a few of the numerous factors that must be considered as work progresses toward development of a comprehensive, synthesized, generally acceptable theoretical schema for understanding the play experience.

BIBLIOGRAPHY

Anderson, Valerie, and Carl Bereiter. *Thinking Games 1.* Belmont, Ca.: Pitman Learning, 1980.

The authors designed their book to illustrate how children may experience enjoyment while exercising thinking abilities. It differs from many other game books in that selections are inexpensive. No special materials are required; those usually readily available can be used. The games emphasize competition between teams rather than individuals. While planned primarily for teachers, the book could be equally as useful with play groups, siblings, and friends in the five-to-nine age range. Inobtrusively the activities aid in development of language, math, strategy, nonverbal communication, perceptual organization, and rhythmic skills.

Axline, Virginia M. *Play Therapy*, rev. ed. New York: Ballantine, 1976.

Axline presents eight different principles of the concept of nondirective, client-centered play therapy. She describes the playroom and suggests materials to be used. She stresses use of the therapist as an indirect participant providing a way for the child to learn about himself and his relationship with others. She discusses establishing rapport and the need for unconditional positive acceptance of the child. Other chapters consider implications for education. Annotated therapy records from individual and group interactions provide clear illustrations of dialogue, demonstrating how this nonthreatening atmosphere can contribute to healthy inner reorganization and well-adjusted forward movement.

Badger, Earladeen. *Infant/Toddler: Introducing Your Child to the Joy of Learning.* New York: McGraw-Hill, 1981.

Badger matches appropriate learning activities, toys, and educational materials bought, improvised, or found around the house to the young child's developmental interests and abilities. A step-by-step teaching model shows the adult how to proceed. Beginning with mouthing, the infant moves through twenty developmental levels, which include such landmarks as visual following, releasing, or letting go, fitting parts to form a whole, and matching. Each activity begins with the learning operation, and the author discusses the role of repetition, incidental learning, and discovery learning. Appropriate materials are listed, followed by a carefully outlined presentation. Ways and methods of observing progress are presented, with space devoted to recording the observations. This is "a-parent-as-teacher" book.

Barnes, Joan, Susan D. Astor, and Umberto Tosi. *Gymboree: Giving Your Child Physical, Mental and Social Confidence Through Play.* New York: Dolphin Books, 1981.

This delightful book extolls the "gymboree" concept as a healthful way for parents and their preschoolers to spend quality time together. A "gymboree" program is a way of understanding children's play, of directing physical coordination and organizing experiences into concepts that set the stage for later mental development, thus leading to optimal learning opportunities.

Bronfenbrenner, Urie. *Two Worlds of Childhood: U.S. and U.S.S.R.* New York: Russell Sage Foundation, 1970.

This study compares child-rearing practices of the world's two largest powers. There are descriptions of children's play in each society and how the play activity is used by the society in terms of their effects on the moral, ethical, and social development of the child. Play is not a specific focus of the study. It is considered one of the many childhood activities that contribute to the development of personality and character. The significance of these activities, including television viewing, is examined in terms of the kind of adult and citizen these activities would tend to foster.

Burtt, Kent Garland. *Smart Toys: For Babies from Birth to Two.* New York: Harper Colophon Books, 1981.

Burtt provides patterns for easy-to-make toys that stimulate a baby's mind and foster skills such as batting, grasping, and manipulating objects. She demonstrates the relationship between an enriched sensory environment and the development of intelligence. Designs are based on educational research. The many drawings enhance a lively text.

Butler, Anne L., et al. *Play as Development.* Columbus, Oh.: Merrill, 1978.

The authors define play as "what children typically and spontaneously do," and they equate it with development by showing how different play activities help a child develop cognitively, physically, and socially. The authors warn against over-structured activities. They include suggestions for using play to help children with special needs. This book is useful for teachers of preschool and elementary school children.

Butterworth, Nancy Towner, and Laura Peabody Broad. *Kits for Kids.* New York: St. Martin's Press, 1980.

This handbook on projects to do, gifts to give, and experiences to share is for children over age three. The first section emphasizes new ways to plan, present, and utilize activities creatively. The second half "spells out" the activity kits. Headings include use at home, in a group, for special occasions, in confined situations, and for going places. There are specific instructions and illustrations of materials. Careful directions facilitate speed and simplicity in gathering and packaging of materials. The kits are a boon for busy adults concerned with children and may be used to occupy a child by himself or with others (peers or adults).

Caney, Steven. *Steven Caney's Play Book.* New York: Workman Publishing, 1975.

This book offers many good projects for children, ages two to ten. Two examples are the making of blocks by stuffing old

newspapers into large grocery bags and the reprinting of newspaper photographs, using a wax candle and white paper. All
materials can be found around the house. It is an excellent
activity source book for both parents and teachers.

Caplan, Frank, and Theresa Caplan. *The Power of Play*. Garden
City, N.Y.: Doubleday, 1973.

The Caplans describe the importance of play as a learning
tool in the lives of children. They discuss how play helps build
and strengthen personality and assists in body building, interpersonal relations, language learning, and creativity. A helpful
list of age-appropriate toys is provided. The volume has been
researched well.

Cass, Joan E. *Helping Children Grow Through Play*. New York:
Schocken, 1973.

Play is stressed as an integral part of the learning process.
There are chapters on social relationships in play, dramatic play,
play at home and school, as well as toy safety and play for the
sick child. The author includes aids to selecting children's books
and a listing of annotated films on play.

Cherry, Clare. *Creative Play for the Developing Child: Early Lifehood
Education Through Play*. Belmont, Ca.: Pitman Learning, 1976.

The author views play as early childhood education at its
best. Her focus is on the value of play in relation to child
development during the first years of life, stressing its importance in developing learning attitudes as opposed to the more
formalized, traditional work-teaching concepts. On the basis of
her research and experience, the author has developed a creative
play program for the early childhood classroom with step-by-
step guide for replication.

Cole, Ann, et al. *I Saw a Purple Cow and 100 Other Recipes for Learning*.
Boston: Little, Brown, 1972.

A "recipe" format makes this guide to preschool activities
easy to use for parents, teachers, and librarians. The varied
activities include stories, music, games, toy making, arts and
crafts, gardening, parties, word games, simple experiments, and
much more. The author offers a practical pot pourri of imagina-

tive ideas for the mutual enjoyment of preschool children and their adult friends.

Frost, Joe L., and Barry L. Klein. *Children's Play and Playgrounds.* Boston: Allyn & Bacon, 1979.

The authors furnish evidence that most American playgrounds are inadequately equipped for young children; in fact, many are inappropriate for the play needs of children. Included is a chapter on play and playgrounds for handicapped children. Stress is placed on the importance of a sensitive and informed play leader as the key to an educationally sound playground environment. This is a book for parents, teachers, and community planners who want to learn how to provide better playgrounds for children.

Garvey, Catherine. *Play.* Cambridge: Harvard University Press, 1977.

Using material from anecdotes, videotaped sessions, and detailed linguistic analyses, the author examines children's play, beginning with such early games as peek-a-boo. Through play, the author contends, the child can experiment with all kinds of actions, roles, and language that have not yet been mastered. Thus play can simulate reality without being bound by it. Many examples are provided.

Grasselli, Rose N., and Priscilla A. Hegner. *Playful Parenting. Games to Help Your Infants and Toddlers Grow Physically, Mentally and Emotionally.* New York: Marek Publishers, 1981.

The authors introduce a program designed to foster the child's development through play. The program is divided into three play groups—diaper play, toddler play, mini play. There are suggestions for warm-up games, finger plays, behavioral guidelines, exploring activities and other sensorimotor experiences.

Hagstrom, Julie. *Traveling Games for Babies: A Handbook of Games for Infants to Five Years Old.* New York: A & W Visual Library, 1981.

Traveling with young children should be fun. This book, the third of a series, offers a number of ways to make it so—be it play with a magnetic board, building blocks, mitten puppets, or an old department store catalogue. There are also suggestions for quiet games to calm an active toddler or games of observation for the older child and games in which an infant can participate. There are step-by-step instructions with each game.

Hartley, Ruth E., and Robert M. Goldenson. *The Complete Book of Children's Play*. New York: Crowell, 1963.

The child who plays is engaged in what is most important to his or her development. This concept is the book's main theme. Play is the way the child learns what no one can teach. It is the way the child explores and orients himself to the actual world of space and time, of things, structures, and people. A detailed appendix is designed to aid parents in selecting the right toy for the right time in the child's development.

Hartley, Ruth E., Lawrence K. Frank, and Robert M. Goldenson. *Understanding Children's Play*. New York: Columbia University Press, 1952.

A classic in the psychological and educational literature dealing with children's play, this volume describes and analyzes the nature of play in nursery schools and kindergartens. The authors show how play with particular materials is an integral part of learning and contributes to the emotional health and general well-being of the child. The authors give diverse anecdotal material to illustrate their points and include an appendix on ways of observing children and recording activities.

Headley, Neith E., et al. *Play: Children's Business*. Washington, D.C.: Association for Childhood Education, 1979.

Ten short essays deal with the relationships between play and cognition, play and development, the dynamics of play, and the acquisition of social values through play. Each essay presents a viewpoint that expands one's awareness of the work of play. Parents will find this volume interesting.

Hendrick, Joanne. *The Whole Child*. St. Louis: Mosby, 1975.

Play serves many valuable purposes in the life of the child. It provides occasions for intense practice of sensorimotor skills. Play facilitates role playing and develops social skills. Play furnishes opportunities to work through emotional problems and to experience the relief of acting like a child instead of an adult. Play serves as an avenue for the child to be creative by using his or her imagination and his or her ability to think in divergent ways. The author ably sets forth these principles.

Hirsch, Eizabeth (ed.). *The Block Book.* Washington, D.C.: National Association for the Education of Young Children, 1974.

An outstanding collection of articles by experts examines the important role of blocks in children's learning and development. Block play helps the child explore the fundamental concepts that foster cognitive growth and esthetic experiences. This volume gives numerous examples of imaginative use of blocks in the early childhood curriculum with pragmatic approaches for teachers and parents.

Kaban, Barbara. *Choosing Toys for Children from Birth to Five.* New York: Schocken, 1979.

This helpful guide, directed to parents and child-care workers, deals not only with developmentally appropriate toys for children at different stages, but also with safety, durability, and care of materials. Six chapters are devoted to toys for children at different age levels. One chapter describes homemade toys and household objects that can function as toys. The pros and cons of TV are discussed as are books and records for young children.

Klein, Melanie. *The Psychoanalysis of Children,* rev. ed. New York: Delacorte/Seymour Lawrence, 1975.

Klein in her classic work presents the play-therapy techniques that she used in child analysis. She writes on early anxiety situations and their effect on the development of the child. She demonstrates that in play the child acts instead of speaks and thereby reveals anxieties to the therapist, who then uses interpretation to alleviate them. She discusses the use of toys and choice of materials in a play-therapy room that aid in play analysis. Case studies illustrate the creative use of make-believe and drama in the therapy.

Koste, Virginia Glasgow. *Dramatic Play in Childhood: Rehearsal for Life.* New Orleans: Anchorage Press, 1978.

The author, an educator as well as theater artist, helps teachers and parents recognize the meaning and form of dramatic play. Her focus is on the importance of dramatic play as practice for real life. Children use play to cope with the concepts, stresses and pleasures in their lives and as practice for dealing with the larger, real world.

Lancy, David F., and B. Allan Tindall (eds.). *Study of Play: Problems and Prospects.* West Point, N.Y.: Leisure Press, 1977.

This book evolved from the First Annual Meeting of the Association for the Anthropological Study of Play. It brings together the thinking of individuals from different disciplines, all fostering the type of research and interaction that would add to the understanding of the nature of play on a global scope. Chapters include such topics as theoretical approaches in the study of play, analysis of play forms, and sociopsychological aspects of play and humor. It is an important book for the serious student.

Lowenfeld, Margaret. *Play in Childhood.* New York: Wiley, 1967.

In this classic, the author points out that too little serious attention has been given to children's play. Play, in fact, is an essential function of childhood basically concerned with the adaptive process that continues throughout life and profoundly affects the ability to survive in the physical and social environments. This book records an experiment in categorization and classification of play as it has been observed by the writer in a clinical situation.

McCoy, Elin. *The Incredible Year-Round Playbook.* New York: Random House, 1979.

There are over 100 excellent and imaginative child-tested activities involving sun, sand, wind, water, and snow. They include ingenious games, unusual recipes, day-long projects, crafts, and science experiments. The directions are clear and workable. It is a great sourcebook for parents and teachers, and it can be used independently by children over seven years of age.

Malehorn, Hal. *K-3 Teacher's Classroom Almanac: A Treasury of Learning Activities and Games.* West Nyack, N.Y.: Parker, 1981.

There are more than 1,000 learning activities and games to spark children's interests. Every day of each month from

September through May has activities. The step-by-step instructions are adaptable to any age or ability level.

Malloy, Terry. *Montessori and Your Child: A Primer for Parents.* New York: Schocken, 1976.

What is your child really like?; What does your child need? How can you help your child? and, What is the Montessori way? are just a sample of some of the questions answered in the well-illustrated Montessori primer for parents. The text is charmingly written in dialogue form, with each page introducing a new question and explanation. There is a personal and comfortable handling of parental feelings while maintaining a "spirit of respect for each individual child."

Marzollo, Jean. *Superkids: Creative Learning Activities for Children 5-15.* New York: Harper & Row, 1981.

Marzollo has written a sparkling book for children who like to do things as well as a guide for parents and teachers looking for activity and play ideas for children. She includes suggestions for dancing games, making musical instruments, putting on a circus show or puppet play, learning how to weave, and many others. Instructions are given for cooking as well as for making films and tapes. A special section is devoted to literature, with booklists arranged according to ages, to rules for essay and letter writing, and to ways for starting a home library.

Marzollo, Jean. *Supertot: Creative Learning Activities for Children One to Three and Sympathetic Advice for Their Parents.* New York: Harper & Row, 1977.

This is a comprehensive activity and idea handbook for parents and teachers of toddlers. It includes lists of age-appropriate toys, discusses developmental stages, and offers supportive advice. It is well organized and nicely illustrated.

Marzollo, Jean, and Janice Lloyd. *Learning Through Play.* New York: Harper & Row, 1974.

The authors have written a common-sense, clearly written, beautifully illustrated catalogue of activities and games. They identify goals and describe activities (complete with materials and instructions) designed to make accomplishing the goals fun for adult and child. For example, they draw from everyday objects and sensations to explain the prenumber concepts of sorting, classifying, counting, and measuring.

Mather, June. *Learning Can Be Child's Play: How Parents Can Help Slower-Than-Average Preschool Children Learn and Develop Through Play Experiences.* Nashville: Abingdon Press, 1976.

Play as a child's work is stressed as are the pleasures and problems encountered in bringing up children who are slower than average. A how-to book, it attempts to show the value of play experiences and to see toys as essential ingredients for physical and intellectual development in childhood. It is a book for parents whose preschool child shows signs of lagging behind.

Millar, Susanne. *The Psychology of Play.* New York: Aronson, 1974.

In an engaging, readable style this comprehensive treatise moves from philosophical, psychological theories of play to pragmatic illustrations of play in the lives of children and adults. Millar defines play as an attitude and offers illustrative material for varied developmental stages. The book will make adults cognizant of the need for play and the types that are beneficial to children as they work through ideas, imitate adults, and use surplus energy.

Millman, Joan, and Polly Behrmann. *Parents as Playmates.* New York: Human Sciences Press, 1979.

The authors provide a variety of activities that parents can enjoy with preschool children. Representing situations that occur in the lives of all children, these activities can serve to stimulate children's imagination and curiosity. Parents can choose those that are applicable to rainy days, traveling, or other times when children tend to become bored. While the author has written this book for parents, it can be used by anyone who interacts with children in the primary grades.

Moustakas, Clark E. *Psychotherapy with Children: The Living Relationship.* New York: Harper & Row, 1979.

Moustakas presents his philosophy of "relationship therapy" using the vehicle of the play session. Well-adjusted, disturbed, and handicapped children demonstrate the value of play in child development. The author's format of an introductory essay followed by verbatim dialogues between patient and therapist and a concluding analysis of the session is very instructive. Particularly good is the chapter guiding parents on the use of play therapy in the home. This book will be helpful to parents, teachers, and all professionals who work with children.

Neser, Gwen, and Janna Gaughan. *Infanttoddler Parenting: Activities for Adult with Child.* Elberoni N.J.: Uni-Ed Associates, 1980.

The authors develop a unique process for infants and toddlers learning together with adults in a group setting or home. This process is adaptable to nursery school, day care, and adult education. The photographs, illustrations, and instructions help the reader to learn and do with their child. Evaluation check sheets and parent discussion topics are included. The appendix suggests ways to start the program.

Newson, John, and Elizabeth Newson. *Toys and Playthings in Development and Remediation.* New York: Pantheon, 1979.

With a focus on the developing child, this book is about the role of toys and play in enhancing development rather than a book about "teaching skills." A considerable portion of the discussion is devoted to the child who has problems in making progress because he or she is in some way handicapped. The authors' refreshing approach emphasizes the normal developmental needs of the child who is also handicapped. Parents and teachers of all young children will find this a delightful and practical book.

Piaget, Jean. *Play, Dreams, and Imitation in Childhood.* C. Gattegno and F. M. Hodgson, trans. New York: Norton, 1962.

This volume is part of the series of studies by Piaget of the mental life of the child. He focuses on cognitive and intellectual development as opposed to psychological development. This volume examines play as a vehicle for the expression of the concerns and interests of the young child. Piaget demonstrates that there is a close similarity between play and dreams in terms of their contents and the way these are assimilated by the child. He thus integrates cognitive development with the "symbolic function." Piaget's theses of the structure of mental life are compared with the theories of other major psychologists: Koehler, Groos, Buhler, Hall, Freud, Jung.

Piers, Maria W. (ed.). *Play and Development: A Symposium.* New York: Norton, 1972.

The papers in this book, presented at a symposium on Knowledge in the Service of Man, were written by Piaget, Spitz, Erikson, and Lorenz. Each writer provides a philosophical framework for play. For example, Erikson traces play from childhood to adulthood. Piers integrates the theories in the epilogue.

Piers, Maria W., and Geneviere Millet Landau. *The Gift of Play.* New York: Walker, 1980.

What is play? What is a child really doing during play? Some educators like to call it child's work. Actually, this definition often leads the adult to use play with the child in adult-directed situations. Play includes a wide range of activities beginning at birth and lasting a lifetime. The authors show that free and imaginative play is much more valuable to the child's development than any structured, goal-oriented program. This book is designed to give educators and parents a fresh appreciation for this vital, complex activity.

Salter, Michael (ed.). *Play: Anthropological Perspectives.* West Point, N.Y.: Leisure Press, 1978.

In recent years the study of play has come into focus, and concentration has been on finding a definition of the term so that it might be operationally employed in a cross-cultural context. Questions are raised by leaders in the field relative to the study of play, and the ideas offered are designed to provide direction to the student in the field.

Schwartzman, Helen B. (ed.). *Play and Culture*. West Point, N.Y.: Leisure Press, 1980.

The papers that make up this book were originally prepared for the Fourth Annual Meeting of the Association for the Anthropological Study of Play, held in 1978. All papers provide ethnographic contributions to the study of play in both traditional and modern cultural contexts and also represent theoretical contributions to the developing research in the field of play. Chapters deal with descriptions of play in a variety of contexts, including analysis of linguistic play, and recent studies of the impact of culture on children's play. The collection works well as a text for the student.

Shapiro, Lawrence E. *Games to Grow On: Activities to Help Children Learn Self-Control*. Englewood Cliffs, N.J.: Prentice Hall, 1981.

Play is the tool that helps children cope with the hurdles that growing up presents. Parents and teachers can help by understanding the value of play in the child's life and the role of play at different developmental stages. Practical ideas with step-by-step directions are given for application at home and in school.

Sharp, Evelyn. *Thinking Is Child's Play*. New York: Dutton, 1969.

The author points out that learning to count is far less important than developing a child's thinking. This book reveals to parents how children learn games through concrete methods of play. Illustrated by forty-two diagrams. This approach shows how children's minds develop and how parents can know when they are ready to grasp prenumber ideas. The book is recommended for teachers, parents, educators, and administrators.

Singer, Dorothy, and Jerome Singer. *Partners in Play: A Step-by-Step Guide to Imaginative Play in Children*. New York: Harper & Row, 1977.

The Singers present a guide to assist adults as they work with young children in stimulating and enriching the children's play. These distinguished educators establish the theoretical basis of imaginative play (its relation to dreams and wish fulfillment) and provide specific activities designed to enhance children's imaginative play experiences. Especially helpful are the chapters on play materials, indoor/outdoor play environments, and activities for children on trips including to the doctor's office. The authors prefer making toys from materials at hand and give instructions for simple toy construction.

Sparling, Joseph and Isabelle Lewis. *Learning Games for the First Three Years: A Guide to Parent-Child Play.* New York: Walker, 1979.

This is a collection of 100 developmentally appropriate activities that adults can engage in with young children. The descriptions, photographs, materials, expected outcomes, and appropriate developmental levels are stated clearly. The book is for parents or early childhood teachers.

Sponseller, Doris (ed.). *Play as a Learning Medium.* Washington, D.C.: National Association for the Education of Young Children, 1974.

The articles in this important compilation focus on the importance of play in relation to learning. They range from the explication of play as a medium for expressing thoughts and feelings, developing problem solving, and social skills to a schema for categorizing play and learning in the child's environment. Sponseller provides the philosophic support for play as learning.

Sternlicht, Manny, and Abraham Hurwitz. *Games Children Play: Instructive and Creative Play Activities for the Mentally Retarded and Developmentally Disabled Child.* New York: Van Nostrand Reinhold, 1981.

Intended for parents and teachers, this book provides play activities designed to stimulate the psychological growth of learning-disabled children. In order to help the parent or professional place the various games in proper perspective, the psychological principles underlying play behavior are given as well as the chronological stages of play development. Included is a helpful section of suggested readings.

Tudor-Hart, Beatrix. *Toys, Play and Discipline in Childhood*. London: Routledge & Kegan Paul, 1972.

The author delineates the interaction between play and discipline in the development of children between the years of two and twelve. She explains the necessity of understanding the impact of play as it relates to daily social and practical experiences. Toys are a means of advancing physical, mental, and emotional progress. The author introduces concepts of "good" and "bad" play materials and explicates the how and why of selection in terms of age appropriateness. This personal and realistic approach is illustrated with vignettes and photographs culled from twenty-five years of teaching. Both parents and teachers will find this book an effective resource.

U.S. Department of Health and Human Services, Public Health Service. *Caring About Kids: The Importance of Play*. Publication No. 81–969. Rockville, Md.: National Institute of Mental Health, 1981.

Children's play is a developmental imperative. But just as crucial is how teachers and parents understand and react to children and their play. Play is a child's rehearsal for life; indeed, play is life to children providing opportunity to try and test all kinds of roles and situations. This short but important publication is available free of charge and makes valuable reading for parents and teachers.

Westland, Cor, and Jane Knight. *Playing, Living, Learning: A World-Wide Perspective on Children's Opportunities to Play*. State College, Pa.: Ventura, 1982.

This detailed and comprehensive study on the various forms and patterns of children's play around the world is designed to motivate and inspire all who are interested in children. It serves as a valuable resource in the worldwide struggle for the recognition of the value of play. Included is a guide to international and national organizations relevant to the subject of play. A Spanish and French edition of the book is in preparation.

Winn, Marie, and Mary Ann Porcher. *The Playgroup Book*. New York: Penguin, 1969.

Using a cookbook approach, the authors offer ideas on how

to plan, organize, and run a playgroup for preschool children. Presented are the fundamentals of playgroups. The authors describe the characteristics of three- and four-year-olds and how they typically behave in groups. Based on preschoolers needs, interests, and potential for learning, detailed activities with suggestions on how to present them to children are included. This book is particularly valuable to parents who seek to help children achieve the advantages to be gained from playgroup membership.

Winnicott, Donald W. *The Piggle: An Account of the Psychoanalytic Treatment of a Little Girl.* New York: International Universities Press, 1977.

This is a verbatim account of the treatment of a little girl who started psychoanalysis at age two. It follows two and one-half years of treatment on demand. Parental letters and therapist's marginal notes provide a complete picture of the child dramatizing her inner world as she gradually invites therapeutic participation. The author's viewpoint points up parental importance in treatment of children.

Winnicott, Donald W. *Playing and Reality.* New York: Basic Books, 1971.

Winnicott views play as a healthy, natural activity within a psychoanalytic framework and links it with creativity and developmental levels. This is an esoteric approach, valuable to researchers and to practitioners who are eager for greater insight into play as it impinges on the lives of children.

Wolfgang, Charles H. *Helping Aggressive and Passive Preschoolers Through Play.* Columbus, Oh: Merrill, 1977.

The author's research leads him to suggest that children in the preschool age who miss out on essential normative play phases are some of the same children who, at a later date, cannot "play the game" of formal schooling during the elementary years. Chapters deal with play and productive behavior, playroom arrangement, introduction to social dramatic play, and play as a vehicle for emotional growth. Included are a behavioral assessment checklist, a list of books for preschool children that touch on family relationships, and descriptions of imitative body games to play in school and at home.

Wolfgang, Charles H., Bea Mackender, and Mary Wolfgang. *Growing and Learning Through Play: Activities for Pre-School and Kindergarten Children: A Parent/Caregiver Book.* New York: Instructo/McGraw-Hill, 1981.

Filled with creative ideas for both home and classroom applications, this book employs an attractive and well-organized format to demonstrate the important and varied role of play in child development. From the definition of play to an explanation of how materials can be fluid or structured, the book moves on to explain how caregivers can interact with their children to enhance constructive, sensorimotor, symbolic, and sociodramatic play experiences. Approximately 100 activities are described in the traditional lesson-plan format: goals; objectives, materials, procedures, observing progress, and follow-up. The materials employed are all inexpensive and readily available, and the activities are structured to encourage creativity and freedom of expression. The volume is a good addition to the collections of professionals in caregiving positions and a must for parents on rainy days!

8
Choices in Child Care and Management of Child-Care Settings

CHILD CARE IN CONTEXT

Vicki Breitbart

Caring for children is supposed to be one of the family's primary functions. Yet, decisions about how to raise children are not made in isolation; they are not merely the result of parents' desires or visions. They are affected by the adults' socialization when they were children, the family's present economic and social conditions, and the values and the state of the society as a whole. Many parents are aware of the contradictions between the way things are supposed to be and the way they really are; they constantly experience the gaps between what they would like to see and the choices they have.

Most of us grew up with a picture of the ideal family where the mother stays at home to raise the children (especially when they are young) and the father goes out to work and earns enough to support them all. But this is far from today's reality. The traditional nuclear family is now in the minority. Families are smaller, and the life span is longer. With labor-saving devices, cooking and cleaning can be completed in less time. But family size and household technology can only account for a partial response to the job market. Family economics is a key factor; financial concerns are perhaps the greatest impetus for mothers of dependent children to enter the labor force.

The movement of married women into the labor force has been one of the most important changes in the American family in the last few decades, and it has had its effect on child-rearing practices. While the sharpest increase in the number of women with dependent children of school age working away from home came during the 1940s and 1950s, in the 1960s it was the mothers of preschool children who were the fastest growing group of women entering the labor market. The trend is for more women to work outside the home, for more of them to be mothers, and for more of these mothers to have young children.

This rising number of women with young children in the labor force is a major factor for providing alternative child-care arrangement. But it is not the only one. The more parents and professionals learn about child development, the more they come to wonder if an early group experience is not valuable for most children. Overall, notions of child rearing are changing; in turn, the need for alternative child care is growing. Our society, however, has not been truly responsive to this need.

Parents who need or want child care are usually left to find their own solutions. Most use other family members, others use babysitters in either the child's home or the provider's home; some use family day care where several children can be in the provider's home; or friends exchange care. In some cases, children are left to take care of themselves. We know less about these informal and less public arrangements for child care. In some cases, though, cooperative arrangements and family day care are written about in glowing terms where parents and children alike find a sense of support and community.

Though it is hard to obtain an overall picture of the more informal arrangements for child care, it is, however, apparent parents who are resorting to make-shift types of child care would prefer day-care center service, if possible.

The solution is not just in an increased number of day-care slots or even better quality centers—though either would be an important step forward. The solution lies in a more imaginative and comphrehensive child-care system, one that can accommodate the parent at home who needs or wants support or a part-time group experience for her or his child, the single parent who works at night, and the family where parents want to share child care.

A look at our history and the present reality of child care in this country demonstrates that we have never come close to this. If we are to change our choices for child care, we then need to change our national priorities as well. As a poster from a Cambridge child-care group says, "It will be a great day when our centers have all the money they need and the navy has to hold a bake sale to buy a battleship." The limits in our child-care alternatives reflect the limits in our society as a whole. Then, we can say we are a society that really cares for its children and gives parents the full range of choices in child care.

CHOICES

Delores Welber and Robert Welber

Parents have knowledge of child-care practices based on what their parents, grandparents, uncles, aunts, and teachers did with them. Parents often treat a child like or completely dissimilar to how they were brought up, depending on what they thought or felt about their own upbringing. "My mother was too strict" or "My father too removed" is often heard or, "My mother let me do anything I wanted. I wish we had had more rules. I didn't think she was interested in me." Choices in child care are based on parents' views of their own experiences.

Children need to be watched and listened to and attended to by a noncontrolling, nurturing adult. Such a caretaker needs to be consciously aware of his or her feelings and attitudes about child rearing. Caretakers need to set a clear, fairly consistent framework that is reasonable and flexible. They need to understand that their job is to help the child grow and develop a strong and independent ego. They are not to gratify their own needs to control, to try to relive their own childhood, or, in ever more subtle and hidden ways, to do to the child what was done or not done to them.

We are all human, and the scene never plays as it is rehearsed. But we can get closer to the ideal if we are attuned to our own feelings and motives and understand the meaning and effect of our own childhood and its influence on us as parents, teachers, or caretakers. Do we get nervous, anxious, or scream when children are too clingy or too silent, withdrawn or too depressed, or too demanding? "Too" means beyond what our impulses can tolerate. Do we get angry with others taking care of our children when they are too much like what we dislike in ourselves, our lovers, spouses, mothers, fathers, etc.?

All children are sometimes disturbed. Childhood is a long distressing journey, filled with feelings that are intense, dramatic, calm, quiet. Often only positive feelings are acceptable to caretakers. "Be nice" often means do not say or do anything that makes me, the adult, uncomfortable. So a discussion with ourselves about what makes us uncomfortable and why can help us control our destructive impulses around children and enjoy them more.

Emotions pass between the adult and the child from the moment of conception; they intensify after birth. The adult who can understand and use these emotions to diagnose what a child needs and is feeling and explore it with the child in creative, noncontrolling ways, both nonverbal and verbal, is the best choice for mother, father, teacher, or caretaker. Such behavior and outlook are the first criteria in looking for a child-care situation that is positive: an adult or adults who are capable and committed to this philosophy. A child who is understood emotionally and develops a strong base of trust can separate from parents and caregivers and begin to develop an ego that has clear boundaries and strong roots.

Physical, social, and intellectual skills and understanding and misunderstanding flower from the emotional roots laid down in early childhood. Caretakers and teachers often find themselves in a position of reeducating children. Parents often develop a new, more usable type of parenting through experience by realizing that all feelings are permissible and what is important is to understand why they feel as they do. There are no right or wrong feelings, only behavior that is acceptable or unacceptable to other human beings.

Children need a lot of individual care before entering a group. Individual care or care in small groups is best for the first years. When a child enters a group, there are, again, issues that need studying before making a choice for the child to join that group.

1. Can the parent work on separating properly, slowly, and gently, with both parent and child and teacher working together and in agreement with the process of separating?

2. Can the child be helped to express his or her needs in the group without it damaging the child or anyone else?

3. Are children allowed to express all their feelings, positive and negative and helped to differentiate between attack and feeling?

Children have strong feelings that they cannot sublimate easily. By verbalizing them and finding them acceptable, they can do the work of early childhood. They can learn to control their impulses, have all their feelings, be able to fulfill their potential creatively, and be a fairly content member of a group. Life is especially frustrating for children. They must study all adults to understand what they must do to survive and to grow up in a healthy manner. The emotional roots laid down in early childhood are the most important. The relationships with the first adults who care for children and have authority over them form the groundwork for a lifetime of ideas about intimacy, work, power, etc. Adults who are willing to tolerate uncomfortable feelings—feelings of failure, inadequacy, delight, yearning, love, hate, sadness—who can understand these feelings and use them, they are the people who should be the first choice for child caretakers.

Children are given few choices in the first years of life. They do not choose their parents or their caretakers. Two-, three-, four-, and five-year-old children are rarely consulted about who will have power over them and be in charge of their care. Children know this. They are masters at understanding who will help them and who will not, who will be sensitive, who will be indifferent.

Adults are the children's advocates. We must make sure that children have caretakers who create environments that are mentally and physically safe and nurturing. We must see that we, the children's advocates as well as the children, are satisfied with the choices made for their care.

MANAGEMENT STRATEGIES FOR CHILDREN'S PROGRAMS IN EDUCATIONAL AND RECREATIONAL SETTINGS

Arnold H. Grossman

Much has been written on "management thought" and "scientific management"; other writings have focused on the "art of management." The main point to be made here is that management encompasses both science and art. Managers must draw on the knowledge of the behavioral sciences as well as on intuition and subjective judgment in order to be effective. A primary objective of this essay is to present some concepts from the behavioral sciences that would be useful to those individuals who find themselves responsible for managing children's programs in educational and recreational settings, while recognizing that there are no general principles of management that apply all the time. As most managers are "doers" and more concerned with action than conceptual frameworks, a second objective of this essay is to present strategies (emanating from the conceptual frameworks) that individuals can use to develop management styles for the effective delivery of educational and recreational services to children.

The humanistic approach to management is producing effective results in product-oriented organizations, so it should produce greater results in service-oriented organizations. The dichotomy between management's approach to employees and the expected approach of employees (including volunteers) to the consumers of the service will be eliminated. No longer will managers have their behavior toward employees "out-educate" their philosophical proclamations of program and leadership.

If we accept the humanistic approach of management as a conceptual framework, then we must accept certain implications for establishing managerial strategies. The following managerial strategies are presented because of their import for the effective delivery of educational and recreational services for children.

Creating an Organization Style

The manager sees the organization as a cooperative team. The members (employees and/or volunteers) serve the organization, but the organization also serves the members. The members have the responsibility of giving their opinions, supplying ideas, and structuring their own work. They participate in establishing the goals of the organization; therefore, they have the motivation to push in the direction of the goals. People at all levels communicate with each other; therefore, they can advise and, in turn, be advised. This creates mutual trust and support. Problems are solved by organizing a group or team to attack them, thus, creating a structure to solve a problem vs. making a problem conform to an already established structure.

In this type of organization, also known as a "developmental organization," formal decision making is decentralized. Decisions are made throughout the organization. Individuals on all levels with knowledge in particular areas are consulted, not just those at the top. The manager becomes an agent of communication more than of control. The manager, as a leader, attempts to stimulate members and coordinate communications between teams so that the best possible decisions and actions result.

This organizational style assumes that individuals like to work and that work can provide satisfaction and can enlist the worker's total commitment. Work also provides opportunity for creativity, and developmental organizations encourage group/team brainstorming and creativity sessions because of the belief that people support what they help create. These types of activities encourage member involvement and cooperation; and cooperation is highly valued.

The developmental organization style fosters independent

(vs. dependent); active (vs. passive), responsible (vs. irresponsible), and outwardly oriented (vs. inwardly oriented) employees and/or volunteers. Is this not what we hope the children whom we service in educational and recreational settings become? Does it not make sense to foster the same characteristics in employees and volunteers so that there is a consistent approach to all individuals in the organization? Should not all the individuals grow and develop? The answers to these questions are apparent. (This section is based on selected concepts from Robinson and Clifford, 1976.)

Leadership

In this context, leadership is defined as "a learned behavioral skill which includes the ability to help others achieve their potential as individuals and team members" (Robinson and Clifford, 1975, p. 2). Although leadership roles, of necessity, must vary depending upon the situation and the individuals involved, the manager in a developmental organization should have a predominant style that is characterized by certain behaviors. This style has been labeled the "activator leadership role" and has the expectation of involving others because teamwork is essential for successful task achievement (Robinson and Clifford, 1975, p. 10). The behaviors associated with this role are initiating (subjects, projects, arousing interest), involving individuals (stimulating, supporting, approving, listening), assimilating (ideas, objections), reinforcing (recognizing, supporting, justifying), and solidifying (reviewing, summarizing, confirming). Although this role will not work in every situation, it is one that provides opportunity for flexibility and permits the manager to modify his or her role depending on the goals of the group, the membership of the group, and the time the group has to accomplish its task.

Motivation

In this context, motivation is viewed from a behavior perspective; and motivated behavior is defined as being "internally activated, but it can be modified by the external conditions in an individual's social environment" (Robinson, Clifford, and Wills, 1975, p. 5). The style of motivation that is consistent with the humanistic approach and the discussion of organizational style and leadership style previously discussed is the positive style for motivating others. It is based on the philosophy that desirable behavior should be rewarded and undesirable behavior should be ignored, with the result being that individuals will more likely continue to perform the desirable behavior. It is characterized by the following behaviors: rewarding (providing intrinsic and extrinsic rewards), including (asking individuals for their opinions, ideas, recommendations), and involving (in groups and teams in decision making). As managers, we want to help individuals to enhance their self-development through this style of motivation, and at the same time, make this development carry over to more effective delivery of educational and recreational services with children. (This section is based on Robinson, Clifford, and Wills, 1975.)

Creating a Synergistic Team and Developing Team Skills

"'Synergism' is defined here as the increased productivity and creativity resulting from the collective influence that people have on one another. That is, the whole is equal to more than the sum of its parts. The output of a synergistic team is greater than the sum of individual inputs by the team members" (Robinson and Clifford, 1977, p. 8).

In order to create synergistic teams, a manager has to help employees and volunteers to develop team skills. This is much easier said than done as American society fosters competition, status, and power; and these lead individuals to learn dominating, attacking, and blocking behaviors as well as the development of vested interests and alliances. These self-roles inhibit the development of effective teamwork. The manager must take the lead in helping members to develop team-centered roles that are characterized by (1) involving (bring out and stimulate every team member), (2) listening (active listening that encourages expression), (3) compromising (give up something to solve a team problem), and (4) supporting (participation, approval, encouragement and building team confidence).

Management is a process that facilitates the achievement of organizational goals. This essay has provided a conceptual framework and management strategies to assist organizations providing children's programs in educational and recreational settings in achieving their goals and thereby enhancing the quality of their services with the nation's most vital resource. It is hoped that child caretakers will follow these strategies.

References

Robinson, Jr., Jerry W., and Roy A. Clifford, *Leadership Roles in Community Groups*. Urbana: Cooperative Extension Service, University of Illinois, 1975.

Robinson, Jr., Jerry W., and Roy A. Clifford, *Organization Styles in Community Groups*. Urbana: Cooperative Extension Service, University of Illinois, 1976.

Robinson, Jr., Jerry W., and Roy A. Clifford, *Team Skills in Community Groups*. Urbana: Cooperative Extension Service, University of Illinois, 1977.

Robinson, Jr., Jerry W., Roy A. Clifford, and A. Christine Wills, *Motivation in Community Groups*. Urbana: Cooperative Extension Service, University of Illinois, 1975.

BIBLIOGRAPHY

Anderson, Scarvia B., and Samuel Ball. *The Profession and Practice of Program Evaluation.* San Francisco: Jossey-Bass, 1980.

The authors have written a clear and a practical guide to program evaluation and offer valuable charts and checklists to aid in the application of evaluation principles. Included are expert discussions of the main issues still confronting this fast-expanding profession. Appropriate methods are pointed out for the different purposes of evaluation, and procedures are described that make for positive communication during the evaluation process. There is a good analysis of ethical responsiblities in evaluation, and a thoughtful discussion of the problems of training "evaluators," and of assessing evaluations.

Auerbach, Stevanne. *Choosing Child Care: A Guide for Parents.* New York: Dutton, 1981.

The author provides reassuring suggestions for the working parent by focusing on three main choices for child care: having a sitter come into the home, bringing the child to a family day-care home, or choosing a day-care center. The advantages and disadvantages of the various alternatives are discussed with checklists for evaluation. There are helpful guidelines for parents from all backgrounds, ranging from the affluent two-career family to the single parent trying to cope.

Auerbach, Stevanne (ed.). *Creative Homes and Centers.* Vol. 3, Child Care: A Comprehensive Guide. New York: Human Sciences Press, 1978.

This volume continues the series' theme of viewing child care as a vital service for all families with emphasis on specific required services. It deals with such topics as infant day care in the black community, family day care, licensing child care, designing a children's center, and creating interior spaces for child care.

Auerbach, Stevanne (ed.). *Special Needs and Services.* Vol. 4, Child Care: A Comprehensive Guide. New York: Human Sciences Press, 1979.

The specific guidelines presented for providing service to handicapped children, working with abused children and their families, and establishing programs designed to meet special needs are based on extensive studies. Stress is on parent participation and community involvement.

Blau, Rosalie, Elizabeth H. Brady, Ida Bucher, et al. *Activities: For School-age Child Care.* Washington, D.C.: National Association for the Education of Young Children, 1977.

This planning book is filled with ideas for activities to use with children, specifically in child-care centers. The authors represent a group of distinguished educators who see a good child-care center as a home away from home where children can play and learn. It is stressed that day care is not a baby-sitting service but a planned program by a professional staff who know the developmental needs of young children. Aside from step-by-step activity suggestions, included are chapters on community resources and how to conduct effective staff meetings.

Breitbart, Vicki. *The Day Care Book: The Why, What and How of Community Day Care.* New York: Knopf, 1977.

Although the reader will find in this book exactly what the subtitle states, this is really a philosophical statement more than a how-to book. The author is an advocate of community day care, and she details how to go about achieving it—such as making key contacts, tapping individual resources, funding, determining board membership, procuring legal help, and finding suitable space. There is a strong emphasis on aggressive and creative outreach to make the system work.

Brown, Susan, and Pat Kornhauser. *Working Parents: How to Be Happy with Your Children.* Atlanta: Humanics Limited, 1980.

The authors emphasize that child rearing must be an individual undertaking. What works in one parent-child relationship may not work for someone else. The focus is on child-care arrangements and the variety of options available. Helpful guidelines are given for making informed choices. Suggestions are also offered for making the home "child comfortable," taking into account the need for a safe environment as well as one that fosters the child's natural curiosity and urge to experiment.

Bruner, Jerome. *Under Five in Britain.* Ypsilanti, Mi.: High/Scope Press, 1980.

This first volume in a series presents an overview of the Oxford Preschool Research Project. Bruner gives details on the care of children in Oxfordshire and presents the research questions and policy issues that the project addressed. The findings relating to the three principal forms of preschool care—playgroups and nursery schools, "child minders," and full-day care centers—are summarized.

Bryant, Bridget, Miriam Harris, and Dee Newton. *Children and Minders.* Ypsilanti, Mi.: High/Scope Press, 1980.

A "child minder" is the British counterpart of the "babysitter" or "home day-care provider." The authors examine the lives and expectations of the child minders and the parents who need their services and describe the relationships that develop between the two. The carefully reported, first-person accounts point up clearly, often poignantly, the experiences of young children in a home away from home. The study shows the need for improving home day-care services but cautions that merely improving child minding is not enough. Provisions must also be made to identify those children who need quite different care and to insure that they get it.

Child Care and Preschool: Options for Federal Support. U.S. Congress. Washington, D.C.: U.S. Congressional Budget Office, 1978.

The pattern of funding as outlined may be obsolete, but there are many valuable guidelines that are relevant today. The Congressional report was designed to provide general information to help make informed choices among a variety of budgetary and legislative options. Although primarily a guide for those involved in making legislative decisions, there are helpful answers for parents to questions that ask what the child-care choices are that families face, how to select among them, and what the major factors are that affect those choices.

Collins, Alice H., and Eunice L. Watson. *Family Day Care: A Practical Guide for Parents, Caregivers, and Professionals.* Boston: Beacon, 1976.

The story of family day care is told by means of imaginary testimony of Givers and Users. Symbolic mothers describe their needs for care, noting the inadequacy of available baby-sitting and the other usual care services, particularly for children under three years of age. Informal family day care, often "hit or miss," has led to more structured programs. The needs of providers and welfare mothers are projected through undocumented interviews. Topics dealt with include quality care replacing custodial care, criteria for evaluation, training accountability, and licensing in family day care.

Decker, Celia Anita, and John R. Decker. *Planning and Administering Early Childhood Programs.* Columbus, Oh.: Merrill, 1980.

The authors present a rationale for thoughtful planning and administration of early childhood programs and give a brief overview of the various types. They point out the importance of developing a philosophical foundation for planning the programs. They then consider all aspects of setting up one. Developing policies, understanding administrative organization, staffing, housing, planning and scheduling children's activities, nutrition and health services, working with parents, assessing, recording, and reporting children's progress, and financing and budgeting are a sample of the relevant topics covered.

Epstein, Anne S., and David P. Weikart. *The Longitudinal Follow-Up of the Ypsilanti-Carnegie Infant Education Project.* Ypsilanti, Mi.: High/Scope Press, 1980.

In this report on the High/Scope approach to home visiting, the focus is on three major issues: the long-term impact of the parent-infant program on mother-child interactions, children's development as learners, and the relation between interaction and development.

Fowler, William. *Infant and Child Care: A Guide to Education in Group
    Settings.* Boston: Allyn & Bacon, 1980.

This is a multipurpose text, intended for students, teachers,
day-care personnel and supervisors. Its design incorporates
total systems for fostering children's development in group
settings. Chapters range from the substantial theoretical
foundations underlying child development to the very practical
and descriptive chapters covering the physical environment of
every possible group setting. Particularly valuable are the following chapters: "The Physical Environment," which details the
influence of physical structures on mental structures, "Toys
and Materials: The Physical Basis for Concepts," and "Play Techniques for Motivating Learning."

Galinsky, Ellen, and William H. Hooks. *The New Extended Family:
    Day Care That Works.* Boston: Houghton Mifflin, 1977.

Galinsky and Hooks analyze fourteen exemplary programs
for infant-toddlers, for preschool and school-aged children that
were set up in family day-care homes, in centers, and at the
work site. By describing the pitfalls and problems that each
program faced and solved, the authors emphasize what works.
The book is a repository of tried and tested information that
will be of great help to parents in selecting or evaluating a
program as well as to professionals working in child care.

Garland, Caroline, and Stephanie White. *Children and Day
    Nurseries.* Ypsilanti, Mi.: High/Scope Press, 1980.

This study clearly demonstrates how policy decisions (both
implicit and explicit) can have a profound impact on the everyday interactions of adults and children in day-care settings. The
authors studied nine day-care sites in Britain (three state day
nurseries and six private nurseries) housed in a variety of
settings from hospitals to industry. The premise is that "the
primary goal of the day nursery should be to establish a climate
within which the two-, three-, or four-year-old child can achieve
the satisfactions of his emotional and social requirements." The
report contains detailed descriptions of the variety of management techniques, daily routines, and interactions of the children
and adults in the nurseries, pointing out clearly both the posi-

tive and negative factors that affect young children in group settings.

Glickman, Beatrice Marden, and Nesher Bass Springer. *Who Cares for the Baby? Choices in Child Care.* New York: Schocken, 1979.

As more and more families look at child care outside the home, a book such as this helps parents make informed decisions. The author suggests that parents look at the variety of options available. The final chapter offers guidelines on how to select day care based on the needs of the individual child and discusses the role government and industry might have in helping provide child-care choices. Included is an appendix that lists agencies that furnish day-care information.

Goldstein, Joseph, Anna Freud, and Albert Solnit. *Beyond the Best Interests of the Child.* New York: Free Press, 1980.

This is a hallmark book in spelling out principles and criteria for determining if separation from the parent and/or placement of a child outside the home is appropriate and how it should be done to maintain the psychological well-being of the child. At times the text is difficult reading, but it is worth the effort. The authors take a firm stand for the needs and rights of the child. Their book is particularly good for child welfare workers, day-care workers, and parents.

Gonzalez-Mena, Janet, and Dianne Widmeyer Eyer. *Infancy and Caregiving.* Palo Alto, Ca.: Mayfield, 1980.

In their text the authors follow the philosophy of Emmi Pickler, and its application in the Demonstration Infant Program in Palo Alto. Bridging the gap between "knowing about" (or theory) and "knowing how" (pulling theory into action), the authors have organized the text with the emphasis on action. It is a practical guide for those involved in caring for and educating the infant. Included is an infant care curriculum as well as a chart that shows how to set up both the physical and social environment to promote development. A wide variety of people will find the material thought-provoking—health professionals, social workers, counselors, parent educators, program and training coordinators.

Griffin, Al. *How to Start and Operate a Day Care Home*. Chicago: Regnery, 1973.

Even though written in the beginning of the 1970s, this volume continues to be a comprehensive guide for those interested in operating a family day-care home. Readers will find useful information on licensing, regulations, zoning, equipment, schedules, program, nutrition, financing as well as many other pertinent topics.

Grosett, Marjorie D., Alvin C. Simon, and Nancie B. Stewart. *So You're Going to Run a Day Care Service!* New York: Day Care Council of New York, 1971.

This 1971 manual remains a classic in terms of guidance in relation to the function of board officers, developing bylaws, incorporating, employing a director, and the many other problems encountered in opening a center. Having been collated soon after the staff unionization at the Day Care Council, the booklet contains helpful guidance in labor relations and negotiations. The authors also describe in simple terms what constitutes good education for preschool and school-age children.

Grossman, Arnold H. *Personnel Management in Recreation and Leisure Services*. South Plainfield, N.J.: Groupwork Today, 1980.

Grossman explores personnel management from a humanistic perspective. There are chapters on policy making, personnel policies, recruitment, and selection, to mention a few. Included are sample applications, position descriptions, policy statements, labor agreements, and evaluation work sheets.

Herbert-Jackson, Emily, Marion O'Brien, Jan Porterfield, and Todd R. Risely. *The Infant Center*. Baltimore: University Park Press, 1977.

With the growing need for group programs for infants, this book is a valuable addition to the literature. Complete with pictures, diagrams, and charts, it provides a wealth of practical information on space arrangement, staffing, scheduling, and programs.

Hewes, Dorothy (ed.). *Administration: Making Programs Work for Children and Families.* Washington, D.C.: National Association for the Education of Young Children, 1979.

The articles in this collection cover a variety of topics of interest to the administrators of programs for young children. Issues in establishing goals and perspectives, running a center, choosing and working with staff, as well as methods for evaluating programs are discussed. It is an extremely useful guide for directors of child-care programs.

Hohmann, Mary, B. Banet, and David P. Weikart. *Young Children in Action.* Ypsilanti, Mi.: High/Scope Press, 1979.

The authors use developmental theory and research to identify the nature of developmental changes that occur in young children. They note their emerging abilities and developmental limitations. The book is filled with specifics on room arrangement, daily routine, team teaching, key experiences for cognitive-social development, examples of teaching strategies, activities, child observation checklists. There is also material on working with handicapped children and bilingual/bicultural education.

Honig, Alice S., and L. Ronald Lally. *Infant Caregiving: A Design for Training.* Syracuse, N.Y.: Syracuse University Press, 1981.

This is a new edition of a guide for those responsible for the training of staff entrusted with the care of infants in a day-care/group setting. Beginning with the premise, "People learn they have ability not by failing, but by succeeding," the authors strive to cover aspects of infant development and education. The book would be most useful when working with paraprofessional staff members who are entering a facility with minimal training or experience. Included in the book are practical suggestions for group and individual activities for the trainees to use with the children assigned to them. Common problems that occur in the day-care setting are discussed. With some modification, this book could be used by parent trainers who wish to increase appropriate parent/child interaction in addition to communicating information about child development.

Hunsaker, Phillip L., and Anthony J. Allessandra. *The Art of Managing People.* Englewood Cliffs, N.J.: Prentice-Hall, 1980.

The authors suggest practical strategies for developing interpersonal skills necessary to improve relations with employees, for understanding the differences among people and behaving appropriately, for assessing and improving current work situations, and for creating a trust between managers and employees. They focus on helping employees achieve their potentials in a supportive environment and the interrelationship with a more productive organization, on reducing stress and conflict in the work force, and on increasing trust and credibility.

Jackson, Brian, and Sonia Jackson. *Childminder: A Study in Action Research.* London: Routledge & Kegan Paul, 1979.

Childminder is the result of an exhaustive investigation in family day care in England. Many aspects of this service—including the problems—are similar to those of day care in the United States.Therefore, the wide range of recommendations are extremely relevant. The authors advocate an initial period of "amnesty" for unlicensed providers, special training programs for those involved in child care, and a charter for childminders.

Kamerman, Sheila B. *Parenting in an Unresponsive Society. Managing Work and Family.* New York: Free Press, 1980.

In the 1980s our society is still not set up to meet the needs of the working mother with young children. The author explores how women manage child care while working, how they deal with their jobs, and how they try to cope with the related problems. Child care, this three-year study shows, is the most important challenge these women have to contend with. The pessimistic title addresses the fact that the problem is for the most part left to the individual to deal with. The chapter "What Do Other Countries Do?" while not a full report, does offer valuable guidelines that might serve as an inspiration.

Kamerman, Sheila, and Alfred J. Kahn. *Child Care, Family Benefits, and Working Parents.* New York: Columbia University Press, 1981.

This book documents a six-nation study of child care. The authors look at the widely differing policies in the United States,

France, West and East Germany, Hungary, and Sweden. These range from government-funded day care to the state paying mothers to stay at home. The authors examine the research in each of the countries, particularly how their policies have affected children and families. They conclude that no industrialized nation can afford any longer to avoid the issue of child care for working parents, nor can any single policy strategy suffice in responding to this complicated work and family product. This volume would be of great interest to all professionals and parents concerned with family, education, and public policy. They would also find the complete bibliography helpful.

Kilmer, Sally (ed.). *Advances in Early Education and Day Care: A Research Annual*, Vol. 1. Greenwich, Ct.: Jai Press, 1980.

This is the first of a series that will focus on original research and develop scholarly references for researchers, educators, and others involved in early education. This volume examines the quality of programs for young children as well as the roles that policy makers, educators, and parents can play in fostering programs of excellence. These important papers are designed to focus on the planning and support of quality child-care programs.

Lambie, Dolores Z., J. T. Bond, and D. P. Weikart. *Home Teaching with Mothers and Infants: The Ypsilanti Carnegie Infant Education Project—An Experiment*. Ypsilanti, Mi.: High/Scope Press. 1981.

This is the initial account of the Ypsilanti High/Scope experiment in home-based parent-infant education. It sets forth the project's philosophy of infant education, describes the families selected for the project, examines the implementation of the program and the experimental design, and gives the initial results of the research. The findings show that the program is effective in supporting communication between mothers and children, which in turn fosters the children's intellectual development.

Levine, James A. *Day Care and the Public Schools: Profiles of Five Communities*. Newton, Mass.: Education Development Centers, 1978.

The author describes the five day-care centers that he observed in Oakland, Ca., Brookline, Mass., and Atlanta, Ga. He compares them as to ages of children served, the children's ethnicity, parent involvement, staff personnel, center financing, and program hours. He notes the historical differences in the patterns of operation as well as the opposing approaches to early childhood education. All the centers did receive Title XX funding. However, supporters of day care in the public schools will find helpful information regarding other sources of financial aid.

Lewis, M., and K. S. Goldman. *Child Care and Public Policy: A Case Study.* Princeton, N.J.: Educational Testing Service, 1976.

This report attempts to identify the difficulties involved in developing an acceptable public policy for child care. It is concerned with the processes by which an effective policy can be established. Several models were drawn from a single document, "Federal Programs for Young Children: Review and Recommendations" by Sheldon White. The report is divided into three parts: (1) structure of the problems to be solved, pitfalls encountered, and conclusions reached, (2) a summary of White's report, and (3) a critique of White's study.

Mayer, Morris Fritz, Leon H. Richman, and Edwin A. Bakerzak. *Group Care of Children: Crossroads and Transitions.* New York: Child Welfare League of America, 1977.

In their review of social-class and changing attitudes toward child rearing, the authors point out the changing concepts of mothering and the role of the family. They discuss the differing philosophical bases among child development programs. Their description of various research models that can be used to evaluate day-care programs is well done and well documented. In scholarly but simple language they present a clear review of what is available in group care of children and how to proceed from this base.

Mitchell, Grace. *The Day Care Book.* New York: Stein and Day, 1979.

The author, an experienced day-care specialist, shows parents how to find quality day care for children. Guidelines are given for what to look for and how to evaluate available facilities, and when to realize that one might have to settle for less than the ideal. Although addressed to parents, this book should be of value to day-care directors and staff, students, and all concerned with quality day care.

Provence, Sally. *Guide for the Care of Infants in Groups.* New York: Child Welfare League of America, 1967.

This guide for caregivers and others responsible for caring for infants without families is in part about how infants develop and in part about how to take care of them in an institutional environment. The author does not advocate such a setting but recognizes that infants depend on people entrusted with their care and that they should be well cared for, whatever the circumstances.

Roby, Pamela (ed.). *Child Care, Who Cares? Foreign and Domestic Infant and Early Childhood Development.* New York: Basic Books, 1973.

This collection of essays although dated, provides an overview of issues related to child care in the United States and abroad. The first part provides an analysis of day-care policies in this country. Part two looks at specific issues including effects of racism and sexism on programs, and part three offers an international perspective by providing a look at programs in Sweden, Finland, Hungary, and Israel.

Schweinhart, L. J., and D. P. Weikart. *Young Children Grow Up: The Effects of the Perry Preschool Program on Youths Ihrough Age Fifteen.* Ypsilanti, Mi.: High/Scope Press, 1980.

Preschool education can help disadvantaged children do better in school for ten years afterward; high-quality early childhood programs pay for themselves—thus reports this latest volume on the landmark Perry Preschool Study. New benefits are documented. Children who went to preschool had higher scores on achievement tests and were more strongly committed to schooling.

Sciarra, June, and Anne G. Dorsey. *Developing and Administering a Child Care Center.* Boston: Houghton Mifflin, 1979.

The vital components in developing and running a child-care center are outlined. Included are chapters on equipping the center, safety, health, and staff relationships. This book is mainly designed for students in early childhood education and professionals who wish to add to their knowledge of supervisory and administrative skills. It may also be helpful to parents who would like to know what makes a child-care center work.

Sjolund, Arne. *Daycare Institutions and Children's Development*. Lexington, Ma.: Lexington Books, 1973.

Still relevant, this translation of a Danish study, takes the form of a review of research already carried out and provides a critical evaluation of methods and results as well as a summary of international knowledge in the field of day care. Included is a study on the effect of institutional care on children with special needs.

Smith, Theresa. *Parents and Preschool*. Ypsilanti, Mi.: High/Scope Press. 1980.

Using both observations in groups and interviews with staff and parents to point out the "shapes and sizes" of parent involvement, the author identifies and describes a number of categories of interaction between preschools and parents. The two overriding dimensions identified are "open/closed" and "professional/partnership."

Streets, Donald T. (ed.). *Administering Day Care and Preschool Programs*. Boston: Allyn & Bacon, 1982.

The purpose of this volume is to provide administrators with the most current and important information for beginning or managing a day-care center or preschool. To this end, the author has called upon contributors who are experts in a specific area. The result is a coherent and comprehensive approach to the total administration of early learning centers. Areas rarely covered in early childhood texts are included, such as fiscal management of day-care and preschool programs and the recruitment and selection of personnel. These are a much-needed addition to the literature.

Sylva, Kathy, Carolyn Roy, and Marjorie Painter. *Childwatching at Playgroup and Nursery School*. Ypsilanti, Mi.: High/Scope Press, 1980.

Preschool or playgroup experiences can stimulate intellectual and social development if careful attention is paid to the setting and the structure of the preschool day. This is the primary conclusion of these authors, who spent hundreds of hours systematically observing play groups and nursery schools in nineteen Oxfordshire Centers. Their volume shows how the observational techniques developed in the project can be used by teachers, day-care personnel, researchers, and others interested in the care of young children.

Trohanis, Pascal L. (ed.). *Early Education in Spanish-Speaking Communities.* New York: Walker, 1978.

This book is designed to serve as a basic reference for the teacher working with Spanish-speaking children. An overview is presented of early education in Spanish-speaking communities, as well as insights into the sociocultural aspects of educating Spanish-speaking children. The appendixes supply lists of resource materials and descriptions of screening materials, and screening procedures are included.

Wagner, Marsden, and Mary Wagner. *The Danish National Child-Care System.* Boulder, Co.: Westview Press, 1976.

The authors have written an informative description of child-care delivery in Denmark. Unlike the United States, Denmark makes a decided commitment to quality care for children. The authors detail the child advocacy system, family support services, group day care, family day care, and the training of child-care workers. Educators, parents, and politicians will find the contents of this book enlightening.

Yocum, Jan C., Donna Franzell, and Gloria C. Simms. *How to Start a Day Care Center.* Washington D.C.: Day Care Council of America, 1981.

This publication describes the necessary steps to help progress from thinking about starting a day-care center to opening the door to care for children. The business aspect is emphasized. Resources are provided to enable the reader to answer the questions raised by the authors.

9
Schooling

READING DEVELOPMENT: THE ROLE OF THE FAMILY

Jeanne S. Chall

Reading is not learned all at once. It is learned over many years. It takes most people about eighteen years to be able to read and understand the kinds of printed materials needed for their work, for keeping informed, for voting intelligently, and for their personal needs in today's complex world. Because most jobs are becoming more technical, the level of reading ability needed by most people continues to rise. It is estimated that a twelfth-grade reading level—a level reached by the typical high school graduate—is needed for the 1980s. This means, roughly, the ability to read, for example, a news magazine such as *Time* or *Newsweek* and the federal income tax instructions. Less than fifty years ago, an eighth-grade level was considered sufficient for most people.

Learning to read begins in the home when children are very young. They acquire some of the background for reading when books are read to them. When they are given a chance to hold the book, they will point out the pictures, name the animals, and sometimes make appropriate noises to identify them. At about four or five, some children learn the letters of the alphabet, and some print their names. They learn these from their parents and siblings and also from watching "Sesame Street," "The Electric Company," and other TV programs. The home is the first teacher, not only because it gives the child the background to learn these things, but because it shows interest in the child's trials and successes. Children will try more things, and harder, if someone appreciates what they do.

During the preschool years, and even during the early school years, books should be read to the child and the child should be encouraged to take part in the reading by being asked what he or she thinks will happen next, why certain events occurred, and the like. After such experiences, the preschool child often pretends to read a story or an entire book from memory. The child points to the pictures and seems almost to do real reading. But this is a kind of "pretend" reading since the words are not really read. It is important for later development, however, because from this kind of activity the child learns that print means spoken words and a story and that certain stories go with certain books.

When children enter kindergarten, they continue these activities, often called "readiness" activities that help prepare them for the reading in first grade. In first grade they learn the sounds that go with the letters and to recognize words, and they read little stories. In second and third grades they learn to recognize more words and learn more advanced phonics. They also read orally and silently longer and more difficult stories. Most of these stories are about familiar experiences.

At about fourth grade, and later, there is a big change in reading for most children. They begin to use reading as a tool for learning about new things in the world—in science, history, literature. The books they read from fourth grade on are also more difficult, requiring knowledge of more words and of more complex sentence structures. At the high school level and above the books they are called on to read become even more difficult; in addition, they are required to read more critically and creatively.

Learning to read, therefore, means learning different things at different levels of advancement. While all children seem to progress through these levels, not all do so at the same pace. Some children can read like the typical first grader at age four or five or even younger. Some cannot achieve this until age eight. This does not mean that the child who starts later will not learn to read. With proper help, such a child can achieve ultimately on the same level as others of the same age. If parents are concerned that their child is not making progress as expected, they should contact the child's teacher and, if needed, request an individual evaluation.

The home also helps students progress in reading by providing appropriate reading materials. During the early school years, parents help children by providing the little easy books that can be read by the child and harder books that are read to the child. During the middle grades and higher, dictionaries, encyclopedias, and other reference books, newspapers, and magazines as well as library books help students advance. Students are also helped when the home is interested in what they are learning and takes pleasure in their achievement.

It is important that children do well in reading because advancement in most other school subjects depends on adequate reading achievement. Therefore, if the child has difficulty in reading, it is important for the parent to make sure that all that can be done is being done—no matter what the age or grade of the student. It is important, also, because poor reading often leads to feelings of inadequacy. Many lose confidence when they fall behind in reading. It has also been found that lack of confidence may bring about inadequate reading. Thus, the support, the love, and the confidence that the home and family provide helps the student achieve full development in reading.

Reading difficulties are more common among boys than girls. Why this is so is not completely understood. Some say it is because of biological differences; some say it is the way they are brought up and treated in school. Both may be involved.

There are many reasons why children can have difficulty with reading. The most important fact for parents to know is that most students with reading problems *can be helped*. Research over many years shows that remedial instruction does help. Those children with reading problems who have received remedial instruction are significantly ahead of those who have not received such help. Thus, parents should take advantage of the services for testing and remedial teaching provided by most schools if they think their child is not doing as well as he or she should.

KNOW THE LEARNER: FIRST STEP IN PLANNING THE EARLY CHILDHOOD LANGUAGE/READING CURRICULUM

Dorothy S. Strickland

Throughout the United States community pressure for an earlier start in reading has shown a steady increase in recent years. Research findings of the 1950s and 1960s revealed that young children were capable of handling higher level cognitive tasks than psychologists and educators had heretofore believed possible. Readiness for learning was no longer considered primarily the result of genetic and maturational influences but a product of the child's prior experiences and learnings as well. These experiences and learnings could, of course, be provided by the home, but the most immediate and profound challenge fell upon the early childhood curriculum.

Early childhood educators, trained to focus on total child development, frequently found themselves unsure as to how to meet this challenge. They were concerned about placing undue stress on cognitive development to the possible neglect and even detriment of the child's emotional, social, and motor growth. They were well aware that ultimately it was combined progress in all of these areas that would determine school success.

Nevertheless, many childhood educators responded to the challenge for more academically oriented programs by hastily implementing activities and practices that had traditionally been geared for older pupils. Formal drills in learning letter names, phonics activities, and word-recognition lessons often took the place of creative dramatics and literature sharing activities. The former offered quick, tangible evidence to parents that something important was happening in the prekindergarten program.

Work sheets and workbook pages were visible proof that children no longer played all day. Uneasiness over apparent contradictions with principles of child growth and development gave way to developmentally inappropriate instruction.

The struggle for a balanced curriculum remains a problem for early childhood educators and for parents seeking to give their children the best possible start. The most logical and responsible place to begin planning, however, continues to be with a thoughtful examination of what is known about how young children learn—and *not* with materials and content. The following principles are offered as guidelines to those who are attempting to incorporate a more cognitively based language/reading curriculum into a child development program:

1. Each child is an individual worthy of dignity and respect for his or her own uniqueness. The language/reading program at any level should be flexible enough to accommodate a variety of cognitive styles and learning rates.

2. Children learn best when they are active participants in the instruction. For the most part, instruction must involve the child in *doing* rather than the teacher telling. Even young children should be given opportunities to make choices about materials and strategies for learning.

3. Children learn to communicate in a variety of ways. They communicate by listening, talking, making body gestures, movements, and facial expressions—as well as by reading and writing. Reading is but one part of a child's total communication system. Activities must be planned to foster development in all the ways that children communicate by integrating the various kinds of language experiences offered.

4. Young children learn best through firsthand experiences with people and materials in their environments. The language/reading program should foster the child's concept development in relation to direct experiences. These direct experiences may then be recounted through oral discussion and translated into written materials through the use of story charts.

5. Children learn and express themselves both through what they know and how they feel. A balanced language/reading program will offer opportunities for children to communicate their feelings and to share in what others are feeling.

6. Young children need opportunities to experiment with language. Since the most productive experimentation is included in their play, they need time to play with provocative materials in interesting settings where they can manipulate materials, test ideas, make mistakes, and discover "new" ways of doing things.

As parents and teachers, we are important decision makers in the lives of children. The decisions we make about the type of language/reading program we offer young children should reflect our concern for their total development. In attempting to help each child reach maximum potential, we must never allow ourselves to foster one area of need at the expense of another. Young children deserve no less than the opportunity to begin the task of learning to read in an atmosphere consistent with what we know about how they develop—naturally.

MAKING PROGRAM CHOICES

Bernard Spodek

Concerns in early childhood education seem to be addressed in waves. We initially respond to those issues that are most pressing; then feeling pressure resulting from another set of issues, we shift our attention from those issues originally addressed, turning our attention elsewhere without ever resolving those issues originally faced. As other pressures arise, we shift again. Possibly because of this never ending lack of resolution, we seem to return again and again to issues of prior eras— or so it seems.

Over the years early childhood education has been used to serve different purposes. It has been viewed as a vehicle for social reform at many periods in its history. Almost from its beginning it has been intertwined with women's roles. It has also been affected by the expansions and contractions of public school offerings. In recent years, for example, the use of early childhood education as a vehicle for social reform can be seen in the development of Head Start, originally a part of the community action programs of the Economic Opportunity Act. Head Start was designed not merely to educate young children, but also to help to reconstruct the communities of the poor and of minorities. Its purpose is not much different from that of the first Infant Schools, developed for young children by Robert Owen in New Lanark, Scotland, and advocated by Bronson Alcott in the United States over a century ago. These were similarly designed to reform society.

A report of the Commission on the Status of Women linked the availability of day-care programs for children to social equality for women. The report suggested that women cannot achieve career development patterns comparable to those of men if they must also be solely responsible for the care, nurturing, and education of their young. Thus, without adequate early childhood services, especially day-care centers, there is no equity for women. In the colonial and Revolutionary period of our nation, women and men worked side by side. There was a shift in the role of women that paralleled the beginning of the industrial revolution where women's place was said to be in the home caring for children and providing support for their husbands. This development in women's roles paralleled the call for "fireside education," the education of young children in their homes by their parents (i.e., mothers) as opposed to in schools outside their homes. The fireside education conceived of women as staying home and the proper form of early childhood education as parent education (Strickland, 1982). Thus, even in those days the status of women and the availability of forms of early childhood education were intertwined.

If we look back to the beginnings of public education in the United States, we find young children enrolled in the public schools. By 1850, 15 percent of the children in the schools of Massachusetts were below the age of five. While it was considered reasonable to enroll three- and four-year-olds in the public schools in the early 1800s, this practice ceased in the last half of the nineteenth century. It was felt that the form of education provided was inappropriate for young children. It was also felt that schools and teachers were serving a child-minding function for such young ones, distorting the purpose of education. In the last decade we have again argued whether young children should be educated in the public schools. At present, well over 80 percent of five-year-olds are enrolled in kindergartens as state after state has mandated the provision of kindergarten education. A much lower proportion of three- and four-year-olds are enrolled either in public or private school programs. We are a long way from establishing a policy to provide public education for children below the age of five.

We can find similar parallels in the cyclical nature of the profession's concern for the content of early childhood education. Over the years, for example, kindergarten programs have been designed to achieve a range of goals including teaching philosophic idealism, socializing children into American culture, building proper habits, serving to prevent emotional problems, and directly or indirectly preparing children or instructing them in the subject matter of the elementary school (Spodek, 1973). One curriculum thread that can be found throughout the year suggests that programs for young children be nurturant and follow the lead of development. This child-centered approach can be seen expressed in different ways in the Froebelian kindergarten, in the progressive kindergarten, in the child development-oriented nursery school, and in more recent "open" approaches to early childhood education.

Another thread has suggested that there should be a greater concern with teaching specific skills than with reflecting emerging patterns of development. Montessori programs represent such a concern. Periodically throughout the history of the field there has been a call for early instruction in the academic skills. Interestingly, one of the early presentations of the kindergarten at the 1876 Philadelphia Centennial Exhibition was criticized by kindergarten educators for encouraging such activities as reading and writing. The inclusion of instruction in these academic skills was defended at that time as a way of Americanizing the kindergarten ideas (Ross, 1979).

Today we again hear a call for teaching basic academic skills in the kindergarten. But long before the "back-to-basics" cry along with the call for continued testing of children to achieve academic progress, there is a call for teaching creative thinking and problem solving in the school from the earliest moment on. The cycles of years past are being revisited.

How does an early childhood educator select a program for young children? Looking at the child and designing a program to "meet children's needs" is not a legitimate criteria for "need" as culturally defined. What children need is essentially what we think they ought to have. Attempting to respond to current popular demands creates other problems for teachers as well. These demands are like fashions in clothing; they are constantly changing. To be responsive continually to popular demands without judging which demands are legitimate and worthy of response is to place oneself in the position of a clothing buyer, attempting to judge whether hems will rise or fall in women's skirts or whether lapels will get wider or narrower in men's jackets. Too often the educators will be caught short, unable to anticipate the desire of a constantly shifting public.

A few years ago I proposed that teachers need to evaluate the worth of educational experiences for young children on three criteria, related to these questions:

Is what is taught to the child developmentally appropriate?
Is what is taught to the child worth knowing?
Is what is taught to the child testable by the child? (Spodek, (1977)

These criteria suggest that knowledge of child development principles can help teachers judge whether a child is capable of benefitting from an educational experience. This knowledge can also help teachers understand how children can learn what we want them to learn. Depending upon the conception of development held, teachers can collect information about what children are capable of doing in order to assess what they are capable of learning.

The *what*, however, is an expression of our values. What we teach children at any point in their lives is based upon what we consider valuable for them to know. Knowledge about the physical and social world, knowledge about ourselves, knowledge rooted in skills that allow us to perform certain tasks, and knowledge embedded in attitudes and values that help us to see what we consider to be right and true are all rooted in a social philosophy that underlies the school. What we teach today, for example, about people of different racial, ethnic, and gender groups is different from what was taught fifty years ago, not so much because the facts about people that are available to us are so different, but rather because how we construe those facts is different.

The values that underlie our educational programs, from the earliest point in the education of children, relate to areas of materialism and work, spiritualism and religion, individualism and freedom, community and power, family and sexuality, and equality and justice. Some of these values are addressed directly, often in the curriculum area of social studies. Other values are addressed indirectly and, unfortunately, often only implicitly by teachers. Thus, when the housekeeping of a preschool is the only setting provided for dramatic play, when the play props offered are only those associated with domestic activities, and when girls predominate in this activity center, then one set of values is being communicated implicitly. On the other hand, if there are a variety of work-oriented settings offered for dramatic play, with boys and girls equally involved, then other values are being communicated. These values are not just transmitted through play activities and play materials but through the books we provide and the way that we, as teachers, organize our classrooms and respond to individual children. The curriculum of the early childhood education is both implicit and explicit.

The third criteria stated is embedded in the notion of autonomy as a goal of education. If children are to be independent, then they need to be able to validate what they learn on their own. When teaching consists primarily of telling—whether directly as in discussions and minilectures or indirectly through books and audiovisual devices—then children remain dependent on the authority, the teacher, as the source of knowledge. When children have the opportunity to explore and investigate, trying out and testing ideas about the physical and social world, then they can become independent learners and problem solvers, a goal consistent with the basic tenets of our society.

Early childhood education has long-term effects. The longitudinal studies of children in "compensatory education" programs of the 1960s showed that there was a difference in these children when compared with children who had no programs. While there are no similar studies of the effects of different programs on children over the long run, these differences surely exist, although they will be more difficult to identify. In selecting program activities for young children and in designing a curriculum, we operate on faith that what we are doing will make a difference. But what kind of difference do we wish to make? We can test the effectiveness of a program by seeking evidence of outcome effects. But how do we test whether program outcomes are in themselves good?

Essentially, the choice we make as teachers is a moral choice. To teach a child to read, to respond innovatively to the world, to value human qualities in others, to help understand oneself and ones' feelings are all possible program goals. They may be attained to some degree by the curriculum we provide in schools. With time and resources so limited, perhaps we cannot provide all possible curriculum options in optimal amounts to all children. In choosing one set of goals to predominate over others, we attribute greater worth to those outcomes and ultimately to these skills, concepts, and attitudes that are reflected in these outcomes. Only by knowing what is possible, by understanding the nature of the curriculum we can offer children, and the possible consequences of these offerings, can we make the best possible choices. Thus, reasoned judgment as well as competency must underlie teaching. The more we know about education, and its consequences, the better we can serve young children.

References

Grant, W. V., and Eiden, L. J. *Digest of Education Statistics 1980*. Washington, D.C.: National Center for Education Statistics, 1980.

Ross, E. *The Kindergarten Crusade*. Athens, Oh.: Ohio University Press, 1979.

Spodek, B. Needed: A new view of kindergarten education. *Childhood Education*, 1973, *49*, 191–197.

Spodek, B. What constitutes worthwhile educational activities for young children. In B. Spodek (ed.), *Teaching Practices: Reexamining Assumptions*. Washington, D.C.: National Association for the Education of Young Children, 1977.

Strickland, C. Paths not taken. In B. Spodek (ed.), *Handbook of Research in Early Childhood Education*. New York: Free Press, 1982.

BIBLIOGRAPHY

Anatasi, Anne. *Psychological Testing*, 5th ed. New York: Macmillan, 1982.

On completing this book, the reader should understand the major principles of test construction, be sensitive to the social and ethical implications of test use, and have gained broad familiarity with the types of available instruments and the sources of current information about tests. In her discussion of the field the author outlines the ethical principles of psychologists, suggests uniform guidelines for employee selection procedures, and gives a suggested outline for test evaluation. This title is for the professional in psychological testing.

Anderson, Scarvia B., and Samuel Ball. *The Profession and Practice of Program Evaluation*. San Francisco: Jossey-Bass, 1980.

Starting with an overview of the rapidly expanding field of program evaluation, the book deals with the major purposes of evaluation, methods of evaluation, ethical responsibilities, training evaluators, and trends in program evaluation. Given are workbook-like tables, charts, and checklists to help in application. This practical guide is for the experienced and beginning evaluator as well as directors of educational and social programs.

Armstrong, David G., Kenneth T. Henson, and Tom V. Savage. *Education: An Introduction*. New York: Macmillan, 1981.

A comprehensive overview of schools at the start of the 1980s, this book concentrates on schools as institutions within a cultural and historical context. Designed to present the "real world" of today's schools, the text addresses college and university students who are thinking about careers in education. Topics also include how curricula are organized (with discussion of both basic and innovative types), the roles of the teacher, contemporary issues, and how to go about getting a teaching job.

Baranoff, Timy. *Kindergarten Minute by Minute*. Belmont, Ca.: Fearon-Pitman, 1979.

As the title suggests, the author lends her expertise in early childhood education through sharing ideas on room arrangements, furniture placement, taking over someone else's classroom, setting up a library center, and dozens of other important activities that take place in kindergarten.

Barzun, Jacques. *Teacher in America*. Indianapolis: Liberty Fund, 1981.

In a classic collection of quotable essays, Barzun expresses his views, applicable to all age levels, on education and good teaching.

Benjamin, Robert. *Making Schools Work: A Reporter's Journey Through Some of America's Most Remarkable Classrooms*. New York: Continuum Publishing, 1981.

The author asked the question "What makes schools work well?" and set out to find some answers. The search began by looking for the best schools in parts of the country reported to have the worst. The approach was qualitative, especially in contrast with more traditional research, but the fascinating findings demonstrate that good schools can be created anywhere.

Bettelheim, Bruno, and Karen Zelan. *On Learning to Read: The Child's Fascination with Meaning*. New York: Knopf, 1982.

The authors offer a psychological explanation of children's responses to reading materials and instructional methods. They examine why children do not like to read and suggest the underlying reasons.

Bissex, Glenda. *GNYS AT WRK: A Child Learns to Write and Read*. Cambridge: Harvard University Press, 1980.

This detailed account of how the author's son learned to write and read naturally traces the patterns of development from five to ten years of age, beginning with the child's use of a system of invented spellings. The author shows how writing ability and reading development are closely intertwined. Her comparisons between the child's work in school and at home and the resulting educational implications are revealing. Bissex's observations and conclusions are of importance to parents, teachers, educational planners, and researchers.

Broman, Betty L. *The Early Years in Childhood Education,* 2nd ed. Boston: Houghton Mifflin, 1982.

This revised edition presents an introduction to the field of early childhood education with a thorough coverage of curriculum and classroom organization. A text for the undergraduate student, the focus is on practical concerns of the beginning teacher. There are detailed skills sequence charts and suggestions for classroom activities and exploration tasks.

Bussis, Anne M., Edward A. Chittenden, Rosalea Courtney, and Kathleen Metz. *Let's Look at Children II: A Guide to Theory and Classroom Observation.* Reading, Mass.: Addison-Wesley, 1981.

The authors provide a framework for observation and guidelines for interpretation of children's thought and language development. For example, procedures for concepts of conservation are included with sample responses at various levels to guide interpretation. Interpretative guidelines contain children's actual responses to the questions and problems introduced by tasks.

Cazden, Courtney B. (ed.). *Language in Early Childhood Education,* rev. ed. Washington, D.C.: National Association for the Education of Young Children, 1980.

Contributors to this book offer parents and teachers a research-based approach to helping children acquire language. They discount myths and provide practical suggestions for developing a total curriculum for young children, suggest criteria to evaluate commercial language programs, consider issues concerning English as a second language, and relate language and reading.

Charles, C. M., and Ida M. Malian. *The Special Student: Practical Help for the Classroom Teacher.* St. Louis: Mosby, 1980.

The focus is on the impact of Public Law 94-142 and on the "least restrictive environment" component that encompasses the mainstreaming of children with special needs. Practical suggestions for appropriate teaching strategies and activities are given as well as guidelines for developing individualized instructional programming.

Cherry, Clare. *Creative Art for the Developing Child: A Teacher's Handbook for Early Childhood Education.* Belmont, Ca.: Fearon-Pitman, 1972.

How creative art becomes a part of the child's growth process is explained, particularly for children in the two- to six-year-old age range. The author discusses, on a practical level, materials for painting, collage, and construction; clay; tools; etc. She suggests objects to make, games to play, and special activities and is always careful to let the reader know the problems and rewards that arise from each type of visual or sensory exploration. This is a sound book for teachers who want to investigate the range of basic techniques, plus a little more.

Cherry, Clare. *Think of Something Quiet: A Guide for Achieving Serenity in Early Childhood Classrooms.* Belmont, Ca.: Pitman, 1981.

Although rarely acknowledged, young children are often stressed and anxious. This truly unique book offers suggestions to assist teachers in the creation and management of learning environments that recognize this fact and work to reduce tension. Carefully thought-out ideas employ music, movement, verbal and nonverbal communication techniques, and room design to aid children to recognize the signs and causes of stress. By helping children to increase their own self-awareness, as well as teaching them actual relaxation techniques and ways to express their feelings, they will not only "get more from rest time," but also function better in our ever more stressful society. This valuable volume is particularly useful for new teachers or those experiencing management difficulties during transition periods. Cherry's true concern and respect for children is evident on every page.

Clay, Marie M. *What Did I Write?* Exeter, N.H.: Heinemann Educational Books, 1975.

Using her extensive observations of five-year-olds in New Zealand schools as the basis for her conclusions, the author delineates patterns of development in children's early attempts to write. She explains and illustrates thirteen concepts and principles of early writing development, using many examples of children's actual work, and argues that there is a strong link between early writing behavior and early reading progress. Written in nontechnical language, this book aims to help teachers develop skills of observation that lead toward a better understanding of the process whereby children develop control of written expressions. The author provides a rating technique for observing children's early progress. The content and style are appropriate for paraprofessionals and parents.

Cohen, Dorothy H., and Marguerita Rudolph. *Kindergarten and Early Schooling*. Englewood Cliffs, N.J.: Prentice-Hall, 1977.

This revision of *Kindergarten, A Year of Learning*, describes kindergartens both historically and currently, the nature of kindergarten children, the nursery school program (language, play, blocks, field trips, and curriculum in general).

The authors also deal with classroom management, discipline and its meaning, and the importance of involving parents. The essence of the authors' message is contained in their words in the preface: "Understanding and respect for the child can be fully realized only when the teacher has kept, along with her increasing wisdom, much of the child in her nature. She must be able to see with a child's eyes, hear with a child's ears, and above all feel with a child's heart."

Danoff, Judith, Vicki Breitbart, and Elinor Barr. *Open for Children: For Those Interested in Early Childhood Education*. New York: McGraw-Hill, 1977.

The authors present a comprehensive overview of the stages of child development as well as the basic skills needed for successful teaching. Emphasis is on curriculum ideas in seven different areas and step-by-step suggestions for practical application as part of the childrens' daily experiences. Included are lists of sources of information, government agencies, suppliers, periodicals, and bibliographies. The book is directed at the early childhood classroom teacher or student.

DeVilliers, Peter A., and Jill G. DeVilliers. *Early Language.* Cambridge: Harvard University Press, 1979.

The authors have written a lucid, nontechnical, and often amusing account of how children develop language from birth to school age. Using many examples, they describe how children acquire sounds, words, grammar, and conversational skills. They discuss the crucial experiences whereby children learn language and the constraints on learning. There is useful information for parents, day-care professionals, and early childhood teachers.

Comer, James P. *School Power: Implications of an Intervention Project.* New York: Free Press, 1980.

This is a report, written by the program's director, of the Yale University Child Study Center's Baldwin-King Program that was started in 1966 in two New Haven inner-city schools. The program was designed to help the children, parents, teachers, and schools. Focus is on the ten-year period between 1968 and 1978 when power was shifted from the school to the students. The author describes how the program worked and how social conditions and academic achievement changed when power was returned to the school authorities.

Copeland, Richard W. *How Children Learn Mathematics,* 3rd ed. New York: Macmillan, 1978.

The text has two major purposes. One is diagnostic, to aid in discerning a child's stage of development as a basic for determining the type of math for which the child is ready. The second is to serve as a primary source for teachers who are interested in developing the techniques for teaching mathematics to children between the ages of four and twelve. The book describes Piaget's theory of intellectual development using many pictures, graphs, charts, and children's drawings.

Doman, Glenn. *Teach Your Baby Math.* New York: Simon & Schuster, 1980.

The book provides concise lessons for parents to follow in order to teach their children certain math concepts through the use of numerical dot cards, number perception, addition, subtraction, multiplication, and division. The content goes beyond simply teaching a child to do math problems. The author discusses why small children should not be taught through a system of reward and punishment and why they learn best at certain times of the day, or in certain surroundings, and how his method encourages love and respect between baby and parent.

Durkin, Dolores. *Getting Started.* Boston: Allyn & Bacon, 1982.

The author offers a number of dynamic activities and classroom materials, as well as teaching strategies, for guiding children into reading readiness. The book shows how to develop a child's comprehension skills based on a language-experience approach that uses instructional materials from the child's everyday experiences.

Durkin, Dolores. *Strategies for Identifying Words,* 2nd ed. Boston: Allyn & Bacon, 1981.

This workbook presents a course of study for the reading methodology. The author is concerned with showing ways designed to help children cope with and figure out unfamiliar words. She sees this goal achieved only through comprehension within the context of connected text. This book should help the reading teacher translate some of the strategies into the classroom situation.

Eliason, Claudia Fuhriman, and Loa Thomson Jenkins, 2nd ed. *A Practical Guide to Early Childhood Curriculum.* St. Louis: Mosby, 1981.

The authors are concerned with quality school experience for young children ages three to six. Many practical suggestions and hundred of illustrations make this a valuable book for teachers or anyone who works with young children. The materials will enable the teacher to provide rich and varied experiences in the content areas of early childhood curricula.

Erikson, Erik H. *Identity and the Life Cycle.* New York: Norton, 1980.

Erikson's theory traces the genetically social character of development of a healthy personality. Caregivers from infancy onward influence the manner in which children solve the conflicts of each stage, such as the development of trust vs. mistrust, or initiative vs. guilt, or industry vs. inferiority. Teachers will be able to fit their guidance and responses more perceptively to meet children's social and emotional needs.

Fowler, William. *Curriculum and Assessment Guidelines for Infant and Child Care.* Boston: Allyn & Bacon, 1980.

Each chapter contains practical step-by-step procedures devoted to learning activities and teaching techniques in the curriculum areas of knowledge, problem solving, language, and play. Sections on assessment devices are included.

Frank, Marjorie. *I Can Make A Rainbow: Things to Create and Do . . . For Children and Their Grown-Up Friends.* Nashville: Incentive Publications, 1976.

This collection of suggestions is intended to serve as a catalyst—a book of beginnings. It provides many ideas for using artistic media and gives hundreds of possible ways to express a single, creative idea. There are many practical suggestions for adapting the art activity for classroom use or relating the artistic experience to a curriculum area. It is for teachers, parents, and students of all ages.

Gaeld, Toni S., and Margaret B. Stern. *Sound/Symbol Activities: Kit A. Decoding Activities: Kit B.* New York: Walker, 1980.

"Consumable" materials for building a reading program for beginning readers are provided by the authors in these two kits using a sound/symbol relationship, as opposed to a symbol/sound approach. Kit A includes letter cards, picture cards, word picture cards, word dominoes (main part and word endings). Organization and management techniques for a reading program are also offered for primary-level teachers.

Gans, Roma. *Guiding Children's Reading Through Experience.* New York: Teachers College Press, 1979.

Children need to be motivated to read through the use of interesting materials and experiences, and the author has suggestions for creating this kind of classroom and home environment. Reading is a most personal process with each reader responding to the literature in a unique way. Developing constructive responses is an essential step toward producing avid, life-long readers. The book sets forth a distinguished educator's sensible and sensitive approach to reading.

Ginsburg, Herbert. *Children's Arithmetic: The Learning Process.* New York: Van Nostrand, 1977.

The author shows how children learn, do, and understand elementary mathematics, especially arithmetic. He also demonstrates how such knowledge can be used to improve mathematics education and to resolve children's difficulties in learning. The text is supplemented by his observations of individual children engaged in mathematical operations.

Glazer, Susan Mandel. *Getting Ready to Read: Creating Readers from Birth Through Six.* Englewood Cliffs, N.J.: Prentice-Hall, 1980.

This book provides adults with the skills and materials needed when helping young children prepare for reading. Each chapter is devoted to an age from birth through six. How to create "learning places" for different activities is detailed. Activities include those that foster growth in reading as well as social, emotional, and physical characteristics of the young child.

Glenn, J. A. *The Third R: Towards a Numerate Society.* New York: Harper & Row, 1978.

Aimed at primary and secondary teachers, this book focuses on "numeracy" (or the numerical equivalent of literacy) and how it can be increased through an enlightened learning program. Numeracy can be basically defined as being able to put numbers to use in a common-sense way to help children solve problems involving sorting, classifying, and ordering.

Griffore, Robert J. *Childhood Development: An Educational Perspective.* Springfield, Ill.: Thomas, 1981.

Concepts and issues in child development are shown as distinctly related to the process of education. Chapters review the history, research methods, and developmental issues as they relate to the educational process. Emphasis is on personality development, intellectual development, as well as parental and familial influences on child development. It is directed to teachers.

Gross, Beatrice, and Ronald Gross (eds.). *Teaching Under Pressure.* Santa Monica, Ca.: Goodyear Publishing, 1979.

The book is designed to comfort the teacher who feels harassed by demands both in and out of the classroom environment. The sixty-four readable articles, by educators as well as students, deal with some of these problems, offering sound and sensitive guidelines.

Gruber, Ellen. *Could I Speak to You About This Man, Piaget, a Second?* Atlanta: Gruber, 1979.

This practical handbook for teachers and parents helps make clear the theories and practices of the late Swiss psychologist, Jean Piaget. Although his work has had far-reaching implications for both child rearing and classroom teaching, his theories are often difficult to understand. This is a highly readable introduction to Piaget that is not only illuminating, but also fun to read.

Hamilton, Darlene Softley, Bonnie Mack Flemming, and JoAnne Deal Hicks. *Resources for Creative Teaching in Early Childhood Education.* New York: Harcourt Brace Jovanovich, 1977.

The authors have compiled a comprehensive handbook for teachers that presents curriculum ideas in a most practical, easy-to-follow format. The text covers an extensive variety of subjects grouped under the general headings of self-concept, families, family celebrations, seasons, animals, transportation, and the world we live in. A section describes games, dramatic play props, and playground equipment that can easily and inexpensively be made by the teacher. It is a well-planned book that offers invaluable teacher resources.

This handbook of curriculum ideas will help educators teach through games, songs, and fun activity concepts, such as classification, comparison, seriation, addition, subtraction, division, equivalence, shapes, measurements, money, and time.

Hansen-Krening, Nancy. *Competency and Creativity in Language Arts: A Multiethnic Focus.* Reading, Mass.: Addison-Wesley, 1979.

Provocative ideas for the introduction of multicultural materials in the classroom are presented. The author advocates the integration of children's experiences and culturally appropriate materials in developing a language arts program, especially where the student population represents a diverse range of ethnic, racial, and language groups. Chapters are arranged to include creativity, sensory awareness, music and listening, art and speaking, basic writing, movement and nonverbal communication, various literary forms, and record keeping. It is a useful source book for teachers interested in a multicultural approach.

Harlan, Jean Durgin. *Science Experiences for the Early Childhood Years.* Columbus, Oh.: Merrill, 1976.

This text is directed to early childhood teachers. The first part gives basic background and rationale, and part two, Concepts, Experiences and Reinforcements, gives specific recipe formula descriptions of activities. These simple, effective suggestions utilize many available materials. References for additional sources are plentiful. It is not necessary to be a science major to understand and use this book.

Hatoff, Sydelle H., Claudia A. Byram, and Marion C. Hyson. *Teacher's Practical Guide for Educating Young Children. A Growing Program.* Boston: Allyn & Bacon, 1982.

This comprehensive guide includes suggestions for observing and recording children's behavior, planning schedules for the entire year, setting up programs, choosing materials, room arrangements, parent involvement, and successful mainstreaming. Illustrations and step-by-step instructions, self-checks, and examples make this a helpful, practical handbook for the classroom teacher.

Hegeman, Kathryn T. *Gifted Children in the Regular Classroom: The Complete Guide for Teachers and Administrators.* New York: Trillium Press, 1980.

Hegeman has written a practical how-to activity manual for teachers, especially those working with the gifted child in the regular classroom. She discusses how to identify the gifted child, and guidelines are given for providing the learning experiences designed to meet the needs of the special child. Included are samples of individual record sheets, outlines of letters to the parents of the gifted child, as well as suggestions for after-school enrichment programs. Although geared to the classroom teacher, this volume should also be of interest to program developers and parents.

Hendrick, Joanne. *Total Learning for the Whole Child: Holistic Curriculum for Children Ages 2 to 5.* St. Louis: Mosby, 1980.

The text centers on the needs of the young child rather than on specific subject areas. It is divided according to the emotional, social, creative, physical, and cognitive selves of children. The bibliography at the end of each chapter is well researched and annotated. The material is solid and substantial for the advanced undergraduate and for the teacher seeking to expand the content of a preschool program.

Henry, George. *Teaching Reading as Concept Development: Emphasis on Affective Thinking.* Newark, Del.: International Reading Association, 1975.

Henry strongly advocates that the emphasis in reading instruction should be on reading as a cognitive and affective experience. He believes that both analysis and synthesis of reading material must occur. "Synthesis in reading has been grossly slighted," according to the author, because reading has too often been presented not as a continuing mode of logic but rather as a number of separate skills. In addition to setting forth the theory supporting the synthesizing aspect of reading, the author provides activities that will emphasize his approach.

Hess, Robert D., and Doreen J. Croft. *Teachers of Young Children.* Boston: Houghton Mifflin, 1981.

Application of research and theory to specific classroom examples gives this teacher-training text relevance and usefulness. Topics covered include safety and health, setting goals for children, helping children use their minds, and developing social skills. Attention is given to work with families and to administrative records and requirements.

Higley, Joan. *Activities Deskbook for Teaching Reading Skills.* West Nyack, N.Y.: Parker, 1977.

The practical ideas for the teaching of reading presented by the author reflect a developmental approach to the subject. In her discussion the author includes oral, motor, visual, and aural skill activities. Chapters are organized to offer a sequential approach to language arts, from simple to progressively more complex reading skills. As a supplement to the classroom reading program, this book is a comprehensive source for teachers.

Hildebrand, Verna. *Introduction to Early Childhood Education,* 3rd ed. New York: Macmillan, 1981.

For educators concerned with children ages three through six, this textbook provides an introduction to professional preparation for nursery school, child care, and kindergarten teaching. Included is an overall view of goals, techniques, and curriculum as well as discussion of child care around the world and future trends in early education. Individual chapters examine the curriculum in detail and provide step-by-step suggestions for practical application. Not only the teacher in the early childhood classroom, but also administrators involved in planning programs, health professionals, librarians, and parents will find this an important resource.

Hill, Dorothy M., *Mud, Sand, and Water.* Washington, D.C.: National Association for the Education of Young Children, 1977.

Young children delight in these messy but necessary ways of learning about the world. Profusely illustrated with pictures showing how children learn through play with mud, sand, and water, the book encourages teachers to take the plunge and make it possible for children to explore these tools to enhance healthy development.

Hohmann, Mary, B. Banet, and D. Weikart. *Young Children in Action: A Manual for Preschool Educators.* Ypsilanti, Mi.: High/Scope Press, 1979.

Key experiences are provided for teachers to enhance cognitive development. Topics include arranging and equipping the classroom, establishing daily routines, planning, and presentation of active learning experiences in language, classification, seriation, number, spatial relations, and time.

Holdaway, Don. *The Foundations of Literacy.* Sydney, Austr.: Ashton Scholastic, 1979.

The author's thesis is that young readers can teach themselves within a properly supportive environment. Holdaway discusses the developmental process and progress of a child who learns to read by being immersed in a literate environment. This practical and theoretical guide is based on years of research by the author.

Holt, Bess-Gene. *Science with Young Children.* Washington, D.C.: National Association for the Education of Young Children, 1977.

Practical information abounds in this text aimed primarily at a teacher audience. The author presents important pointers in teaching science to young students. Her poisonous plant chart is an excellent teaching resource.

Hoover, Kenneth H., and Paul M. Hollingsworth. *A Handbook for Elementary School Teachers,* 3rd ed. Boston: Allyn & Bacon, 1982.

The teaching strategies detailed are adaptable to a variety of classroom settings. Sample lesson plans are provided as well as discipline approaches and testing methods. Suggestions and techniques are given for teaching multiethnic children. There are ideas for parent involvement and mainstreaming guidelines, serving to make this an easy-to-use handbook.

Jarolimek, John, and Clifford D. Foster. *Teaching and Learning in the Elementary School.* New York: Macmillan, 1981.

In this text for the experienced as well as the student teacher, the focus is on universal skills that can be applied in a wide range of subjects. Discussed are purposes of education, teacher roles, classroom management, planning, and strategies for cognitive and effective learning. Included are bibliographies for further professional studies and lists of relevant articles in professional journals.

Johnson, David W., and Roger T. Johnson. *Learning Together and Alone: Cooperation, Competition, and Individualization.* Englewood Cliffs, N.J.: Prentice-Hall, 1975.

This study of teaching principles and techniques is influenced by humanistic values. It is a realistic analysis of different goal structures, learning processes, and social myths that have bearing on education. Many apt literary quotations and some personal references make it a lively and thought-provoking book for early childhood educators who are concerned not only with methods of teaching, but also with values in living.

Kamii, Constance, and Rheta DeVries. *Group Games in Early Education: Implications of Piaget's Theory.* Washington, D.C.: National Association for the Education of Young Children, 1980.

What are good group games? Why use group games? How do competitive games contribute to children's development? The authors answer these and many other questions and provide directions for playing many games for children from ages three through ten.

Kamii, Constance, and Rheta DeVries. *Physical Knowledge in Preschool Education: Implications of Piaget's Theory.* Englewood Cliffs, N.J.: Prentice-Hall, 1978.

In clear terms the authors explain Piagetian theoretical position and rationales to help four-year-old children to construct their own knowledge of the physical world. The authors assume that the reader has previous understanding and is in the field. Through exploring the materials, mostly through their own initiative (sometimes with teacher modeling or using questions), the children begin to understand the physical properties of water, force, balance and other phenomena of physics.

Kamii, Constance, and Rheta DeVries. *Piaget, Children and Numbers.* Washington, D.C.: National Association for the Education of Young Children, 1979.

The purpose of the book is threefold: (1) to explore Piaget's theory concerning the nature of numbers, (2) to outline the principles of teaching numbers that can be derived from this theory, and (3) to describe situations that the teacher can use to teach according to these principles.

Kaplan, Sandra Nina, Jo Ann Butom Kaplan, Sheila Kunishima Madsen, and Bette Taylor Gould. *Change for Children: Ideas and Activities for Individualizing Learning.* Santa Monica, Ca.: Goodyear Publishing, 1980.

Easy-to-follow guidelines are provided for a wide range of

materials and activities that foster the concept of individual freedom within the classroom structure. Included is a flow chart that should be helpful to teachers as an outline to follow when implementing the individualized learning classroom.

Kusnetz, Len. *Your Child Can Be a Super Reader.* Cockeysville, Md.: Liberty, 1980.

This small book is especially helpful for its specific recommendations for increasing children's vocabulary in order to help them read with ease. The author provides a directory of publishers that offer good books for youngsters and also lists recommended periodicals for children.

Languis, Marlin, Tobie Sanders, and Steven Tipps. *Brain and Learning: Directions in Early Childhood Education.* Washington, D.C.: National Association for the Education of Young Children, 1980.

The authors suggest strategies for teachers to promote integration of right and left hemisphere ways of knowing based on recent research. The evidence supports using a hands-on curriculum, accommodating to children's different learning styles.

Larrick, Nancy. *Children's Reading Begins at Home—How Parents Can Help Their Young Children.* Winston-Salem, N.C.: 1980.

This paperback, geared for parents, contains suggestions for reading aloud, talking, singing, and listening. The value of reading as an entire family activity is stressed.

Larrick, Nancy. *Encourage Your Child to Read: A Parent Primer.* New York: Dell, 1980.

This book includes specific things-to-do at home in daily family activities to encourage children to read. The author explains how reading is taught in school and the development of oral language skills. She describes the relationship of play to reading. Books are suggested as well as activities for informal ways to make home a center for learning.

Lay-Dopyera, Margaret, and John Dopyera. *Becoming a Teacher of Young Children,* 2nd ed. Lexington, Ma.: Heath, 1982.

Teachers and prospective teachers are guided in developing four crucial qualities—commitment to the profession, sensitivity to children's development and behavior, resourcefulness in providing learning activities, and organizational abilities for establishing and maintaining successful classroom programs. The book maintains a personal, practical, and skills-oriented approach. It also considers alternative approaches and the orientations toward child development that they reflect.

Lee, Doris M., and Joseph B. Rubin. *Children and Language*. Belmont, Ca.: Wadsworth, 1979.

Based on research and theories, this comprehensive textbook, presents a rationale for building a language arts program that makes maximum use of children's natural capacity to learn language. Intended for prospective teachers, it is a valuable resource for in-service practitioners as well. Serious questions are raised about widespread practices used in schools to promote language development. The text is discussed under four sections: Communication: The Purpose of Language, Oral Communication: Talking and Listening, Written Language: Recording and Retrieving Thoughts, and Epilogue—The Language Arts Program in Action. The authors explain the significant role language plays in personal, social, and cognitive development; stress the interrelationships among talking, listening, reading, and writing; and emphasize the importance of a child-centered approach. Each chapter includes guidelines and practical experiences to promote a major aspect of language and ends with lists of useful learning experiences for prospective teachers, recommended readings with comments on each, and strategies designed to be used with children that are appropriate to the topic of the chapter.

Lemlech, Johanna K. *Handbook for Successful Urban Teaching*. New York: Harper & Row, 1977.

Lemlech presents a functional approach to the urban teaching experience. Throughout the book she provides the necessary information and ingredients for becoming a successful urban teacher. Her six chapters focus on what she believes are the critical areas for the urban school. After discussing the necessary theory, Lemlech systematically outlines workshops for the reader to participate in.

Lewis, Claudia. *Writing for Young Children*. New York: Doubleday, 1981.

Anyone interested in children's language should read this volume. Lewis helps the reader appreciate children's use of language. She points out how awareness of its usage can be applied by the adult living and working with children.

Lillard, Paula Polk. *Children Learning: A Teacher's Classroom Diary*. New York: Schocken, 1980.

Although the basic content is in the form of a classroom diary, the book is in essence a structured presentation of academic learning in a class of four- to five-year-olds with a Montessorian approach. The teaching is carried out with a full range of Montessori materials in a carefully "prepared environment." The author's own curiosity and questions as well as her honest recording of discouragements and of astonishing individual achievements make this work a unique contribution to educational literature dealing with the kindergarten.

Lindberg, Lucile, and Rita Swedlow. *Early Childhood Education: A Guide for Observation and Participation*, 2nd ed. Rockleigh Boston: Allyn & Bacon, 1980.

Providing both theoretical and practical background information, the authors, both leading educators, offer specific techniques and suggestions plus detachable worksheets for easy application in the classroom. Each chapter includes objectives, behavioral indicators, pre- and posttests and resource materials.

Lindfors, Linda. *Children's Language and Learning*. Englewood Cliffs, N.J.: Prentice-Hall, 1980.

This is not a traditional language arts methods book. It is a comprehensive treatment of five dimensions of language: structure, acquisition, its relation to cognition, its use in social contexts, and language variation. Rich in theory yet practical, the chapters in each section synthesize and explain theory and research related to each of the dimensions, discuss how theory and research findings can be incorporated into classroom practice, and suggest exercises and projects that are well thought out to develop teachers' observational skills and their awareness of children's language abilities.

Lorton, Mary Baratta. *Workjobs: Activity-Centered Learning for Early Childhood Education.* Reading, Mass.: Addison-Wesley, 1972.

In this functional resource book for beginning and experienced teachers of preschool children. Pictures effectively demonstrate each of the activities suggested. These activities are primarily centered on language and math development through its use of photographs and narrative. The excellent photos and interesting and concrete text make the reader want to do the activities suggested at that very moment.

Mack, Faite R-P, and Melvin Wesley Wells. *Learning Games: Through Games-Objective Based.* Novato, Ca.: Academic Therapy Publications, 1981.

There are two hundred lesson plans, each self-contained with behavioral objectives, materials to be used, and step-by-step procedures. Topics include, among others, comprehension, dramatic play, literacy forms, and body awareness. It is a useful guide for a teacher in the primary grades or a teacher working in an independent environment.

McCarthy, Melodie A., and John P. Houston. *Fundamentals of Early Childhood Education.* Cambridge, Mass.: Winthrop, 1980.

The book is written as a guide for the new, future, or relatively inexperienced teacher in a preschool, nursery school, or child-care center. As such, it is clearly organized with sufficient attention to the primary areas of early childhood education. It does not overwhelm and may therefore serve a significant purpose in preparing beginning teachers.

McCaslin, Nellie. *Creative Drama in the Classroom.* New York: Longman, 1980.

The author intends this book for the nonspecialist teacher who wishes to introduce dramatic activities into the classroom and who needs guidelines and help in starting the program. Against a rich background of information, the author shows creative drama as an art form, a socializing activity, and a teaching and learning tool. She also discusses movement and rhythms, pantomime, improvisation and how to build plays from stories and use poetry. Of particular interest is a chapter that concentrates on creative drama in special education.

Margolin, Edythe. *Teaching Young Children at School and Home.* New York: Macmillan, 1982.

This book offers both the parent and the early childhood classroom teacher numerous suggestions for activities and programs for use with young children. Additionally, the book stresses the importance of adult attitudes and how these critically affect the way children are raised and educated.

Marion, Marian C. *Guidance of Young Children.* St. Louis: Mosby, 1981.

The presentation is divided into three parts. The first section focuses on child/teacher interaction in the developmental process. The next section deals with discipline techniques and behavioral concerns, giving specific suggestions for promoting positive behavior based on self-esteem, and the last part outlines specific programs based on the behavioral, Adlerian, and Rogerian philosophies. Both parents and teachers will find this book helpful.

Martin, Robert J. *Teaching Through Encouragement: Techniques to Help Students Learn.* Englewood Cliffs, N.J.: Prentice-Hall, 1980.

The author's objective is to get teachers to interact more effectively with children. To achieve this, specific practical suggestions are given for coping with nonproductive student behavior and encouraging communication and self-responsibility. Although addressed to the teacher, the content should be helpful to parents as well.

Menyuk, Paula. *Sentences Children Use.* Cambridge: MIT Press, 1972.

The author examines children's acquisition of language and experimental approaches that have been employed to help children expand their use of language. The structure of the language, sentences children use, as well as data from relevant studies are discussed. The text is linguistics oriented, but Menyuk intends to reach all readers interested in technologies of language development and acquisition.

Moe, Alden J., Carol J. Hopkins, and Timothy Rush. *The Vocabulary of First-Grade Children*. Springfield, Ill.: Thomas, 1981.

Especially suitable for language arts and reading teachers, this study lists and analyzes words spoken by over 300 children during a seven-year span. Chapters include a history of word counts, collections, analysis and lists of children's oral language, vocabulary diversity, and the use of vocabulary lists in teaching reading.

Montessori, Maria. *The Montessori Method*. New York: Schocken, 1977 (21st printing).

The world-famous physician and educator explains her theories and work with "deficients" and deprived children in the slums of Rome early in this century. Montessori's humanitarian concerns, scientific approach, and educational use of practical work plus her "education of the spirit" enabled hopeless children to become successful learners. Her methods of "education of the senses" are relevant to the educational principle of sensory experiences in early childhood education today.

Morrison, George S. *Early Childhood Education Today*, 2nd ed. Columbus, Oh.: Merrill, 1980.

The text is written in an imaginative style, which makes for interesting reading and study. The material is arranged according to particular topics that are helpful in organizing concepts and practices. The chapter entitled "Historical Influences" discusses the impact of early educators' ideas upon subsequent generations of teachers. A chapter on Jean Piaget highlights his contributions to cognitive development and includes an illustration of an educational curriculum based on his theories.

Mosse, Hilde L. *The Complete Handbook of Children's Reading Disorders: A Critical Evaluation of Their Clinical, Educational, and Social Dimensions*. New York: Human Sciences Press, 1982.

This work in two volumes examines the reading process from an innovative perspective. Mosse describes how clinical examination of children can unravel all the various factors involved in the causation of reading disorders. For educators, health professionals, parents, and anyone involved in the life of a child experiencing a reading disorder, this is a valuable resource.

Oettinger, Anthony G. and Sema Marks. *Run, Computer, Run: The Methodology of Educational Innovation, An Essay.* Cambridge: Harvard University Press, 1969.

Written more than a decade ago, this controversial and pugnaciously written evaluation of the state of educational technology in the 1960s is fun to reread in the light of developments in the 1980s. Oettinger, in looking to the future, urges more risk taking: "The technology-there-is fails in the schools-as-they-are. No one can tell for sure how to marry the technology-that-could-be with the schools-that-might-be."

Ollila, Lloyd O. (ed.). *The Kindergarten Child and Reading.* Newark, De.: International Reading Association, 1977.

In this overview of the infusion of reading instruction filtered down to the kindergarten level, the author raises questions of interest not only to teachers and administrators, but also to boards of education and parents. How much formal reading should exist in kindergarten and how should it be taught are discussed. It is a good informational handbook relating to this topic.

Ornstein, Allan C., Harriet Talmage, and Anne W. Juhasz. *The Paraprofessional's Handbook: A Guide for the Teacher-Aide.* Belmont, Ca.: Fearon, 1975.

This is a valuable handbook for the teacher's assistant who works in the classroom and has instructional duties to perform. Guidelines are given for working with the staff, understanding the children, promoting good discipline, planning for instruction, and using audiovisual aids.

Page, William D., and Gay S. Pinnell. *Teaching Reading Comprehension.* Urbana, Ill.: National Council of Teachers of English, 1979.

This book provides a much needed review of the relevant research on linguistics, instruction, and curriculum. The material is presented in a clear, concise fashion.

Paley, Vivian Gussin. *White Teacher.* Cambridge: Harvard University Press, 1979.

The author examines and challenges society's values as reflected in the classroom. In light of these, she relates how she helps her kindergarteners develop the tools needed to face the world as it is and move it toward what it can be. This is a moving personal account of the author's experiences in an integrated school in a white, middle-class neighborhood.

Papert, Seymour. *Mindstorms: Children, Computers and Powerful Ideas.* New York: Basic Books, 1980.

Papert, in this timely book, discusses the role of the computer in education. Two major themes are prevalent: that children can learn to use computers in a masterful way and that learning to use computers can change the way they learn everything else.

Petty, Walter T., Dorothy C. Petty, and Marjorie F. Becking. *Experiences in Language: Tools and Techniques for Language Arts Methods*, 3rd ed. Boston: Mass.: Allyn & Bacon, 1981.

A comprehensive language arts text is offered by the authors who have written extensively in this area. Special education, learning disabilities, language diversity, and library skills are examined. Each chapter contains explanatory and/or resource notes and ends with references, activities for pre-service and in-service teachers, and independent activities for children. The volume is useful as a college textbook as well as a resource for teachers.

Petty, Walter T., and Julie M. Jensen. *Developing Children's Language.* Boston: Allyn & Bacon, 1980.

This inclusive text ranges from language development theory to the achievement of complex writing skills. The authors' presentation reflects a philosophical orientation that is reality-based, i.e., one that understands the complexities involved in children learning to read and the exigencies of teaching reading. Pre-service and in-service teachers, as well as students in undergraduate language arts courses will find the material very useful.

Pflaum-Connor, S. *The Development of Language and Reading in Young Children.* 2nd ed. Columbus, Oh.: Merrill, 1978.

Language growth is described during the preschool years. Detailed explanations are given of the specific auditory, visual, cognitive, and experiential skills necessary for preparing children for reading.

Pickering, C. Thomas. *Helping Children Learn to Read: A Primer for Adults.* New York: Chesford, 1977.

Questions asked by parents and answers to these questions begin this book that speaks to parents about early reading instruction. How reading is taught in schools is described with sample pages from textbooks. One chapter shares ideas for coordinating home and school instruction. Award-winning books for children are listed. Basic word lists used in most beginning reading materials are included at the end of the volume. Parents who think of reading as "learning words" will find these lists helpful.

Pinnell, Gay Su (ed.). *Discovering Language with Children.* Urbana, Ill.: National Council of Teachers of English, 1980.

There are twenty-six brief, nontechnical articles by recognized authorities in the field of language acquisition. Each essay summarizes current knowledge about an aspect of children's language, uses examples to support and illustrate points, discusses implications for practice, and provides references for further study. Includes three sections: the first, Language and the Young Learner, deals with how children learn language before formal schooling and what teachers and other adults need to know in order to foster continued development; the second, Language Growth in Educational Environments, focuses on language development in school, emphasizing classroom contexts that promote growth in oral language, reading, and writing; the last, Evaluation in Language Education, addresses the issue of accountability, discusses alternatives to standardized tests, and describes theoretically based procedures and techniques for continuous assessment of children's language development. This informative volume is of value to teachers, parents, and others who want guidance on how to support and encourage language learning.

Pope, Lillie. *Guidelines to Teaching Remedial Reading.* Brooklyn, N.Y.: Book-Lab, 1975.

This is a manual for tutors who work with handicapped individuals outside of the established educational structure. Here, the tutor is guided in organizing an effective program and given helpful suggestions for useful materials, evaluating the student's reading level as well as establishing a positive relationship.

Porter, Judith, D. R. *Black Child, White Child: The Development of Racial Attitudes.* Cambridge: Harvard University Press, 1971.

This is a probing study of young black and white children that supports the findings that racial attitudes are learned during the preschool years. The author undertook a study of the genesis of prejudice and its effects with the hope that this study would provide a foundation for changing negative attitudes.

Postman, Neil. *Teaching as a Conserving Activity.* New York: Dell, 1980.

Reversing or, at least reinterpreting, his position in the 1960s (expressed in an earlier book *Teaching as a Subversive Activity*), Postman suggests that schooling should always be "thermostatic," i.e., countercultural. If the culture is tight and prescriptive, schools should open up new ideas and values for children. But if the culture is permissive and ill-defined (as is the TV culture of the 1980s), then children need disciplined study of their heritage.

Resnick, Lauren B., and Phyllis A. Weaver (eds.). *Theory and Practice of Early Reading,* Vols. 1-3. Hillsdale, N.J.: Lawrence Erlbaum Associates, 1979.

The editors have assembled articles by recognized theorists and practitioners representing different disciplines and points of view. Articles in each volume address six issues: (1) the centrality of decoding in early reading, (2) the nature of skilled reading, (3) the relation between language and reading, (4) factors that interfere with learning to read, (5) the acquisition of reading competence, and (6) the relations between theory and practice. A discussion section contains chapters that synthesize, clarify, and criticize points raised in previous chapters. The series is a valuable resource for researchers, reading educators, program designers, and teachers. It provides a comprehensive picture of the state of the art of early reading theory and practice.

Riessman, Frank. *Inner City Child*. New York: Harper & Row, 1976.

Primarily addressed to urban educators, this volume serves as an introductory review of the current issues in the education of inner-city children. Recent research findings are presented with practical value for educators in that the strengths of the children and their families and social background are illuminated.

Rogovin, Anne. *Let Me Do It!* New York: Crowell, 1980.

Rogovin includes over 300 projects suitable for both the exceptional and the normal child and supplements them with illustrations. Activities include puppet making; using bottles, boxes, plants, and animals to teach concepts; and suggestions that incorporate nursery rhymes, fables, and stories. The book is particularly useful for beginning teachers because of the simplicity of the activities and the clarity of the directions and illustrations.

Roth, Marian. *Creative Movement for Young Children*. Chicago: Ellie Enterprises, 1980.

This excellent, well-illustrated book on body movement for young children can be very helpful to the in classroom teacher. The teacher, however, should try out each movement before trying it with the children. Some of the activities may be difficult for three-year-olds, and the author's cautions should be kept in mind. Her ideas for props and adding words and songs while doing the movements are particularly intriguing.

Russell, Helen Ross. *Ten-Minute Field Trips*. Chicago: Ferguson, 1973.

This volume is an absolute must for every classroom! It will help teachers organize and plan in detail their trips both in the building and outside. Numerous ideas and extensive background material make this a veritable Bible for teaching science. The book is divided into science units, cross-referenced for easy access. A valuable annotated bibliography and useful annotated list of children's books are included.

Rutherford, Robert B., Jr., and Eugene Edgar. *Teachers and Parents: A Guide to Interaction and Cooperation.* Boston: Allyn & Bacon, 1979.

The authors consider systematic procedures that teachers can follow when confronted with a variety of problems. They believe that effective teacher-parent interaction involves cooperation and exchanges of information. These procedures, they say, promote a level of trust and help resolve value conflicts, but require parent participation. At the preschool stage and at all further levels of schooling, they insist, it is important to have shared feelings about goals and clarification of values. The authors have developed a problem-solving model that teachers can apply when working with parents to resolve their children's problems. This model provides a step-by-step approach through the use of skills derived from applied behavior analysis, interpersonal communication, and assertiveness.

Schuman, R. Baird. *Elements of Early Reading Instruction.* Washington, D.C.: National Education Association, 1979.

This small book documents influences upon beginning reading instruction, including descriptions and comparisons of various programs (basals, etc.) as well as dialectical differences and how they affect instruction and learning. Readiness, the aspects of language, and psycholinguistics all come into play, and the author clearly discusses each in depth.

Schwebel, Andrew I., et al. *The Student Teacher's Handbook: A Step-by-Step Guide Through the Term.* New York: Barnes & Noble, 1979.

The authors understand the psychology of student teaching. In their book they help students examine their own expectations and cope with the great variety of problems they face in the classroom. Especially interesting are the excerpts from the logs of student teachers. This book is of great value not only to student teachers, but also to cooperating teachers and college supervisors.

Seaver, Judith W., Carol A. Cartwright, Cecilia B. Ward, and C. Annette Heasley. *Careers with Young Children: Making Your Decision.* Washington, D.C.: National Association for the Education of Young Children, 1979.

Students in early childhood teacher education programs or adults who because of burnout, layoffs, or the need for new challenges are seeking new careers using their knowledge of children will find this book the ideal source for information. Interviews, questionnaires, and job descriptions suggest a variety of ways in addition to classroom teaching that adults can serve the needs of children and families. It is an indispensable resource for libraries in high schools and colleges of education.

Shallcross, Doris J. *Teaching Creative Behavior: How to Teach Creativity to Children of All Ages.* Englewood Cliffs, N.J.: Prentice-Hall, 1981.

In this teacher's handbook designed to foster creativity in the classroom, the author shows how creative behavior can be established in numerous ways and illustrates this through sequenced activities. Chapter titles are descriptive of the discussion, for example, "Setting the Climate for Creative Behavior," "Overcoming Barriers to Creative Thinking," "Measuring Student Growth," and "Incorporating Creative Processes into Existing Curricula." Included is a list of resources for teachers and children.

Shapiro, Lawrence E. *Games to Grow On: Activities to Help Children Learn Self-control.* Englewood Cliffs, N.J.: Prentice-Hall, 1981.

Although not a book that speaks directly to teaching reading, this small volume will be of great help to parents as well as classroom teachers who always say, "I can't get my child to sit still!" Games that help children build the necessary self-control for reading activities are included. Activities for following directions, slowing down in order to concentrate, learning to think before acting, and more are well illustrated.

Sharp, Evelyn. *Thinking Is Child's Play.* New York: Avon, 1970.

Sharp introduces parents and teachers to child psychologist Piaget's stages of mental development in children. She also describes games that involve prenumber concepts, such as classification, seriation, and one-to-one correspondence. These are the tools a child needs to fully understand how to reason through instead of merely memorizing the ideas that he or she will later call arithmetic.

Sime, M. *A Child's Eye View.* London: Thames & Hudson, 1973.

Sime presents a nonclinical approach to Piaget's theories and how they may be practically applied in the beginning stages of problem solving. Since this is, in fact, the basis of any math concept, understanding these theories should prove helpful in aiding a child's grasp of prenumber and number concepts.

Smith, Frank. *Reading Without Nonsense.* New York: Teachers College Press, 1979.

This book is meant for anyone interested in the topic of reading. No specific methodology for teaching reading is given, but rather information about the nature of the reading process is presented in a clear, concise manner. Smith believes that the most important set of facts for teachers to learn are those that contribute to the nature of reading. He makes the point that children learn to read by reading. In all cases, the reading for the learner must be meaningful. This is one of the most sensible books on the entire topic of reading.

Snyder, Martha, et al. *The Young Child as Person: Toward the Development of a Healthy Conscience.* New York: Human Sciences Press, 1980.

The authors provide teachers of young children with a theoretical background for common-sense ideas about children. Therefore, the book can be useful in helping teachers to formulate a philosophy of instruction. It can be used as a reference book or as a classroom text in a course in early childhood education. The book is well written and easy to understand.

Sparkman, Brandon, and Jane Saul. *Preparing Your Preschooler for Reading: A Book of Games.* New York: Schocken, 1977.

The authors present practical and sequential ideas relating to reading readiness activities, organized to include parents' role, experiences, and visual and listening games. Ideas are coupled with the rationale of why they are important and how they fit into the learning-to-read process. There are lists of records and children's literature. This short, concise, and clearly presented text can be a useful resource to parents and paraprofessionals.

Spodek, Bernard. *Teaching in the Early Years.* Englewood Cliffs, N.J.: Prentice-Hall, 1978.

Spodek considers educational philosophies and practices in preschools and the early grades that reflect contemporary society and special needs, such as programs for disadvantaged children. The text is an overview of a variety of subjects taught in schools today and of the different methods used.

Spodek, Bernard (ed.). *Teaching Practices: Reexamining Assumptions.* Washington, D.C.: National Association for the Education of Young Children, 1977.

These essays addressed to teachers, are a selection of papers presented at the June 30–July 3, 1976, Bicentennial Conference on Early Childhood Education. The topics range from the theoretical underpinnings of learning activities in nursery schools to the need to harness the pro-social impact of television. The focus throughout is a humanistic one, toward expanding learning possibilities and improving the child's environment in the present and the future. Appropriately, the last essay is entitled "A Code of Ethics: The Hallmark of a Profession."

Tiedt, Sidney W., and Tiedt, Iris M. *The Elementary Teacher's Complete Ideas Handbook.* Englewood Cliffs, N.J.: Prentice-Hall, 1980.

The Tiedts have filled this handbook with delightful ideas for making learning interesting and exciting for the elementary school child. The techniques presented are easily understood. The chapter called "Improving the Reading Program" supplies important information and ideas for any adult interested in enriching the early reading experience of a child.

Todd, Vivian Edminston, and Helen Hefferman. *The Years Before School: Guiding Preschool Children,* 3rd ed. New York: Macmillan, 1977.

This text has been a popular and useful one. It aims for

completeness in describing curriculum and practices in preschools for those considering entering the field. Bibliographies at the end of each chapter are not only clearly annotated but contain almost all the relevant references of the early 1970s and 1960s. As such, this text well serves a researcher's interests.

Traub, Nina, with Frances Bloom. *Recipe for Reading: A Proven Program for Reading, Writing and Spelling.* New York: Walker, 1977.

Beginning with specific letter sounds and going on to more complex units, this step-by-step program by a nationally recognized and successful reading teacher can equip even inexperienced adults to be effective tutors. There are daily lesson plans, specific teaching techniques, remedial techniques for dyslexic children, instruction for correct letter formation, games and activities, and tests to review previous material.

Walker, Hill M. *The Acting-Out Child. Coping with Classroom Disruption.* Boston: Allyn & Bacon, 1980.

This book spells out numerous of effective techniques for easing the learning and behavior problems of the disruptive child as well as for managing the overall classroom environment in a positive manner.

Weber, Evelyn. *Early Childhood Education: Perspectives on Change.* Belmont, Ca.: C. A. Jones, 1970.

New developments in the field of early childhood education are discussed with consideration of constants that cannot be ignored. The author reviews the philosophies from Froebel to Dewey; child psychology from Gesell to Piaget; and the impact of the outside environment on child learning theories. Value objectives in learning are uniqueness, creativity, and relevance. The author after a year of intensive research and observation arrived at strong convictions about many learning centers. In her view, inner growth results from an individual's strength to solve his or her own problems. Bank Street School (New York City) and the Infant School in England are given as examples where learning can be made into an exciting and meaningful procedure.

Weber, Evelyn. *The Kindergarten: Its Encounter with Educational Thought in America.* New York: Teachers College Press, 1971.

Weber has written an in-depth presentation and critique of kindergarten, from its idealistic beginning with Froebel in Germany to its migration and practical adaptation to changing American society. The historical account of the kindergarten movement brings to life the important American educators, including Wheelock, Peabody, Kilpatrik, and Dewey. Weber explains their philosophies in relation to different kindergarten curricula.

Weikart, D. P., J. T. Bond, and J. T. McNeil. *The Ypsilanti Perry Preschool Project: Preschool Years and Longitudinal Results Through Fourth Grade.* Ypsilanti, Mich.: High/Scope Press. 1978.

The well-known study of the long-term effects of preschool education on a group of "high-risk" disadvantaged children in Ypsilanti, Michigan, is shown to be one of the definitive educational research projects of recent times. This monograph, second in a series on the Perry Project, analyzes data obtained on the experimental and control groups as they progressed through fourth grade. Here is solid evidence, grounded in a rigorous methodological framework, that preschool did indeed make a difference for children. Its impact on their school achievement and grade placement has been positive and sustained.

Winsor, Charlotte B. (ed.). *The World of Words: Writings by Bank Street College Faculty.* New York: Bank Street College of Education, 1980.

This collection of papers by leaders in the field serves to bring together the many facets of experiences by which children develop as full members of our culture and community. The focus is on books and storytelling as vital teaching tools. The articles also cover recent research, as well as classroom programs in early reading.

Yamamoto, Kaoru, (ed.). *Children in Time and Space.* New York: Teachers College Press, 1979.

The author examines the development of children's understandings of time and space and explores the implications for teaching and learning in school.

Yeomans, Edward. *The Shady Hill School: The First Fifty Years.* Lincoln, Neb.: Windflower Press, 1979.

This is another fascinating story of the founding and development of an unusual school—one of the giants of progressive education—still going strong in Cambridge, Mass. A group of Harvard professors, scholars in their own fields, worked together to educate their children by adapting their subjects to young children.

Zaichkowsky, Leonard D., Linda B. Zaichkowsky, and Thomas J. Martinek. *Growth and Development: The Child and Physical Activity.* St. Louis: Mosby, 1980.

This book is designed for undergraduate and graduate students who are preparing for a career in physical education as well as those in the teaching, recreation, and health professions. The authors give a new dimension to the teaching of motor development by showing human development as a process in which psychomotor, cognitive, and affective or social-psychological factors interact during a life span.

Zaslavsky, Claudia. *Preparing Young Children for Math: A Book of Games.* New York: Schocken, 1979.

The author tells quite specifically how to use simple materials and games as well as everyday home and school situations to heighten children's awareness of and responsiveness to math. The book is addressed, in plain language, to teachers, parents, and other caregivers of young children over two years of age. It focuses on mathematical aspects of traditional games, those from other cultures, and specially devised games. These range in complexity from simple manipulation and sensory discrimination to abstract mathematical operations. The eighty-five illustrations contribute to the immediacy and clarity of the math aspect of objects and games.

10
Literature

CATCH 'EM IN THE CRADLE:
LEARNING TO LOVE LITERATURE

Bernice E. Cullinan

In all the research on reading failure, one fact stands out: there is *no* association between reading and pleasure. This is one reason, among others, that many children do not have a strong desire to learn to read, and, of those who do learn, many do not choose to read. It is ironic that in a country that produces the world's most beautiful and engaging books for children we have some who do not wish to share the abundance.

Perhaps part of the fault lies in the way in which we associate reading with work. This work-related concept of reading is evident in the way that reading is taught and practiced throughout much of a child's schooling. Children asked to fill in work sheet after work sheet in the guise of "learning to read" or developing reading skills experience little joy from literature. For many children we make reading a chore with our work-mentality approach; it is not fun, it is plain drudgery to be drilled on long vowel sounds and consonant blends. The road to reading is laborious when children only learn skills without ever reading good stories.

The resources cited in this section do not call for the elimination of teaching reading skills, but they do not ask us to balance the scales a bit in a child's reading experience. The greatest amount of reading a child does should be from the sort of trade books listed in this section. When the daily reading-aloud sessions become a time of pleasure, children build a love of story from their earliest days.

The wealth of literature for children is offered as the real reason to read. Parents and other caregivers can forge the connection between reading and pleasure if they share with children some of these treasures. The professional and popular books cited here lead to good books for children. Many not only list good books, but they tell you how to find other good books on your own and how to use them with children. Children need to discover that learning to read is worth the effort; good books lead them to laughter—and tears—and other worthwhile experiences. We cannot turn children into avid readers when what they find in print is unlively and joyless. The promise that learning to read will someday enrich their lives is an empty promise for children; they must be nurtured every day with alluring stories of magic and irresistible charm.

The most important gift we can give children is the gift of reading for pleasure. It is given to them primarily by reading aloud; stories read aloud by an enthusiastic reader endow the child listener with a love of stories. This love of story paves the way for reading alone and establishes early the reason to read.

Children who have stories read aloud to them often pick favorites that they want read time and time again. The adult who says "Oh, no, not that one again" is the only one who tires of repetition. Children thrive on it and soon take the words of the story for their own. The repetition is a replay of a happy experience. Children possess their favorite books in more than one way; they carry them around, pore over them, say bits and pieces of the story until they come close to approximating the words in the book and gradually can tell the story almost verbatim. This reading-like behavior is a critical step in learning to read. When children "read" and "reread" their own version of a favorite story, it leads to a stage called emergent reading and often is the beginning of authentic steps to literacy.

Reading can develop naturally if it is nurtured by a supportive environment. Children who teach themselves to read do have role models; they have people who read to them and answer their questions about "What does this say?"

Reading aloud to infants and toddlers actually means repeating the nursery rhymes and lullabies sung and recited from memory or recognized in recent collections. These draw children to the magic of oral language while teaching them its rhythm and intonation. When children are about a year old, they attend to the colorful pictures in an illustrated Mother Goose, simple picture book, or a cloth book. Soon they want to help turn the pages and begin to label the pictures they see. The "lap method," a child snuggled comfortably in a loving adult's arms, directs attention to the book held front and center. When children correct the reader on the slightest deviation from the text, they have made the words of literature their own.

Picture books become the mainstay for reading aloud during the early childhood years. Renowned artists devote endless talent to produce books of lasting beauty. Donald Crews, Leo and Diane Dillon, Janina Domanska, Pat Hutchins, Ezra Jack Keats, Anita and Arnold Lobel, and Maurice Sendak are only a few of the illustrators whose work a child should know.

Poetry is the spontaneous language of childhood. The easy rhythm of lilting verse follows naturally from a full measure of Mother Goose to delight the child's ear. David McCord, Aileen Fisher, Karla Kuskin, Myra Cohn Livingston, and Mary Ann Hoberman are poets whose work children should know and learn to love. Favorite verses read over and over are committed to memory voluntarily and are drawn upon to brighten a moment for years to come.

Wordless books in which the entire story is told through illustration bridge the gap for the reader who does not know how to read print. Mercer Mayer, John Goodall, Pat Hutchins, and Paula Winter create the magic of story through ingenious art. Children who tell their own versions of these enchanting tales are growing in their knowledge of story, and they are rehearsing language that they associate with books. Wordless books appeal to all ages; their humor and clever design have universal appeal.

Reading aloud to children produces visible evidence of the joy it brings. Giving such joy cannot help but reward the giver.

PICTURE BOOKS AND THE PUBLIC LIBRARY

Naomi Noyes

"No!"

And for the first time in his two-and-a-half years, Jahmoiaya shut a book firmly before he had heard the story to the last page. But that was not all, for he slid off my lap, moved with the book to the other end of the sofa, and proceeded to create his own story. He turned each page carefully and for each had a statement:

"Somebody knock at the door."

"Crocodile opy the door."

"Crocodile sit next to Elizabeth." and on to the very last page.

Wonder blocks my total recall. The book that precipitated this burst of creativity was *A Roundabout Turn* by Robert Henry Charles, illustrated by Leslie Brooke. A friend had mentioned it as a memorable childhood favorite, but said later she had not meant for me to read it to such a little child. (This is the tale of a British toad who sets out to make sure the world is round, as he has heard. By chance he gets on a roundabout at the fair, after which he staggers dizzily home to the bosom of his loving wife, his curiosity considerably dimmed.)

At this time, our reading relationship was only two or three weeks old, but it was passionate. It began when Jahmoiaya came to visit and announced proudly, "I Spiderman." As a children's librarian I could not let this go unchallenged and brought home Gerald McDermott's *Anansi the Spider*, especially fitting because my friend's mother was born in Jamaica. We read it first on a hot August night when the three of us had taken refuge on the apartment house roof. And that night there was an early rising full moon! How wonderful it was to point to it at just the right time in the story: "What is this? A great globe of light? O mysterious and beautiful, I shall give this to my son, . . . to the son who rescued me."

Such early reading experiences are sheer delight. They can begin with the infant stretched across a grandparent's lap listening to the cadence of a voice reading nursery rhymes, go on to Jahmoiaya's age, and on and beyond to the time when a child learns to read. Reading aloud is a real pleasure throughout life since it fosters intimacy and sharing in addition to giving added dimension to the printed page.

The source for all this pleasure is so obvious that surprisingly enough it is often overlooked. New parents may be familiar with the public library from their student days and not think of it in terms of picture books for little children. They may rely instead on the sometimes more easily available mass market books displayed at the supermarket check-out. With a few exceptions, these books, so similar in format and style of illustration, become monotonous and eventually unappealing both to the child looking and listening and to the adult reading them aloud. In these inflationary times, the cost of any noticeable number of quality picture books becomes prohibitive, although their place as gifts for a child's home library should always be remembered.

Even a small public library offers a wide variety of books markedly different in size, style of illustration, and, most significantly, in theme. The well-illustrated picture book is a child's first introduction to art and, as such, its significance must not be underestimated. Good picture books present a wide range of themes, those from the past as well as those reflecting the present and the familiar. Brian Wildsmith and Paul Galdone take us back to Aesop, and the child who sees Walter Crane's *Baby's Own Aesop* is blessed indeed. Beginning with the assumption that the illustrator's art is good, the decision as to what a child will like should be left to him. Jahmoiaya taught me that lesson. Professionally, I would never have believed that a child of two-and-a-half would respond so completely to Gerald McDermott's bold graphics!

The advent of picture books presenting individual fairy tales widens the audience for these links to the past. Philosophy, psychology, and preparation for life are in them, and by collecting them, Perrault, Grimm, and Asbjornsen have preserved the roots of Western civilization down to the present day. These furnish a child's mind with the human wisdom and traditions written down two or three hundred years ago but going all the way back to the Middle Ages and beyond.

The latter part of the nineteenth century saw children's books released from the chains of didacticism and piety. When Randolph Caldecott and Leslie Brooke came on the scene with some of the earliest examples of picture books, the delight and humor of their work together with their skill as artists created a world of abiding pleasure. A child familiar with Caldecott, probably now to be found only in public libraries, is prepared to picture Jane Austen's world in his or her mind. Even if a child never reads Jane Austen, think of the wonderful images there! And then there is Beatrix Potter, whose little books so right for lap reading are familiar to and loved by a good four generations.

Some will say these worlds are no longer relevant, and it is true that we are separated from them by time and inevitable social change. Once again, though, consider letting the child decide, whatever his or her world. Programming children is to be avoided because it deprives them of the right of choice and, most of all, of breadth of vision and imagination.

Although we seem to be on the brink of another didactic age whose presence is making itself felt even in children's picture books explaining the world and its problems to the very young, they are a significant part of the children's reading background for they do represent the present-day world, the world in which they live. Such books do need to be judiciously mixed with those inspired by the past. Identification with the familiar is a comforting experience, and books depicting it may well be a larger part of the reading experience. But it is the mixture that breeds that kind of excitement that will promote early reading skills and, one can surely hope, lifelong pleasure in reading.

In addition to the books themselves, the public library provides other resources promoting reading with young children. Chief among them can be the librarian, hopefully one trained in children's services but certainly one interested in children and their books. It is the librarian who often chooses the books in the collection, who reads them, who observes their use, and who can provide informed advice and suggestions. One can also meet in the library other adults who share books with young children and share ideas and experiences with them. Programs for preschool children are burgeoning as the significance and needs of that age group are becoming more recognized. Toddler programs in particular are on the rise and are rewarding in spite of the careful preparation they require. Preschool programs are a regular part of life in many libraries, and often add finger plays and simple crafts to the reading of picture books. Films and filmstrips for preschoolers are possibly the form of programming easiest for the library staff. However, with our current and real concern for the great drop in reading skills a watchful eye should be kept on the consistent use of books with young children. Today when even babies watch television, films and filmstrips at the library generally do not provide a different or mind-expanding experience.

Books can provide memorable experiences. *Anansi*, read over and over to Jahmoiaya (even on one occasion twice before seven in the morning), was enough a part of his consciousness that when he moved to Florida and we could talk only on the telephone, he could still say, "AntiNoyes, you read me my *'nansi?'*"

READING BEGINS AT HOME

Nancy Larrick

Teachers of young children often comment, "I can always spot the children who have been read to. They come in full of talk. They are eager to read because they have learned that books and reading bring delight."

The first four years of a child's life have been called the peak language-learning years. This is the time when children learn most easily. How much they learn and how successfully they respond will depend upon the opportunities provided by the older, more experienced members of their family: their parents primarily, but also grandparents, older siblings, and caregivers.

Yet few adults seem to realize that a baby's experience with language in the first months and years will strongly affect his or her skill in speaking, listening, reading, and writing at school. It is in the preschool years that children must acquire the skills basic to reading. It is in this period that they develop eagerness to read, provided they can handle words easily and know that books and reading bring pleasure.

Children who have not been encouraged to talk and question, who have had no experience with storytelling and books, either hearing them read aloud or exploring their illustrations, may be language cripples when they enter school.

They may lack the vocabulary and the confidence for simple conversation. Often they are so insecure that they avoid the risk of asking questions, expressing independent ideas, or exploring the printed page. These handicaps begin at home.

There are three important ways in which families can help their children prepare for reading:

1. By promoting fluency in the use of oral language
2. By building interest in reading printed language
3. By providing rich experiences that will broaden the child's vocabulary and background of understanding

Oral language is the foundation for reading and writing. And experience with oral language can begin as soon as the baby is born. The soothing songs and gentle talk of parents should be part of an infant's life right from the start. It can be a good-morning song to start the day, a lullaby at bedtime, or spontaneous commentary when the baby is being bathed and dressed. This is the time when the parent can introduce nursery rhymes and songs. Many of the old Mother Goose rhymes fit easily into the small child's routine: "Rub-a-dub-dub" while having a bath, for example, and "One, two, buckle my shoe" when being dressed.

Many of the old songs suggest activities the baby can take part in—bouncing to the tune of a bouncy song, for example, and later skipping to the rhythm of a skipping song.

With "Pat-a-cake" and "This little pig went to market," the baby can take part even before he or she can join in the words. It will not be long until the baby will be saying an occasional word, then part of a line or repeated phrase. Finally, the three-year-old will be able to say the whole rhyme simply from pleasure in repeating what has been heard so many times.

The simple events of the day can be the start of a friendly conversation that will add to the young child's vocabulary and understanding: talk about foods as they are being prepared and served, talk about pets and people in the household, talk about the weather and how it changes from day to day, talk about such simple games as "peek-a-boo" for the youngest or the way to fly a kite for an older child.

When taking children for a walk, parents can comment on situations of interest: the old man riding a bicycle, the cat dashing across the yard, the boy carrying a bundle of newspapers. Soon the child will note people and situations to comment on.

Experience with printed language is a natural partner to experience with oral language. In the kitchen there may be labels on boxes and cans. On the street there are traffic signs. On television words may be pronounced as they appear on the screen. With a little help, children pick up the sound of each word and relate it to the printed word.

In the newspaper children can find pictures to talk about and then words that they can identify.

The well-illustrated children's book gives many opportunities for listening to oral language, finding clues in the pictures, talking about pictures and story, and later relating the sound of words to the printed words.

At first the experienced reader will have to take the lead in noting details and relating words to pictures for the child. But with practice even the six-month-old infant is capable of identifying stories by the picture and of pointing out the biggest bear. In a few more months such a child will be able to use words for identification of pictures.

Reading aloud in the family is probably the most valuable aid to children's reading. New books can be introduced. Intriguing details in text and illustrations can be noted. Questions can be raised. Enjoyment can be shared.

New experiences add immeasurably to the child's vocabulary and general understanding. Little children should have a chance to explore their neighborhood, to visit the market, the post office, the public library. City children need to visit the country, and country children need to see something of the city. All will revel in a visit to the airport to see different kinds of planes.

Think of the conversation such experiences could generate! Think of the new vocabulary! The concepts, the reasoning, the questioning! Possibly the follow-up reading that would add another dimension to the whole experience!

Parents must realize that reading is a two-way process with the reader bringing his or her experience to extend the meaning of the printed page. It is in the family that children have the greatest opportunity to build the background of information and experience that will make reading appealing and satisfactory. As one expert has said, "The more we know before we read, the more we know after we read."

POETRY AND YOUNG CHILDREN

Claudia Lewis

Poetry—it is the most natural way to begin our storytelling, language play, or reading aloud with our young children. Don't we all find ourselves chanting, "This little pig went to market, this little pig stayed home . . ." as we play with our babies? We do it more or less instinctively because we ourselves heard the chant when young and it comes so naturally.

"Natural" is the keyword here. Rhythmic movement, chanting, and repetition—these are all one for the infant and toddler. We comfort babies by rocking them and singing to them; and they, as they begin to talk and walk and play, move into our world in their own rhythmic way, accompanying their bounces and jumps with sounds. They chant over and over words that match their movements—"bingo, bango, bingo, bango" a two-year-old sings out, pounding with a toy hammer.

We know all this well, of course, and perhaps without analyzing just why we have done it, we have kept Mother Goose alive for centuries, repeating the clear-cut lines and catchy words to our very youngest, who beg to hear the verses again and again. No matter that the words do not always make sense to the child or to us, the sense is in the ear appeal of the sounds, the brisk accents, the lively run of the lines.

"But are these Mother Goose rhymes poetry?" the reader may ask, thinking of "The Daffodils" by Wordsworth and Whitman's "O Captain! My Captain!" Yes, they are poetry, and perhaps the whole trouble with "poetry" can be traced to a misconception about the term. That there has been trouble is clear, or there would not be so many adults who shudder at the word, remembering uncomfortably the poems forced upon them in their early school days—poems without either relevance to child life or the magical sounds that can be heard and enjoyed by children.

Poetry is for enjoyment, and the way to begin is simply with the age-old play chants such as "This little pig" or "Pat-a-cake, pat-a-cake," moving on to Mother Goose and any other playful (or serious) rhymes, poems, chants that the adult loves and wants to read or speak aloud. It might even be William Blake's two mysterious lines:

> Tyger Tyger, burning bright
> In the forests of the night;

Poetry lies there waiting in some of the best-loved picture books, too. The whole quiet bedtime story, *Goodnight Moon* by Margaret Wise Brown is actually a poem. So is *May I Bring A Friend?* by Beatrice Schenk de Regniers and *"I Can't," Said the Ant* by Polly Cameron, a favorite of five-year-olds. Others can easily be discovered among the picture books.

The poetry books recommended here have been chosen with several criteria in mind: they invite browsing and choosing; they avoid the intimidating long nineteenth-century poems that can indeed still be loved by adults and older children but could only turn away the six-year-olds and their younger brothers and sisters; and among them are the many new voices of today's poets who are experimenting with poetic shapes and sounds and often writing without rhyme. Young children can understand this rhymeless poetry because they themselves create poems or chants that are full of rhythm and form but have no emphasis on rhyme. For instance, three-year-old Bobby running exuberantly around a table chants:

> One Bobby outside
> One Bobby inside
> One Bobby outside
> One Bobby inside
> Bob-bee, Bob-bee
> Bob-bee, Bob-bee

And a five-year-old girl, painting a picture with flowers and trees in it sings as she paints:

> Flowers are growing in springtime,
> It's springtime, it's springtime,
> Springtime is here.

At about age six or seven, when children often want to start writing their own poems, the easy thing for them to do is to make up rhyming, funny jingles. After all, they hear these a great deal every day in the commercials on television, and most of them are familiar with Mother Goose. Certainly there is nothing wrong with their beginning in this way, but sticking too closely to the need to rhyme can lead to trouble, as all who practice the craft of poetry know well. Better no rhyme than a forced rhyme. Children can appreciate the rhythmic flow, the poetic images, and the quality of perception that are caught in unrhymed poems such as Langston Hughes' well known "April Rain Song" (found in many anthologies), with its description of "the little sleep-song" the rain plays on the roof at night; or in Lilian Moore's "New Sounds" (in *Little Raccoon and Poems from the Woods*), about the dry leaves that talk in "hoarse whispers."

Perception so often is the life of a poem, or perhaps I should say "new perception," the sudden discovery of likenesses. Young children are themselves constantly making these discoveries, and for this reason they have often been called natural poets. A three-year-old notices that "skywriting is fuzzy like a kitten." Another observes that "jello is like rubber," while a five-year-old tells us that in the springtime you feel all light inside, "like a green snowflake."

Thus, it is up to us to take the cue from children themselves. Read to them, or speak from memory, at any time of day the poems that seem to match their own perceiving and their own rhythmic and rhyming play—match it, and carry it a little further. Often we will find that children will want to listen to those poems that we ourselves obviously find very appealing, no matter whether they are new or old, for adults or for children. Of course it is possible to put a record on and let children hear the voices of poets or accomplished readers. This is a valuable experience to have, but infinitely more effective and more loved is our own reading, our communication of our own pleasure in poetry.

BIBLIOGRAPHY

American Library Association. Association for Library Service to Children. *Opening Doors for Preschool Children and Their Parents*, 2nd ed. Chicago: The Association, 1981.

Compiled by librarians working with preschool children, this comprehensive bibliography is an invaluable guide to all concerned with young children. Against a background of information on parenting, films, puppetry, and preschool play, books for children are grouped according to picture books, wordless books, participation books, ABC books, Mother Goose, concept books, as well as those dealing with special needs such as adoption, death, divorce, new baby, etc. There is also a useful section on nonprint materials, such as films, filmstrips, recordings, and toys.

American Library Association. Association for Library Service to Children. *Programming for Very Young Children*. Chicago: The Association, 1980.

First in a series of pamphlets on library service to children, this one focuses on the how, why, and what of programming for preschool groups. The techniques described would be helpful to day-care teachers, hospital workers, and volunteers interested in providing story-centered activities for this age group. A good reading list for adults is included.

American Library Association. Association for Library Service to Children. *Selecting Materials for Children with Special Needs*. Chicago: The Association, 1980.

Though directed to librarians, this useful reference pamphlet is equally suitable for parents and teachers. Of particular value is the clearly designed chart defining six broad categories of special-needs children. It summarizes the general characteristics of each group and sets forth guidelines for evaluating materials to meet their needs.

Applebee, Arthur. *The Child's Concept of Story*. Chicago: University of Chicago Press, 1978.

Applebee has written a scholarly presentation of the developmental stages in children's understanding of stories from age two to seventeen. Results of a research study based on Piaget's theories of child development and James Britton's concept of language development are provided. The volume is required reading for those interested in children's responses to literature.

Association for Childhood Education International. *Bibliography of Books for Children*. Washington, D.C.: The Association, 1980.

Since its first edition in 1937, this book has been a valuable guide to quality children's literature. This updated version includes new titles and over 1,500 annotated entries with major awards noted. In addition, there is an expanded reference section.

Bader, Barbara. *American Picturebooks from Noah's Ark to the Beast Within*. New York: Macmillan, 1976.

This large and handsome volume is a lavishly illustrated survey of the development of picture books in the United States from colonial times to the present. Over 600 illustrations present examples of picture books representing major historical trends and the work of significant illustrators, including Wanda Gag, Roger Duvoisin, Marcia Brown, and Maurice Sendak. The effects of social and technological change as well as the influence of comic strips and motion pictures are discussed. There is an extensive bibliography.

Baker, Augusta, and Ellin Greene. *Storytelling: Art and Technique*. New York: Bowker, 1977.

As a comprehensive manual for contemporary storytellers, the book explores all aspects of the art—the history of storytelling, its purpose, as well as the selection, preparation, and presentation of material. Special features include a section on telling stories to children with special needs, a practical chapter on the planning of story hours, and a glossary of terms and definitions.

Baskin, Barbara H., and Karen Harris. *Books for the Gifted Child*. New York: Bowker, 1980.

The authors describe the gifted in society, their identification, and intellectual aspects of the reading experience. They also develop criteria for books that are intellectually demanding and give annotations for about 150 books. These are based on principles of literary criticism and emphasize the reader's cognitive development.

Baskin, Barbara H., and Karen H. Harris. *Notes from a Different Drummer: A Guide to Juvenile Fiction Portraying the Handicapped*. New York: Bowker, 1977.

In this excellent statement of criteria for selecting books portraying the handicapped the reader will find high-quality literary analyses in addition to the evaluation of the portrayal of the handicapped.

Bauer, Caroline Feller. *Handbook for Storytellers*. Chicago: American Library Association, 1977.

This is a how-to book designed to assist the storyteller in the effective use of the varied ways of presenting stories to an audience. The author includes suggestions for using film, music, crafts, finger plays, chalkboard stories, fold-and-cut stories, and other unique ways of presenting stories.

Bettelheim, Bruno. *The Uses of Enchantment: The Meaning and Importance of Fairy Tales*. New York: Knopf, 1976.

This scholarly work discusses folk and fairy tales from the viewpoint of a Freudian psychologist, making a strong case for the inclusion of such tales as part of every child's cultural experience. Folktale characters and situations are seen as providing symbols through which children may vicariously overcome such developmental challenges as Oedipal and sibling rivalry and their own awareness that "they are not always good." Although he writes of "overcoming infancy with the help of fantasy," Bettelheim is concerned with fantasy in folklore, not in modern literary fairy tales or fantasies. About two dozen folktales or folktale themes are analyzed in detail in this book.

Bingham, Jane, and Grayce Scholt. *Fifteen Centuries of Children's Literature: An Annotated Chronology of British and American Works in Historical Context.* Westport, Ct.: Greenwood Press, 1980.

A chronological annotated bibliography of significant work written for or appropriated by British and American children, this volume is a valuable tool for historical research. Each historical period is briefly described and attitudes toward children portrayed. These serve as a backdrop for the listings of books.

Butler, Dorothy. *Babies Need Books.* New York: Atheneum, 1980.

Although directed to parents, the practicality and scope of content suggest this as a basic title for the professional reference shelf. The initial chapter persuasively argues the case for books in every child's life; succeeding chapters, organized according to stages of development from infancy to age six, suggest titles appropriate to the characteristics of each age. Included are annotated lists of recommended books.

Butler, Dorothy. *Cushla and Her Books.* Boston: Horn Book, 1980.

The book documents the role of literature in transforming a severely handicapped baby into a competent young child. An intensely moving and compassionate study, it is a valuable resource for professionals and parents alike.

Cameron, Eleanor. *The Green and Burning Tree: On the Writing and Enjoyment of Children's Books.* Boston: Little, Brown, 1969.

This is a collection of critical essays about children's literature written by an author and critic with great vision. She discusses style, characterization, a sense of place, and a sense of reality found in her own books and those of other writers.

Carlson, Bernice Wells. *Listen! And Help Tell the Story.* Nashville: Abingdon, 1965.

Wells has compiled a delightful collection of easy participation stories and related activities. She includes finger plays, action verses and stories, and poems and stories with sound effects. While especially good for beginners, more experienced storytellers will also find this book useful.

Chambers, Aidan. *Introducing Books to Children*. London: Heinemann Educational Books, 1977.

The book was written for those people who want to make children become avid, willing, enthusiastic readers. It takes a straightforward look at ideas, methods, and approaches for bringing children and books together.

Champlin, John, and Connie Champlin. *Books, Puppets and the Mentally Retarded Student*. Omaha: Special Literature Press, 1981.

For the teacher working with the educable mentally retarded child, this is a useful guide that suggests a variety of ways for providing literature experiences, including rhyme and verse, stories, and puppets. Although designed for use with the child identified as delayed, the authors provide ideas for working with all young children.

Children's Book Council. *Children's Books: Awards and Prizes*. New York: The Council, 1981.

This is a compilation of all national and international awards for children's books. Books cited for each award are listed by the year the award was given. It is a valuable guide for locating outstanding books.

Children's Book Council. *Children's Choices for 1982*. New York: The Council, 1982.

This bibliography includes titles with annotations of 500 selected children's trade books published the previous year. It is a most useful list for teachers, parents, and all concerned with children's literature and can be obtained free of charge by sending a self-addressed stamped envelope to the Council.

Cianciolo, Patricia (ed.). *Picture Books for Children*, 2nd ed. Chicago: American Library Association, 1981.

The introduction provides a full discussion of the variety and use of current picture books as well as criteria for evaluating them. There are four categories: Me and My Family, Other

People, The World I Live In, and The Imaginative World, each of which contains annotations (with age-level indications) from picture books of fiction, nonfiction, and poetry. The annotations and illustrations reflect our pluralistic world. This volume is a valuable resource with an extensive title/author/illustrator index. It is a beautifully presented book with black-and-white illustrations throughout.

Cohen, Monroe D. (ed.). *Excellent Paperbacks for Children.* Washington, D.C.: Association for Childhood Education International, 1979.

This annotated bibliography includes only titles that "met high standards in both content and format." Four developmental level designations are used—ranging from nursery through adolescence—to accommodate "the great divergence in both interests and coping abilities." A resource guide, a list of publishers, a title index, and a subject index are appended.

Cullinan, Bernice E., M. C. Karrer, and A. M. Pillar. *Literature and the Child.* New York: Harcourt Brace Jovanovich, 1981.

This comprehensive literature text, with richly filled pages of professional information and practical teaching suggestions, illustrates the pleasure and fulfillment that result when teachers share good books with children. Part I, The Child, discusses a child's interaction with various kinds of books at different developmental stages, reviews the evolution of children's literature, and describes the prominent role it plays in language development. Part II, The Books, includes all genres with full discussions and implications for each. Part III, The Child and the Books, treats current issues and concerns, including the needs of the disabled and the gifted and talented, and offers suggestions for literature curricula and programs.

DeWit, Dorothy. *Children's Faces Looking Up: Program Building for the Storyteller.* Chicago: American Library Association, 1979.

Those interested in bringing literature to children through the oral tradition will find this a readable and practical manual. Chapters on selecting, preparing, and modifying tales precede an excellent section of demonstration programs that include suggestions for integrating media or crafts projects with stories

when appropriate. An extensive bibliography of source materials
is appended.

Durkin, Dolores. *Children Who Read Early: Two Longitudinal Studies.*
New York: Teachers College Press, 1966.

The research studies detailed in this volume revealed the
characteristics of children who learned to read early. The role of
reading to children and providing opportunities for them to write
and handle books is clearly demonstrated.

Early Childhood Experience: A Bibliography. Garden City, N.Y.: Children's Services, Nassau Library System, 1978.

Subtitled *The Right Book for the Right Situation—for Parents,
Teachers, Librarians, and Other People,* this useful pamphlet is organized under topics touching young children: concepts, emotions, health care, physical disabilities, siblings, to name a few.
Here are listed appropriate picture books that can help children
work their way through a variety of situations.

Evans, Edmund (ed.). *The Reminiscences of Edmund Evans.* Ruari
McLean, ed. Oxford, Eng.: Oxford University Press, 1967.

This is the autobiography of Edmund Evans, the engraver
and printer of books by Kate Greenaway, Randolph Caldecott,
and other notable contributors to children's literature. It is an
example of beautiful bookmaking itself and gives personal insights into the early development of books for children.

Favat, F. Andre. *Child and Tale: The Origins of Interest.* Urbana,
Ill.: National Council of Teachers of English, 1977.

In his scholarly examination of the sources of appeal in folk
literature, Favat parallels the stages of children's development
and their characteristic ways of responding to the characteristics
of folk and fairy tales.

Fisher, Margery. *Who's Who in Children's Books: A Treasure of the
Familiar Characters of Childhood.* New York: Holt, Rinehart and
Winston, 1975.

The text is arranged alphabetically by the character's name.
The vignettes about characters and the work in which they
appear are written in a lively style.

Georgiou, Constantine. *Children and Their Literature.* Englewood Cliffs, N.J.: Prentice-Hall, 1969.

This book is designed as a reference for the professional and parent interested in children's literature. Presented within a carefully planned arrangement are an historical account of children's books; literary genres differentiating among fiction, nonfiction, poetry, and prose; approaches in criticism; analysis of books; and comprehensive bibliographies annotated and classified according to subject and age appropriateness.

Gillespie, John T., and Christine B. Gilbert (eds.). *Best Books for Children: Preschool Through the Middle Grades.* New York: Bowker, 1981.

This annotated bibliography was designed to be used as a tool for evaluating and expanding existing collections, as a guide for the preparation of bibliographies and reading lists, and as an aid for giving reading guidance to children. In addition to a subject index, there are indexes of authors and illustrators, book titles, and subjects of biographies. It is a most helpful book for all interested in a comprehensive overview of the best titles for children.

Glazer, Joan I. *Literature for Young Children.* Columbus, Oh.: Merrill, 1981.

A comprehensive guide to the field, this text shows the many ways in which children's books enrich the aims of early childhood education. Each chapter deals with development and includes an introduction to the current research, goals for teaching, books designed to support these goals, as well as summaries and suggestions for further reading. Although educators and day-care providers will find the book most useful, it will also be of interest to parents.

Greene, Ellin, and Madalynne Schoenfeld (compilers). *A Multimedia Approach to Children's Literature: A Selective List of Films, Filmstrips, and Recordings Based on Children's Books,* 3rd ed. Chicago: American Library Association, 1982.

The reader is provided with brief annotations both for the children's books cited and the audiovisual materials based on them. This is an invaluable guide for finding excellent interpretations of children's books.

Gruber, Ellen, and Carol Schwartz. *Tell It Again: An Integrated Approach to Sharing Literature with Young Children.* Atlanta: Gruber, 1981.

The authors provide a useful guide for inviting children to experience books. They suggest using "storyboxes," creative activities, and motivational ideas for subject areas centered around fifty-seven popular children's books. There are sections on how to present literature to children, the scope of children's literature, and integrating creative activities. This is a resource tool for librarians, students, media specialists, and parents.

A Guide to Subjects and Concepts in Picture Book Format, 2nd ed. Yonkers Public Library. Dobbs Ferry, N.Y.: Oceana, 1979.

Although not annotated, this is a comprehensive guide to picture books dealing with particular subjects, ideas, and themes for the preschool and early elementary school level. Divided into fifty-five main subject categories ranging from adoption to zoo, it is a useful tool for finding materials suitable for the young child.

Haviland, Virginia (ed.). *Children and Literature: Views and Reviews.* Glenview, Ill.: Scott, Foresman, 1973.

Haviland has compiled a collection of outstanding articles about the history of children's literature, the classics, writers and writing, illustrators and illustrations, folk literature and fantasy, poetry, fiction and realism, historical novels, and criticism. Included are some of the best commentary on children's books available.

Hearne, Betsy, and Marilyn Kaye (eds.). *Celebrating Children's Books: Essays on Children's Literature.* New York: Lothrop, Lee and Shepard, 1981.

This volume of essays devoted to the art of writing and publishing children's books is dedicated to Zena Sutherland, a respected reviewer, teacher, anthologist, and leader in the field. Authors, illustrators, and critics probe story, imagination, and quality in children's books.

Heins, Paul (ed.). *Crosscurrents of Criticism: Horn Book Essays, 1968–1977*. Boston: Horn Book, 1977.

Heins has put together a collection of outstanding articles on criticism of children's literature which appeared in *Horn Book* magazine. Writers discuss standards, criticism, and particular genre to develop a framework of mature critical thought.

Hopkins, Lee Bennett. *The Best of Book Bonanza*. New York: Holt, Rinehart and Winston, 1979.

In each of the articles in this selection from *Teacher* magazine Hopkins shares his enthusiasm for using books in every arena of life. A host of ideas and activities built around the books that appeal to children are described.

Huck, Charlotte S. *Children's Literature in the Elementary School*, 3rd ed. New York: Holt, Rinehart and Winston, 1979.

This volume gives a comprehensive and well-written overview of the subject, covering the historical background to children's literature and thoroughly describing books and authors in each subject area. Although the activities described are geared for classroom use, many are readily adaptable to other settings.

Johnson, Ferne (ed.). *Start Early for an Early Start: You and the Young Child*. Chicago: American Library Association, 1976.

Johnson presents a well-organized collection of articles on parent/child activities related to literature that is specifically oriented toward the needs and interests of the preschool child. Each article includes suggested activities, materials, and readings. The section on Experiencing Literature covers group programs suitable for the library setting.

Karl, Jean. *From Childhood to Childhood: Children's Books and Their Creators*. New York: John Day, 1970.

Among some of the topics discussed are Why a Children's Book?, What Children's Books?, Is It a Good Book?, and Reading a Children's Book. Karl writes that one of the greatest needs for children today is books of humor. Other kinds of books needed are those in which the ordinary person proves himself/herself to be a hero and how-to books that stimulate children's creativity and productivity. Karl explains in this book how teachers can destroy children's love of reading through their insistence on bombarding children with meaningless literal questions.

Lamme, Linda L. (ed.). *Learning to Love Literature (Preschool Through Grade 3)*. Urbana, Ill.: National Council of Teachers of English, 1981.

This is a book designed to help teachers bring children's literature into the mainstream of their curriculum. Its nine chapters combine theory and practice. Included are reproducible classroom material suitable for literature enrichment. The main goal of the techniques presented is to establish "a completely integrated curriculum with literature as its base."

Lamme, Linda L., Vivian Cox, Jane Matanzo, and Miken Olson. *Raising Readers: A Guide to Sharing Literature with Young Children.* Committee on Literature in the Elementary Language Arts, National Council of Teachers of English. New York: Walker, 1980.

This book is designed for parents. It shows them a variety of ways for insuring that their children will grow up with a love for literature, complete with practical suggestions for each age level—infant, toddler, prereaders, and beginning readers. There are also annotated lists of children's books for each stage of development plus suggestions for young children's magazines and a list of publishers of children's books. The ideas for developing good family reading habits and the use of books in the family library are constructive.

Lanes, Selma. *Down the Rabbit Hole; Adventures and Misadventures in the Realm of Children's Literature.* New York: Atheneum, 1976.

This is a "frankly idiosyncratic" collection of essays by a well-known reviewer and critic of children's literature. Kate Greenaway, Arthur Rackham, Dr. Seuss, Maurice Sendak, and Joan Walsh Anglund are among authors and illustrators for the very young that are critically reviewed. Lanes also discusses publishing for children, the phenomenon of books in series, and racial stereotyping in children's books. An annotated list of books for the very young is provided as an appendix.

Larrick, Nancy. *A Parent's Guide to Children's Reading*, 4th ed. New York: Bantam, 1975.

This inclusive guide for parents describes methods and materials to use for reading at home and suggests good books for youngsters. Readers will learn how to find and buy good books, and how to use books, films, puppets, records, and slides to create a love of literature. There are excellent suggestions about how to get children to talk about books, read on their own, and find stories, poems, and magazines that appeal to their interests. This book is a *must* for all parents of young children. It is often used as a supplement to a text in methods courses in the language arts.

Meek, Margaret, Aidan Warlow, and Griselda Barton. *The Cool Web: The Pattern of Children's Reading*. New York: Atheneum, 1978.

Stories, whether read, told, or played, are central to a child's experience and a basic instrument for making sense of the world. This collection of essays by fifty distinguished commentators on children's literature and language emphasizes the basic role of stories in children's lives.

Monson, Dianne L., and Day Ann K. McClenathan (eds.). *Developing Active Readers: Ideas for Parents, Teachers, and Librarians*. Newark, Del.: International Reading Association, 1979.

Experts in reading instruction and children's literature offer a variety of articles on book selection, using the library with children, and involving children with books and other media.

Moore, Vardine. *The Pre-School Story Hour*, 2nd ed. Metuchen, N.J.: Scarecrow Press, 1972.

The sound advice for children's librarians presenting programs to young children can be easily adopted for use by staffs in day-care centers and by any adults involved with groups of children. Topics covered include selecting books, planning programs, the storyteller, and related activities.

Morrow, Lesley Mandel. *Super Tips for Storytelling*. Dansville, N.Y.: Instructor Publications, 1981.

The art of storytelling is creatively described. Photographs and illustrations guide parents and teachers to good books and techniques for sharing these books with youngsters. The book shows how to use puppets, photographs, flannel boards, and music in record and song to help tell stories. Original stories for family fun are included.

Peterson, Carolyn Sue, and Brenny Hall. *Story Programs: A Source Book of Materials*. Metuchen, N.J.: Scarecrow Press, 1980.

The emphasis is on the planning of story programs for young children. The materials are suitable for toddlers (ages two to three), preschoolers (ages three to five), and primary-grade children (ages six to eight). The first chapter outlines sample programs, each including a balance of books, songs, finger plays, and dramatic activities, based on a particular theme and suitable for the age group specified. Succeeding chapters provide an annotated bibliography of picture books and the texts of many recommended stories and verses with detailed instructions for their presentation.

Polette, Nancy, *E Is for Everybody: A Manual Intended for Bringing Fine Picture Books into the Hands and Hearts of Children*. Metuchen, N.J.: Scarecrow Press, 1976.

This practical guide to storytelling for young children gives specific suggestions for activities based on specific children's books. Most notable is the Art and Media with Literature section, which includes information on displays, slides, puppets, papier-mâché, drawing, painting, and book making.

Rahn, Suzanne. *Children's Literature: An Annotated Bibliography of the History and Criticism*. New York: Garland, 1981.

This is a comprehensive annotated bibliography of the development of children's literature. Some of the topics covered are historical studies, genres, and authors. It is an excellent resource for the serious student of children's literature.

Rollock, Barbara. *The Black Experience in Children's Books*. New York: The New York Public Library, 1979.

The extensive listing of picture books and easy books included in this bibliography makes it especially useful as a source of books for use with all preschoolers, not only those who are black. It is a valuable tool for intercultural relations. Even more it is a source for delightful reading experiences.

Self, Frank, Nancy De Salva, and Faith Hektoen. *Resource List for Adults of Materials to Use with the Very Young Child (Up to Age Three)*. Hartford: Connecticut State Library, 1981.

This valuable annotated list of materials for young children includes cloth and board books, alphabet books, books of nursery rhymes, and picture books. There are also music books, records, and films and a list of toys ranging from the very simple homemade to the more complex commercial ones. Its brief section of parenting books is useful.

Stewig, John Warren. *Children and Literature*. Chicago: Rand McNally, 1980.

Stewig's comprehensive text focuses on how to share literature effectively with children of all ages. For those who work with children from infancy through eight years of age, the chapters on the alphabet book, picture books, poetry, and wordless picture books are up-to-date and exciting.

Stewig, John Warren, and Sam L. Sebesta (eds.). *Using Literature in the English Classroom*. Urbana, Ill.: National Council of Teachers of English, 1978.

This small paperback contains six articles that are full of practical and innovative ideas for teachers to try. Two discuss how children's vocabularies can be enhanced through trade books. Creative dramatics, the role of reading in writing, book illustrations as the key to visual and verbal literacy, and the use of trade books to facilitate children's understanding are other topics that teachers will find interesting.

Strickland, Dorothy (ed.). *Listen Children: An Anthology of Black Literature.* New York: Bantam, 1982.

Although this collection of prose and poetry by black writers is addressed to black children learning about their heritage, it is a collection of writings for *all* children, one that will teach them to value themselves in the process of growing up and understanding themselves. The book is arranged developmentally within affective areas of joy, pain, and self-concept. The well-written introduction by Coretta Scott King encourages reading various authors' literary works to children.

Sutherland, Zena, Dianne Monson, and May Hill Arbuthnot. *Children and Books,* 6th ed. Glenview, Ill.: Scott, Foresman, 1981.

This is a basic comprehensive text for librarians and teachers. Genre divisions with groupings by authors are used to present outstanding books.

Sutton-Smith, Brian. *Folkstories of Children.* Philadelphia: University of Pennsylvania Press, 1980.

The author presents a unique collection of stories told by children, naturally and without adult direction. The text is designed to help teachers appreciate the importance of storytelling for children's language awareness and to guide them in using storytelling as a tool for curriculum development.

Tucker, Nicholas. *The Child and the Book: A Psychological and Literary Exploration.* New York: Cambridge University Press, 1981.

Tucker presents a scholarly examination of the developmental stages of children and books that appeal at each stage. Child development and psychology undergird the literary analyses and the basis of books' appeal to children.

Poetry and Verse

Adoff, Arnold. *Make a Circle, Keep Us In: Poems for a Good Day.* Illustrated by Ronald Himler. New York: Delacorte, 1975.

Short poems about family living are presented in an imaginative format. The words are arranged among the lively black-

and-white pictures in ways that suggest to the reader how to accent their rhythms and bring out their meanings.

Brown, Marc. *Finger Rhymes.* New York: Dutton, 1980.

Parents, teachers, and librarians will enjoy this easy-to-learn collection of fourteen, familiar finger-play rhymes. The illustrations and the picture book format make this book especially well suited for both individual and group use.

Cromwell, Liz, and Dixie Hibner. *Finger Frolics: Fingerplays for Young Children.* Livonia, Mich.: Partner Press, 1976.

Hundreds of finger plays are organized in a subject-oriented format, including such topics as seasons, holidays, counting, nursery rhymes, activity verses, animals, community helpers, and more. A brief introduction explains the educational as well as recreational value of finger-play activity for the preschool child.

Fisher, Aileen. *Cricket in a Thicket.* Illustrated by Feodor Rojankovsky. New York: Scribner, 1963.

These poems about nature and the small creatures of the outdoors are short and fun to read for their sounds. Even the headings for the sections have an appeal: for example, Six Legs and Eight, Sunflowers High and Pumpkins Low. Black-and-white drawings by an outstanding illustrator enliven the pages.

Geismer, Barbara Peck and Antoinette Brown Suter. *Very Young Verses.* Illustrated by Mildred Bronson. Boston: Houghton Mifflin, 1945.

Organized under a variety of topics of appeal to the younger child, this collection will be useful in group situations as well as at home. Although published in 1945, this book remains a valuable tool.

Hannum, Sara, and Gwendolyn E. Reed (compilers). *Lean Out the Window: An Anthology of Modern Poetry.* Decorations by Ragna Tischler. New York: Atheneum, 1965.

James Joyce, Robert Frost, Elinor Wylie, Gwendolyn Brooks, e.e. cummings, and William Carlos Williams are some of the poets represented. Many of the poems could be read to five- and six-year-olds; others can wait for the years ahead. Both rhymed and unrhymed poems are included. It is a useful volume for introducing children to the idea that poetry does not always have to rhyme.

Hoberman, Mary Ann. *A Little Book of Little Beasts.* Illustrations by Peter Parnall. New York: Simon & Schuster, 1973.

These short poems about small animals and insects are most appealing, but what makes this book unique is its distinctive layout. The poems and pictures trail across the pages, if necessary, to make the shape of the poem match its content. For instance, we see the mole running through a burrow that curves over all of a two-page spread and the next spread also in a poem that follows these contours.

Hopkins, Lee Bennett (ed.). *I Think I Saw a Snail.* Illustrations by Harold James. New York: Crown, 1969.

There are short poems for young children about child life by such well-known poets as Langston Hughes, Gwendolyn Brooks, Richard Wright, Eve Merriam, Dorothy Aldis, and Aileen Fisher. The large charcoal drawings of children of various racial backgrounds are unusually full of life and make this a distinguished poetry picture book.

Ireson, Barbara (ed.). *The Barnes Book of Nursery Verse.* Illustrated by George Adamson. New York: Barnes, 1960.

The poems, rhymes, riddles, and jingles in this large treasury are by no means just for the nursery. Here are all the ear-catching verses for young children up to ages seven or eight that one could hope to find collected in one volume. The organization is helpful, and the pages are uncrowded, inviting the eye. It is a beautifully designed book, enlivened with abundant small black-and-white drawings.

Kuskin, Karla. *Near the Window Tree: Poems and Notes.* New York: Harper & Row, 1975.

This is a book for many ages—for children who want to try their own writing as well as for younger ones who will just enjoy these short poems that so clearly reflect the special quality of Karla Kuskin.

Livingston, Myra Cohn (ed.). *Listen, Children, Listen: An Anthology of Poems for the Very Young.* Illustrated by Trina Schart Hyman. New York: Harcourt Brace Jovanovich, 1972.

All of these poems are short, filled with the rhythmic and sound qualities young children love. The size of the book, too, about 6" × 8", is appealing, and the small black-and-white drawings on almost every page add to the artistry of the volume. Two of the editor's own poems, especially loved by young children, are included.

Love, Katherine (ed.). *A Pocketful of Rhymes.* Illustrated by Henrietta Jones. New York: Crowell, 1946.

Charming poems by well-known poets about real and imaginary, personages, plants and animals, and heavenly bodies are collected here and will delight both reader and listener.

McCord, David. *One at a Time.* Illustrated by Henry B. Kane. Boston: Little, Brown, 1977.

This collection of McCord's poetry illustrates the fine work available for young children. McCord was the first winner of the National Council of Teachers of English Award for Excellence in Poetry for Children. He is considered the dean of children's poets.

Milne, A. A. *Now We Are Six.* With decorations by Ernest H. Shepard. New York: Dutton, 1927.

Some of these well-known poems can be read aloud even to the youngest children, who can enjoy their sounds if not their sense. This Milne-Shepard volume has become one of our true poetry classics for children.

Moore, Lilian. *Little Raccoon and Poems from the Woods.* Drawings by Gioia Fiammenghi. New York: McGraw-Hill, 1975.

The watercolor pages make this a beautiful picture book. The short, catchy poems are written in a way that is distinctly Moore's own.

Opie, Iona, and Peter Opie (eds.). *The Oxford Nursery Rhyme Book.* With additional illustrations by Joan Hassall. New York: Oxford University Press, 1955.

Every reader will find a favorite among the volume's 800 "rhymes and ditties," from baby games through wonders and riddles to ballads and songs. It is an inexhaustible treasury for reading aloud and child participation. Eye-catching pages are filled with small black-and-white decorative pictures between the poems, most of them from chapbooks and toy books of the eighteenth and early nineteenth centuries. All ages, including the preschool child, will enjoy the selections.

Richards, Laura E. *Tirra Lirra: Rhymes Old and New.* Boston: Little, Brown, 1955.

First published in 1902, these short poems—over a hundred of them—never go out of date because of this poet's skill and playfulness with rhymes, sounds, and rhythms. Not all of the poems are for children under six, but favorites can easily be found for reading aloud.

Ring a Ring o' Roses: Stories, Games and Fingerplays for Preschool Children. Flint, Mi.: Flint Public Library, 1979.

Finger plays old and new are illustrated in this comprehensive collection of teacher- and librarian-tested finger-play rhymes. Also included are lists of stories and folktales suitable for the preschool child and a first-line index.

Rockwell, Anne (compiler). *Gray Goose and Gander and Other Mother Goose Rhymes.* New York: Harper & Row, 1980.

The attractively designed book features colorful illustrations (by the compiler)—one to a page—executed in a flat, poster-like, child-oriented style. Selections, based upon the preferences of Rockwell's own children, feature some of the less familiar Mother Goose characters as well as the more widely known ones.

Schick, Eleanor. *City Green.* New York: Macmillan, 1974.

Each one of these short, unrhymed poems is about some aspect of city life, and each one has a full-page picture by the author to illustrate it. It is suitable for preschoolers as young as three.

Updike, John. *A Child's Calendar.* Illustrated by Nancy Ekholm Burkert. New York: Knopf, 1965.

There is a poem for each month, in verses that "trip" along in easy rhyme and rhythm, accompanied by distinguished pictures in color. Children of all ages would enjoy owning this calendar.

Watson, Clyde. *Father Fox's Pennyrhymes.* Illustrated by Wendy Watson. New York: Macmillan, 1971.

These irresistible short rhymes reflecting New England country life have the appeal of Mother Goose. There are charming little pictures, full of miniature foxes in human clothing going about their business. It is a book for preschool and elementary school children.

11
Expressive
Arts

THE ARTS

Frances W. Aronoff and Steve Yarris

Most of us are filled with awe and wonder when we experience the works of great artists. What makes an artist? What makes a person able to give us insights into universal feeling and indeed into our own emotional lives? What is so special about the artist's use of paint, of sound, of movement?

Aestheticians provide a variety of theories and models of the creative individual. But there are certain themes that appear repeatedly. The artist, they concur, is egocentric; he speaks his piece. He is apt to break established rules as he injects his feeling about the subject, the world, and himself into his creation. Finally, motivated to create, to communicate, he takes the action to do so.

Now let us focus on the young child. By his very nature, the young child is egocentric. Decisions are invariably tied to inner feelings. And the child is not a passive observer; his or her immediate response is to act. These are the very qualities identified in the artist! Obviously, the maturity and skills of the artist cannot be approached by the very young. But the challenge for educators is to nurture these qualities along with the child's academic needs.

Freedom to explore in the various media needs careful channeling if the learning is to be productive and satisfying. The structure can be the most elementary awareness of the basic elements, whatever the art, and their most direct expressive potential. The adult who becomes involved with enthusiasm, commitment, and discipline provides opportunities for the child's increased perception and, in turn, joyous and satisfying responses.

When education is properly defined as the process of intellectual and emotional growth, the role of the arts becomes clear. Because the arts are about knowing—knowing through the senses because they deal directly with the development of sensibility and because they are available to very young children in forms they can use and understand, the arts must be an integral part of education in the early years. The books noted in the bibliography of this chapter will help both parents and teachers open up the world of the arts to young children.

THE LEARNING CONNECTION: MUSIC AND MOVEMENT

Frances Webber Aronoff

Music is an eminently practical and particularly appropriate expression for the young child. One's voice, clapping hands, and tapping feet are built-in, portable sound sources. The body is the child's instrument for learning as the youngster discovers the essences of music's expressive qualities.

Education in the arts is learning that develops the senses, making one more able to perceive with discernment. It is particularly crucial to the child's search for his or her special and unique self and to learning of how he or she will deal with that self and the surrounding world. Related kinesthetic and aural experiences, as in music-movement activities, are easily tailored to the age when knowing and feeling are so very tightly intertwined. The safe character of such activities encourages spontaneity, in that emphasis is always on process rather than product.

The teacher must aim beyond the traditional goals of (1) language development from the words of songs, (2) social skills, and (3) release of energy after "serious" study. Purposeful music-movement experiences can lead directly to the child's acquisition of concepts of the elements of music. Research has verified that a basic structure of these concepts can be acquired by the very young and that indeed such a structure is essential for further musical growth. Can a parent or teacher not trained in music make this happen? Absolutely! He or she can guide a child to use, enjoy, and understand music by exploiting its learning connection with movement.

Music has its roots in movement. Observing the child's unself-conscious use of body in play, we accompany the movement with an instrumental rhythm, a song, an improvised chant. As the child moves in many different ways, we provide matching sounds. The child is always in time with the music because he or she establishes the beat! When the procedure is reversed, the music starts and the child moves accurately and appropriately, drawing on accumulated experience. These are the beginning strategies of Emile Jaques-Dalcroze (1875-1950), a Swiss musician and educator who evolved eurhythmics, strategies for constant interaction between aural awareness, movement, and improvisation.

These music-movement activities allow for subjective, spontaneous responses; at the same time, they focus on the basic concepts of the elements of music. The parent or teacher needs only to recognize the most obvious contrasts in the use of movement to begin: Is the child using lots of energy or little? Is the movement slow or fast? Is the movement the same or different in shape, in flow? Recognizing these contrasts, the adult can easily make the sound support the child's actions, eventually inspiring movement by sound. This interchange in both directions is the basis of the music learning process.

In each instance, the individual child's affective response is taken into account. Children generally act out their feelings with a gesture, a facial expression, sometimes even a verbal response. They naturally join in the singing of simple folk songs, especially if they have been involved physically as they hear the melody over and over. "Move the way the music tells you." There need be no wrong ways of moving because the song or rhythm pattern may always be adjusted to "the different drummer."

The music-movement learning connection is especially valuable in early childhood because it can be nonverbal, even preverbal, on the child's part. Parents or teachers who participate physically with enthusiasm and abandon invariably discover personal joys of music for themselves, with exciting possibilities for their own development.

VISUAL ART AND YOUNG CHILDREN

Joy L. Moser

Young children are instinctive art makers. The early swirling world of sight, sound, sense, and taste begins to be captured and understood as the child gathers and expresses his or her concepts of the universe. As we grow older, some of the ease of expression and magic seems to evaporate, but at three, four, and five anything that is imagined can be symbolized on paper or in clay. To the young child, "If I make it and name it, it is." Early art expression is not random play or making "things"—it is the serious business of establishing self through the materials of art.

Adults often stand in wonder as they view the freshness of the color, line, and form of children's art. Some are bewildered at what appears to be either chaos or abstraction. However, research over the last seventy years has documented that from the first scribble at age two, children's drawings have meaning and form. A pattern of growth is evident as paintings evolve from early lines to circles, squares, and aggregates of shape that demonstrate the evolution of a visual symbol system. These visual growth stages closely parallel those of verbal and mathematical thought articulated by Piaget. Early scribbles are dominated by a kinesthetic or "felt" sense of the world; as perception becomes more complex, the child begins to describe the seen as well as the felt world. Increasingly, there is a drive toward the concrete, and at six or seven years of age visual expression begins to focus on making it look like it "is."

This unfolding of visual expression is universal. Unlike language, we all share the same visual world. Whether children reach for a crayon in New York City or a stick in the Sahara

Desert sand, they all begin to make their mark in the same way. Though children may vary in age and method as they express and describe, all go through similar stages. From two to seven, we see a steady emergence of increasingly complex visual configurations.

Since we know there is a natural unfolding of art expression, we might ask ourselves as parents and teachers, "What is our role? Do we simply stand aside and let nature take its course, or do we play a part?"

Parents and teachers are crucial in this evolution. By our understanding of the meaning and process of visual development, we are able to provide the proper materials and learning environment at the appropriate age and stage. Very young children need large paper, big brushes, fat chalks, and materials that allow them to explore their work; manipulation is dominated by gross motor control and a kinesthetic or "felt" sense of the world. We do not give preschool children small paper, complex cutting tasks, rigid dittos, or pre-formed "smiling faces." The essential aspect of the art experience for the young child is "the act of doing," the manipulation, the gathering, the forming —gaining control rather than a neat finished product.

For the fours, fives, and sixes, the richest materials are thick tempera paint, rich moist clay, a varied supply of collage materials, and good drawing tools, such as thick markers and big chalk. Gimmicks, such as painting with straws or chocolate pudding, are unnecessary. The catalyst for a rich art experience is a sensitive parent or teacher who creates a comfortable place to work and provides the tools for a child to achieve the effect that the child is searching for.

CREATIVE DRAMA

Nellie McCaslin

Of all the arts, drama/theater is the most inclusive. The mind, body, feelings, and social relationships of the player are all involved in the experience and are of equal importance. Most parents and teachers are aware of the young child's response to drama, though it was not until the pioneering work of Winifred Ward in the 1920s that the spontaneous drama of children was given a name and a structure for use in the elementary classroom. The name, *creative dramatics*, coined by Ward, has been used ever since—though the terms, improvisation, child drama, and creative drama are preferred by some. Whatever we choose to call it, however, it may be defined as the spontaneous enactment of a story or situation, original or literary, without the use of a script.

Unlike formal theater, creative drama is not designed for an audience. When occasionally young players wish to share an improvised play with outsiders, it should be done as a demonstration or presentation of a group project, which has culminated in a script for performance. Most educators are in agreement that such programs should be kept low-key and infrequent. Older children, on the other hand, enjoy the discipline of a production and can profit from the experience.

The values of creative drama include:

1. An opportunity to use and stretch the imagination.
2. Improvement in the language arts, particularly oral communication.
3. Social growth through working cooperatively with others.
4. Greater understanding of persons different from oneself through assuming their roles.

5. Development of poise and self-confidence.
6. Appreciation of good literature through dramatizing it.
7. Additional learnings, both as specified goals or as by-products of the experience (English, math, history, etc.).
8. An introduction to the theater as an art form.
9. The pleasure that play making affords.

Some of these values will be stressed more by one instructor than another, for groups and individual children vary in interests and needs. Not all values are realized at one time or within a single semester. A good teacher will discover a way of working as well as techniques that lead to desired goals. By starting where the children are, the teacher can lead into new areas and develop abilities that have heretofore been given scant time or attention.

To have a successful experience in creative drama, certain conditions are necessary.

1. A group of no more than fifteen or twenty children.
2. A large open space rather than a stage. If a classroom is used, desks should be pushed back to allow for free movement.
3. A sound-proof room or an area removed from other classrooms. The noise level may be high at times and constant reminders to "quiet down" inhibit creativity.
4. A piano, record player, and drum.
5. A costume closet or box of garments to dress up in and stimulate the imagination.
6. Sturdy boxes and light-weight chairs.

It would be impossible to describe in so short a paper even a few selected procedures for teachers of creative dramatics classes. The following guidelines, however, will suggest directions that may be taken. The books included in the bibliography will help both beginning and experienced teachers to plan activities, evaluate results, and share our oldest art form with children. Meanwhile, the following sequence is one often followed:

1. Large physical movement—this is both a warm-up and a physical expression recommended as a beginning activity for participants of all ages.
2. Group pantomimes—these involve familiar activities such

as throwing a ball, feeding a dog, dressing, etc.; characters in action; animals.

3. Enactment of well-known and favorite stories.
4. Original stories and situations based on real or imagined events—their accomplishment is more difficult and better left to a time when teacher and children have become accustomed to working together.
5. An integrated project—a project of this nature may be developed cooperatively over a longer period. Many skills are involved.

Creative dramatics works well in combination with puppetry. Indeed, puppetry may be preferred when the playing space is small or when a class has special needs or handicapping conditions. Storytelling is another related activity that may be included as a way of presenting material or as an enrichment in itself.

Most important to remember is that the leader's primary concern is process—not product, though obviously the two are interrelated. Teachers schooled in formal theater techniques often find this a difficult concept to accept, for they see "the show" as proof of success rather than the growth and development of the young players. It is for this reason that putting on a play for an outside audience is discouraged. The teacher knows each child's interests, limitations, and needs; an audience does not. What may appear to an outside observer as a weak or limited effort may in fact represent a giant step forward for a shy boy or girl. Also, the group that has had trouble working together may achieve its greatest triumph in a cooperative effort, discounting for the time being other goals.

Drama/theater, through its inclusion of the literary, performing, and visual arts, has an important contribution to make to the lives of children. Its several components—physical, mental, emotional, social, and moral—make it unique among the arts. Most children respond to drama from earliest childhood and, if encouraged, find it a source of pleasure and profit for the rest of their lives. It has been said that if drama were to vanish overnight, it would be invented all over again tomorrow, not by adults but by children.

CHILDREN'S DANCE

Judith G. Schwartz

Children move. Children are energetic. Children are curious. All these are essential resources for learning. By channeling their movement, energy, and curiosity, one can mobilize these qualities into a structured learning experience. How? Through dance. Dance combines movement, energy, and curiosity. Moreover, it is a vehicle through which children can express feelings that help them learn about themselves and their environment.

Movement is one of the most important elements in dance. Movement alone, however, is not dance. I define dance as movement that utilizes force and takes place in space and time coupled with imagination and expression. In creative dance for children, the emphasis is placed on the developmental process of building and using a movement vocabulary to be used expressively and creatively to interpret the interest, needs, and feelings of children. The body, "the Me," is used as an instrument for discovery, exploration, interpretation, and creation. Thus, dance is the most personal of all learning as it involves the total body to develop cognitive, communicative, and expressive growth. It, therefore, contributes to the physical, intellectual, emotional, social, and artistic development of the child.

Dance included in the school curriculum is another means of learning and expressing. Dance is particularly appropriate for young children who have not yet developed verbal proficiency. The child is provided an opportunity to express his or her thoughts and feelings through nonverbal communication.

Dance, since it represents a synthesis of the arts—incorporating music, visual arts, and drama—also enables children to experience all the arts and perceive their relationship to each other.

Children in urban areas, many living in small overcrowded apartments, have little space in which to move, "to let go," to release tension. Further, the many hours most children spend passively watching television makes it imperative that youngsters be presented with space and opportunities for constructive emotional and physical outlets in a structured and controlled environment. It is important to encourage children to use large-muscle activities, but also to use movements that are relaxing. In this way youngsters become aware of their bodies in motion and at rest.

A well-rounded dance program, involving movement in time and space and using force, provides children with the physical means for developing strength, control, and coordination—all of which, it should be stressed, become lifelong assets. Through movement, young children become aware of their bodies and learn its parts and their relationship. They explore, via body movement—bending, stretching, twisting, shaking, swinging, collapsing—and locomotor movement—running, walking, leaping, jumping, hopping, skipping, galloping, sliding; and they combine two or three or more of these movements, depending on their age and capabilities, into short sequential dance phrases.

Movement takes place in space. Spatial concepts are easily learned and understood by young children as they discover the shapes their bodies can assume: the different levels in which they can move; the direction, range, and floor and air patterns they can take. Youngsters learn through the use of polarities. Placing one's body up/down, in/out, in front of/in back of, under/over, lateralities of right/left, to name a few, reinforces the learning of these concepts, which, of course, are precisely the concepts so essential in learning to read and write, to master mathematics, and to understand the use of symbols.

Rhythm and movement are inexorably intertwined. As the child moves, he experiences the elements of music, which are pulse or beat, rhythmic patterns, accent, tempo, phrasing, and dynamics. Further, to accompany specific dance movements and studies or to inspire dances, children use songs and chants, instruments, and a wide variety of music such as folk, modern, classical, and jazz. Thus, we begin to expose and introduce children to the rich variety of music as well as dance.

The concept of force in dance encourages the child to use expression, which adds emotional and intellectual color to his or her movement. These qualities of movement—heavy, light, sharp, smooth, and vibratory—can, in and of themselves, suggest dance ideas.

It is also valid to use stories and ideas initiated by the children and the teacher. Dance is so exciting because it can be inspired by so many sources—school subjects, dance fundamentals, stories, dance concerts, feelings, holidays, and, of course, the arts.

Many educators agree that knowledge is best acquired when individuals are allowed to make their own discoveries, that cognitive development occurs when emphasis is placed on activity, concrete manipulation, and self-discovery. Hence, by employing creative problem-solving techniques, children, working independently or in groups, are encouraged to find their own solutions to movement problems. As a result, many solutions are encouraged. Dance thus represents not only a learning experience for the child but, equally important, provides an ideal setting and stimulus for group interaction.

Of course, it is the teacher (parent, classroom teacher, specialist) who is the vital connection between the child and what takes place in a dance session. The teacher must find his or her own way of releasing and exposing youngsters to a myriad of dance experiences so that learning becomes exciting, stimulating, challenging, and joyful. In order to achieve these goals, the teacher must establish an open, accepting, and flexible environment in which mutual trust can prevail—an atmosphere where pupils are encouraged to share their feelings, thoughts, and knowledge and feel free to find and create new ways of expressing and learning; an environment in which limits, structures, and controls are mutually set and understood by the teacher and the students; a place where emotions can be released and dealt with in a supportive setting, thereby aiding students to understand and establish limits for themselves. In such a setting, concepts can be understood, school subjects personalized, learning reinforced, and creativity developed.

The many books listed in the bibliography contain excellent suggestions on the why, what, how, and when for the teacher of dance. The hope is that each individual will select those books that answer his or her needs and interests. Since no text can be appropriate for all situations, effective utilization of these resources implies that the teacher be flexible and open and not rigidly bound by the material. Rather, the ideas presented in the literature should serve as a jumping-off point to stimulate creativity in the teacher, who, in turn, can stimulate creativity in the students.

BIBLIOGRAPHY

Creative Arts

Allen, Janet. *Exciting Things To Do with Color*. Philadelphia: Lippincott, 1977.

This book is one in a series of Look and Make Books. Other books in the series illustrate things to make with paper, wool, and materials from nature. These do-it-yourself craft books give clear step-by-step illustrated directions. A section in the beginning called Useful Things to Know has good hints on organizing materials and using found objects. Some segments also introduce a simple activity related to a more difficult one, so that one can get a feel for the process and materials.

Bland, Jane Cooper. *The Art of the Young Child*. New York: Museum of Modern Art, 1968.

The author in short, clear descriptions explains how young children (those three to five years of age) create art and ways adults can help. The setting is the Peoples Art Center at the Museum of Modern Art, and the experiences described grew out of classes for parents and children working together. Beautiful photographs elaborate on the text.

Bos, Bev. *Don't Move the Muffin Tins*. Carmichael, Ca.: Burton Gallery, 1978.

Focus is on art activities for the young child in the age range of two to five. Simple-to-read rules for adults to follow, lists of materials, and a multitude of processes in art that are appropriate for the very young child make up the major portion of the book. Many suggestions for using materials readily available around the home make it valuable for parents and teachers. Guidance is given for those needing help in arranging the physical environment for art as well.

Brittain, W. Lambert. *Creativity, Art and the Young Child.* New York: Macmillan, 1979.

In this comprehensive report in simple language on research in young children's visual art development and expression, the emphasis is on the importance of creative activity in relation to cognitive development. The information is of value to the preschool teacher. The book's particular strength is its clear statement of how art influences other aspects of learning.

Cherry, Clare. *Creative Art for the Developing Child.* Belmont, Ca.: Fearon, 1972.

This book, derived from the personal experiences of the author as she worked with nursery school children, is presented as a guide for teachers. Its many practical suggestions for art materials, activities, physical arrangements, and adult guidance are equally applicable to day care and home practice. The reader will find it necessary to discriminate between those art experiences presented that really provide opportunities for children to be expressive and those that are merely busy work. The sections of the book on woodwork and other construction activities are especially good.

Cobb, Vicki. *Arts and Crafts You Can Eat.* New York: Harper & Row, 1974.

There are instructions for creating such artistic cuisine as mosaic salad, cheese intaglio, carved chocolate, pasta mobile, and peach-pit ring. The author tells how to make all these and more with detailed instructions and illustrations. It is written for adults with recipes that children as well as adults will enjoy.

Cohen, Elaine P., and Ruth S. Gainer. *Art: Another Language for Learning.* New York: Citation Press, 1976.

This is a thoughtful text that is replete with philosophical discussion rather than how-to recipes. Its pervasive message is the importance and serious nature of child art as a means of communication and as a medium for enhancing learning. The book is crammed full of anecdotal illustrations of the points made about children and their art. It is a must for elementary school teachers' reading lists as well as for parents of all children. The chapter devoted to the unique needs of "special"

382 Resources for Early Childhood

children is a welcome addition, infrequently found in recent texts in the field.

Cumming, Robert. *Just Look: A Book about Paintings*. New York: Scribner, 1979.

Cumming has written of the few books available to introduce children to the art of seeing paintings. A short text accompanies most of the plates (all of which are in color!) and asks appropriate questions, with the answers at the back of the book. It provides an excellent introduction to painting and would well serve as an initiation to a museum or art gallery because many of the questions could be asked of paintings in general.

Dimonstein, Geraldine. *Exploring the Arts with Children*. New York: Macmillan, 1974.

This work is most appropriate for the professional educator with prior background in the arts. It presents information about the importance of the arts in a sophisticated manner. Sections are devoted to dance and poetry as well as painting and sculpture. The text is composed primarily of anecdotal descriptions of teacher/child interaction in the elementary school. This book would be an excellent addition to graduate courses in early education. The activities are geared primarily for children ages five to twelve.

Downer, Marion. *Children in the World's Art*. New York: Lothrop, Lee & Shepard, 1977.

Downer presents an overview of art from around the world —all containing images of children. The text is aimed at older readers, but even very young children would take great pleasure in examining the paintings, etchings, drawings, and three-dimensional artworks. Parents and teachers might profitably explore the pictures and engage children in discussion of them.

Fiarotta, Phyllis. *Snips and Snails and Walnut Whales: Nature Crafts for Children*. New York: Workman, 1975.

There are over 100 projects with easy-to-follow, step-by-step instructions for making a variety of useful and decorative objects using raw materials from nature. This volume is suitable for parents and teachers to use with children of all ages.

Fiarotta, Phyllis, and Noel Fiarotta. *The You and Me Heritage Tree*. New York: Workman, 1976.

The Fiarottas have assembled a collection of craft ideas from twenty-one ethnic, national, or native groups that have settled in the United States. The activities are divided into categories such as beads, eggs, fabric, nature, paint, paper, and yarn. Each activity is presented in four parts: the drawing, the instructions, a brief history of the ethnic background, and a list of materials needed to complete the project. Some projects are simple enough for young children to do; others require more skill and are better suited to older groups. The last section gives suggestions for planning a heritage bazaar. Teachers, parents, and children will find this an excellent source for craft activities. Instructions and illustrations are clear, and the materials used are easy to obtain.

Fisher, Elaine Flory. *Aesthetic Awareness and the Child*. Itasca, Ill.: Peacock Publishers, 1978.

To enable teachers and others to help the child become an artist in his or her own right, this book regards art as a truly integrated experience of life—not merely a segmented component of the school curriculum. It deals with kindergarten through seventh grade with a special emphasis on young children. The author has developed a comprehensive approach to art curriculum design, with appropriate goals for a school art program.

Gardner, Howard. *Artful Scribbles: The Significance of Children's Drawings*. New York: Basic Books, 1980.

The stages of children's growth are examined in light of the developmental factors that influence changes in connection with children's art. Gardner, in addition, wrestles with the question of the artistic merits of child art. Since Gardner writes both as a parent and educator, this basic, informative, and carefully written text serves as a reference for either group.

Garritson, Jane S. *Childarts: Integrating Curriculum Through the Arts*. Reading, Mass.: Addison-Wesley, 1979.

This work is addressed to teachers of kindergarten through third grade, but it could be adapted for other age groups. The author capitalizes on three starting points—child interests, the art material, and a specific concept—and then builds a series of classroom experiences. Neophyte teachers should find the book especially helpful for planning, since each procedure for carrying out a visual art experience is preceded by rationale for its inclusion. The instructions are carefully delineated, and a list of vocabulary words that the child will learn are included for each activity. A good bibliography of related books for both teacher and child is a helpful addition to each experience as well. Since some of the art experiences are quite sophisticated, and require well-developed manual dexterity, the adult will have to try them before deciding on their appropriateness for his or her children.

Goffstein, M. B. *An Artist*. New York: Harper & Row, 1980.

This work contains only about 100 words and an exquisite series of watercolors depicting The Artist—his goals, his limitations, his frustrations. All this is accomplished in a manner which is readily accessible to very young children (if the text is read to them), older children, and adults alike. It is a book that speaks volumes with just a few words, shapes, and colors.

Gruber, Ellen. *Learning Can Be Fun: A Learning Center Approach to Creative Activities*. Atlanta: Gruber, 1978.

The author's how-to text bears out her title. She provides a clear, visual, motivating, easy resource guide for inexpensive projects including painting, printing, music, movement, puppets, drama, clay, papier-mâché, weaving, and cooking. It is for teachers and parents who want to incorporate creative activities into everyday experiences of young children.

Gruber, Ellen, and Verl Short. *Creative Fun for Everyone: A Learning Center Approach to Creative Activities*. Carrollton, Ga.: Southeast Educators Services, 1976.

This is a book designed to help adults offer a variety of creative activities to children. The authors encourage integrating creative activities into all aspects of the curriculum: language arts, math, science, and social studies as well as art, music, and physical education programs. Categories include painting and printing, box construction, collage, chalk and crayon, clay and papier-mâché, cooking, music and movement, puppets and drama, stitchery, weaving and cloth, wood, and rocks.

Guttman, Dena. *Teacher's Arts and Crafts Almanack*. West Nyack, N.Y.: Parker, 1978.

This collection of over 100 practical ideas is based on holidays and special events for every month and is intended to serve as natural motivators for art activities and learning center activities. The suggestions, which are supplemented by step-by-step illustrations throughout, can be used with children in kindergarten through sixth grade. The author stresses materials that are free or inexpensive and easily obtainable.

Haskell, Lendall. *Art in the Early Childhood Years*. Columbus, Oh.: Merrill, 1979.

In this collection of tried-and-true ways for arranging art experiences for children, the organization of the chapters, according to age-appropriate activities, supports the less knowledgeable reader's quest for ideas. The working philosophy set down by the author has a sound base in psychology and in practical experience. Several sections of the book are unique in the field. For example, a chapter on making art games and the parts of the appendix related to the masters and their works are well conceived for early elementary school grades.

Herberholz, Barbara. *Early Childhood Art*, 2nd ed. Dubuque, Ia.: William C. Brown, 1979.

This comprehensive text seems most appropriate for teachers of children in kindergarten and the early primary grades. A chapter on the stages in children's expression with art materials, suggestions for motivation of child art, and ideas for related activities such as museum visits makes the book particularly practical for both the practicing and prospective teacher. It is profusely illustrated with children's artwork and also children at work. The wide variety of art/craft processes included and the recipes given are excellent.

Highlights Editors. *132 Gift Crafts Kids Can Make*. Columbus, Oh.: Highlights for Children, 1981.

This volume of the Highlights Creative Craft Series contains ideas for gifts for family members, friends, or pets. The suggested materials, for the most part, can be obtained free of charge or for a small charge. To make the gifts, minimum supervision is required. The projects can be simplified or elaborated upon to match the age, skill, and creativity of the maker. The small book is a valuable classroom or home teaching tool.

Highlights Editors. *127 Anytime Crafts Kids Can Make.* Columbus, Oh.: Highlights for Children, 1981.

Another of the Highlights Creative Craft Series, this one has a variety of craft activities suited to a wide range of age and ability levels. Children enjoy the satisfaction of working independently and making varied creations, and there are ample ideas for them to do so suggested in this volume. Crafts covered include puppetry, mobiles, construction, drawing and painting, and cutting and pasting. Parents and leaders of children's groups as well as teachers will find the suggestions useful.

Jenkins, Peggy D. *Art for the Fun of It.* Englewood Cliffs, N.J.: Prentice-Hall, 1980.

This text contains numerous ideas for guiding and sparking children's creative expression with art materials. This, coupled with a concise coverage of the philosophic support for art as valuable for young children, makes the book a good reference for parents and beginning teachers. All suggestions for activities are written succinctly, making the book easy reading. Some readers may find the cartoonlike illustrations attractive and helpful in explaining the text.

Karnes, Merle B. *Creative Art for Learning.* Reston, Va.: Council for Exceptional Children, 1979.

This is an arts curriculum designed for young children. Activities are supported by suggestions for introducing and reinforcing materials. Subgoals of the curriculum include "fostering the development of concepts, skills and attitudes, enhancing self-concept, promoting curiosity and motivation to learn and developing inner controls, self-discipline, and increased attention span."

Kellogg, Rhoda. *Analyzing Children's Art.* Palo Alto, Ca.: National Press Books, 1969.

The development of children's art is traced as it reflects the mental development of children ages two to eight. Presenting the observation that every child draws his or her own personal sun (until shown the "right" way by an adult) is an example of how this book creates a new awareness for both teacher and parent about the connection between the child and his or her artwork.

Kellogg, Rhoda, et al. *The Psychology of Children's Art*. New York: Random House, 1967.

The text illustrates the development of children through their art. It starts with the scribble begun around the age of two and follows the different stages of growth in their art until the age of seven. There are beautiful color illustrations of children's art from around the world. Parents, teachers, and anyone who wishes to begin to understand the development of children and their art will find this interesting and easy to read.

Lasky, Lila, and Rose Mukerji. *Art: Basic for Young Children*. Washington, D.C.: National Association for the Education of Young Children, 1980.

The contents are based on the authors' broad experience in working with young children and with prospective teachers. The aim is to give the reader specific information about how to set the climate for and how to guide the young child's engagement in the creative process. Throughout there are well-documented statements about the value of art for the child's total development. The largest chapter describes a variety of art processes, materials, and necessary arrangements for children's participation. Sections are also devoted to the integration of visual art with the other arts as well as other curriculum areas. Photographs and drawings enhance the text and support the authors' statement, "When we value art as basic education and as a distinctive way of knowing, we can appreciate the importance for children of education through art."

Lowenfeld, Viktor, and W. Lambert Brittain. *Creative and Mental Growth*, 6th ed. New York: Macmillan, 1975.

The senior author of the text is a leader in art education who is largely responsible for the inclusion of visual arts in the school curriculum. He reviews "ages and stages" of children's art including research that further documents the educational value of this art form.

Mayesky, M., D. Neuman, and R. Wlodkowski. *Creative Activities for Young Children*. New York: Delmar, 1980.

The authors describe the various facets of child development that impinge on children's creative play. They carefully delineate interrelationships among the different types of creative responses young children are likely to make. These include experiences in arts, crafts, drama, and explorations of the environment. One section is devoted to helping teachers plan and arrange activities that will encourage creative responses.

Montgomery, Chandler. *Art for Teachers of Children*, 2nd ed. Columbus, Oh.: Merrill, 1973.

The author presents a series of excellently conceived experiments in which adults are led to participate in order to understand the nature of the creative experience firsthand. Subjects included are: printmaking, three-dimensional construction, experiments with color, line, space, and sound, and others with clay and puppets. The practical suggestions related to the teacher's role in organizing and implementing an art program for children and the ideas for encouraging creativity make this book a "must" for prospective and practicing teachers. The large number of explanatory photographs serve to further enhance this text.

Preslan, Kristina. *Group Crafts for Teachers and Librarians on Limited Budgets*. Littleton, Co.: Librarians Unlimited, 1980.

The author shares with educators, librarians, and group leaders some of the activities found to be most successful in providing opportunities for free expression through creative activity. The forty-five activities can stimulate more ideas for new crafts or be used in conjunction with other projects. There are no age limits. Professionals will decide the capabilities of their own group.

Rainey, Sarita R. *Weaving Without a Loom*. Worcester, Mass.: Davis, 1966.

The author presents simple and imaginative weaving techniques that she has developed through her exploration of weaving as a designer-craftsman and illustrates them with photos that she took. She explains some of the techniques and materials for weaving without a regular loom. The book is suitable for parents and teachers to use with any age child.

Richardson, Elwyn S. *In the Early World: Discovering Art Through Crafts.* New York: Pantheon, 1973.

Although the artwork and writing that are used as examples to support the author's ideas are those of older elementary school children, the ideas themselves are universally applicable. Through his descriptions of children at work with clay, making prints, or writing poetry, the author stresses his essential concern for the developing child as a creative being. This book is a classic! It is important background reading for all adults living and working with children.

Seidelman, James E., and Grace Mintonye. *Shopping Cart Art.* New York: Macmillan, 1970.

The authors explore possibilities for creating paintings, prints, puppets, sculpture, and collage from materials found in any grocery shopping cart. They explain how to turn your grocery list into an art supply list. All will have hours of fun with these easy-to-follow instructions. For parents, teachers, and students, this small volume has activities for all ages.

Short, Pat, and Billee Davidson. *Totalaction: Ideas and Activities for Teaching Children Ages Five to Eight.* Santa Monica, Ca.: Goodyear Publishing, 1980.

This source of ideas and activities for teachers has a triple thematic approach—colors, shapes, and sizes; circus sights and sounds; and water, water, everywhere. Within the three units are work-card sets, graphs, booklets, games and tasks, projects, handwork, physical activities, and work sheets.

Wiseman, Ann. *Making Things: The Hand Book of Creative Discovery.* Boston: Little, Brown, 1973.

This book about improvisation for hands of all ages, creating delight and discovery out of available materials, is truly a collection of discoveries and resources of simple and important concepts. Children will find it full of revelations and adventures in logic, experiences both concrete and abstract. Although designed for parents and teachers, its simple drawings and words also show children how to do activities.

Music, Dance, Movement, and Drama

Aronoff, Frances Webber. *Move with the Music: Songs and Learning Strategies for Young Children*. New York: Turning Wheel Press, 1982.

Aronoff suggests strategies for discovering the elements of music through twenty-six American and (easy) foreign-language folk songs. Keyboard explorations, designed for one child or a small group, are related to each song. Model adult-child interactions adapt easily to individual teacher's style; previous music training is not required. The loose-leaf format allows for flexible use, such as additions and memoranda.

Aubin, Neva, Elizabeth Crook, Erma Hayden, and David Walker. *Silver Burdett Music: Teacher's Edition, Early Childhood*. Morristown, N.J.: Silver Burdett, 1981.

The 113 (mostly folk) songs are organized into twenty-four sequential experience modules for increasing skill, sensitivity, and imagination in music activities. Included are sample-related arts lessons, using paintings, poems, a guide to recordings, and activities for individual evaluation; sound stories; progress charts; and song guides to concepts and activities.

Barlin, Anne Lief. *Teaching Your Wings to Fly: The Nonspecialist Guide to Movement Activities for Young Children*. Santa Monica, Ca.: Goodyear Publishing, 1979.

Barlin, in her pictorial guide for movement education (ages three to twelve), includes exploring body techniques, relating to others, spatial awareness, relaxation, rhythm and music, and emotional expression. She provides original choreography with individual and class activities. Objectives, notes to the teacher or parent, and explicit directions make this book a worthwhile source.

Batchelder, Marjorie. *The Puppet Theatre Handbook*. New York: Harper & Row, 1947.

Of special interest for the teacher in this clear, comprehensive, still very relevant book about all aspects of the puppet theater are the chapters on playwriting for the puppet theater, planning the puppet show, the uses of puppetry in education, recreation, therapy and rehabilitation, and bibliographies (of source material for plays and of records). Teachers may also welcome Batchelder's materials list. The book includes plans for wheel-chair and hospital-bed puppet stages.

Bayless, Kathleen M., and Marjorie E. Ramsey. *Music: A Way of Life for the Young Child.* St. Louis: Mosby, 1978.

Written for adults who work with young children, this book provides a developmental approach to children's musical experiences. Theory is combined with practical suggestions for teaching children from infancy to five years of age. Sections on using music with the exceptional child and music as an integral part of a total educational environment are valuable additions. Each chapter includes simple songs notated for piano and chordal instruments and an extensive list of references and suggested readings.

Beall, Pamela Conn, and Susan Hagen Nipp. *Wee Sing and Play: Children's Songs and Fingerplays,* 4th ed. Los Angeles: Price, Stern, Sloan, 1981.

The collection of over seventy songs and finger plays is grouped under headings of holiday, meal time, daily happenings, traveling, active workouts, and bedtime. The simple music and directions are designed to foster language development, body coordination, auditory discrimination as well as simple enjoyment of music and song.

Boardman, Eunice, and Barbara Andress. *The Music Book: Kindergarten Teacher's Reference Book.* New York: Holt, Rinehart and Winston, 1981.

In this explicit guide the authors describe and organize clear musical objectives for children's performing. Although geared to the four-to-six age group, the activities can be easily adapted for younger children. Each lesson identifies a concept, activities for its discovery, and ways to extend the concept. There are eighty songs (composed, folk, and Mother Goose), poems, picture charts, and a guide for thirty-three instrumental listening lessons.

Dimondstein, Geraldine. *Children Dance in the Classroom*. New York: Macmillan, 1971.

The strength of this book lies in its clearly articulated theoretical rationale for creative dance for children in the classroom. The author deals with dance as "knowing" (the internalization of movement concepts through exploratory experiences) and "feeling" (the use of dance as a medium for creative expression). She discusses the creation of an atmosphere for dance in the classroom and the classroom teacher's (preschool and elementary) role as a dance educator. She advocates and provides examples of the creative problem-solving approach to movement. Each chapter introduces the elements of movement—space, time with force—and elaborates upon these concepts; examples of specific problems and possible solutions follow. Life-size photographs beautifully illustrate movement fundamentals. Resources at the end of the book include records, dance and song books, and films.

Dorian, Margery. *Ethnic Stories for Children to Dance*. San Mateo, Ca.: BBB, 1978.

Dorian includes stories from around the world with suggestions for rhythmic accompaniment on drums and other instruments. Years of experience as a dancer and as a teacher of dance give the author knowledge and insight. The choice of material is a valuable addition to the resources available to teachers in lower grades and preschool settings.

Dorian, Margery, and Frances Gulland. *Telling Stories Through Movement*. Belmont, Ca.: Fearon, 1974.

Thirty-one children's stories including folk tales from Africa, China, and Russia as well as such classics as *Rosie's Walk*, *The Snowy Day* and *The Three Billy Goats Gruff* are in this book. Each story is summarized with an eye to its interpretation in movement and has "appropriate rhythm patterns, themes, instruments, and exercises." These activities are delightful when combined with the actual book, which can be read at story hour. However, they also work alone as a means of stimulating dramatic improvisation without the original book. No musical accompaniment is needed, but ideas are provided for using simple percussion instruments. The book encourages teachers to use their own material as a basis for movement improvisation. All the action and directions are directed toward preschoolers.

Engler, Larry, and Carol Fijan. *Making Puppets Come Alive: A Method of Learning and Teaching Hand Puppetry.* Photographs by David Attie. New York: Taplinger, 1973.

This systematic, progressively organized approach to teaching puppetry includes puppetry movement exercises for solo and duet work. Beautiful, clear, and interesting photos illustrate how to move puppets. Specific movements are taught; they show that puppets can do more than just bob up and down. Some of the movements may be beyond the abilities of a preschooler. With this book teachers will acquire an understanding about the use of puppets.

Etkin, Ruth. *The Rhythm Band Book.* New York: Sterling, 1978.

Delightful songs from around the world abound in this book. Each musical selection has a simple piano accompaniment. It does not have chord symbols for guitar or autoharp. All selections have simple, concrete suggestions for use with rhythm instruments and directions to make one's own rhythm instruments. The rhythm band scores are inappropriate for preschoolers. There are excellent photographs of children playing rhythm instruments and of the instruments themselves, both commercial and homemade.

Evans, David. *Sharing Sounds: Musical Experiences with Young Children.* New York: Longman, 1977.

The author divides his text into three parts. Part I contains straightforward observations and informal speculations about "powerful, intelligent and interesting" behavior of babies (to approximately two years) with practical suggestions for adults' encouragement of their musical development. Evans emphasizes linking baby's movement with sound and adults' close-range, unaccompanied singing. Part II explores enjoying others' music making, live and recorded; early use of musical instruments, what and when; and includes a sensible section on formal musical skills. Part III discusses music in the play group and nursery school. There are practical how-to's for dealing with differences in levels of musical experience in large-group music.

Fleming, Gladys A. *Creative Rhythmic Movement: Boys and Girls Dancing*. Englewood Cliffs, N.J.: Prentice-Hall, 1976.

Fleming provides kindergarten and elementary school teachers with ways of initiating and planning a developmental program in creative rhythmic movement for children. Two threads are interwoven throughout this text. The first is the emphasis on creativity; the process of stimulating, nurturing, and releasing creativity in both teacher and children. The second furnishes examples of movement sessions. Reproducing the interaction between teacher and student serves to illustrate the dynamic process that occurs when joint solutions to movement problems are explored. In beginning chapters the nature of dance is defined and the role of dance in the school program is clarified. Following chapters focus on methods of starting movement, using sounds, chants, and songs, and ways of making percussion instruments. The elements of dance are grouped into movement, space, time with force, and finally, there are suggestions for creating dance compositions.

Gilbert, Anne G. *Teaching the Three Rs Through Movement Experiences*. Minneapolis: Burgess, 1977.

Gilbert demonstrates the use of movement in the classroom as another way of learning, of motivating children to learn, and of making learning a total body and mind experience. After a brief discussion of the fundamentals of movement and problem-solving techniques, she offers movement suggestions for the various subject areas of the school curriculum. Her knowledge of the school program is extensive. She covers subject areas in language arts, mathematics problems, science problems, social studies, and natural resources but has an all too limited chapter on art problems. This text will serve as an excellent aid for the classroom teacher.

Glazer, Tom. *Eye Winker, Tom Tinker, Chin Chopper: Fifty Musical Fingerplays*. Garden City, N.Y.: Doubleday, 1973.

Piano arrangements and guitar chords accompany fifty song/ finger-play activities that were selected from folk resources of the recent and more distant past. Many of the songs are familiar, with some interesting new ones included.

Glazer, Tom. *Do Your Ears Hang Low? Fifty More Musical Finger-plays*. Garden City, N.Y.: Doubleday, 1980.

Following the success of his earlier volume (*Eye Winker, Tom Tinker, Chin Chopper*), Glazer has arranged (for piano, guitar) fifty more fun folk-based songs that lend themselves to finger-play activity. Illustrations by Mila Lazarevich provide a delightful accompaniment to the songs.

Hawes, Bill. *The Puppet Book*. San Diego: Beta Books, 1977.

Hawes in his comprehensive book examines all aspects of puppetry, plus many excellent practical suggestions. Most early childhood educators will not need the depth of coverage the book provides. The chapter, "A Puppet Philosophy for Schools," offers innovative suggestions about appropriate educational uses of puppets from kindergarten through sixth grade, and another offers a discussion of the strength of puppetry as an artistic medium.

Heinig, Ruth B., and Lyda Stillwell. *Creative Drama for the Classroom Teacher*. Englewood Cliffs, N.J.: Prentice-Hall, 1974.

This text begins with simple activities and techniques and moves to more complex and sophisticated material. Emphasis is on story drama. A chapter is devoted to the group process and classroom management. It is a teacher's training manual with clear step-by-step development of the dramatic process with the elementary school child.

Hoffman, Hubert A., Jane Young, and Stephen E. Klesius. *Meaningful Movement for Children: A Developmental Theme Approach to Physical Education*. Boston: Allyn & Bacon, 1981.

The field-tested practical activities detail how physical education can contribute to the goals of the classroom curriculum. Topics include establishing basic movement capabilities, increasing self-reliance and confidence in moving, working with others, and communicating through movement. Lesson plans present movement experiences and related classroom activities. Managerial guidelines are also included.

Horton, John. *Music.* New York: Citation Press, 1975.

The author describes the aims and approaches of music programs in informal British infant and primary schools. Much of the theory and practice borrow from the Orff and Kodaly methods. The music curriculum is presented as an integral part of an educational environment that stresses problem solving and the development of children's expression in many art forms. A 33 rpm recording of original compositions played by children on Orff-type instruments is included.

Hunter, Ilene, and Marilyn Judson. *Simple Folk Instruments to Make to Play.* New York: Simon & Schuster, 1977.

This illustrated guide gives step-by-step instructions for making over 100 authentic musical instruments. Useful for preschoolers as well as adults, these "recipes" range in difficulty from extremely simple to complex. A preface includes suggestions for teachers and recreation leaders and provides information pertinent to the acquisition and use of materials and tools. Presentations are organized in six divisions: Rhythm Sticks and Rasps; Jingle Bells and Rattles; Gongs, Blocks and Zylophones; Drums and Vibrating Membranes; Zithers and Dulcimers; and Flutes, Whistles, and Horns. Each section is introduced with a historical, cross-cultural overview.

Jacobson, Ruth. *Music and Movement.* Queens, N.Y.: Queens College Day Care Project, 1980.

The booklet is a pragmatic approach to lesson planning designed for classroom teachers, librarians, and caregivers who have no background in music or movement. It is conveniently divided into Hello Songs, Warm-ups, Finger Plays, Classification Chants, Choosing Rhymes, Movement Songs, Songs from Other Countries, and Goodbye Songs. All the songs are simple. They have the steady beat underlined so that they may be used by an inexperienced person for clapping rhythms and rhythm band exercises. One song from five categories will make a twenty-minute lesson. The material, all of which has been tested in day-care centers, stresses classification and listening skills.

Jenkins, Peggy Davison. *The Magic of Puppetry: A Guide for Those Working with Young Children.* Englewood Cliffs, N.J.: Prentice-Hall, 1980.

This book, geared to early childhood teachers, is worth reading from cover to cover! The chapter on rationale for using puppets is superb: it gives clear, valid reasons for its thesis.

Jones, Genevieve. *Seeds of Movement: Philosophy of Movement with Techniques Applied to the Beginner.* Pittsburgh: Volkwein, 1971.

That children through series of movement explorations and experiences discover their own way of moving toward their fullest potential is the thrust of this book. Aimed at the classroom or specialist teacher of young children, each chapter is preceded by an introduction with specific suggestions and instructions that serve as a guide for teaching. The text is organized so that each chapter builds on the previous one, episodes correlating with the objectives of that chapter so each falls in place and finally, at the end of the book, creates a movement lesson plan. Chapters deal with movement games—elements of movement explorations, sounds, music, ideas to motivate movement, exercises, relaxation, imitations. Scores for songs and music are provided.

Joyce, Mary. *First Steps in Teaching Creative Dance*, 2nd ed. Palo Alto, Ca.: Mayfield, 1980.

The first fifty pages give an inexperienced teacher an excellent introduction to the theory and methods used in creative dance. There is special emphasis on the teaching of Rudolph Laban. Most of the book has actual lessons that are age graded and are paired with photographs. Though the material works best with children five and over, much of the material can be used with four-year-olds.

Konowitz, Bertram Lawrence. *Music Improvisation as a Classroom Method; A New Approach to Teaching Music.* Sherman Oaks, Ca.: Alfred, 1973.

Konowitz introduces an interesting new way for the music teacher or the classroom teacher to incorporate music learning and skill development into the curriculum. Based on the principles of music (tempo, dynamics, form, etc.), the book provides a sequence of creativity sources and enrichment activities that are designed into lesson plans for the teacher with even moderate musical understanding. Improvisation is wonderful for children at any age and, based on recent research in music learning theory, essential at an early age if optimal musical development is to occur. This book provides uncomplicated and effective methods of improvisation.

Koste, Virginia R. *Dramatic Play in Childhood: Rehearsal for Life.* New Orleans: Anchorage Press, 1978.

A thought-provoking book filled with anecdotes and personal experiences by an actress/educator working with children, it provides penetrating glimpses of the roots of child's play—its meaning and form. Koste does not attempt to define "creativity," "play," or "drama," but allows the reader to experience the meaning through vivid images and descriptions. This is a unique book about play as well as the basic development of art.

McCaslin, Nellie. *Creative Drama in the Classroom.* New York: Longman, 1980.

The author examines virtually every aspect of teaching creative dramatics and its relation to children. She covers creative dramatics as a socializing activity and a way of learning; movement, rhythms, and dramatic play; pantomime; improvisation; dramatic structure; drama as a teaching tool; creative drama for the special child; and more. She discusses poetry and stories as source material and gives specific examples throughout for improvisation. She deals with organization of the session and how to handle a practical problem arising out of a child's physical or emotional difficulties. Various types of class situations—giving a speech, performing for an audience, and a miscellany of other topics related to creative dramatics—are covered in this essential handbook for the creative dramatics instructor. It is illustrated extensively, and there is a detailed bibliography.

McCaslin, Nellie. *Puppet Fun: Performance, Production and Plays.* New York: Macmillan, 1977.

Here is a book with special value for the teacher of very young children. Based on sound educational principles, it is a guidebook for the stimulation of creativity through music, mime, movement, and language arts. It is clearly written and presented in an attractive format with good illustrations. It is highly recommended.

McCaslin, Nellie (ed.). *Children and Drama*, 2nd ed. New York: Longman, 1981.

In this important collection of twenty essays on theater and creative dramatics, authorities in their field present their own (and frequently refreshingly diverse) viewpoints. The result is a rich source of thought-provoking material—from basic concepts of what drama and theater are and can be to the participating child through different goals, approaches, teaching methods, and criticism. The editor, who has contributed an introduction, has gathered a number of deeply felt and clearly articulated opinions, all of which deserve the consideration of the creative dramatics instructor.

McDonald, Dorothy T. *Music in Our Lives: The Early Years*. Washington, D.C.: National Association for the Education of Young Children, 1979.

What musical experiences are best for infants? Which instruments are most suitable for young children, and how can teachers encourage their use in groups? From birth through age six, the author explores musical experiences, songs, teaching strategies, purchasing information—all developmentally based.

Mitchell, Donald, and Carey Blyton. *Every Child's Book of Nursery Songs*. New York: Crown, 1968.

The authors have compiled an excellent collection of songs designed not only for parents, but also for use by teachers of young children. "Humpty Dumpty," "Mary Had a Little Lamb," "Little Boy Blue," "Jack and Jill," "Old King Cole," "Simple Simon" and "Wee Willie Winkie" are only a few of the Mother Goose characters found between the covers of this book. The authors have also included some little-known songs that will become favorites of the children and adults who use this book. Simple piano arrangements accompany the tuneful, jaunty rhymes. The illustrations are in rhythmic and enchantingly childlike agreement with the verses and the music they interpret.

Moving Learning Action Pack. Chicago: McDonald's Corporation, 1979.

A select group of physical educators and writers collaborated to produce this "action pack" which is full of material on the movement education approach through eight themes. Each theme can be used for lesson or a month of lessons. Readers are encouraged to build on the base material presented and are given suggestions of how to do this. There is one ditto master for each theme to help children conceptualize about some phase of their movement work.

Nelson, Esther L. *Singing and Dancing Games for the Very Young.* New York: Sterling, 1977.

The forty-four singing and dancing games in this delightful book are brief, to the point, and designed for instant success, so that children get an immediate sense of satisfaction. The music is simple, and there are many familiar melodies such as "Twinkle, Twinkle Little Star," "This Old Man," "Rock-a-Bye Baby," "Where Is Thumbkin" and "Open Shut Them." The dance for each song is simple and easy for the young children to do. There are lovely black-and-white photographs of children throughout the book.

Nye, Venice. *Music for Young Children*, 2nd ed. Dubuque, Ia.: William C. Brown, 1979.

This basic book for teachers and parents of young children relates theories of child development to current methods of teaching music. Suggestions stress an exploratory, improvisational approach to musical experiences. Chapters on using music as part of an integrated curriculum and in classrooms where children with handicapping conditions are "mainstreamed" are valuable additions. The suggested songs have guitar or autoharp chords. A comprehensive bibliography/discography is also included.

Panabaker, Lucile. *Lucile Panabaker's Song Book.* Toronto: Peter Martin, 1968.

Learning to sing in tune is a slow developmental process for most children, and they need to be given songs within a range that their voices can master. The author offers her original songs for very young children. These are perfect for developing the child's voice as they are within the C to A range, with an occasional song leading into higher or lower notes. The songs provide an opportunity for frequent repetition of a melody with original verses suggested by the children. The delightful black-and-white illustrations for each tune make this a picture book for children as well as a song book. Teaching suggestions and guitar and autoharp chords are given for each melody.

Peck, Judith. *Leap To the Sun.* Englewood Cliffs, N.J.: Prentice-Hall, 1979.

According to the author, her book is designed to "motivate teachers and group leaders to develop expressive movement with children." The stories, for children three to eleven, can be read during story hour and then acted out. The first part of the book contains many excellent movement and theater games to stimulate movement and improvisation. Especially interesting are the fifteen stories "to stimulate movement" offered in the last part of the book. These are marked with a P when they are meant for preschoolers.

Philpott, A. R. *Dictionary of Puppetry.* Boston: Plays, Inc., 1969.

A unique book, this dictionary provides a guide to technical and historical aspects of puppetry, information about films and puppetry books, and biographies of puppeteers. It is for the specialist.

Post, Henry, and Michael McTwigan. *Clay Play: Learning Games for Children.* Englewood Cliffs, N.J.: Prentice-Hall, 1973.

Profusely illustrated by Diane Martin's photographs and delightful drawings, this slender volume explores the joys children can find in working with clay and suggests ideas to spark their imagination in using the materials. Comments in the back of the book by Mihalri Csikszentonihaly enumerate for adults the advantages other than pure fun that children derive from playing with clay.

Renfro, Nancy. *A Puppet Corner in Every Library.* Austin, Tx.: Nancy Renfro Studios, 1978.

Though this book is specifically designed for use by librarians, it is appropriate for anyone who would like to explore the fascinating world of puppets. It provides clear illustrations and instructions on how to make a variety of puppets and puppet stages. It contains ideas for motivating creative play with the puppets. There are excellent ideas for integrating puppetry into the curriculum.

Riggs, Maida L. (ed.). *Movement Education for Preschool Children.* Reston, Va.: American Alliance for Health, Physical Education, Recreation and Dance, 1980.

This booklet is designed for those who work with preschool age children. It discusses the why, what, how, and where of movement education for the preprimary child and what the adults who work with those children can do. It is a helpful aid for preschool teachers and parents.

Russell, Joan. *Creative Dance in the Primary School,* 2nd ed. London: Macdonald & Evans, 1975.

This text serves to clarify and demonstrate the application of Rudolph Laban's analysis of movement for teaching children's dance. The author discusses teacher aims, role of the teacher, and offers guidance for assessing children's progress. Her detailed chart of Laban's classification of movement—based on space, effort, time, and flow; relationship of body parts; and individual and group interaction—serves as a fine summary and guide for developing movement lessons. The lessons are explicit and easy to follow for the teacher with dance experience. Along with sample lessons are action photographs of children that help illustrate the written text.

Seeger, Ruth Crawford. *American Folk Songs for Children.* Garden City, N.Y.: Doubleday, 1980.

This collection of tune-tested songs for children is especially suitable for preschoolers. Songs are indexed as to subjects— including occupations, animals, insects, birds, horses, counting, goodbye, greeting, snow, sunshine. There is also a rhythmic index that includes clapping, rhythm band, galloping, knocking, jumping, hopping, marching, rolling, running, skipping, stretching, swinging, and walking. The pictures by Barbara Cooney are charming. Most of the songs offer ideas for dramatic play experiences and improvisation. Some play party games are included. The indices of quiet songs and games using toe play, finger play, name play, and drama are invaluable. This classic, originally published in 1948, remains one of the best collections in the field of preschool music from the point of view of musicianship, practical application and historical accuracy.

Sheeves, Rosamund. *Movement and Educational Dance for Children.* Boston: Plays, Inc., 1980.

Sheeves presents a detailed, structured and directive approach to the teaching of dance in the schools based on Rudolph Laban's movement analysis. The first section of the book discusses the meaning of and methods for teaching dance. The second suggests a multitude of stimuli to encourage movement ideas and themes—flash cards, movement patterns, objects, people, moods, emotions, nature, shapes, sculptures, sounds, poetry, etc. The third offers a collection of sample lessons based on the preceding material. Each lesson is accompanied by a diagram of stated objectives and serves as a summary of the activity. Even the inexperienced teacher will find these lessons easy to follow.

Siks, Geraldine. *Drama with Children.* New York: Harper & Row, 1977.

This book, designed specifically for teacher training, is rich with the experiences and insights of an expert. Siks develops a conceptual framework for the dramatic process that presents the child with three distinct roles—player, playmaker, and/or audience.

Spencer, Ruth Albert. *Early Childhood Music Kit—The First Year.* New York: Trillium Press, 1980.

Spencer has written a practical introduction to music for young children that can be used by nonmusically trained early childhood educators. There are ninety lesson plans with forty-five variations, designed for periods of ten to fifteen minutes. There are cassettes with all music for the class plus music background for teachers. Teachers are provided with rhythm, movement, pitch, listening, conducting, ensemble, and notation activities.

Stecher, Miriam, Hugh McElheny, and Marion Greenwood. *Music and Movement Improvisation.* New York: Macmillan, 1972.

The authors detail ways to include spontaneity in the classroom as a support and enrichment of the total curriculum. Vivid anecdotes clearly illustrate how to use the suggestions given in a variety of early childhood environments.

Torbert, Marianne. *Follow Me: A Handbook of Movement Activities for Children.* Englewood Cliffs, N.J.: Prentice-Hall, 1980.

The movement activities designed to stimulate and support life-preparing skills are described for young children. Each chapter presents specific play activities and lists the benefits derived from each. Developmental skills gained through these games include motor ability, attention span and concentration, listening skills, release of tension and excessive energy, self-control, social growth, and so on. The play activities are simple, and instructions are easy to follow for both teachers and parents.

Way, Brian. *Audience Participation Theatre for Young People.* Boston: Baker, 1981.

The author is the British director/playwright who has been a pioneer of participatory theater for children in Great Britain and the United States. He develops his theories in detail, stressing the honesty that must be inherent in all participation theater, whether for young children or those in secondary schools. The book has photographs of performances, diagrams of a variety of playing spaces, and descriptions of ways to solve problems of concept and production. The text is an explanation and justification of the author's viewpoint, still a controversial one among theater professionals and educators on both sides of the Atlantic.

Way, Brian. *Development Through Drama.* New York: Humanities Press, 1967.

In this classic in creative drama literature the emphasis is on the use of drama in the development of the whole child. Way underscores its value in nurturing inner resourcefulness. In addition to a strong philosophical rationale for the use of drama, he provides many exercises and techniques for use in the classroom with children of all ages.

Wiener, Jack, and John Lidstone. *Creative Movement for Children: A Dance Program for the Classroom.* New York: Van Nostrand Reinhold, 1969.

Written by two educators for classroom teachers, this book discusses the purpose and process of creative movement for children. The authors' position is that creative experience originates with the individual and develops from deep, personal feelings. A main objective of the teacher in providing movement experiences is to help the child become aware of the power to use the body as a medium in dance to express feelings and thoughts. After a brief discussion of basic movement vocabulary, the authors describe the system they have developed that employs familiar imagery to help the child experience qualities of movement in a concrete and sentient way. The main qualities explored include heaviness (clay), hardness (wire), lightness (rubber band), and softness (piano). Giving children the experience of sustaining the sensation of movement qualities develops their sensitivity and widens their physical and emotional repertoire. Dramatic photographs illustrate the authors' teaching concepts and styles.

Wilder, Rosilyn. *A Space Where Anything Can Happen.* Rowayton, Ct.: New Play Books, 1977.

Wilder has written a practical handbook for teaching creative drama to the middle grades in urban public schools. The author suggests ways to involve children, creating a comfortable atmosphere for imagining and improvising, and building the trust needed for critique. The book is full of ideas—and the ideas work.

Winn, Marie, Allan Miller, and Karla Kuskin. *What Shall We Do and Allee Galloo!* New York: Harper & Row, 1970.

Here is a unique collection of songs for young children. It includes old favorites as well as less familiar songs. There are songs to sing in the car, songs to sing while waiting for the bus, songs for nursery schools or playgrounds, songs for bedtime— in short, an abundance of delightful children's songs for all times and occasions. Each song includes an activity in addition to the actual singing—clapping, jumping, falling down, making animal sounds, echoing words. Although all the songs and games in this book are suitable for use by groups, this collection includes only those that can be sung and played by just one child and a parent. The piano arrangements are well within the musical range of beginning pianists, and guitar chords are given for each selection. Karla Kuskin's delightful and whimsical illustrations capture perfectly the feeling and mood of each song.

Witkin, Kate. *To Move To Learn*. Philadelphia: Temple University Press, 1977.

Although designed particularly for movement educators dealing with the slow learner and the physically handicapped, the material presented can work successfully for any young student. Witkin blends her experience in musical comedy and education to give a series of imaginative and enticing lesson plans with the practical detail and sensitive evaluation that teachers appreciate.

12
Multicultural
Education

PERSPECTIVES

Beryle Banfield and Robert B. Moore

Research on children's racial awareness shows that by four years of age, children in our society have a fairly well-developed conception of race and racial differences, particularly in terms of the status ascribed to persons on this basis. This early racial awareness will significantly shape not only children's perceptions of themselves but also their perceptions of others and will mold their behaviors and interactions in the future. A 1979 study of racial awareness in kindergarten children, designed to replicate a 1966 study, concluded that "white children have not been moved . . . from the biased views of their counterparts of thirteen years ago. The tendency to view white peers positively and black peers negatively was strong then, and is even more comprehensive in scope today. Whatever social forces have influenced contemporary American society, none seem to have altered the patterns of racial bias toward blacks in the rearing of white children" (Olson, et al., 1981).

In a society in which isolation continues to characterize the racial experience of millions of children, images and information about various racial and cultural groups assume particular importance. Indeed, research suggests that children's views of other races are shaped less by actual contact with people of other races than by contact with the images and attitudes that prevail in their communities about those peoples. Those images and attitudes are conveyed by significant adults, TV, books, games and toys, and a variety of other communicative media. Implicit and explicit notions of superiority and inferiority that are so conveyed warp children's humanity and limit the human potential of all children.

Thus, it is essential for those who seek to assist children to develop in healthy, humane, pluralistic, and nonbiased directions to intervene early and strongly to counter the traditional socializing influences. It is equally essential to provide youngsters with experiences, activities, information, and images that will help them develop a respect for the essential equality of all human beings, an appreciation for the great diversity of peoples and cultures, and a concern for the well-being of others that will be translated into efforts to bring about a more just, equitable, and inclusive society.

This has important implications for parenting and educating. For educators, it means the responsibility of ensuring that, from early childhood on, children are exposed to a sound program of education that is multicultural (EMC)—the type of education that is consciously designed to enable them to function effectively in a culturally diverse society. This goes far beyond the type of multicultural experiences that focus solely on the preparation of ethnic foods, the honoring of ethnic heroes, and the celebration of ethnic festivals.

Education that is multicultural is at once corrective and preventive—correcting those misconceptions concerning gender, race, and disability that children gain early in life and preventing the further development of stereotypic attitudes. Education that is multicultural is pervasive, reflecting itself in every aspect of the total early childhood educational environment: staffing, curricular adaptations, instructional practices, selection and use of materials, administrative procedures, classroom practices, and school-community relationships.

A thoroughly rounded program of EMC assumes staffing patterns that provide for the presence of minority groups, women, and disabled persons in varying positions of responsibility. Curricular adaptations that reflect sensitivity to the demands of minority groups for adequate and accurate presentation of their life, history, and culture are key elements in such a program. The history, folktales, and music that comprise such an important part of a people's culture should be utilized as a means of gaining insight into that culture and should be incorporated naturally into all curriculum areas. Teachers must adapt instructional styles and strategies to the different needs of different learners. They must become aware of ways in which classroom practices impinge upon the customs and traditions of various cultural and racial groups.

The selection of books and instructional materials is of vital importance in any program of EMC. Since these materials play a major role in creating and reinforcing children's stereotypic perceptions, it is essential that they be selected in accordance with such bias-free criteria as those developed by the Council on Interracial Books for Children and other concerned organizations. It is incumbent upon early childhood educators to equip themselves with the skills and information that will enable them to detect race, sex, and handicap bias in instructional materials and in trade and picture books in areas such as illustrations, language and terminology, characterization, historical background, and presentation of stereotypic situations. Where biased materials are used, instructional techniques must be employed that will develop children's abilities to recognize the racial, sex, and cultural biases in these materials.

Given the preschool age by which children are socialized, parents must accept the responsibility for combatting the racist, sexist, and handicappist messages conveyed not only by children's picture books and trade books but also throughout the media. Parents, too, must be familiar with bias-free criteria so that they can make careful selections. They must equip themselves with the skills that will enable them to discuss TV presentations even with their preschool children in a manner that will develop the children's skills of critical thinking.

We must all raise our own awareness of the manifestations of racial and cultural bias that regularly assault children's minds. Such consciousness raising is crucial in order to avoid those child-rearing practices that might unintentionally promote bias. This awareness will assist us in countering the influence of racial/cultural bias by assisting children to recognize its various manifestations.

The tasks facing parents and educators are many. But if we are to develop a truly just and pluralistic society, we must accept the challenge to rear a generation of children who will be unburdened by the constrictive biases now imposed on children at such an early age.

Reference

Olson, James, et al. Racial awareness in kindergarten children: A decade of progress? *Integrateducation*, Spring 1981, pp. 98–100.

BIBLIOGRAPHY

Abrahams, Roger D., and Rudolph C. Troike (eds.). *Language and Cultural Diversity in American Education*. Englewood Cliffs, N.J.: Prentice-Hall, 1972.

This anthology of essays is still relevant in the 1980s. The focus is on the effects of the diversity of languages and cultures in the United States on the educational system, especially as they pertain to linguistic and culturally different persons. The essayists attempt to analyze and understand the life-ways of Americans who are linguistically and culturally different from mainstream, middle-class America—that is, from those who for the most part formulate our educational policy and for the most part run our schools. The editors hope to provide a fuller understanding of the nature and uses of diversity.

American Speech-Language-Hearing Association. *Partners in Language: A Guide for Parents/Compañeros En El Idioma: Guia para Los Padres*. Rockville, Md.: The Association, 1981.

In this easy-to-read and easy-to-follow English/Spanish guide, parents will learn ways to foster their child's language development and how to model speech behavior for very young children. A broad outline on children's development from birth to three and one-half years of age is also included.

Aquino-Mackles, Alexis, David C. King, and Margaret S. Bronson. *Myself and Others*. New York: Global Perspectives in Education, 1979.

This handbook of activities is intended to prepare children for the world they will be living in. The authors provide experiences to help children see that interconnections and human commonalities extend to people throughout the world, not just people in their immediate surroundings. Through varied activities, such as songs, art, discussions, and trips, children can learn ways that people communicate with one another and achieve a sense of belonging.

Banfield, Beryle. *Black Focus on Multicultural Education*. New York: Blyden Press, 1979.

In this handbook on multicultural education there is special emphasis on the black experience. The author suggests practical and specific strategies for the presentation of language arts and social studies activities. The experiences are adaptable for kindergarten through sixth-grade classes.

Banks, James A. *Multiethnic Education: Theory and Practice*. Boston: Allyn & Bacon, 1981.

Students and teachers will learn about various facets of pluralistic education—the historical development of multiethnic education (the goals, problems, and current practices) as well as the conceptual and philosophical issues. The author describes teaching strategies, student characteristics, and curriculum reform. He concludes with sections on continuing issues and guidelines in multiethnic education. An annotated bibliography and evaluation guidelines are helpful.

Banks, James, and William W. Joyce. *Teaching Social Studies to Culturally Different Children*. Reading, Ma.: Addison-Wesley, 1971.

This anthology considers various aspects in the lives of linguistically different youths. In addition, the authors present effective strategies for teaching about diverse cultures.

Barrera, Rebecca, and Mari Rojas. *Amanecer*. San Antonio: Intercultural Development Research Associates, 1979.

The authors have prepared a preschool curriculum composed of eleven sets of materials, including twenty-four booklets, file cards, language profiles, master checklists, and training filmstrips. The theoretical base for the program is eclectic; the authors combined elements from Piaget, Montessori, and Maslow. Instruction is presented in the children's language preference, and close linkages between the home and the school are actively encouraged. This bilingual-multicultural program was sponsored by the Head Start Strategy for Spanish-Speaking Children, Administration for Children, Youth, and Families, DHEW/OHDS.

Carter, Thomas P., and Roberto D. Segura. *Mexican Americans in School: A Decade of Change.* New York: College Entrance Examination Board, 1979.

The authors offer a thoughtful view of the education of Mexican Americans in this revision of the timely book that appeared in 1970, *Mexican Americans in School: A History of Educational Neglect.* It is especially recommended for teachers.

Colangelo, Nicholas, Cecelia H. Foxley, and Dick Dustin (eds.). *Multicultural Nonsexist Education: A Human Relations Approach.* Dubuque, Ia.: Kendall/Hunt, 1979.

Topics on multicultural education, nonsexist education, special education, gifted children, and many others are discussed within the framework of human relations. Each section ends with discussion questions, projects, and activities. The volume can be used as a college text and for in-service workshops. Parents will also find several topics to be helpful.

Coleman, Madeleine (ed.). *Black Children Just Keep On Growing: Alternative Curriculum Models for Young Black Children.* Washington, D.C.: Black Child Development Institute, 1977.

This book is the result of an analysis of ten alternative preschool programs in seven states. The first part deals with the methodology of the programs, a review of the literature, and a description of the alternative programs. The second part contains readings pertinent to curricula for black children and to the growth and development of the black child. The appendixes include samples of the research instruments that were used to gather the research data. The programs described were developed by black educators expressly for young black children.

Coles, Robert. *Children of Crisis*, Vol. 4. *Eskimos, Chicanos, Indians.* Boston: Little, Brown, 1978.

The author presents a penetrating look at three groups of American children. The volume is one of a series of sociological writings that vividly depict the lives of poor children in the United States and the people and forces that influence them. This is timeless literature for parents, students, teachers, and everyone who is interested in children.

Coles, Robert. *Children of Crisis*, Vol. 2. *Migrants, Mountaineers, and Sharecroppers*. Boston: Little, Brown, 1977.

The second volume in the author's acclaimed series is a clear and penetrating report on rural life and on the people in rural America, most particularly the children, "who live uprooted lives, who have been stranded, who are hidden."

Comer, James P., and Alvin F. Poussaint. *Black Child Care*. New York: Pocket Books, 1980.

Comer and Poussaint have written the first child-care manual that concerns itself with the issues of raising black children. The book is replete with helpful, easy-to-read information on the growth and development of the black child from infancy through adolescence. The guidance provided is preceded by background information on American society and its attitude toward black children since the days of slavery. The authors have addressed the book to "all people." It is must reading for every person who has a role in the development of black children.

Cordasco, Francesco. *Bilingual Schooling in the United States: A Source Book for Educational Personnel*. New York: McGraw-Hill, 1976.

This basic source book for specialists in bilingual education is a compendium of documents, program constructs, theoretical-practical statements, and related materials. It provides an instructional-learning tool for the pre- and in-service teacher. It is intended as a classroom text for undergraduate classroom adoption.

Cotera, Martha, and Larry Hufford (eds.). *Bridging Two Cultures: Multidisciplinary Readings in Bilingual Bicultural Education*. Austin, Tx.: National Educational Laboratory Publishers, 1980.

In this series of articles on educational needs of all linguistic and cultural minorities, anthropology, linguistics, sociology, history, and economics are among the disciplines represented. The contributions of these disciplines offer new insights into matters that are by tradition the province of the educational theorist. Their presence demonstrates the editors' belief that bilingual bicultural education should consider nontraditional ideas.

Cox, Barbara, Janet Macaulay, and Manuel Ramirez, III. *New Frontiers: A Bilingual Early Learning Program/Nuevas Fronteras: Un programa de aprendizaje bilingue para niños.* Elmsford, N.Y.: Pergamon Press, 1981.

This curriculum for young children strongly emphasizes cultural diversity, individual differences, and cultural democracy. It also stresses the need and importance for teachers to know their preferred teaching style and the preferred learning or cognitive styles of the children in their classrooms. The materials include a training manual for teachers, child assessment materials, curriculum guide, unit materials on thirteen subjects, storybooks, and ideas for parent and community involvement. The volume is one of four bilingual multicultural curriculum models sponsored by the Head Start Strategy for Spanish-Speaking Children, Administration for Children, Youth, and Families, DHEW/OHDS.

Cross, Delores E., G. C. Baker, and L. J. Stiles (eds.). *Teaching in a Multicultural Society: Perspectives and Professional Strategies.* New York: Free Press, 1977.

The authors have assembled a series of readings on multicultural education. Suggestions on teaching strategies are provided, especially in the language arts.

Davis, Florence V., and Barbara Z. Presseisen. *Multicultural Education for Practitioners.* Philadelphia: Research for Better Schools, 1979.

As the title states, this publication is geared to educators, particularly administrators, supervisors, or trainers. The first part traces the history of multicultural education, dealing with such topics as assimilation, cultural pluralism, and separation. A working definition of multicultural education is presented along with the approaches of various national councils and state education departments. The second part contains guidelines for multicultural education in the school and covers such topics as knowledge, skills, and attitudinal goals, curriculum, policy and procedures, school/community relations, and staff.

Dunfee, Maxine. *Ethnic Modification of the Curriculum*. Washington, D.C.: Association for Supervision and Curriculum Development. National Education Association, 1970.

This report of a conference held in St. Louis in November 1969 addresses the problem of appropriate ethnic emphases in the school experiences of children and youth. The curriculum in the United States in general highlights the achievements of Western civilization at the expense of what has been contributed by Africa, Latin America, or Asia. The salient question dealt with is the matter of curriculum modification to meet the distinctive needs of children from a variety of backgrounds.

Friedman, Delores L. *Education Handbook for Black Families*. Garden City, N.Y.: Doubleday, 1980.

Friedman provides a broad reference guide for parents on educating the black child from preschool to college. Readiness activities are listed to help prepare children for reading, writing, and expressing themselves successfully so they will do well later on in school. There are criteria that will be useful for parents when choosing play groups, child care, books, toys, and field trip experiences that will enhance their child's self-image as a black child. In addition, the author guides parents in dealing with aspects of their child's education, such as teacher attitudes about minority children, images of black family life, culture, and history as it is presented in the child-care or educational setting. This book would interest all concerned with making education more responsive to the needs of black families.

Gabel Liebowitz, Dorothy. *The Vocabulary Builder, for Teaching Basic Second-Language Skills in Six Different Languages*. Skokie, Ill.: National Textbook, 1979.

This book is a vehicle for teaching or reinforcing vocabulary in English, Spanish, French, Italian, German, or Russian. It includes suggestions for practice and reinforcement of skills. Games and other activities are used to teach a second language. It also contains multilingual duplicating masters.

Giese, James. *Multicultural Education, A Functional Bibliography for Teachers.* Omaha: Center for Urban Education, University of Nebraska, 1977.

The bibliography was compiled to accompany *In Praise of Diversity: A Resource Book for Multicultural Education.* It is a multicultural listing of references on topics that affect individual ethnic groups, such as discrimination and prejudice. There are materials for use at elementary, secondary, and adult levels. Special consideration is given to those that emphasize group values, social institutions (such as family and child rearing), as well as the community, neighborhood, and work situations.

Gold, Milton J., Carl A. Grant, and Harry N. Rivlin (eds.). *In Praise of Diversity: A Resource Book for Multicultural Education.* Washington, D.C.: Association of Teacher Education, 1977.

This book provides specific information about America's pluralism and the professional skills and materials needed to move toward education that is truly multicultural. It furnishes information to teachers seeking elements about pluralism in the United States that were omitted from their education at all levels.

Gonzalez-Mena, Janet. *Program for English Experiences.* Silver Spring, Md.: Institute of Modern Languages, 1975.

This book is designed to teach English-as-a-second-language to preschoolers and kindergarteners. It emphasizes the skills of listening and speaking. It is a good aid for teachers who work with children who speak languages other than English.

Granger, Robert C., and James C. Young (eds.). *Demythologizing the Inner City Child.* Washington, D.C.: National Association for the Education of Young Children, 1979.

The editors selected readings on the inner-city child that emanated from a conference in 1976. The diverse topics and their development compel the serious reader to rethink and reevaluate existing myths and stereotypes concerning the inner-city child. They also provide mechanisms by which research findings can be analyzed. This book could prove helpful to college students, child-care workers, and teachers.

Grant, Carl A. (ed.). *Multicultural Education: Commitments, Issues, and Applications.* Washington, D.C.: Association for Supervision and Curriculum Development, 1977.

The articles in this booklet of readings cover a wide range of topics related to multicultural education and provide teaching strategies and applications appropriate for all grades.

Grant, Gloria (ed.). *In Praise of Diversity: Multicultural Classroom Applications.* Omaha: Center for Urban Education, University of Nebraska, 1977.

Teachers will find this book of fifty-one activities very helpful as they involve their students—at all grade levels—in practical multicultural activities. References are made to sections of the accompanying handbook, *In Praise of Diversity: A Resource Book for Multicultural Education.*

Greeley, Andrew M. *Why Can't They Be Like Us? Facts and Fallacies About Ethnic Differences and Group Conflicts in America.* New York: Institute of Human Relations Press, 1980.

This short treatise discusses various aspects of ethnicity in the United States society—the meaning and function of ethnicity, the steps in becoming assimilated, and the future of ethnic groups in the United States.

Hanes, Michael L., Marina I. Flores, Jose Rosario, and David P. Weikart. *An Open Framework/Un Marco Abierto.* Ypsilanti, Mi.: High/Scope Press, 1979.

This preschool bilingual-bicultural curriculum is an adaptation of the Cognitively Oriented Preschool Curriculum Model. The program subscribes to a guided "open-framework" approach rather than to specified lessons or activities. Adults help to support and maintain the children's first language and culture by emphasizing key experiences in both languages. Parent involvement is a vital component of the program, and parents and community people are encouraged to participate in the total program. The materials include a teacher's guide, in-service training materials, with audiovisual programs, and bilingual booklets for parents. The curriculum is one of four models that were sponsored by the Head Start Strategy for Spanish-Speaking

Children, Administration for Children, Youth, and Families, OHDS/DHEW.

Harrison-Ross, Phyllis, and Barbara Wyden. *The Black Child.* New York: Berkley, 1974.

The authors state they have written their book for everyone —black parents, white parents, and teachers. The intention is to counteract the effects of bias, both black and white. The content was developed from case studies from the clinical practice of one of the authors and her work with children in preschool programs in New York City.

Hill, Robert B. *The Strengths of Black Families.* New York: National Urban League, 1971.

This National Urban League research study contravenes the predominant trends in sociological literature that focus on indicators of instability or pathology in the black family. Five characteristics—strong kinship bonds, strong work orientation, adaptability of family roles, strong achievement orientation, and strong religious orientation—are viewed in terms of adaptation for survival in the hostile environment experienced by blacks in America.

King, Edith. *Teaching Ethnic Awareness: Methods and Materials for the Elementary School.* Santa Monica, Ca.: Goodyear Publishing, 1980.

A handbook for anyone interested in an activity-based approach to multiethnic education, this volume of field-tested projects was developed through courses and research at the University of Denver's Center for Teaching International Relations and the School of Education from 1975 to 1978. Activities listed are for three groups: ages four through seven, eight through ten, and ten through twelve. The activities recommended incorporate background information, objectives, procedures, and extension activities. Guidance is given as to how to use parents, the local community, and other resources to begin preparing children for a world of ethnic diversity. The book is effectively illustrated with children's drawings.

Kloss, Heinz. *The American Bilingual Tradition.* Rowley, Mass.: Newbury House, 1977.

The author isolates, describes, and analyzes the characteristic of a seemingly all-dominant monolingualism and a tradition of bilingualism, chiefly below the national level. This tradition depended on bilingual schooling and legislation. The text bears directly on the problems of non-English or bilingual schools in the United States.

Kwok, Irene. *Chinese Cultural Resource Book.* Fall River, Mass.: National Assessment and Dissemination Center for Bilingual Education, 1976.

The materials are based on the author's research and personal experiences as a child in Canton. Six sections include songs, games, poems, stories, art projects, and recipes relating to the five major Chinese holidays: Moon Festival, Winter Festival, Chinese New Year, Ching Ming, and Dragon Boat Festival. Kwok also writes about the family in China and other topics of interest. The activities make a good introduction to Chinese customs for children.

Longstreet, Wilma S. *Aspects of Ethnicity: Understanding Differences in Pluralistic Classroom.* New York: Teachers College Press, 1978.

The book provides a definition of ethnicity and a new insight into the dynamics of verbal and nonverbal behavior. Five aspects of ethnicity are identified—verbal communication, nonverbal communication, orientation modes, social value patterns, and intellectual modes. In addition, the author examines relevant social science research findings, classroom management techniques, and a language/communication analysis system.

McNeill, Earldene, J. Allen, and V. Schmidt. *Cultural Awareness for Young Children.* Dallas: The Learning Tree, 1975.

The authors describe a program that covered six cultures within its educational setting. Each culture is considered from seven perspectives—family living, creative arts expression, nature and science, language development, music and dance, manipulative and game center, and special events. A selected bibliography of multicultural resources concludes the book. This volume should prove a useful guide to teachers in developing their own cultural activities.

Maxwell, Marilyn, and Caryl Hamilton. *Feelings and Friends.* New York: Global Perspectives in Education, 1980.

There are curriculum ideas to help children (up to third grade) be self-aware, to feel positively about themselves first, and then to expand their knowledge and concerns to their family, class, neighborhood, city, state, country, and world. Children learn both verbal and nonverbal skills, how people are both different and similar, how to manage conflict situations, and to understand our interdependence at all levels. The book is primarily a handbook for teachers but community workers would also profit from it.

National Multilingual Multicultural Material Development Center. *Language Development in a Bilingual Setting.* Los Angeles: National Dissemination and Assessment Center, California State University, 1979.

This volume brings together thinking in five areas important to the success of bilingual programs: legal aspects of bilingual education, philosophies, social factors, language and content, and assessment. The final paper discusses practical application of programs and materials for bilingual education.

Pialorsi, Frank (ed.). *Teaching the Bilingual: New Methods and Old Traditions.* Tucson: University of Arizona Press, 1974.

This is a selection of writings by linguists, psychologists, anthropologists, and educators relating to the education of the child. The book begins by advocating the exercise of cultural understanding by teachers in order to facilitate and foster communication in the classroom. Theories of language acquisition and learning first and second languages, including psychological implications, are discussed. The discussion provides a natural base for the field surveys and the practical classroom applications that follow. This volume should be an asset to teachers of preschool children as well as to professors in teacher-training programs.

Saville, Muriel R., and Rudolph C. Troike. *A Handbook of Bilingual Education*. Washington, D.C.: Teachers of English to Speakers of Other Languages, 1975.

This handbook is considered a classic. The authors take the reader from the historical perspective of bilingual education on to its psychological, social, and cultural factors and then to such practical considerations as design of a program, the structure of language, planning a curriculum, and teaching approaches. A selected bibliography is provided at the end of each chapter.

Saville-Troike, Muriel. *Foundation for Teaching English as a Second Language: Theory and Method for Multicultural Education*. Englewood Cliffs, N.J.: Prentice-Hall, 1976.

The author presents the theory of language in its psychological, linguistic, and cultural foundations and suggests a wealth of practical teaching approaches. Although limited in scope, the chapter on ESL in bilingual education should help readers to understand how both disciplines complement each other. The book is a resource for teachers and teachers-in-training of English as a Second Language (ESL) and bilingual education.

Saville-Troike, Muriel. *A Guide to Culture in the Classroom*. Rosslyn, Va.: National Clearinghouse for Bilingual Education, 1978.

The author explores the relationship of language, culture, and education; recommends in-service and pre-service training procedures for developing cultural competencies in teachers; and suggests applications of cultural information to classroom practices, curriculum development, and evaluation. The text helps to sensitize teachers to new positive awareness of cultural differences so they can ease the adjustment of children from other cultures and help the rest of the class see differences among peoples in a positive way.

Schmidt, Velma E., and Earldene McNeill. *Cultural Awareness: A Resource Bibliography*. Washington, D.C.: The National Association for the Education of Young Children, 1978.

The authors have compiled a multicultural bibliography of books and materials for children and adults. The books for children have been used for several years with young children in The Learning Tree in Dallas, Texas. Teachers and college students from different cultures have used the adult materials and books and responded to their evaluations. A list of criteria developed by the Council on Interracial Books for Children for evaluating resources is included.

Simoes, Antonio, Jr. (ed.). *The Bilingual Child: Research and Analysis of Existing Educational Themes.* New York: Academic Press, 1976.

This volume is intended to indicate trends of research on bilingual children and their educational needs. The chapters are concerned with literacy in the minority home language plus literacy in another language learned in school, an analysis between immersion and submersion programs, the school environment as a variable in learning how to read, interactions that are meaningful for successful teaching, and community and school expectations, among others.

Werner, Emmy E. *Cross-Cultural Child Development: A View from the Planet Earth.* Monterey, Ca.: Brooks/Cole, 1979.

The author looks at the development of Third World children (in Asia, Africa, Oceania, and Latin America). She considers the effect of an interrelationship of factors during the transition from traditional to modern living. In her discussion of social, physical, and cognitive development, she examines cultural diversity and anticipated universal sequences. Each of the sixteen chapters assists the reader in recognizing cross-cultural similarities inherent in development as well as the socioeconomic conditions affecting the developmental process.

Williams, Leslie R., Iris R. Sutherland, and Charles H. Harrington. *Alerta—A Bilingual Multicultural Early Childhood Curriculum.* New York: Institute for Urban and Minority Education, Teachers College, Columbia University, 1979.

This is a child-centered program that was developed from intensive classroom and community observations and whose theoretical foundation is based on child development, learning, anthropological, and sociolinguistic theories. The curriculum encourages both child-initiated and teacher-directed activities that are carried out bilingually within a nonthreatening, multicultural environment. The materials are in English and Spanish, and they include a manual for teachers and assistants, a manual with suggestions for pre-service and in-service training, a file of suggested activities, and an annotated bibliography.

Wilson, Amos N. *The Developmental Psychology of the Black Child.* New York: Africana Research Publications, 1978.

The development of the black child is traced, beginning with the prenatal period. Thus the subject matter necessarily deals also with the physical and mental health of the expectant mother. The author discusses in each chapter areas of differences between black and white children that he considers to be critical. Among the subjects covered in the book are psychosocial development and race, psychogenic brain damage, play activities and the black child, socialization, achievement and the black child, language and cognitive style, and cultural determinism.

Wilson, Geraldine. *An Annotated Bibliography of Children's Books: An Introduction to the Literature of Head Start's Children.* Washington, D.C.: U.S. Department of Health, Education, and Welfare, 1978.

Wilson lists multiethnic, multicultural materials for the preschool level.

Wilson, Geraldine L. *Multi-Cultural Cookbook.* New York: New York City Head Start Regional Training Office, New York University, 1978.

By exposing children to the foods of many different cultures and involving them in the process of their preparation, it is hoped that they will gain an appreciation of other cultures. In addition to the recipes for meals and snacks, the text includes a list of goals for children to be attained by using this book, questions to help teachers prepare successful cooking experiences, planning charts for preparation and evaluation, charts delineating the tasks of both teachers and children for each step in the cooking process, a chart of the nutritional value of foods, a resource listing of where to purchase foods, and a list of other cookbooks with recipes from different ethnic groups.

13
Special Needs

THE UNCOMMON AS THE COMMON

Michael Lewis

Webster's Dictionary defines "uncommon" as "not ordinarily encountered." This definition suggests that uncommonness is neither positive nor negative, but it does imply that uncommonness is to be judged against some type of normative value. The feature of such a definition is that it is relative rather than absolute. In one culture or setting, a particular behavior may be common, whereas it may be uncommon in another. Nonstandard English, for example, may be common in a poor inner-city community but uncommon in the suburbs. While some might hold to an absolute standard, say, for example, in mental health, against which deviation in any culture or setting could be viewed as uncommon, we prefer the more relative view as implied in the definition as given. We shall hold uncommon to mean (1) that there exists a norm, (2) that this norm is relative, and (3) that all deviance is to be viewed in terms of that relative norm.

In discussing the sources of uncommonness, we need first to focus on the various potential forces that, because of their distinction, may affect developmental outcome. With some exceptions, it can be argued that the single-culprit-variable approach to deviation is incorrect. That is, uncommon development cannot be caused solely by any one of the potential sources of distinction.

The two primary potential sources of uncommonness, like the sources of development in general, can be identified to include both biological and social environmental factors. In the case of chiefly biological potential sources of uncommonness of a child, the uncommonness is located in the organism. The deviation we study pertains most to the unusualness of the

429

child himself. These potential sources are highlighted in the studies of Down's syndrome. The second potential source of deviance in the child pertains to the external environment or social setting in which each child develops. These have been identified as malnourishing, maltreating, neglectful environments. Neither the biological nor environmental forces working alone can be used to predict uncommonness, rather it is the interplay of various sources that is necessary to produce any particular developmental effect. This, of course, applies to both common or deviant development.

Having defined the primary potential sources of uncommonness, we need to focus attention on how the development of distinction may occur. Explicit in the biological notion of uncommonness, either in terms of some positive outcome such as superior IQ performance or in terms of a negative outcome like Down's syndrome, is the view that the deviant characteristics of the individual are an intrinsic property of the individual. This conception likens the uncommonness to a trait or attribute of the individual that acts on the developmental process to effect distinction. Certainly, such explanations appear reasonable in terms of some forms of uncommonness. The Down's child is a good example of such a view. It would be difficult to argue that the behavior or even physical appearance of this child is not solely a function of his or her particular chromosomal makeup. Nevertheless, even here the simple notion of a trait explanation for the developmental end product appears somewhat less than adequate. One developmental outcome associated with Down's syndrome is fairly profound retardation as measured by standard IQ tests. As has been repeatedly pointed out, the IQ score of Down's children is generally below 50. Thus, poor mental scores are associated with a potential biological source of deviation. Even with such a biological source, this simple model of development fails. Removing Down's children from institutions and returning them to family care in their own homes has substantially increased their IQ scores.

We have been discussing the potential sources of uncommonness in terms of the influence of biological and environmental factors. In terms of the child's own psychological processes, the child's internal sense of uncommonness also derives from several sources. Certainly, as indicated above, the social world, depending upon environmental circumstances, may label the child of any cluster of characteristics as uncommon; whether the terms used imply a positive valence (e.g., "gifted" or "precocious") or a negative one (e.g., "different," "handicapped," or "strange"), the communication of the way in which the child is perceived within his own social nexus will affect the infant's developing sense of self. At the same time, there are direct effects of the developing child's interaction with the surrounding environment and the perceived comparisons of the relative performance of others; thus, even in the absence of any attribution by others of uncommonness, such a self-concept may emerge in the child. Not surprisingly, we may expect the social-attributive and self-evaluative factors to interact in shaping the child's perception of this fundamental facet of self—the feelings of either identification with and belonging to or a difference and apartness from those who surround us. This point of view suggests, however, that the internal sense of uncommonness may not always reflect a true perception of the child's world and his place within it, either on the child's own part or on the part of others that play a role in influencing the developing sense of self. Moreover, the same child placed in different environments, which require different characteristics for achievement or failure in which salient features may be mastered with ease or difficulty, can emerge with different feelings of uncommonness. Thus, for example, the spastic child who performs poorly when confronted with a world of staircases may function without handicap in a world of elevators and ramps.

The general principle represented in this example reverts to our initial definition of uncommonness. Not only does the physical and social environment exert forces that may shape uncommonness, the same domains provide the very basis upon which uncommonness may be defined. Change the norms and you redefine uncommonness; change the environment and that which was previously uncommon now fits the norm.

CHILDREN WITH SPECIAL NEEDS: DISABILITIES AND HANDICAPS

Barbara Mates

Much of our popular literature, motion pictures, television, and other media fare tends to promote the notion that childhood is a relatively trouble-free, idyllic state of being. Any stresses that come along for the child are mainly of the innocuous, social *faux pas* type, easily resolved and secretly tittered at or disdained by adults as being really unimportant. Perhaps, in our heart of hearts, each of us wishes that it had really been that way for us in our own childhood and clings to the belief that if it was not that way for us, for others it really was halcyon. Real problems of young children are often dramatically portrayed as notable exceptions to general youthful tranquility, all the more tragic because the difficulties are those of a young person. The notion that stresses of working through childhood problems may be as real as those of dealing with adult problems is one that some adults seem to have difficulty accepting. Even more alien to some is the fact that children, including preschoolers and even infants, are prey to the gamut of disabilities and problems that face their adult counterparts.

The question of dealing with the special needs of infants and preschoolers with disabilities and handicapping conditions is a complicated one for several reasons. The infant and child are constantly changing—developing, though imperceptibly, from moment to moment. The picture of a particular preschooler that we had yesterday may be altered today because of developments that are taking place. Often, we cannot clearly say when the transition from one picture to another has occurred, how that change takes place, or what has prompted it to take place.

So, our attempts to discover the pattern and picture of the young child's problems are complicated, as are our attempts to plan a program to help the child overcome or ameliorate the problems.

Further complications arise because until an infant has developed to the point where we might expect him or her to be able to carry out a certain activity, we may not be able to tell that the child will have difficulty with it. Knowledge of what to expect and of the present problem areas of the individual child may lead us to watch for certain difficulties and thus enable us to help the child as soon as special needs present themselves. On the other hand, an infant or preschooler with mild or minimal problems may not be noted by the adults around him or her to need help until the problem has developed into a much larger one, later on.

In a sense, we all have special needs. We all have our areas of strength and weakness. What distinguishes the special needs of the disabled from those of the bulk of the population is that without specialized help or attention these difficulties can prevent the individual from attaining his or her maximum capability in one or more areas of life. There is, too, that area of shading in which weakness is neither great enough to be clearly disabling nor slight enough to be easily dealt with. Sometimes this situation presents a more difficult problem than a clear-cut case; it is not easily recognized as a real problem and the child is blamed for not achieving or, perhaps worse yet, for not trying. And if the disability is recognized, its slight nature may make appropriate settings for treatment or remediation difficult to find.

Problems from which infants and preschoolers may suffer may have occurred before birth, during infancy and babyhood, or at any later time during development. Some children may have a single impairment. For others, a multiplicity of disabilities may occur. Classification of kinds of disability may vary with the viewpoint of the classifier. However, more important than the way in which the listing of disabilities is arranged is that they are all encompassed and that the classification system leads to some effective approach or approaches to treatment and/or amelioration. The classification system used here cuts across various approaches and taxonomies. It is intended only as a general approach to inclusiveness for the convenience of the reader. Terms used are descriptive rather than definitional. Specific areas of disability of infancy and early childhood include problems of general health—conditions such as allergies, asthma, and other respiratory problems, cardiac problems, and other physical difficulties. Orthopedic, bodily, and motor movement problems include manifestations of conditions such as cerebral palsy, spina bifida, various kinds of paralyses, amputations, and results of accidents. Children may have total or partial sensory impairments, such as blindness or low vision and deafness or partial hearing. Language-processing problems and/ or speech difficulties may become apparent as the infant or preschooler develops or may have occurred following some specific causal situation. Developmental disabilities have been noted to include conditions such as various kinds of mental retardation and other intellectual and developmental difficulties. Learning disabilities may be manifest in certain areas of function despite potentially adequate intellectual ability. Reading, writing, spelling, arithmetic, or other educational problems may sometimes be predicted and eased by observation of earlier appearing developmental difficulties. Emotional problems, behavioral dysfunction, various neurologically based disorders, and rarer conditions of other types may also be found in the infant and preschool population.

Considerations arise other than those of identifying and dealing specifically with particular problems in infants and preschoolers. Some of the questions transcend various conditions and are common to a number of them, if not to all children with disabilities, their families, and those who work with them. Included are matters of educational rights of disabled children, a legal concept but one having immediate relevance to the people who are involved in implementing it. Related to this is the matter of appropriate educational curriculum and setting: shall the individual child be best served in a mainstream setting, a specialized program within the mainstream, a self-contained group, or in a residential environment? Still another area to consider deals with the problems of the child who must be hospitalized for a prolonged period of time or of the child who must return to the hospital intermittently. Other ramifications of disability are the psychosocial aspects: how does the disability affect the developing child *vis à vis* his or her milieu? And what of the parents and family of the disabled child—the child and parent do not exist in a vacuum. Often there is more than a single child, a matter relatively little dealt with by the literature. Another area of concern is the management of the child with a disability by parent, educator, and practitioner. These and related areas are more or less spottily examined in the literature.

To be a parent of or a practitioner for such children presents unique problems that are often not encountered by parents and professionals whose involvement is generally restricted to children whose specialized individual needs do not call attention to themselves. The parent or family member of a child with a disability may be fortunate enough to have found an adequate source of information and direction for promoting the child's development and education. Others, who have a child with a lesser known or as yet unidentified problem, may be in a situation of being bounced from setting to setting, practitioner to practitioner, in search of an adequate answer. Similarly, the practitioner trying to work with a family and/or child whose disability is not clear-cut may be seeking sources of information. For those parents and professionals seeking information and guidance in various areas dealing with the special-needs child, this chapter attempts to provide a base of departure.

The references cited cover a number of areas relevant to both general and specific types of disabilities. They are intended to give the parent or professional practitioner a basic view of some of the literature available. Because the breadth and scope of the available literature varies greatly from area to area, this sampling of what may be found reflects both that variability and the selection of the contributors in the various disabilities and related areas.

For parents and professionals seeking more specific or detailed information or information about rarer conditions, the listings of organizations, newsletters, and periodicals for parents and professionals noted in the Resources chapter of this volume may prove useful.

NURTURING GIFTEDNESS AND CREATIVITY IN THE EARLY YEARS

Renee Queen

All children need responsive parents, stimulating environments, questions to support curiosity, and explorations to extend creativity. But for gifted and potentially gifted and talented children the lack of such an environment may make the difference between reaching for and attaining their full potential and functioning at a less than challenging level of aspiration. And this environment must be provided in infancy and toddlerhood as well as the first years of schooling if children with unique intellectual, social, physical, and creative attributes are to fulfill their identification of giftedness.

For many adults, giftedness is synonymous with intellectual function or high IQ scores. It is necessary here to sound a cautionary note about stressing intellectual expansiveness while paying scant attention to physical, psychological, and creative development. Balance is a must: the fun of adventuring, risking, learning to be free, questing, and questioning will help young children accept themselves as unique beings, comfortable in their pursuits of interests that often are not on the same level as those of their age or peer group. *All* children must be free to test their growth in varied areas, which includes being free of the pressure of adults who expect some of them to excel in all areas.

Gifted and talented children rarely fit into preconceived developmental slots; their graph of growth is neither uniform not balanced. For this reason parents and teachers would do well to mesh learning and teaching experiences with each child's level of interest and readiness for reaching and at the same time realize that gifted children need time to play, to discover, to be themselves.

It is important to temper the vision of the gifted child as a verbally precocious, high-IQ scientific and mathematical whiz with the inclusion of traits inherent in children who will eschew the school-oriented paths for iconoclastic paths of daring. In all learning encounters, planned and spontaneous, creativity is a vital force. Laurence Kubie, a psychiatrist who worked extensively with creativity, holds it to be an important human resource, inseparable from and essential to human progress. When gifted children tirelessly pursue a topic, stay unrelentlessly with an object or activity, explore and press for answers, the frazzled adult too often stifles the curiosity, the springboard for creativity. Creativity and giftedness are sparked through varied stimulations with open-ended materials and myriad experiences beginning in infancy and continuing throughout the school years. When teachers or parents feel comfortable with curiosity and seeking and nurture them, they encourage the child to take the step beyond, to listen to the small intuitive voice within. It is only through challenging beliefs, systems, self, and aspects of society that creative spurts and contributions are possible. Awareness of these traits enable parents and educators to implement effective programs and experiences for children with special gifts.

Early experiences have a far-reaching influence on the attainment of capacity. Gifted children are not always self-motivated. They need understanding, encouragement, and respect for their efforts to grow.

The very young will respond to an effective stimulating environment and demonstrate their giftedness in early physical development, precocity in reasoning and verbal ability, social responsiveness, dogged curiosity and an intense, protracted attention span. Educators have come to recognize the multidimensional nature of giftedness, and most definitions move on from intellectual ability to include task commitment, talent in visual or performing arts, and superior psychomotor ability. Children often demonstrate giftedness in more than one area.

Awareness of the varied dimensions will alert those who work and live with young children to the need to use flexible criteria in recognition and extension of gifts and talents.

In all aspects of giftedness, the responsibility of adult care-givers and program planners is to develop the habit of excellence in pursuits for themselves and for the children. Expectations and belief in the possible lead to excellence in achievements, contributions to society, and self-fulfillment.

BIBLIOGRAPHY

Coping with Disabilities

Adams, Barbara. *Like It Is: Facts and Feelings About Handicaps from Kids Who Know*. New York: Walker, 1979.

Young people with handicaps tell how they feel about their problems, what those problems are, how they look at the world, what their fears and accomplishments are, and, most particularly, how they would like to be treated by their nonhandicapped peers. The handicaps dealt with include hearing, speech, and visual impairment, orthopedic disabilities, developmental disabilities, and behavioral disorders.

Anderson, Elizabeth M., and Bernie Spain. *The Child with Spina Bifida*. Denver, Col.: Love Publishing Co. 1977.

Although this book is about spina bifida and hydrocephalus, many of the special needs described are shared by children disabled in other ways. The authors provide comprehensive information about all aspects of the condition through a multidisciplinary approach. Additionally, practical suggestions are given to the parents and professionals for helping the child cope with physical as well as social and emotional problems.

Atheim, Daniel D., and William A. Sinclair. *The Clumsy Child: A Program of Motor Therapy*. St. Louis: Mosby, 1979.

This book is designed to be used by the physical education specialist, movement therapist, special educator, and classroom teacher. The goal is to help the professional assist the child who, because of physical, mental, or emotional factors, is awkward in motor behavior. The approaches and methodologies offered by the authors are taken from many years of working with motor-deficient children. In this comprehensive guide, complete with step-by-step instructions, there are valuable tables that outline gross motor, fine motor, and social and adaptive behavioral characteristics.

Ayrault, Evelyn West. *Growing Up Handicapped: A Guide to Helping the Exceptional Child.* New York: Seabury Press, 1977.

To have a disability is not synonomous with being handicapped. Those living or working with special needs children will learn how to prevent the disabled child from becoming a handicapped one. Drawn from the author's case histories, chapters deal with the attitudes of parents ranging from rejecting, passive, fearful, overindulgent, to adjusting. Guidelines are given for coping with all sorts of problems, such as temper tantrums, using the disability as an excuse, toilet learning, and discipline. Discussed are the pros and cons of school for the young child, the various aspects of rehabilitation, the work of the rehabilitation team, and qualifications needed for staff members treating the disabled. Appendixes list rehabilitation agencies, sources of financial information, and national organizations that provide services.

Barkley, Russell A. *Hyperactive Children: A Handbook for Diagnosis and Treatment.* New York: Guilford Press, 1981.

Professionals working with hyperactive children and their families will find this book comprehensive. Although the text advocates intervention based upon the principles of behavior modification, there is an excellent chapter on drug management techniques. There are suggested scales and assessment instruments that should help to clarify the particular problems a child may be experiencing. Of most importance would be the outlines of actual programs. Parent training methods are thoroughly explored, as are methods for implementing programs in classroom settings. In addition to a review of the literature, there is an interesting section on the more radical theories concerning the etiology and treatment of this often baffling disorder.

Berko, Frances C., Martin J. Berko, and Stephanie C. Thompson. *Management of Brain-Damaged Children: A Parents' and Teachers' Guide.* Springfield, Ill.: Thomas, 1970.

This practical book gives concrete advice in such important management areas as development of feeding and eating habits, facilitation of early speech development, management of hyper-activity, toilet training, home and school discipline, personality training and growth, and development of attention and perception. There are definitions and descriptions of the brain-damaged child and how the child may be diagnosed. The text deals with the special problems presented by the brain-injured child to his family, to his teacher as well as to his community.

Brown, Diana. *Developmental Handicaps in Babies and Young Children: A Guide for Parents.* Springfield, Ill.: Thomas, 1972.

This slim volume is an informal source book for parents and those concerned with the welfare and learning development of developmentally handicapped babies and young children. The author is concerned with the areas of prevention of handicaps, general developmental problems, and seeking resources. The chapter "A Special Dictionary for Parents" provides parents with good definitions of terms written in lay person's language. Early intervention is explored, and there is emphasis on diagnostic evaluation and counseling.

Brown, Sara, and Martha Moersch (eds.). *Parents on the Team.* Ann Arbor: University of Michigan Press, 1978.

Parents as well as professionals have contributed their own perspectives to this volume that stresses the need for a partnership in the care of handicapped children. The background material is drawn from experiences in the Early Intervention Program for Handicapped Infants and Young Children in Michigan. The volume includes four useful appendices: a list of general resources found in most states, a list of national organizations, a list and short description of the major laws that provide protection and services to handicapped persons, and a well-annotated bibliography.

Corrigan, Dean, and Kenneth Howey (eds.). *Concepts to Guide the Education of Experienced Teachers with Implication for PL 94-142.* Reston, Va.: Council for Exceptional Children, 1980.

This book is addressed to teachers and teacher trainers. Focus is on the preparation and in-service training with focus on Public Law 94-142, which insures the right of all handicapped children to a free public education in a least restrictive environment.

Crow, Gary A. *Children at Risk.* New York: Schocken, 1978.

Crow has written this book to alert parents or professionals to potential problems most frequently encountered with children between the ages of five and eight at home and in the classroom. He lists 450 signs and symptoms of early childhood difficulties, and practical advice is given on how to deal with the various problems.

Cruickshank, William M. *Concepts in Special Education.* Syracuse, N.Y.: Syracuse University Press, 1981.

This volume, the first of a series on special education, consists of the author's own selected papers that have previously been published as speeches or in professional journals. Each paper is preceded by a brief introduction or followed by a summary that illuminates more fully the topic discussed. Some of the essays included deal with: arithmetic ability of mentally retarded children; the impact of physical disability on social adjustment; group therapy with physically handicapped children and pioneer studies in the field of learning disabilities. A scholarly work and valuable contribution to the literature in special education.

Deppe, Philip R., and Judith L. Sherman. *The High-Risk Child: A Guide for Concerned Parents.* New York: Macmillan, 1981.

The authors have written this book for parents of children with learning or physical disabilities, health care professionals and parents concerned with understanding the factors that often place a child at risk of developing an impairment through heredity, fetal injury during pregnancy and post-natal problems. Chapters deal with expected developmental milestones, identifying disabilities, financing and supporting the special child, utilizing community resources and keeping "home, hearth and self together" when faced with raising a disabled child.

Faas, Larry A. *Children with Learning Problems: A Handbook for Teachers.* Boston: Houghton Mifflin Co., 1980.

The author provides a wide range of diagnostic and remedial

suggestions for teachers of children with learning problems. The emphasis is on learning problems rather than learning disabilities to allow for a flexible frame of reference that highlights similarities rather than differences among children who have trouble learning. The text discusses types of learning problems, prevalence, legal provisions, diagnostic procedures, recording student progress, developing instructional plans as well as working with parents of children who have learning problems.

Featherstone, Helen. *A Difference in the Family.* New York: Basic Books, 1980.

This is a valuable contribution to the literature about and for families of handicapped children. The author combines the feelings, sensitivities, and reflections of a parent who has lived through the experiences, with the clear insight of a professional. Sensitive, yet not maudlin; critical and angry, yet not destructive, Featherstone has written a genuinely helpful book.

Forehand, Rex L. and Robert J. McMahon. *Helping the Noncompliant Child.* New York: The Guilford Press, 1981.

This book is intended for professionals and paraprofessionals who work with parents of children with special needs. Provided is a detailed description of a treatment program developed to teach the parents how to modify their children's deviant behavior problems. The chapters offer the reader with an introduction to the problem of noncompliance, overview of the suggested treatment, treatment program and parent training program.

Heisler, Verda. *A Handicapped Child in the Family: A Guide for Parents.* New York: Grune & Stratton, 1972.

The author, herself a victim of polio in childhood, has written a direct and compelling book about feelings, attitudes, stress, conflict, resolution, and growth, of a handicapped person based on her own experiences and as a practicing psychotherapist working with parents of handicapped children. The focus is on the psychological adjustment of parents to the special problems of their child's handicap, and the overriding concern is for the emotional needs of the handicapped child and the development of the handicapped child as a person. In addition to parents, this book will provide valuable insights to all professionals who provide services to families of children with any kind of mental or physical handicap.

Curriculum for Special Education

Alvin, Juliette. *Music for the Handicapped Child*, 2nd ed. London: Oxford University Press, 1976.

The author describes her own approach to using music to aid in the development of the other aspects of the child's total development. Individual chapters deal with intellectual and social development, music for the mentally limited, autistic, cerebral palsied, blind, deaf, and physically handicapped. Some musical materials are recommended but are not included in the text. It is designed for anyone working with the handicapped.

Anderson, Frances E. *Art for All the Children*. Springfield, Ill.: Thomas, 1978.

In her comprehensive text in arts for the handicapped, Anderson provides a description of exceptionality, evaluation and assessment of creative potential, and arts experiences in mainstreamed settings. Each activity includes a rationale, motivating technique, listing of materials, description of procedure, evaluation, and suggestions for adaptations.

Bangs, Tina. *Birth to Three: Developmental Learning and the Handicapped Child*. Hingham, Mass.: Teaching Resources Corp., 1979.

This book is meant primarily for the professional, though a concerned parent could benefit from its clear and precise information about development of children during the first three years of life. While problem solving, social/personal and motor skill development are discussed, emphasis is placed on language acquisition. Bangs provides a useful curriculum guide for normal children, performance objectives, and lesson plans for six age groups between the birth to three-year range. She then provides curriculum guide adaptations for children with handicapping conditions.

Baskin, Barbara, and Karen Harris. *Notes from a Different Drummer: A Guide to Juvenile Fiction Portraying the Handicapped*, New York: Bowker, 1977.

The book contains thoughtful, sensitive annotations of children's books that contain characters who have special needs. The authors provide plot summaries and comment on the accuracy of each book and its usefulness in teaching. This book is recommended to those interested in children's literature or handicapped children. It will be a valuable tool to those seeking to integrate disabled children into mainstream programs.

Bergmann, Thesi and Anna Freud. *Children in the Hospital*. New York: International Universities Press, 1974.

The reader will gain an understanding of hospitalized children. The volume is illustrated with case studies using children's conversations and stories and describes use of play and art therapy. It is aimed at the medical professions, but it is a good introduction for people who are involved with physically ill or handicapped children.

Connors, Frances P., Gordon G. Williamson, and John M. Siepp. *Program Guide for Infants and Toddlers with Neuromotor and Other Developmental Disabilities*. New York: Teachers College Press, 1978.

This book was developed during ten years of service to and learning about young children with special needs. The authors worked closely with the National Collaborative Infant Project, which was sponsored by United Cerebral Palsy Associations. The book has three parts. Part One "discusses the fundamentals of a sound developmental program"; Part Two "describes developmental sequences of normal and atypical children and intervention strategies in five areas—movement, pre-speech, language, cognition, and social emotion"; and Part Three "presents practical applications of the curriculum."

Cunningham, Cliff, and Patricia Sloper. *Helping Your Exceptional Baby*. New York: Pantheon, 1980.

In this guide to the development of the mentally handicapped infant during the first years of life, the authors draw on their extensive work in the study of Down's syndrome and offer practical information that will show parents how to help their child master the skills of the first years. Written in a clear, direct, and supportive way, the tone emphasizes the importance of the quality of the intervention.

Ginglend, David R., and Winifred E. Stiles. *Music Activities for Retarded Children.* Nashville: Abingdon Press, 1965.

Although this book was written for children in special education classes, its material is excellent for all preschoolers. The book is divided into a number of categories: "All About Me" (self-realization), "Listen" (auditory), "Ten Little Fingers" (finger plays), "I Can, Can You" (following directions), "Holidays," "Things to Learn," "Let's Pretend" (dramatic play), "Just for Fun" (nonsense songs), "Come to the Party" (simple structured dances). The music has piano accompaniment and simple chords for autoharp and guitar. Each song is followed by suggested activities that are especially helpful for a classroom teacher who wants to introduce more music into the class.

Gould, Elaine, and Loren Gould. *Arts and Crafts for Physically and Mentally Disabled.* Springfield, Ill.: Thomas, 1978.

The authors suggest 120 craft projects for exceptional people. A discussion of adapting materials to meet their unique learning and social needs is included.

Graham, Richard M. (ed.). *Music for the Exceptional Child.* Reston, Va.: Music Educators National Conference, 1975.

The emphasis is on music therapy in special education and in school settings. Readings include music therapy for the speech handicapped, hearing and sight impaired, retarded, emotionally disturbed, and learning disabled. In addition, there are programs for the gifted. Excellent resources and bibliography make this very useful for the music educator and those interested in music therapy in educational settings.

Hardesty, Kay. *Silver Burdett Music for Special Education.* Morristown, N.J.: Silver Burdett, 1979.

Designed to assist the general music teacher to adapt conventional music materials for use with children having special needs. Written to be used with Silver Burdett Music series, used in many schools, it contains many detailed musical activities using body motion, singing, instruments, and games. There are lesson plans and many activity songs and other activities. Two soft-vinyl records are included with sample songs. The book is an excellent resource for anyone interested in using music with group activities.

Jones, Reginald L. (ed.). *Mainstreaming and the Minority Child.* Minneapolis: Council for Exceptional Children, 1976.

This book offers a collection of papers dealing with the "double-jeopardy" issue of the handicapped child who is also a minority child. The contributors report on a variety of crucial aspects such as assessing the minority child and teaching specific minority children in mainstream programs. The total work offers a strong basis for developing an appropriate mainstreaming program.

Kay, Jane G. *Crafts for the Very Disabled and Handicapped.* Springfield, Ill.: Thomas, 1977.

In this collection of product-oriented art projects the activities are clearly presented and well illustrated. Patterns are provided and level of difficulty and fine motor coordination are included for each activity.

Kirk, Samuel A., and James J. Gallagher. *Educating Exceptional Children*, 3rd ed. Boston: Houghton Mifflin, 1979.

This edition of this title clearly, and succinctly discusses children who are gifted, mentally retarded, hearing and visually impaired, learning disabled, emotionally disturbed, and multi-handicapped. Classroom application for all of these situations is included. It is highly recommended.

Kokasha, Sharon Metz. *Creative Movement for Special Education.* Belmont, Ca.: Fearon, 1974.

These lesson suggestions work very well with preschool children three to five, though they are presented for special education. They start with "Back to School," continue through all the holidays and seasons and end with "The Summer Season."

Any melodies used are extremely simple and most of the exercises require no musical accompaniment beyond storytelling directions or chanting. The movement lessons are suitable for both an experienced or inexperienced teacher.

Krone, Ann. *Art Instruction for Handicapped Children.* Denver: Love Publishing, 1978.

Krone discusses the stages of artistic development and techniques for the selection of art activities appropriate for children with special needs. Included are project descriptions, materials, and motivational approaches. The appendix contains formulas for preparing art materials.

Lillie, David L. (ed.). *Teaching Parents to Teach: Education for the Handicapped.* New York: Walker, 1977.

Total parent involvement is increasingly seen as a critical factor in effectively teaching the disabled child. Guidelines are given on how to plan and implement programs for parents of children with special needs. Some of the recommendations are appropriate for all parents.

Long, Kate. *"Johnny's such a Bright Boy, What a Shame He's Retarded": In Support of Mainstreaming in Public Schools.* Boston: Houghton Mifflin, 1977.

Long combines her own experience in the field of special education with several years of research in writing this book about the education of the mentally retarded and the critical role that mainstreaming must play. She also includes detailed descriptions of legislation and policy making in special education. This readable and relevant book for parents, caretakers, educators, and other professionals working with the mentally retarded child has important implications for the future.

McElderry, Joanne S., and Linda E. Escobedo. *Tools for Learning, Activities for Young Children with Special Needs.* Denver: Love Publishing, 1979.

The text was developed for teachers of students with learning problems or handicapped children. It is also useful for preschool or kindergarten educators, parents, or paraprofessionals and volunteers in these settings. A variety of materials and techniques to make learning of basic skills fun for teachers and children are demonstrated.

Piazza, Robert, and Roz Rothman (ed.). *Pre-School Education for the Handicapped*. Guilford, Ct.: Special Learning Corporation, 1979.

The editors have organized their selection of articles about the young handicapped child into five sections: Early Intervention, a Rationale, Identification and Assessment of a Preschool Population, Programs, Parents, and Future Trends. Various conditions and program strategies are described. The articles constitute an overview of current practices and may be used as a guide to more intensive reading. It is part of a special education series. Parents as well as professionals will find it of value.

Pope, Lillie, Deborah Edel, and Abraham Hakley. *Special Needs: Special Answers. A Resource of Reproductable Exercises and Activities for Special Education and Early Childhood Programs*. Brooklyn, N.Y.: Book-Lab, 1979.

This activity book is designed for the teacher or tutor to use with students with learning problems. It is especially useful for working with children in the early grades who have difficulties with basic mathematical concepts or prereading or perceptual skills.

Reger, Roger (ed.). *Preschool Programming of Children with Disabilities*. Springfield, Ill.: Thomas, 1974.

This small volume is a collection of articles written by educators of preschool children with disabilities. One particularly valuable chapter is concerned with a parental viewpoint of preschool programs. The articles in this book deal with such areas as: Evaluating Children; Language; Perceptual-Motor Development of the Young Child. The author presents a clear picture of the various stages of development in the young child.

Reynolds, Maynard C., and Malcolm D. Davis, Eds. *Exceptional Children in the Regular Classroom*. Minneapolis, Minn.: University of Minnesota, 1977.

This book presents a number of cogent essays by leaders in the field of special education concerned with offering the best possible educational environment for children with disabilities. Focus is on how to manage disabled children in the regular classroom and how to develop strategies for improving regular educational services for children with special needs.

Sherrill, Claudine. *Creative Arts for the Severely Handicapped.* Springfield, Ill.: Thomas, 1979.

A rationale for the inclusion of the creative arts into educational and recreational programs for exceptional children is offered. Supporting chapters include "Adapting Wheelchair Dance to the Severely Disabled," "Self-Expression Through the Arts," and "Creating a Children's Theatre for the Deaf." Parents and teachers of children with special needs will find it an excellent reference text.

Siegel, Ernest, and Ruth F. Gold. *Educating the Learning Disabled.* (With contributions by David Levinsky and Joan Lange Bildman). New York: Macmillan, 1982.

The authors note that the learning disabled are easily misunderstood because of the very mildness of many conditions and set out to present both sides of a question, when possible reconciling differing viewpoints as well as offering their own opinions. The text serves as an introduction to learning disabilities for preservice and inservice teachers and parents and as a reference to other professionals. Discussed are general teaching principles, suggestions, curriculum implementation and instructional sequencing.

Whittaker, James K. *Caring for Troubled Children.* San Francisco: Jossey-Bass, 1979.

This book presents a comprehensive examination of residential childcare for children with severe emotional problems or severe learning disabilities. This book is written for childcare workers, child psychiatrists, educators of exceptional children, as well as planners charged with developing new programs. A chapter that deals with the importance of parent involvement will be especially helpful to parents of children with special needs.

Wiederholt, J. Lee, Donald D. Hammill, and Virginia Brown. *The Resource Teacher: A Guide to Effective Practices.* Boston: Allyn and Bacon, 1978.

A guide and reference for resource teachers and those in teacher in-service training programs. Divided into three parts, the book describes in part one the resource program and the role of the teacher; part two details the organizing and managing of the program, with the last part focusing on planning appropriate individual programs. Comprehensive in scope, this book is filled with effective step-by-step guidelines.

Wilson, Sue. *I Can Do It! I Can Do It! Arts and Crafts for the Mentally Retarded.* Newport Beach, Ca.: Quail Street Publishing, 1976.

Wilson has assembled a collection of highly motivating arts and crafts activities coded for children's levels of special needs. This small volume is an excellent home reference for parents of exceptional youngsters.

Frith, Greg H. *The Role of the Special Education Paraprofessional.* Springfield, Ill.: Thomas, 1982.

The author addresses this introductory text to the teacher assistant as the emerging new professional. Starting with a historical perspective of the special education movement, the chapters deal with the various stages involved in screening, referral, placement, re-evaluation of disabled children, the instructional process, therapeutic play programs, classroom activities and the paraprofessional's role and responsibility as an individual who provides direct or indirect services to children with special needs and their parents.

Meisels, Samuel J. *Development Screening Guide in Early Childhood: A Guide.* Washington, D.C.: National Association for the Education of Young Children, 1978.

Meisels outlines all the steps necessary to set up an exemplary screening program for young children in a community. Service groups, social agencies, and other community planners will find this practical guide invaluable as a source for identifying, evaluating, and serving children with disabilities.

McNamara, Joan, and Bernard McNamara. *The Special Child Handbook.* New York: Hawthorn Books, 1977.

As professionals in the field of handicaps, and as parents of five children with special needs (four adopted), the authors have written a good reference book. Chapter headings include "When Special Needs Appear," "Getting the Right Diagnosis," "Your Feelings and Your Child's," "Where to Find Support," "Financial Problems," and "Legal Rights." Each chapter is supplemented by a resource directory to books and services. But the book is more than a director to services; it offers valuable insight into some of the major issues for parents and professionals.

Moore, Coralie, and Kathryn Gorham Morton. *A Reader's Guide for Parents of Children with Mental, Physical, or Emotional Disabilities.* Rockville, Md.: U.S. Department of Health, Education, and Welfare, 1976.

The authors have compiled a well-organized, annotated guide to the literature available for parents of handicapped children. Selections in Part I are relevant to all disabilities and include basic readings, how-to books, books based on personal experiences, and books dealing with special issues. Part II lists books about particular disabilities; Part III, books for children about children with handicaps. Part IV contains sources of information, organizations, agencies, directories, and a listing of popular journals on various disabilities. This guide is comprehensive, and the references are well selected by authors who are knowledgeable and sensitive to parents' needs.

Morse, William C. (ed.). *Humanistic Teaching for Exceptional Children.* Syracuse, N.Y.: Syracuse University Press, 1979.

This collection of essays by leaders in the field of special education focuses on the child with special needs as a human being with emotional needs shared by all children. Guidance is given to parents as well as both classroom and resource teachers on helping children prepare for life in the mainstream of society. Chapters deal with learning disabilities, socio-emotional impairment, gifted children, vision and hearing problems, physical handicaps, cerebral palsy, and the problems and promise of special education.

Pope, Lillie. *Guidelines for Teaching Students with Learning Problems.* New York: Book-Lab, 1982.

This is a practical guide for teachers, clinicians, tutors, and parents who are concerned about the students in any grade with learning or behavior problems. Guidelines are provided for assessing the needs of the child who may have difficulty with the standard curriculum.

Learning Disabilities

Gliedman, John, and William Roth. *The Unexpected Minority: Handicapped Children in America.* New York & London: Harcourt, Brace, Jovanovich, 1979.

In this report, prepared for the Carnegie Council for children, the authors for the first time apply a civil rights concept to the problems of both handicapped children and adults, charging that the traditional use of a medical mode has generated attitudes and practices by which social aspects of a disability stunt the lives of many handicapped children and adults. The authors call for a more active role by parents in controlling services provided to their children.

Hammill, Donald D., and Nettie R. Bartel. *Teaching Children with Learning and Behavior Problems.* Boston: Allyn & Bacon, 1978.

The authors provide an overview of various methods used in educational programs for children with learning disabilities. Descriptions of assessment and remediation procedures are provided for the following areas: math, spelling, reading, writing, language development, perceptual-motor development, and classroom management. Also included is a comprehensive bibliography of relevant literature.

Jordan, June B., and Rebecca F. Dailey (eds.). *Not All Little Wagons Are Red: The Exceptional Child's Early Years.* Reston, Va.: Council for Exceptional Children, 1973.

This shared effort by the leaders in the field of early childhood education for children with special needs is for professionals and parents. Its main topics are rationale and historical perspective for early intervention, identification of children needing special help, program models and resource materials, training personnel, initiating and implementing change. The clear and concise language, the illustrative photos, and the philosophical base of "special children need what all children need as well as additional support and adaptations" make this a valuable book.

Lagos, Jorge C. *Seizures, Epilepsy, and Your Child: A Handbook for Parents, Teachers, and Epileptics of All Ages*. New York: Harper & Row, 1974.

Lagos has written a practical guide, to the nature, diagnosis, treatment, and management of epilepsy. The author, a pediatric neurologist, goes beyond the medical treatment to the impact of epilepsy on the rest of the family as well as suggestions on how to deal with behavioral and psychological problems. Written in clear, layman's language, this book should be an aid to parents, teachers, and other professionals in the better understanding of the epileptic child.

Osman, B. B. *Learning Disabilities. A Family Affair*. New York: Random House, 1979.

The book effectively provides information on how parents and others interested in learning-disabled children can help them to develop with positive feelings. It describes early signs of learning disability, how schools can deal with learning-disabled children, and ways for parents and school to improve these children's social difficulties. There are appendixes listing, among other relevant facts, the names of special schools, camps, and colleges for such children.

Pope, Lillie. *Guidelines for Teaching Students with Learning Problems*. Brooklyn, N.Y.: Book-Lab, 1982.

Teachers, parents, clinicians and tutors who are concerned about the student in any grade with learning and/or behavior problems will find this a practical source. The book provides guidelines for assessing the needs of the learner who may have difficulty with the standard curriculum and for planning an individualized instruction program to meet these needs. A brief description of child development supplies the reader with enough background to appreciate developmental patterns in children and to be aware of the more common type of dysfunction encountered in those with learning problems. The chapters that deal with language development reading, and behavioral and academic disabilities provide a wealth of suggestions on how to deal with common problems. In addition, answers are given to 100 questions most frequently asked by teachers and parents.

Pope, Lillie. *Learning Disabilities Glossary*. Brooklyn, N.Y.: Book-Lab, 1976.

The main purpose of this glossary is to define the meaning of much of the technical terminology used in the field of special education. Arranged in alphabetical order, the terms selected by the author for inclusion are those that are current and not self-explanatory.

Rosner, Jerome. *Helping Children Overcome Learning Difficulties*. New York: Walker, 1979.

Walker has developed a revolutionary program for parents whose children are not doing well, or are failing, in school. With the help of this book, a parent can teach the skills that will enable the child to master reading, writing, and arithmetic. The program can be followed in less than half an hour per day. Grounded in a sound theoretical and research base, this revised and expanded edition of the original work gives parents and teachers an eminently practical plan of action.

Ross, Alan O. *Learning Disability: The Unrealized Potential*. New York: McGraw-Hill, 1977.

This book can be useful for both the professional and the concerned parent. Ross' thesis is that the learning-disabled child's primary symptom is his inability to "focus" his attention; if anything, this child pays attention to almost everything around him rather than only one thing at a time. Ross is quite certain, citing research findings, that what the learning-disabled child needs is special education rather than medicine, gymnastics, or visual-motor (perceptual) exercises.

Ross, Alan O. *Psychological Aspects of Learning Disabilities and Reading Disorders*. New York: McGraw-Hill, 1976.

Ross examines major research in the field of learning disabilities and discusses the implications of this research for classroom teaching. Main goal of the book is a much needed attempt to integrate research and practice. Ross covers the following major categories: defining learning disabilities, perception, attention, memory, information processing, hyperactivity and medication, and reading disorders. Difficulty with selective attention is cited as the underlying problem of learning-disabled children. The author stresses that the failure of a child to learn should be viewed as a deficiency in the program rather than the child. Although geared to educators, the material may be of interest to parents and caretakers.

Ross, Bette M. *Our Special Child: A Guide to Successful Parenting of Handicapped Children.* New York: Walker, 1981.

A parent of a Down's syndrome child aims to help other parents who find themselves in a similar situation. Ross guides parents through the new and conflicting emotions and situations that they will doubtlessly experience. The philosophy of organizing and dealing with agencies and service providers to obtain needed assistance is clearly outlined. Many sections give references for further reading. From the decision to bring your baby home or not through the encouragement of independence, Ross offers the reader examples of the experiences many families have had. There is an awareness throughout of the feelings and adaptations parents, siblings, and grandparents make as they grow and learn with their handicapped child. This is an uncomplicated and "upbeat" book that achieves its goal of being informative, yet supportive.

Safford, Phillip. *Teaching Young Children with Special Needs,* St. Louis: Mosby, 1978.

Organized around identified areas of special needs, including giftedness, this book serves as a basic reference for regular and special education teachers, as well as parents. Combining theory with practical application, the author provides information concerning handicapping conditions of children from birth to eight years of age, and teaching suggestions on how to offer individualized learning opportunities in the "least restrictive" environment.

Samuels, Shirley. *Disturbed Exceptional Children: An Integrated Approach.* New York: Human Sciences Press, 1981.

Samuels has written a comprehensive guide to the emotional needs and problems of exceptional children, integrating psychodynamic, behavioristic, medical, and ecological treatment modalities. Possible emotional reactions of exceptional children with physical, medical, hearing, visual and speech disorders, mental retardation, learning disabilities and multihandicaps are systematically examined. Guidance is given for recognizing psychological difficulties in gifted children and for developing individualized remediation programs for social, cognitive and psychomotor development. Although for the professional, it is also valuable for the parent of an exceptional child.

Smith, Sally L. *No Easy Answers: The Learning Disabled Child at Home and at School.* New York: Bantam, 1981.

This is a book that can be read and reread (each page is a goldmine of insights) by either a professional or a concerned parent. Smith's main point is that the learning-disabled child, though often average or above average in intelligence, cannot get himself "organized"; he fidgets, he forgets, he trips over his own legs, his nervous system develops slower than the rest of his body. To help such a child (more often a boy than a girl), the parent and the teacher must provide "structure" and "organization" in addition to educational remediation.

Spredemann, Sharon D. M. Ed. *The Bookfinder: A Guide to Children's Literature About the Needs and Problems of Youth Aged 2–15*, 2 vols. Circle Pines, Mn.: American Guidance Service, 1981.

This reference work lists over 1,031 annotations of children's books according to more than 450 psychological, behavioral and developmental topics of concern to young people. Books were selected that could help children increase their knowledge and self-esteem, clarify values, expand their understanding of people and dealing with real life situations before or after they actually encounter them. Books may be found under the subject, author, or title indexes. There is a synopsis of the book and a commentary that restates the book's main message and the age level for which it is appropriate. Picture books for young children are included under such headings as Africa, Afro-American, Appalachia, Buddhist, Chinese, Roman Catholic, Appearance, Dependence/Independence, Belonging, Differences, Body Concept, Self.

Webster, Elizabeth, J. *Counseling with Parents of Handicapped Children.* New York: Grune & Stratton, 1977.

Webster examines ways in which educators and other professionals can provide meaningful help to the parents of handicapped children. Since counseling refers to "a number of situations in which people communicate," ideas and suggestions are presented to develop and improve communication skills. Helpful examples of parent interviews and counseling sessions are included. Exercises and study guides at the end of each chapter also make it a useful text for student training in the field of special education, social work, counseling, and the like.

Weihs, Thomas J. *Children in Need of Special Care.* New York: Schocken, 1979.

The author, an educator of the handicapped for many years, writes of the development of handicapping conditions in children. He stresses that handicapped children need an environment that provides love, understanding, and social acceptance.

The Cerebral-Palsied

Cruickshank, William M. (ed.). *Cerebral Palsy: A Developmental Disability*, 3rd ed. Syracuse, N.Y.: Syracuse University Press, 1976.

Compiled by a group of distinguished authors, this book meshes viewpoints of the medical, psychological, therapeutic social work, and rehabilitation professions. The chapters that deal with the impact on the family may be especially helpful to parents too. It is a comprehensive text.

Finnie, Nancy R. *Handling the Young Cerebral Palsied Child at Home,* rev. ed. New York: Dutton, 1975.

This important book for parents and professionals has been translated into many languages, including Spanish. It covers all phases of cerebral palsy as well as educational, psychological, and family implications. The language is simple, and there are excellent illustrations for adapted equipment and excercises that can be helpful to parents, nurses, teachers, and others handling the cerebral-palsied child. It is a must for every family with a cerebral-palsied child.

Haeussermann, Else. *Developmental Potential of Preschool Children.* New York: Grune & Stratton, 1958.

The author was a pioneer in the development of individualized evaluations and programs for multihandicapped children, primarily those with cerebral injury or insults. This book remains important for teachers and for support staff of children with cerebral palsy and other neurological impairments. It aptly points out the complexity of evaluation and programming and the time and patience required to understand the potential strength of such children. It is also suggested for parents, as it is written positively and helps them understand the need for modifying each child's evaluation according to his or her strength and disability.

Language and Speech Disorders

Bangs, Tina E. *Language and Learning Disorders of the Pre-Academic Child: With Curriculum Guide.* New York: Appleton-Century-Crofts, 1968.

This is an introductory book for those interested in development of language and related language and learning disorders in the pre-academic child. It contains guidelines and exercises for promoting language development.

Berry, Mildred F. *Language Disorders of Children: Bases and Diagnoses.* Englewood Cliffs, N.J.: Prentice-Hall, 1969.

Berry covers various aspects of disorders of language in children. She discusses neural substrates of language and language disorders, evaluates language problems, traces the development of language, and considers remediation. Her book is useful for interested practitioners.

Bloodstein, Oliver. *Speech Pathology: An Introduction.* Boston: Houghton Mifflin, 1979.

This introductory survey presents information about the nature and remediation of various language, speech, and hearing disorders. There are discussions of normality vs. abnormality, differential diagnosis, and the treatment of various areas of disorder, including cleft palate, stuttering, and voice problems. It is useful for beginning students, parents, and practitioners from other fields seeking information.

Hubbell, Robert D. *Children's Language Disorders: An Integrated Approach.* Englewood Cliffs, N.J.: Prentice-Hall, Inc., 1981.

In this broad coverage of language disorders, the author discusses language as both a cognitive and emotional process and suggests that working with language-disordered children is a problem-solving process. How best to enhance the language skills of each child is the focus of this book with guidelines for clinicians and teachers on how to use the outlined problem-solving strategies most effectively.

Gregory, Hugo H. (ed.). *Controversies About Stuttering Therapy.* Baltimore, Md.: University Park Press, 1979.

The contributors to this book, all active clinicians, have set out to clarify controversial issues surrounding the evaluation and treatment of stuttering by reviewing the literature and by making comparative analyses of the differing approaches. The issues presented include psychotherapy for stutterers, management of stuttering in children, and criteria for assessing the results of stuttering therapy, with the focus of the book on the evaluation and guidelines for treatment.

Ingram, David. *Phonological Disability in Children.* New York: Elsevier, 1976.

A linguistic approach to an area of language disability—phonological disorders with primary focus on assessment, analysis and treatment. The author focuses on those aspects of linguistics which have direct connection to a child's pronunciation difficulty. Written for the professional therapist, educator, and linguist, the scope of this book brings together the areas of speech therapy, remedial teaching, teaching of the deaf, and educational psychology.

Irwin, Ann. *Successful Treatment of Stuttering*. New York: Walker, 1981.

The author, a widely experienced speech therapist, clears away many of the popular misconceptions about the frustrating affliction, stuttering. Special attention is given to therapy for child stutterers in a section devoted to early therapy. The author's "Easy Stuttering" program helps relax the speech organs, eliminates the involuntary repetition of sounds, and is a welcome practical method for dealing with one of the most psychologically damaging "minor" disabilities.

Irwin, John V., and Michael Marge (eds.). *Principles of Childhood Language Disabilities*. Englewood Cliffs, N.J.: Prentice-Hall, 1972.

The purpose of this collection of essays by an interdisciplinary team of leaders in the field is to bring together findings from recent studies relevant to language disabilities in young children. The authors have provided information about new linguistic and psycholinguistic approaches to understanding language and its acquisition by the child, the characteristics of language disabilities, evaluative techniques and management procedures.

Mosse, Hilde L. *The Complete Handbook of Children's Reading Disorders*, 2 Vols. New York: Human Sciences Press, 1982.

The purpose of these two comprehensive volumes is to describe how careful clinical evaluation of children is the only valid basis for establishing realistic guidelines for prevention and treatment of reading disorders. Dr. Mosse sees use of the clinical method as imperative for the understanding of reading and its pathology and talks about real children and their real, not theoretical, reading problems. Detailed guidelines are offered for application in the actual situation with step-by-step suggestions to teachers and parents.

Weiss, Curtis, E., and Harold S. Lillywhite. *Communicative Disorders: Prevention and Early Intervention*. St. Louis: Mosby, 1981.

This resource addresses both teachers and communication specialists, with emphasis on the vital role of the classroom teacher in discovering communication problems. Normal speech and hearing development is discussed, with guidelines for recognizing when intervention for possible remedial action may be required.

Weiss, Curtis E., Harold S. Lillywhite, and Mary E. Gordon. *Clinical Management of Articulation Disorders.* St. Louis: Mosby, 1980.

This book concentrates on articulation development and disorders and their management. Special focus is placed on assessment, using articulation only recently developed, as well as on approaches and techniques that have evolved out of the latest research and clinical practice at the time of writing. It is recommended for the student in the field of communication and its disorders.

The Blind, Visually Impaired, Deaf, and Deaf-Blind

Alonso, Lou, M. Pauline Moor, and Sherry Raynor. *Mainstreaming Preschoolers: Children with Visual Handicaps.* Washington, D.C.: U.S. Government Printing Office, 1978.

This book is a guide for teachers, parents, and others who work with preschool visually impaired children. It describes mainstreaming, visual handicaps, the development of the visually impaired child, activities for encouraging development, and resources for children and families. The text is written clearly, well organized, and illustrated with many photographs and line drawings. It is an excellent source of practical information.

Drouillard, Richard, and Sherry Raynor. *Move It!* Washington, D.C.: American Alliance for Health, Physical Education, and Recreation, 1977.

This booklet is a sequel to *Get a Wiggle On* (*see* Raynor, Sherry). It contains suggestions for persons working with blind and visually impaired toddlers. It emphasizes the importance of teaching blind children to be curious, and to use their other senses. There is one suggestion to a page accompanied by examples and a full-page line drawing. This booklet provides practical information that can be put to use at home or in school.

Kastein, Shulamith, Isabelle Spaulding, and Battia Scharf. *Raising the Young Blind Child: A Guide for Parents and Educators*. New York: Human Sciences Press, 1980.

The authors combine clear descriptions of the development of the blind child with suggestions for dealing with day-to-day situations. Sections are labeled according to functional activities so that an individual using it as a reference can locate such things as drinking from a cup, running, helping around the house, and pre-braille. The book provides a realistic picture of the blind child and a positive approach for parents and educators.

Keller, Jerry D. *Recreation Programming for Visually Impaired Children and Youth*. New York: American Foundation for the Blind, 1981.

This volume brings together two professional fields of endeavor, leaders from the field of vision and recreation. Here they have pooled their resources and expertise in order to enrich community services. Mainly designed for the recreation consultant or trainer concerned with providing services and programs for the visually impaired child, the text will also be of interest to the therapeutic recreation practitioner or vision expert.

Meadow, Kathryn P. *Deafness and Child Development*. Berkeley: University of California Press, 1980.

The author stresses the fact that the effects of early childhood deafness are so far-reaching that some basic knowledge of linguistic, cognitive, social, and psychological aspect of human development is needed if an understanding of any one specialized area is to be possible. In this comprehensive work, an informed and balanced approach is provided for the professional who works with deaf children. Practical suggestions are given for ways to apply the findings.

Myklebust, Helmer R. *The Psychology of Deafness*. New York: Grune & Stratton, 1964.

This work deals with deafness in individuals of various ages. Parents and practitioners working with young children may be interested in it for its overview of the area.

Raynor, Sherry, and Richard Drouillard. *Get a Wiggle On*. Washington, D.C.: American Alliance for Health, Physical Education, and Recreation, 1975.

This booklet is a collection of suggestions for persons who are in contact with blind and visually impaired infants. It stresses the critical importance of appropriate early assistance so that blind children will develop "a framework within which they can interact with the world around them." Every suggestion is stated clearly on a separate page and is accompanied by examples and a full-page line drawing. All suggestions are written as if the infant was talking to the caregiver (e.g., "When you're feeding me, put my hand on the spoon").

Riekehof, Lottie L. *Talk to the Deaf*. Illustrated by Betty Stewart. Springfield, Mo.: Gospel Publishing House, 1963.

This is a practical guide for anyone wishing to learn sign language and the manual alphabet. The author stresses that whatever method used in communicating with the learning impaired, nothing can surpass the clarity of expression of sign language. Provided in this manual are about 1,000 signs. The book should be helpful to parents and professionals.

Warren, David H. *Blindness and Early Childhood Development*. New York: American Foundation for the Blind, 1977.

Warren provides extensive information in all areas of development, as well as, suggestions for future research and a review of the issues in research methodology in the area of visual impairment. It is a clearly written, comprehensive text that is essential reading for the professional working with young visually impaired children.

Wright, David. *Deafness*. New York: Stein and Day, 1975.

The author and poet David Wright relates his own story of deafness at a young age. His personal insights give the reader firsthand information on what it is to be deaf and gifted in a hearing world. The book is divided in two parts: Part I concerns the author's life. Part II traces the history of the education of the deaf.

The Mentally Retarded

Alpern, Gerald, and Thomas Boll. (eds.). *Education and Care of Moderately and Severely Retarded Children.* Seattle: Special Child Publications, 1971.

A compendium of ideas for use by parents and teachers of children evidencing intellectual deficits, this book provides general information, philosophy, and a vast array of ideas for meeting the specific curriculum needs of this group of special children. It will help inquiring parents become a vital part of the educational team working with their child.

Cunningham, Cliff, and Patricia Sloper. *Helping Your Exceptional Baby: A Practical and Honest Approach to Raising a Mentally Handicapped Child.* New York: Pantheon, 1980.

Originally published in Great Britain, this easy-to-read, comprehensive guide deals with the ways in which family members can facilitate the growth and development of Down's syndrome children during the first two years of life. The developmental checklists are augmented by a series of clear line drawings and photographs. The teaching suggestions are carefully outlined and do not require the purchase of specialized equipment. As the subtitle promises, this guide is not pedantic and verbose. It is excellent for helping parents become skilled observers of their children. The authors give advice for all manner of problems and situations that occur during a retarded child's first years and help families to exploit the learning potential of the home environment. This is an excellent addition to the library of professionals also, as many of the suggestions and activities can be used with children exhibiting developmental delays other than Down's syndrome.

Curry, Judith Bickley, and Kathryn Kluss Peppe. *Mental Retardation: Nursing Approaches to Care.* St. Louis: Mosby, 1978.

The purpose of this informative text is to serve as a resource for nurses already working with retarded persons as well as for students who may be entering the field. There is first an overview of nursing in mental retardation, then guidelines for nursing practices helpful in working with mentally retarded individuals and their families. The last section deals with prevention, genetic counseling, interventive techniques, and program planning. The overall theme focuses on humanistic, family-centered services.

Edgerton, Robert B. *Mental Retardation: The Developing Child.* Cambridge: Harvard University Press, 1979.

This small volume contains a great deal of current information about the topic. Edgerton furnishes the reader a vivid picture of the reality of mental retardation in a humane and concrete manner. Aspects of the care of the mentally retarded are discussed as well as the role of society in preparation for the acceptance of the retarded as productive and happy persons.

Erickson, Marion J. *Teaching the Retarded Child: A Developmental Approach.* New York: Garland STPM Press, 1980.

Following Piaget's theories of intellectual development, this work stresses what the child can do. It provides concrete suggestions for enhancing individual capabilities on an ongoing basis. There is a useful bibliography.

Hunter, Marvin, Helen Schucman, and George Friedlander. *The Retarded Child from Birth to Five: A Multidisciplinary Program for the Family and Child.* New York: John Day, 1972.

This book is based on the work of the Shield Institute, a pioneering agency on the field of specialized services to young retarded children and their families. Stress is on early identification and the importance of the multidisciplinary team approach. Included are detailed descriptions of programs as well as case histories to illustrate the value of techniques used.

Johnson, Vicki M., and Roberta A. Werner. *A Step-By-Step Guide for Retarded Infants and Children,* 3rd ed. Syracuse, N.Y.: Syracuse University Press, 1981.

The authors have prepared a helpful handbook for parents or preschool teachers of retarded infants and children. They share a successfully tested systematic training program designed to help the child learn the needed skills for development, self-care, social interaction, gross and fine motor skills, perceptual and cognitive development. A checklist of abilities is given to aid in the selection of the appropriate curriculum. The program can be used with an individual child or in a group setting.

Lewis, M., and Leonard Rosenblum, (eds.). *The Uncommon Child: The Genesis of Behavior*, Vol. 3. New York: Plenum, 1981.

This volume brings together theoretical research and empirical data in such areas as infant biology, developing infant capacities, animal models, and the impact of various social forces in an attempt to examine uncommonness in children. It views uncommonness as either the result of a child's unique characteristics (such as Down's syndrome) or the result of an environment characterized by such extremes as schizophrenic parents. The initial chapter describes the ecological perspective in viewing uncommonness in children. Down's syndrome, temperament differences, gender dysfunction, intellectual giftedness, and the sick and dying infant are then discussed in detail by a variety of experts in the field. Specific characteristics of the child's interactions with the environment are detailed. Subsequent chapters discuss the impact of uncommon environmental conditions on infant development. Topics considered in the final chapters include the effects of malnutrition, maltreatment, and disordered socializing experiences, such as nontraditional family and social structures.

Menolascino, Frank J., and Michael L. Egger. *Medical Dimensions of Mental Retardation*. Lincoln: University of Nebraska Press, 1978.

Intended as a comprehensive, yet nontechnical reference, this book is for all who are concerned with mental retardation of childhood and beyond. Presented is an overview of the causative factors and symptoms in regard to general and developmental dimensions as well as discussion of treatment and management.

Mercer, Jane R. *Labeling the Mentally Retarded: Clinical and Social System Perspectives on Mental Retardation*. Berkeley: University of California Press, 1973.

An eight-year-study was conducted to understand the nature and extent of mental retardation in an American community. This book details the findings . Along the way, the authors found that not only do schools label more children mentally retarded than any other agencies, but also by relying on a unicultural perspective, the schools place the poor and ethnic minorities at a decided disadvantage. Policy recommendations are offered as well as suggestions for IQ tests that do away with cultural biases and inequities.

Sarason, Seymour B., and John Doris. *Educational Handicap, Public Policy and Social History: A Broadened Perspective on Mental Retardation.* New York: Free Press, 1979.

Sarason and Doris have made an important contribution to the literature in mental retardation. They examine the changing character of the field and see these changes reflected in the larger society. The point is forcefully made that to confuse change with progress is to set the stage for disappointment. The development of special education is traced, and it is suggested that the label "mentally retarded" is deeply intertwined with immigration policy, urbanization, poverty, and universal compulsory education. The authors also look at the traditional concepts of diagnosis and management, the training of professionals, and institutionalization. Much is seen as culturally biased and of limited benefit to the individual, the family, and the community. Alternative approaches are suggested.

The Emotionally Disturbed

Axline, Virginia. *Dibs: In Search of Self.* New York: Ballantine, 1964.

This is a moving account of an emotionally disturbed child's experience in play therapy. Axline views play as an expression of a child's innermost feelings. Through Dibs' experience in play therapy, he was able to achieve great strides in his search for self. This success story has major implications for establishing those conditions that facilitate positive growth. It is an important book for parents, caretakers, and professionals interested in the emotionally disturbed child.

Bernheim, Kayla F., and Richard R. J. Lewine. *Schizophrenia: Symptoms, Causes, Treatment.* New York: Norton, 1979.

This book serves to provide a basic understanding of schizophrenia, its symptoms, causes, and treatment. Addressed also are the myths and mystique surrounding the illness. A general model is given for understanding why and how schizophrenia develops. The text is written in nontechnical language for schizophrenic patients and their families as well as mental health professionals and students in the field.

Bettelheim, Bruno. *The Empty Fortress: Infantile Autism and the Birth of Self.* New York: Free Press, 1967.

The author, a famous psychoanalyst, presents a detailed clinical discussion of the treatment of three children suffering from childhood autism/schizophrenia. The presentation of theory is relatively jargon-free and focuses more on the everyday aspects of child development and their significance. The discussions include many descriptions of the play of these children in their special treatment setting and of the meaning of these play activities in terms of the child's preoccupations and difficulties.

Holmes, Beth. *The Whipping Boy.* New York: Marek, 1978.

In her novel based on the actual experience of a mother's plight to help her "emotionally abused" son, Holmes traces the struggle to find an appropriate educational setting and highlights the difficulties encountered. This is a powerful and important novel that offers the educator and parent a sensitive description of the family dynamics at the core of this child's emotional problems.

The Gifted

American Association for Gifted Children. *On Being Gifted.* New York: Walker, 1979.

Writing about themselves, twenty gifted teenagers offer special insight into the experience of growing up gifted in today's America. Their frustrations and dreams, accomplishments and failures are revealed with candor and individuality in this extraordinary collection. The volume is a must for parents, teachers, the four million-plus talented young people in the United States, and all people concerned about educational opportunities available today.

Arts, Education, and Americans Panel. Rockefeller, David, Chairman. *Coming to Our Senses. The Significance of Arts for American Education, A Panel Report.* New York: McGraw-Hill, 1977.

Programs for gifted and talented stress intellectual growth. The Arts, Education, and Americans Panel developed this report to heighten awareness of the need for arts in education. Parents and educators of gifted and talented children, anxious to plead this cause, would do well to read this report. It traces the role of arts in America while underscoring the place of arts in the schools: "Arts are the language of a whole range of human experiences; to neglect them is to deny children the full development that education should provide."

Barbe, Walter, and Joseph Renzulli. *Psychology and Education of the Gifted.* New York: Irvington Publishers, 1981.

There are articles by such noted experts in the field of gifted education as Terman, Torrance, and Guilford. Topics include historical development, characteristics, development, and encouragement of the gifted, and teaching of the gifted. Each article has an extensive bibliography.

Baskin, Barbara, and Karen Harris. *Books for the Gifted Child.* New York: Bowker, 1980.

Three well-thought-out and well-expressed chapters on the gifted in society, on identification of gifted children, and on the reading experience especially as a force promoting cognitive thinking, accompany this fully annotated bibliography of excellent children's books, many of which are suitable for the young child.

Clark, Barbara. *Growing Up Gifted.* Columbus, Oh.: Merrill, 1979.

This book is a good place to start in garnering knowledge about giftedness. It is well organized with supportive research data, charts, outlines and study questions. The section on infancy describes effective, responsive behaviors for the adult caregivers with pertinent references to the work of Maslow, Kohlberg and other luminaries in early childhood education.

Delp, Jeanne L., and Ruth A. Martinson. *The Gifted and Talented: A Handbook for Parents.* Ventura, Ca.: National/State Leadership Training Institute on the Gifted and Talented, 1975.

Simple, easy to understand, and very practical, this book covers a broad range of parenting areas.

Dickinson, Rita Mitton. *Caring for the Gifted.* North Quincy, Mass.: Christopher, 1970.

Dickinson's observations are applicable to most school-age children, but the references to younger children are particularly apt. His book is written primarily for parents. Suggestions are practical and realistic.

Ehrlich, Virginia Z. *The Astor Program for Gifted Children: Prekindergarten Through Grade Three.* New York: Teachers College, Columbia University, 1978.

This is the story of a highly successful program for gifted children, ages four through eight. Philosophy of education, curriculum practices, administrative problems, teaching and management approaches are all discussed.

Ehrlich, Virginia Z. *Gifted Children: A Guide for Parents and Teachers.* Englewood Cliffs, N.J.: Prentice-Hall, 1982.

Ehrlich presents a coordinated philosophy for rearing and guiding gifted children from the nursery through the school years. The discussion deals with identification, problems of giftedness, parent and teacher roles, schooling opportunities, career education, tests and their meanings, and legislative provisions. Special attention is given to the needs of the very young child in the prekindergarten/primary grades.

Fortna, Richard O., and Bruce O. Boston. *Testing the Gifted Child: An Interpretation in Lay Language.* Reston, Va.: Council for Exceptional Children, 1976.

The authors stress that tests are simply devices for ranking the performance of children against averages. Tests do not really measure how "smart" a given child is or how much has been achieved. Parents and educators, regardless of how they feel about testing, are faced with the reality that standardized tests are constantly used, despite the fact that much is being said about the possible racial, cultural, and socioeconomical biases in testing. Provided are descriptions of tests, what they are and how they function, in nontechnical language.

Freeman, Darlene, and Virginia Stuart. *Resources for Gifted Children in the New York Area*. New York: Trillium Press, 1980.

This is an invaluable compendium of information describing programs, curriculum materials, books and games for gifted children. The Appendix is a guide to vital sources of information for parents and teachers. For example, there is a list of museums with descriptive data and ages for whom the exhibits are best suited. Although the places to visit are geographically accessible to New York and surrounding areas, the other information included in the book is applicable for children in all parts of the country. Parents and teachers could use the format to develop miniguides for their own geographic and interest areas.

Gallagher, James J. *Teaching the Gifted Child*, 2nd ed. Boston: Allyn & Bacon, 1976.

Gallagher discusses the gifted child primarily in terms of his/her school experiences. He includes suggestions for curriculum modification, stimulation of productive problem solving, and dealing with special problem areas such as underachievement and the culturally different gifted. The extensive bibliography includes a listing of relevant organizations as well as books and articles.

George, William C., Sanford J. Cohn, and Julian Stanley. *Educating the Gifted: Acceleration and Enrichment*. Baltimore: Johns Hopkins University Press, 1979.

This reader provides an overview for the historical controversy surrounding the enrichment vs. the achievement debate. It is recommended for parents and workers of pre-schoolers to help them understand that there is a battle going on between the two strategies, and it is simply not an either/or issue.

Ginsberg, Gina, and Charles H. Harrison. *How to Help Your Gifted Child—A Handbook for Parents and Teachers*. New York: Monarch Press, 1977.

This how-to book for parents of gifted children covers such

topics as how to understand gifted children and how to organize parent groups in order to provide enrichment for these children. Although adequate in its scope, the reader should seek out additional publications dealing with this topic.

Goertzel, Victor, and Mildred Goertzel. *Cradles of Eminence.* Boston: Little, Brown, 1978.

While not a contemporary treatise on child development, this classic work provides a glimpse into the childhood of gifted people of the past.

Gowan, John C., Joe Khatena, and E. Paul Torrance. (eds.). *Educating the Ablest: A Book of Readings.* Itasca, Ill.: Peacock Publications, 1979.

Various aspects of giftedness are discussed in these articles by a variety of persons recognized as experts in the field. Emphasis is on role of parents and teachers, and stress is placed on creative aspects of giftedness. Each article includes an extensive bibliography.

Hall, Eleanor, and Nancy Skinner. *Somewhere to Turn: Strategies for Parents of the Gifted and Talented.* New York: Teachers College Press, 1980.

This brief book spans topics essential for parents. It includes identification procedures for children who are gifted, a questionnaire for parents to determine their own giftedness in parenting, resources to extend their own learning, and examples of parent effectiveness, thus enabling parents to become the principal motivators for their child's optimum development. The questionnaire on parenting emphasizes activities to extend the child's interests and talents. The caution for readers is to understand the identification components as suggested benchmarks rather than definitive, inflexible standards.

Hopkins, Lee Bennett, and Annette Frank Shapiro. *Creative Activities for the Gifted Child.* Belmont, Ca.: Pitman Learning, 1969.

This pamphlet contains more than 100 ideas for enrichment activities suitable for the gifted. Although they are not classified by age or grade level, many are suitable for the younger child. They also are useful for gifted children in regular classrooms who need special attention.

Kanigher, Herbert. *Everyday Enrichment for Gifted Children at Home and School*. Los Angeles: National/State Leadership Training Institute on the Gifted and Talented, 1980.

Hundreds of ideas are suggested for parent/child activities. The book can double as an activity guide for teachers in primary and intermediate grades. The book is divided into subject areas: art, music, language and reading, math, science, and geography. Besides lead-off and follow-up questions, there are suggestions for research and experimentation.

Kaufmann, Felice. *Your Gifted Child and You*. Reston, Va.: Council for Exceptional Children, 1977.

Primarily for parents, this book describes the identification of the gifted, their creativity, and possible social problems. Included is information about parent groups, lists of resources, and a bibliography.

Laubenfels, Jean. *The Gifted Student: An Annotated Bibliography*. London: Greenwood Press, 1977.

This annotated bibliography is a rich resource for parents and educators in need of information, books, articles, organizations, tests, etc., on the gifted. In many instances the information is simply listed without explicative data but it is a good place to start in researching the topic. Although the emphasis is not on early childhood, readers will be guided to materials in their specific area of need in regard to the young gifted.

Lewis, David. *How to Be a Gifted Parent*. New York: Norton, 1981.

The basic premise in this book is that every child deserves the right to develop his or her potential for intelligence, creativity, and physical and social prowess. The author suggests parental responses to encourage thinking and problem solving. "Gifted children begin with gifted parents" but a word of caution: Readers should use the insights and activities as suggested approaches, not dictum.

Martinson, Ruth A. *The Identification of the Gifted and Talented*. Reston, Va.: Council on Exceptional Children, 1975.

This discussion of screening and identification of the gifted emphasizes the need for early identification. For the professional who is seeking innovative identification procedures.

Miller, Alice. *Prisoners of Childhood.* New York: Basic Books, 1981.

The focus of this book is on the gifted child and the self-centered parent, with the emotional difficulties that may result. Although this book uses sophisticated psychological terminology, it is written in a very clear, concise style. It conveys the subtle and not so subtle ways that unresolved parental problems can damage the growing child's personality.

Passow, A. Harry (ed.). *The Gifted and the Talented: Their Education and Development.* Chicago: National Society for the Study of Education, 1979.

This is a practical and important book on education, identification, development, and programs for the gifted and talented. Distinguished people in gifted education have contributed to this book.

Perino, Sheila C., and Joseph Perino. *Parenting the Gifted: Developing the Promise.* New York: Bowker, 1981.

This comprehensive, practical handbook for parents is designed to foster an understanding of gifted and talented children. The scope is from infancy to adolescence. The authors throughout stress child rearing, identifying the gifted, understanding tests and measurements, and selecting appropriate programs. Included are a model constitution and by-laws for establishing a parent advocacy group, a glossary of terms, and a selected bibliography.

Renzulli, Joseph, and Elizabeth Stoddard (eds.). *Gifted and Talented Education in Perspective.* Reston, Va.: Council for Exceptional Children, 1980.

The authors have culled articles from the educators well versed in the field of giftedness. Though most helpful for those who work with older children, the articles provide information on identification, programs, and philosophy of import to all parents and educators.

Roedell, Wendy Conilin, et al. *Gifted Young Children*. New York: Teachers College Press, 1980.

This is must reading for teachers and parents of the young. The authors investigate the nature and characteristics of giftedness, identification techniques, and workable programs. The issue of early school entrance is examined in a balanced and helpful manner.

Shallcross, Doris J. *Teaching Creative Behavior*. Englewood Cliffs, N.J.: Prentice-Hall, 1981.

Creativity is everybody's business. This book is filled with ideas to plan for the step-by-step development of the creative response present in human beings of all ages. The activities outlined will help the reader gain a better understanding of the nature of creativity and how it can be fostered and supported.

Stein, Morris. *Gifted and Talented Young People, Studies in Excellence: An Annotated Bibliography and Guide*. New York: Garland, in press.

This annotated primary and secondary bibliography and guide to English-language materials presents some of the major classic works and a representative selection of the more critical contemporary works within the past ten years. Designed specifically for researchers and educators who are looking for the most reliable information in the field. Excellent appendixes list pertinent organizations and periodicals, etc.

Vail, Priscilla. *The World of the Gifted Child*. New York: Walker, 1979.

Vail discusses the multidimensionality of giftedness, and what parents and schools can and should do for gifted children. She includes an excellent list of age-appropriate books (for parents to read to children and for children to read themselves), suggestions for games and other activities, and a brief bibliography.

Whitmore, Joanne Rand. *Giftedness, Conflict, and Underachievement*. Boston: Allyn & Bacon, 1980.

Whitmore describes a ten-year study in the Cupertino School District in California to aid underachievers. Besides providing an historical perspective of education for the gifted, the author shares the strategies that help underachievers become successful learners and people. One cannot help but wonder if these techniques that help build self-esteem, and social skills and help close the academic lag are not applicable to all underachieving students. Those who work and live with preschoolers would do well to read this for preventive medicine.

14
Nonsexist
Education

REARING AND EDUCATING CHILDREN FOR THE TWENTY-FIRST CENTURY

Barbara Sprung

A nonsexist upbringing and education should be the birthright of every child. That is a very strong statement and one to which this author, after a decade of working to bring this about, remains totally committed. This essay will examine some elements of nonsexist child rearing and education, and why I consider them to be essential for today's children, children who will be adults in the postindustrial world of the twenty-first century.

In his closing address to the First National Conference on Nonsexist Early Childhood Education in 1976, Patrick C. Lee of Teachers College, Columbia University, stated:

> As I see it, there are two models of interaction between culture and the rate of sex-role change that are of interest here. In the first model, sex-role change moves ahead too quickly, thus threatening to throw the carefully wrought interconnections of culture into disorder and chaos. The second model is the converse of the first. In this model, *sex role threatens cultural integrity* by *changing too slowly.* . . . I think that the second model applies to North American middle-class society. I will argue strongly for this proposition— that is, that change in the sex roles is proceeding too slowly, that the traditional sex roles have become nostalgic anchoring points in an era that closed down at the end of the Second World War, that they linger on like ghosts from the past while American society careens into the future. (Lee, 1978, p. 138; italics added.)

I agree with Lee, except that I think that the slow pace of change affects all classes, not just the middle class. While traditional sex-role socialization is still the "norm" in most homes and schools, it is increasingly out of tune with the realities of our society. Parents and teachers have the task of helping young children understand and feel comfortable in the real world. Yet we continue to rear children for a world that no longer exists, if indeed it ever did. We foster myths about the nuclear family with the male parent being the sole breadwinner, when in reality these families constitute less than 15 percent of all families ("*Who* is . . . ," 1978, p. 43). Many of us still bring up girls with the expectation that marriage will be their only career, despite statistics that show that well over 90 percent of them will enter the work force and that many will work for over thirty years. We do not bring up boys with the understanding that nurturing children is a shared responsibility of parenting or girls who are capable of being the sole head of household, if that becomes necessary. When we perpetuate the teaching of cultural modes that are no longer relevant, we do an educational disservice to our children.

What is nonsexist child rearing? It is a humanistic approach to raising children. It is looking at a child as a person with a variety of personality, intellectual, physical, and emotional traits stretched along a human continuum. Some of these traits may be traditionally thought of as male, others female. But, if children are to realize their fullest human potential, they will need a full complement of traits from both ends of this continuum. While rearing children along rigidly divided sex-role lives deprives them of the opportunity to reach their maximum growth and development, nonsexist child rearing provides an environment that exposes children of both sexes to a wide variety of options.

Nonsexist parents allow their girl children the same amount of independence and freedom of movement that their boy children enjoy. And they provide their boy children with as many opportunities to try on nurturing roles as they do their girls. Nonsexist parents understand that gender is a given; children are born male or female, and by the age of five or six they attain "gender constancy," that is, they know unequivocally that they will always be male or female. Children know this without benefit of frills or football helmets or any other of the culturally designated "appropriate" props. Nonsexist parents are not threatened if their children experiment in dramatic play situations with props and behaviors normally attributed to the opposite sex because they know this is a learning process, a totally appropriate way for young children to try to understand the adult world. They do not say to a three-year-old boy with a scraped knee "Big boys don't cry" because they know that a scraped knee hurts terribly whether you are a girl or a boy. They do not tell a three-year-old girl at a party that "ladies don't make noise" because making noise is one of the delights of childhood, regardless of sex.

Parents who rear their children in nonsexist ways choose toys, clothes, and room decorations that are functional, age appropriate, and fun, not sex typed and rigidly different for girls and boys. They do not dress their girls in pink and then tell them not to get dirty, thereby inhibiting their urge to explore or be physically active. They give blocks to girls as well as boys because blocks teach spatial analytic skills and math concepts better than any other toy. And they provide paper, scissors, and crayons to boys as well as girls because these are the toys that develop small motor skills.

Underlying the myriad day-to-day things that nonsexist parents do is a commitment to equality between the sexes. One sex is not valued more than the other. Nor are the traditional roles of dominance by the male and subordination by the female considered acceptable or desirable. There is equal respect for the male and female in all of us in the nonsexist home.

To create a nonsexist environment for children takes a concerted effort between the home and school. Cooperation and harmony of purpose between the two major forces in the young child's life are essential, especially in the face of the sexist barrage they will encounter in the media and in the larger community.

Nonsexist education (especially at the preschool level) is not radically different from nonsexist child rearing in the home, except that the teacher has the opportunity to work with groups of children as well as individuals. And he or she can seize the "teachable moment" to solve a conflict in a nonsexist way or intervene in subtle ways to help children fully utilize the learning environment. How can this be done without being heavy-handed, obtrusive, or generally out-of-tune with the traditionally open-ended, free choice atmosphere of the preschool program? Let's look at a few ways:

1. *The Teacher as a Magnet.* Research has shown that when a teacher places herself/himself in an area of the classroom, he or she becomes a "magnet" for the children. Therefore, if the teacher sits or works in the block corner, children who do not usually elect to play with blocks (typically girls) will be drawn to that area simply because the teacher is there. He or she can then involve the newcomers in the innumerable possibilities and sheer joy of working with blocks (Serbin, 1980).

2. *Reinforcing Analytic Skills.* Research has shown that when a boy comes to the teacher with a piece of finished work such as a puzzle, she or he will analyze how the work was done, i.e., "Johnny, you did such a fine job on the puzzle. You took out all the pieces, turned the painted sides up, put in all the corners, put in the wheels of the car," etc. However, when a girl comes up with a finished puzzle, the remarks are, "Sue, you did a good job. Now put the puzzle back on the shelf and find something else to do." In one study it was found that teachers interact with boys *eight* times as often as with girls. (Serbin, 1978, p. 85.)

3. *Reversing Traditional Sex Roles.* Often when a preschool classroom does have a male teacher (a fairly rare occurrence), he takes on "traditional" male roles as the active outdoor person or the block area teacher. Have a male teacher (or a father or grandfather or other carefully selected male volunteer) assume the more nurturant role in the classroom by conducting a cooking activity or by stationing himself in the housekeeping area while his female counterpart oversees woodworking or block building. This will demonstrate concretely to the children that males and females can do many different things. One of the ways children learn is by imitation, and a nonsexist example set by adults will say more to them than "message" books or verbal discussions.

Seizing the teachable moment is one of the real satisfactions of teaching—being there when the "teachable moment" arises and being able to step in and move children into new growth. Every teachable moment is different, but here's a typical one:

> Several children are in the housekeeping corner, and the boys are getting ready to "go to work." A girl says she's "going to work" also, and the boys challenge her, saying, "You can't. You're a mommy—you have to stay home." An argument ensues and the children are stuck on dead center —so the teacher intervenes (after giving the children a reasonable amount of time to work it out) and helps them work out their differences. She or he could ask the involved parties if any of their mothers work or point out women that the children know who do work outside the home. The teacher could follow up the discussion by arranging a trip to see women at work (preferably mothers of children in the group) or by inviting women with various careers into the classroom to demonstrate and talk about their work. Books about women at work can be added to the class library at this point, and discussions following story time can be made into experience charts or classroom books about the topic.

The few examples given above are typical early childhood teaching techniques, but with a nonsexist focus. Once a teacher has gained awareness and is committed to a nonsexist approach, there will be countless opportunities to integrate curricula activities, materials, and "teachable moments" into the typical school day. The result will be a nonsexist school environment which, in concert with a nonsexist home, can create a generation of children who will be able to make life decisions from a pool of options that far exceeds the one that has existed in our sex-role divided society.

Is the struggle to create a nonsexist home and school environment worth it? After all, it is not easy to change deep-seated cultural values and the larger community including the extended family, the media and the governmental and educational institutions offer little or no support for the effort. They seem very much caught in the "nostalgic anchoring points" that Patrick Lee spoke about in 1976.

Of course, it is worth it, despite ridicule, institutional backsliding, peer pressure, and an intransigent media. It is worth it because as we approach the twenty-first century our society has changed dramatically and rapidly. The child-rearing and educational practices that trained women for totally domestic lives of subordination to men are obsolete, as are the practices that trained men for domination and a superior sense of their worth. In the future, our society will need to realize the full potential of its men and its women. One of the key ways to make this happen is to free children now from the limiting effects of sex-role stereotyping. We must hurry—the twenty-first century is just around the corner.

References

Lee, Patrick C. Sex role and human culture. In Barbara Sprung (ed.), *Perspectives on Non-Sexist Early Childhood Education*. New York: Teachers College Press, 1978.

Serbin, Lisa. Play activities and the development of visual-spatial skills. *Equal Play, 1* (No. 4), 6–8, Fall 1980.

Serbin, Lisa. Teacher, peers, and play preferences: An environmental approach to sex-typing in the preschool. In Barbara Sprung (ed.), *Perspectives on Non-Sexist Early Childhood Education*. New York: Teachers College Press, 1978.

"Who Is the *Real* family?" *MS Magazine*, p. 43, August 1978.

BIBLIOGRAPHY

Adell, Judith, and Hilary Dole Klein, comps. *A Guide to Non-Sexist Children's Books.* Chicago: Academy Press, 1976.

An annotated listing of over 400 books for preschool through twelfth-grade levels. Both fiction and nonfiction titles are included. The annotations are brief, without critical evaluation.

American Association of University Women. *Books with Options; An Annotated Bibliography of Non-Stereotyping Books for Children and Young People,* Boulder, Co.: The Association, 1976.

There are short, uncritical annotations for preschool through young adult levels.

Astin, Helen S., Allison Parelman, and Anne Fisher. *Sex Roles: A Research Bibliography.* DHEW No. 75-166. Rockville, Md.: National Institute of Mental Health, 1976.

This annotated bibliography of 346 journal articles and 54 books focuses on sex-role research as well as 49 chapters in other books with a broader focus. The selections, published between 1960 and 1972, come from the disciplines of sociology, psychology, child development, anthropology, political science, economics, medicine, and education. It is a useful resource for those interested in broad-based research on sex roles.

Bracken, Jeanne, and Sharon Wigutoff. *Books for Today's Children: An Annotated Bibliography of Non-Stereotyped Picture Books.* Old Westbury, N.Y.: Feminist Press, 1981.

In this critically annotated listing of about 200 picture books published between 1972 and 1977, books are categorized as Highly Recommended, Recommended, Recommended with Some Reservations, and Not Recommended.

Carmichael, Carrie. *Non-Sexist Childraising*. Boston: Beacon Press, 1977.

Interviews with families who are struggling with the daily problems of sexism offer a glimpse of parents and children in the act of change making. The author's popular, journalistic style makes such issues as female chauvinism and homophobia accessible to the casual reader. Chapters on children's books, sexist language, and unequal education balance the discussion between the influences of the home and the larger culture.

Council on Interracial Books for Children. *Guidelines for Selecting Bias-Free Textbooks and Storybooks*. New York: The Council, 1980.

There are helpful criteria and checklists for evaluating sex bias and cultural bias in school materials and children's literature. Included is the council's concise and valuable guide, "Ten Quick Ways to Analyze Children's Books for Racism and Sexism."

Council on Interracial Books for Children. *Human (and Anti-Human) Values in Children's Books: A Content Rating Instrument for Educators and Concerned Parents*. New York: The Council, 1976.

There are detailed critiques of 235 books published in 1975 with Third World, feminist, or social-issue themes. Books are analyzed for racism; sexism; "ageism"; elitism, materialism, and individualism; and escapism and conformism. Guidelines for selecting antisexist and antiracist literature are included.

Davis, Enid. *The Liberty Cap: A Catalogue for Non-sexist Materials for Children*. Chicago: Academy Press, 1977.

This valuable combination of critical analysis of relevant issues followed by critical reviews of individual book titles includes picture books, easy readers, and fiction and nonfiction for older children. There are also analyses of toys, games, records, and films. Davis notes further resources for parents and professionals.

Fair Play: A Bibliography of Non-Stereotyped Materials, 2 vols. Vol. 1 by Ferris Olin. Vol. 2 by Marylin A. Hulme. New Brunswick, N.J.: Training Institute for Sex Desegregation, Rutgers University, Vol. 1, 1976; Vol. 2, 1977.

The combined volumes include over 2,000 listings of teacher

resources for kindergarten through grade twelve, including brief sections on recommended fiction for the various grade levels. Volume 1 includes both print and nonprint materials; Volume 2, mostly print materials.

Gallagher, Kathleen, and Alice Peery (compilers). *Bibliography of Materials on Sexism and Sex-Role Stereotyping in Children's Books.* Chapel Hill, N.C.: Lollipop Power, 1982, revised annually.

This is one of the most comprehensive listings of published articles and books on the subject. The annual booklet also includes bibliographies of nonsexist children's books and addresses of "alternative" publishers.

Greenberg, Selma. *Right from the Start: A Guide to Nonsexist Child Rearing.* Boston: Houghton Mifflin, 1978.

This book contains narrative, anecdotes, and sound advice from an early childhood specialist with a loving respect for children. Although directed primarily to parents, the book provides theoretical insights (particularly about the meaning of the inside and outside world) that can challenge scholars as well. An effective mixture of the practical and philosophical, this book should appeal to educators and other child-care practitioners as well as parents.

Guttentag, Marcia, and Helen Bray. *Undoing Sex Stereotypes: Research and Resources for Educators.* New York: McGraw-Hill, 1976.

This book contains a report of research on a nonsexist intervention project conducted in kindergarten, fifth, and ninth grade classrooms. There are also curriculum suggestions and bibliographies for nonsexist education on the early childhood as well as higher grade levels.

Interracial Digest, 2 vols. New York: Council on Interracial Books for Children, Vol. 1, 1976; Vol. 2, 1978.

Each volume contains ten significant articles from the *Bulletin* of the Council on Interracial Books. These include critical analyses of many famous children's books, in regard to sex and race bias.

Jenkins, Jeanne Kohl, and Pam Macdonald. *Growing Up Equal:
   Activities and Resources for Parents and Teachers of Young Children.*
   Englewood Cliffs, N.J.: Prentice-Hall, 1979.

Teachers and parents who want to know about activities,
games, and actions that have been tried and tested for promoting sex equity will find this volume a useful source.

Little Miss Muffet Fights Back. Feminists on Children's Media.
   Whitestone, N.Y.: Feminist Book Mart, 1974.

This bibliography is the result of questionnaires sent to
librarians, teachers, and feminists across the country in a 1970
study of outstanding books that present girls and women in a
positive role. Also included is information on how to order
books, how to work for change in children's books, where to
find articles, and reports on sexism in children's books.

Maccoby, Eleanor Emmons, and Carol Nagy Jacklin. *The Psychology
   of Sex Differences.* Stanford, Ca.: Stanford University Press,
   1974.

For those interested in research on sex differences, this is an
invaluable resource. The authors systematically summarize and
interpret research findings from approximately 1,600 studies,
published for the most part between 1966 and 1973. The studies
cover sex differences in intellect, achievement, and social behavior as well as works on the origins of psychological sex
differences. There are many tables that summarize findings in
the text as well as an annotated bibliography of the studies.

*Maximizing Young Children's Potential: A Non-Sexist Manual for Early
   Childhood Trainers.* Non-Sexist Child Development Project.
   Developed by Project T.R.E.E. under a grant from the U.S.
   Department of Health, Education, and Welfare, Women's
   Educational Equity Act. Newton, Mass.: EDC, 1980.

This manual contains material to be used with teachers and
parents to develop their awareness of the educational, psychological, and occupational consequences of sex typing children
during the early years.

Miles, Betty. *Channeling Children: Sex Stereotyping on Prime Time.* Princeton, N.J.: Women on Words and Images, 1975.

Miles focuses on the effect upon American children on sex-role stereotyping in television. She explores the televised relationships between men and women and discusses children's attitudes and feelings about those relationships. This booklet ably assists parents in understanding some of TV's intended messages.

Pogrebin, Letty C. *Growing Up Free: Raising Your Child in the 80's.* New York: McGraw-Hill, 1980.

In this ground-breaking book on nonsexist child rearing, Pogrebin provides a blueprint that outlines the way toward what she calls "role-free family life." The author, backed by research, sees traditional child-rearing methods, which restrict children based on their sex, as harmful. In this comprehensive guide she offers convincing advice on every aspect of family life based on new, nonsexist approaches to parenting.

Romer, Nancy. *The Sex-role Cycle: Socialization from Infancy to Old Age.* New York: McGraw-Hill, 1981.

Sex-role socialization throughout the life span is described. In language free of jargon, the author synthesizes a great deal of information, based on research and theory. The first two chapters focus on infancy and early childhood, respectively. This is an excellent introduction to the topic of sex-role socialization for those who are concerned with nonsexist education.

Rosenberg, B. G., and Brian Sutton-Smith. *Sex and Identity.* New York: Holt, Rinehart, and Winston, 1972.

For those interested in theories of sex-role development, this is a good introduction. Published as a "small textbook," it summarizes theories from a number of disciplines including comparative psychology, psychoanalysis, social learning theory, biology, sociology, and anthropology.

Sadker, Myra, and David Sadker. *Now Upon a Time: A Contemporary View of Children's Literature.* New York: Harper & Row, 1977.

The Sadkers discuss how various stages in the life cycle are represented in today's literature, as well as cultural pluralism in children's books, the controversy over censorship, and how to teach literature creatively.

Safilios-Rothschild, Constantine. *Sex Role Socialization and Sex Discrimination: A Synthesis and Critique of the Literature*. Washington, D.C.: National Institute of Education, Department of Health, Education, and Welfare, 1979.

An analysis is provided of research related to sex-role socialization and sex discrimination, most of which was conducted between 1960 and 1978. The sections focusing on young children include studies on such topics as sex differences, sex-role preferences, parental behavior toward boys and girls. The author's critiques of the research are insightful and relevant.

Shapiro, June, Catherine Hunerberg, and Sylvia Carter. *Growing Up Equal: Activities and Resources for Parents and Teachers of Young Children*. Englewood Cliffs, N.J.: Prentice-Hall, 1981.

The authors offer hundreds of imaginative and varied activities for creating and maintaining a climate of nonsexist learning.

Sprung, Barbara. *Non-Sexist Education for Young Children: A Practical Guide*. New York: Citation Press, 1975.

The text suggests materials and offers ideas and insights about what is necessary to eliminate sexist messages from the early childhood environment.

Sprung, Barbara (ed.). *Perspectives on Non-Sexist Early Childhood Education*. New York: Teachers College Press, 1978.

This book contains a collection of essays, research reports, and discussions on the issue of equity in education and the contributions that teachers, administrators, researchers, and parents must make to realize equality of educational opportunity.

Weitzman, Lenore J., et al. *Sex-role Socialization in Picture Books for Preschool Children*. Pittsburgh: Know, Inc., 1972.

The authors have made an important analysis of how children's books can serve to socialize children into roles that limit them.

Women on Words and Images. *Dick and Jane as Victims: Sex Role Stereotyping in Children's Readers*, 2nd ed. Princeton, N.J.: Women on Words, 1975.

This booklet details the results of the now classic research project on sexism in children's reading texts. The study examined the most widely used series of elementary school textbooks. A slide show with synchronized cassette tape and script, that ably complements the booklet is available from the publisher.

15
Film
and
Television

MEDIA: IMPLICATIONS AND INFLUENCES

Luberta Mays and Deidre Breslin

Media is defined as means of communication that reach the general public, the substance through which an effect is transmitted. One of the most significant developments of the twentieth century has been the innovations in media. Mass communications and telecommunications have transformed the world and what people see and hear. The media's assault on our personal environment through the senses has brought about a radical reconstruction of children's auditory and visual experience and has affected the way children perceive and learn about the world. Film and television have been the media that have had the most effect on children, even as early as infancy, and it is television in particular where parents have felt the most helpless and frustrated in their attempts to monitor their children's viewing. Despite the birth of Action for Children's Television (ACT) at the end of the 1960s parents feel that they have too little say in either the type of children's programming scheduled by the networks or the commercials that keep these programs on the air.

To be responsible parents and teachers, it is imperative that we develop a critical response to the media and have a thorough knowledge of the ways in which television and film contribute to feelings and attitudes and influence behavior. Knowledge of how this occurs will provide insights regarding the influence media has on young children, whether in news broadcasting, advertisements, documentaries, or feature films. In short, parents and teachers need to be aware of not only the fact that visual media manipulates them but the degree to which they and their youngsters are affected through viewing.

497

In an article entitled "Children and Media," Mays and Pagano (1978) state:

> Television has taken on a major and permanent role in classroom instruction and in learning outside of school. It is a medium with which all children identify and which all educators must regard as a teaching tool. Current television technology needs to be explored and utilized by educators at every level of childhood learning in order to maximize its potential as a positive means to affect the mental and social growth of young children.

How can teachers use television positively, or teach children how to view television critically? We want youngsters to develop the ability to view television in a way that promotes the most desirable social outcomes. Development of critical viewing skills, assistance to parents for mediating their children's viewing, planned classroom use of current television programs and actions to influence program content and advertisements are significant actions in the right direction.

Television and Social Behavior

More than any other medium television furnishes a common body of information for the early socialization of children. Television can present to the audience many examples of positive social behavior. Mister Rogers of "Mister Rogers' Neighborhood" with his message of "I like you just as you are" can help the viewer have an understanding of the beauty of diversity, individuality, and acceptance. Shows like "Villa Allegre," "Sesame Street," and "The Big Blue Marble" present a vast array of positive solutions to everyday problems. Television programming carefully chosen will present to the young viewer human beings functioning appropriately and sensitively in the real world.

Perhaps the most obvious and therefore most researched, discussed, and analyzed aspect of television content is violence. Most of the research has focused on trying to establish a simple cause-and-effect relationship between the child watching a program termed violent by an adult and the child engaging in some violent behavior after viewing. The research, despite the millions of dollars spent on it, is still unclear. The vital questions remain unanswered. We need more information on how the young viewer perceives all television content and violent content in particular. Is the TV message different when the child sees any show with an adult present? Does the effect of all content and violent content in particular change when the message is discussed or analyzed with a loving, caring adult? These questions need answering.

The chief part television plays in the lives of children depends at least as much on what the child brings to television as on what television brings to the child. Therefore, the role of the adult is the critical one in determining what the young child learns about social behavior through the television experience.

Television and Reading

Learning to read with understanding, enthusiasm, and joy is a lifelong learning experience that starts long before the child ever gets to school. Television presents a broad, diverse curriculum. This curriculum can be an asset in the acquiring, development and enrichment of those skills necessary for literacy in general and print literacy in particular.

The television viewing experience can present a potentially valuable body of information to the viewer of any age. Concepts, general knowledge, facts, and vocabulary can be nourished and expanded via the TV curriculum. However, the young viewer has no opportunity to synthesize the material presented and then act upon it. Therefore, the amount of understanding the child has of this TV curriculum is unknown. Adults need to spend some time watching television with children. In this way, they can build on the experience. Events, ideas, and general information can be broadened and made more meaningful by dialogue between the adult and the child viewer. Connections between the child viewer and the television curriculum will be initiated and strengthened by this kind of participatory viewing experience. The viewer who participates with the television will be talking and thinking. Therefore, the same skills utilized by the reader to acquire meaning from print will be utilized by the viewer to acquire meaning from television viewing. Both reading and television viewing will become active experiences. Thus, the habits necessary for reading are enriched and supported by the viewing of television.

Vocabulary is the cornerstone of the child's understanding of both the oral and the written language. Television will become a tool for increasing vocabulary if the viewer is encouraged to interact with the program. If an argument is presented on the television tube, have children take sides. This strategy will enable children to acquire a personal meaning for the vocabulary presented.

Communication, in general, and reading, in particular, require thinking. Television viewing when taken seriously by both the child and adult viewer increases the quality of the experience. Television therefore demands thinking. Thus television can be one of the most powerful aids to the child who is starting on the road to reading.

Film: A Medium For Learning

Lindberg and Swedlow (1981) indicate that films have been an important form of communication for parents, teachers, and others who are concerned with improving their ways of working with young children. Films can be used with either large or small groups.

While educators have frequently used film in the classroom as kind of a "special treat," their film choices have, more than likely, been based on assumptions about children and film. Rarely are the films previewed by adults and even more rarely by children of an anticipated audience. Without a preview evaluation, the selected audience may not comprehend the objectives of the film showing, if indeed there were objectives. Lindberg and Swedlow (1981) suggest that films should be used only after it has been determined that this medium is likely to sharpen the intended message. This means that there are specific objectives to be addressed with each particular film. Lindberg and Swedlow strongly urge that adults using film, review their objectives to determine whether the particular visuals will indeed enhance the presentation. Neither film nor any other medium should be used merely because of availability or convenience.

Previewing by adults is of utmost importance and careful consideration must be given, as to how the film presentation will assist in achieving overall goals of a program or lesson.

Children, too, play a vital role in the selection of films chosen to benefit their age group. The Media Center for Children stresses the importance of film evaluation with children. The center has three objectives in film evaluation. The first is "to make inexpensive, practical, and child-centered infomation available to people who select films for or use with children." Since most distributors' materials are designed to entice people to use their films, the distributors suggest materials without field testing them and the materials are based on what adults think children would like. Thus, the second objective of the Media Center's film evaluation program is to provide information to film makers about what children understand and what they like or dislike about particular films and why. The third objective is to improve children's media and make them more child-oriented.

After determining which films are appropriate for a particular audience, parents and educators should consider their importance as a teaching tool. We agree with Lindberg and Swedlow (1981) who suggest that actual situations can be brought to the viewer's attention with film and it is possible to focus on a specific behavior or material.

> As desired, films can be used to provide a common frame of reference through which an audience can examine an issue or look at a piece of life together. They can serve as a primary source of information for those who are not likely to read books, and are a supplementary source for others. Although everyone in an audience sees the same frames, all do not really see the same things, nor do they interpret them in the same ways because each person brings his own experiences to them.

Because showing a film is primarily an adult-controlled operation (unless on TV, films cannot be turned on and off by small children), parents and teachers are fortunate in that they really can select the best in children's film. Further, this allows them every opportunity to choose films that will assist them in meeting their stated program goals, whether at home or in the classroom. Some of the thoughts previously discussed coupled with the following bibliographic entries in this area should provide information of vital importance regarding effective use of films with young children.

While television and film represent the most common use of media with children, they do not represent the total picture. Educators in the classroom often use overhead projectors, phonographs, and tape recorders. In the home, tape recorders, audiovisual tape cassettes, and movie cameras are used in increasing numbers. These types of equipment enable parents to diversify their teaching methods in the informal setting of the home as well as enable teachers to do so in structured classroom situations. Both settings may provide an atmosphere that enhances the ongoing social, emotional, and intellectual growth of young children.

The purpose of this chapter is to provide essential information to parents and teachers that will assist them in pursuing media education in a meaningful, constructive manner. Further, its purpose is to serve as an introduction to areas for consideration, wholly necessary, prior to making any decisions about what, when and how to use media effectively as a learning tool in the home or in the classroom.

References

Mays, Luberta, and A. Pagano. Children and media. In A. Pagano (ed.), *Social Studies in Early Childhood: An Interactionist Point of View.* Washington, D.C.: National Council of Social Studies, 1978.

Lindberg, Lucile, and R. Swedlow. Film: A medium for learning (unpublished paper), New York, 1981.

BIBLIOGRAPHY

Association for Educational Communication and Technology. *Selecting Media for Learning: Readings from Audio Visual Instruction.* Washington, D.C.: The Association, 1974.

These valuable suggestions should be considered when selecting films for many types of programs.

Barker, R. K., and S. J. Ball, (eds.). *Violence and the Media.* Washington, D.C.: U.S. Government Printing Office, 1975.

This staff report to the National Commission on the Causes and Prevention of Violence sums up and discusses some of the research. The authors point up some of the conclusions that suggest that some of the violence in our society might have its roots in the media presentation of life.

Barcus, F. Earle. *Commercial Children's Television on Weekends and Weekday Afternoons.* Newtonville, Ma.: Action for Children's Television, 1978.

An eminent university professor of communications gives a definitive content analysis of children's TV programming and advertising.

Bobker, Lee. *Elements of Film.* New York: Harcourt Brace Jovanovich, 1979.

This work will appeal to the serious students of film as well as the general reader. The emphasis is between the how to-do-it and the way to-do-it in film making.

Brown, James W., Richard B. Lewis, and Fred F. Harclerood. *Audio-Visual Instruction: Technology, Media and Method*, 5th ed. New York: McGraw-Hill, 1976.

The special values of films as media for instruction are noted. One chapter is concerned with choosing media. A directory of sources of media information is included.

Brown, Les. *Television: The Business Behind the Box.* New York: Harcourt Brace Jovanovich, 1971.

This book takes the reader behind the scenes to look at the industry. Describes competitive relationship between the major networks and their affiliate stations. The work emphasizes how children and adults are sold by TV; as products of commercial television. Television decision-making is discussed, as well as the limitations and power of the Federal Commerce Commission (FCC). This volume is useful for parents and teachers.

CBS Office of Social Research. *Communicating with Children Through Television: Studies of Messages and Other Impressions Conveyed by Five Children's Programs.* New York: Columbia Broadcasting System, 1977.

This work describes how television programs determine what social and/or factual messages are internalized by child viewers. The report analyzes the data collection approach used in the three-year study on which the text is based and discusses children's responses to selected entertainment programs.

Charren, Peggy, and Martin Sandler. *Watching Television: A Practical Guide for Practically Everybody.* Reading, Mass.: Addison-Wesley, 1982.

This illustrated book provides the background for understanding television and offers practical advice for using it better. It is an authoritative and enjoyable guide to what parents, teachers, children, and everybody else needs to know about television.

DeFranco, Ellen B. *TV On/Off: Better Family Use of Television.* Santa Monica, Ca.: Goodyear Publishing, 1981.

While not negative toward television, this book gives guidelines on how to regulate viewing habits that will serve to turn watching into a positive learning experience for the whole family. Suggestions include setting up family discussions about programs as well as ideas for alternative activities that do not include television. For the overindulging famiy a useful "TV diet" is given.

Goldsen, Rose K. *The Show and Tell Machine.* New York: Dial Press, 1977.

Well-researched, this book speaks to both the parent and professional. Especially interesting is the treatment of children's programs and the impact of television on young children. The book effectively points up the power of television and the commercialism that is the industry's guiding force.

Gropper, George L., and Glasgow, Zeta. *Criteria for the Selection and Use of Visuals in Instruction.* Englewood Cliffs, N.J.: Educational Technology Publications, 1971.

Criteria are carefully developed for selecting visual materials and should prove helpful in formulating guidelines for the use of films.

Harmonay, Maureen (ed.). *Promise and Performance: ACT's Guide to TV Programming for Children.* Vol. 2, *The Arts.* Cambridge, Mass.: Cambridge, Mass.: Ballinger, 1977.

This is an unprecedented collection of articles and resources about the ways in which television programming can be used to benefit one of the most neglected broadcasting constituencies: children with handicaps.

Harmonay, Maureen (ed.). *Promise and Performance: ACT's Guide to TV Programming for Children.* Vol. 2, *The Arts.* Cambridge, Mass.: Ballinger, 1979.

This is a valuable tool for educators, arts professionals, communications students, libraries, broadcast executives and TV producers—in short, anyone who is concerned about the current status of children's television. This is a one-of-a-kind compilation of articles and resources on one of the most nourishing but least available elements of a child's television diet, the arts.

Harmonay, Maureen (ed.). *Promise and Performance: ACT's Guide to TV Programming for Children.* Vol. 4, *The Sciences.* Cambridge, Mass.: Ballinger, 1982.

This practical guide examines television's influence on children's attitudes about science. The book includes a series of case studies that explore ways in which television programs can inform children and teenagers about science.

Kaye, Evelyn. *The ACT Guide to Children's Television: How to Treat TV with T.L.C.,* rev. ed. Boston: Beacon, 1979.

This basic handbook for parents and concerned citizens was prepared in cooperation with the American Academy of Pediatrics. It provides information and practical guidance about how to make television a positive and rewarding experience in children's lives.

Kinder, James S. *Using Instructional Media.* New York: Van Nostrand, 1973.

Chapters concerned with the media and change, communication and learning, using pictorial graphics and creating a learning environment are especially suitable for those who wish to include the use of films in their programming.

Laybourne, Kit, and Pauline Cianciolo. (eds.). *Doing the Media: A Portfolio of Activities, Ideas, and Resources.* New York: McGraw-Hill, 1978.

There is much information and ideas about photography, film making, video, and other media that teachers and parents will find helpful. There are suggestions on how tc teach children to use the media in as many ways as possible.

Logan, Ben. (ed.). *Television's Awareness Training: The Viewer's Guide for Family and Community.* Nashville: Abingdon Press, 1980.

This collection of articles focuses on television awareness training. The reader will develop an awareness of how we use TV, what the intended and unintended messages are, and the strategies for change in areas of concern. The positive use of television is stressed. There are work sheets and assignments appropriate for elementary youngsters as well as parents and teachers.

Mankiewicz, Frank, and Joel Swerdlow. *Remote Control: Television and the Manipulation of American Life.* New York: Times Books, 1978.

This book discusses the wide changes evident in American life as a result of the age of television. Chapter six gives a detailed explanation of the changes in reading and learning behavior, which the authors believe are traceable to television.

Melody, William. *Children's TV: The Economics of Exploitation.* New Haven: Yale University Press, 1973.

In this still relevant study of the economics of children's TV, the focus is on the forces that make most television geared for children more concerned on riveting children's eyes to the product than delivering quality programs to the children.

Moody, Kate. *Growing Up on Television.* New York: Quadrangle, 1980.

Moody considers the effect television has on children and what can be done about it. She focuses on experiences of teachers trying to teach children who find it difficult to concentrate when using nontechnological school materials. She discusses the trend away from the print medium and the consequences of such learning behavior. The book is directed to the parent and caregiver group.

Postman, Neil. *The Disappearance of Childhood.* New York: Dell, 1981.

The author, a commentator on media, points toward its effects on young people. He documents his thesis—that the period called childhood is disappearing—with vivid examples including those from books, films, and television.

Singer, Dorothy, Jerome L. Singer, and Diane M. Zuckerman. *Teaching Television: How to Use TV to Your Child's Advantage.* New York: Dial Press, 1981.

The authors, leaders in the field of psychology and founders of the Yale University Family Television Research and Consultation Center, show how parents can utilize television to further their child's growth and development. The authors review significant aspects of programming and how children perceive what they watch. They explain how shows are put together and examine the differences between fantasy and reality that may be unclear to children. Here is a practical guide to help parents help children develop the kinds of critical skills that will last a lifetime.

Trojan, Judith. *American Family Life Films*. Metuchin, N.J.: Scarecrow Press, 1981.

Both short and feature-length documentary and dramatic films that deal with a wide range of family life are listed and annotated.

Winick, Mariann Pezella, *Films for Childhood Educators*. Washington, D.C.: Association for Childhood Education International, 1977.

This pamphlet includes guidelines for choosing films and suggestions for using them. Films concerned with such subjects as open classroom, child development, readiness, and family living are described and evaluated. Sources and rental fees are included.

Winn, Marie. *The Plug-In Drug*. New York: Viking, 1977.

Any parent or teacher who is disturbed by a child's overuse of TV will find ample support in this book. Turn the set off is the message, before it's too late.

16
Resources for
Service and Information

INTRODUCTION

Bertha Campbell

In this chapter we have listed pertinent organizations, periodicals and newsletters that will enable the reader to obtain additional information on the topics covered in the first fifteen chapters. Of necessity, these listings are selective rather than exhaustive in scope. The listings may not be mutually exclusively; thus an organization for children with special needs may also furnish information or assistance to involve parents and professionals. For the most part, national or regional rather than state or local organizations have been cited; however, some specialized organizations of smaller scope that have relevant materials have been included. In every metropolitan area there is a wide range of human resources available that can be of assistance in a myriad of fields relevant to early childhood development, ranging from professional organizations, to service agencies and organizations, to local government departments to volunteer parent groups. Departments of early childhood education and psychology, among others, at colleges and universities may contain service centers or resource personnel that can be of assistance. The yellow pages of the local telephone directory is still an invaluable source for those seeking both information and help concerning children. Most relevant organizations would be listed under the heading, Social Service Agencies.

The public library as well as the libraries of local hospitals or colleges and universities should be consulted when seeking pertinent data. If you consider ordering materials from any resources, visit the library's periodical department to see if they are available there so that you can examine them and then determine if

the materials will answer your needs. But here is a starting
point.

Newsletters

ACT Newsletter
Action for Children's Television
46 Austin Street
Newtonville, MA   02160

Action for Children Newsletter
1426 H Street NW
Washington, DC   20005

Advocacy for Children
U.S. Department of Health &
   Human Services
Washington, DC   20201

Bank Street Reporting
Bank Street College of Education
610 West 112th Street
New York, NY   10025

Bulletin
Interracial Books for Children
Council on Interracial Books for
   Children
1841 Broadway
New York, NY   10023

Council on Children and Families
Empire State Plaza
Agency Building
Albany, NY   12223

Center for Parent Education Newsletter
55 Chapel Street
Newton, MA   02160

Childcare Information Exchange
C-44
Redmond, WA   98052

Children in Crisis
ATCOM Inc.
2315 Broadway
New York, NY   10024

*CWA Critten Reporter on School-Age
   Parenting*
Child Welfare League of America
1346 Connecticut Avenue, N.W.
Washington, DC   20036

Day Care & Child Development Reports
2626 Pennsylvania Avenue NW
Washington, DC   20037

*Early Childhood Education Alumni
   Newsletter*
College of Staten Island
130 Stuyvesant Place
Staten Island, NY   10301

EDC News
Educational Development Center
55 Chapel Street
Newton, MA 02160

ECEC
Early Childhood Education
   Council of NYC
66 Leroy Street, NY   10014

Edu-Letter
NYS Association for Retarded
   Children, Inc.
175 Fifth Avenue
New York, NY   10010

Education for Parenthood Exchange
W. Stanley Kruger
400 Maryland Avenue, SW
Washington, DC   20202

Equal Play
Woman's Action Alliance, Inc.
370 Lexington Avenue
New York, NY   10016

ERIC/EECE Newsletter
College of Education
University of Illinois
805 West Pennsylvania Avenue
Urbana, IL   61801

ETS Developments
Educational Testing Service
Princeton, NJ   08541

Family Dynamics
600 Lexington Avenue
New York, NY   10022

Family Life Developments
Cooperative Extension
U.S. Department of Agriculture
Roberts Hall, Cornell University
Ithaca, NY   14853

Gifted Children Newsletters
Gifted Children Newsletters
P.O. Box 115
Sewell, NJ   08080

Good Parenting
International Education
   Association
21 Charles Street
Westport, CT   06880

Growing Child
22 North Second Street
Lafayette, IN   47902

Growing Parent
22 North Second Street
Lafayette, IN   47902

Hotline
Day Care & Child Development
   Council of America, Inc.
1602 17th Street, NW
Washington, DC   20009

Head Start Newsletter
U.S. Department of Health &
   Human Services
Washington, DC   20201

Human Development News
Office of Human Development
   Services
U.S. Department of Health &
   Human Services
Washington, DC   20201

Impact
Institute for Family Research and
   Education
Syracuse University
760 Ostrom Avenue
Syracuse, NY   13210

Insights
Center for Teaching and Learning
Corwin Hall
University of North Dakota
Grand Forks, ND   58202

Let's Find Out
Scholastic Magazines
902 Sylvan Avenue
Englewood Cliffs, NJ   07632

Living with Young Learners
Cooperative Extension
U.S. Department of Agriculture
Roberts Hall, Cornell University
Ithaca, NY   14853

NAEYC Affiliate
National Association for the
  Education of Young Children
1834 Connecticut Avenue, NW
Washington, DC   20009

Newsletter of Parenting
2300 West Fifth Avenue
P.O. Box 2505
Columbus, OH   43216

News of the World's Children
United States Committee for
  UNICEF
331 East 38th Street
New York, NY   10016

New York Early Education Reporter
117 Euclid Avenue
Albany, NY   12203

New York Parent-Teacher
119 Washington Avenue
Albany, NY   12210

Nurturing News
187 Caselli Avenue
San Francisco, CA   94114

Nutrition News
National Dairy Council
6300 North River Road
Rosemont, IL   60018

Parent Child Center Newsletter
55 Wheeler Street
Cambridge, MA   02138

Parenthood Education Report
Box 81
Peabody College
Nashville, TN   37203

Parents Helping Parents
Parents Anonymous
121 North Fitzhugh Street
Rochester, NY   14614

*Parents and Friends For Children's
  Survival Newsletter*
  Includes bibliography of books
on threat of nuclear war for parents, children, and teachers by
Educators for Social Responsibility. To get on mailing list, call
691-4709 or write Box 986, Old
Chelsea Station, NY, NY   10013

Practical Parenting Newsletter
Meadowbrook Press, Inc.
1813 Minnetonka Boulevard
Deephaven, MN   55391

Organizations in the United States

Academy of Dentistry for the
  Handicapped
1726 Champa
Denver, CO   80202
  Publishes a free *Membership Re-
ferral Roster.*

Action for Children's Television
  (ACT)
46 Austin Street
Newtonville, MA   12160
  A national organization working to upgrade the quality of television for children.

Adoption Resource Exchange of
  North America
Child Welfare League of
  America, Inc.
67 Irving Place
New York, NY   10003
  Makes national referrals to li-
censed agencies throughout the
United States for adoptable chil-
dren with special needs.

The Alexander Graham Bell
Association for the Deaf
Headquarters
The Volta Bureau
34–17 Volta Place, N.W.
Washington, DC   20007

The American Academy of
Husband-Coached Childbirth
(AAHCC)
The Bradley Method
P.O. Box 5224
Sherman Oaks, CA   91413

American Alliance for Health,
Physical Education, Recreation
and Dance
Reston, VA   22091

Offers comprehensive publications in the areas of health, physical ed for adults-children

American Center of Films for
Children
Division of Cinema, University of
Southern California
University Park
Los Angeles, CA   90007

Encourages the production, distribution, and exhibition of high-quality films for children. Maintains a clearinghouse of information on children's films and a rental library of films for children.

American Council on Science &
Health
1995 Broadway
New York, NY   10023

Provides information on food and nutrition.

American Dental Association
211 East Chicago Avenue
Chicago, IL   60611

American Diabetes Association,
Inc.
2 Park Avenue
New York, NY   10016

Helps families and professionals who deal with diabetes. Fifty-five affiliates around the country.

American Diagnostic Learning &
Reading Center
2211 Broadway
New York, NY   10024

Guidance on various aspects of infant and toddler normal development and disability.

American Dietetic Association
430 North Michigan Avenue
Chicago, IL   60611

American Digestive Disease
Society, Inc.
7720 Wisconsin Avenue
Washington, DC   20014

American Foundation for the
Blind, Inc.
15 West 16th Street
New York, NY   10011

American Heart Association
205 East 42 St
New York, NY   10017

American Home Economics
Association
2010 Massachusetts Avenue, NW
Washington, DC   20036

Provides information on food and nutrition.

American Institute of Nutrition
9650 Rockville Pike
Bethesda, MD   20014

American Library Association
50 East Huron Street
Chicago, IL   60611
    Publishes pamphlets, bibliographies, and relevant materials.

American Medical Association
    (AMA)
535 North Dearborn Street
Chicago, IL   60610

American Montessori Society, Inc.
175 Fifth Avenue
New York, NY   10010

American Public Health
    Association
1790 Broadway
New York, NY   10019

American School Food Service
    Association
4101 East Cliff Avenue
Denver, CO   80222

American Society for Clinical
    Nutrition
9650 Rockville Pike
Bethesda, MD   20014

American Speech-Language-
    Hearing Association
10801 Rockville Pike
Rockville, MD   20852
    Publishes *Guide to Clinical Services in Speech-Language Pathology and Audiology*

Anti-Defamation League of B'nai
    B'rith
345 East 46th Street
New York, NY   10017
    Distributes teaching materials related to racial and ethnic diverse minorities. Also conducts training sessions on human relations.

Association for Anthropological
    Study of Play
P.O. Box 297
Alamo, CA   94507

Association for the Care of
    Children in Hospital
3615 Wisconsin Avenue NW
Washington, DC   20016

Association for Childhood
    Education International
3615 Wisconsin Avenue, NW
Washington, DC   20016
    For professionals concerned with the child from infancy through early adolescence.

Association for Children and
    Adults with Learning
    Disabilities
4156 Library Road
Pittsburgh, PA   15234
    Publishes *Directory of Education Facilities for the Learning Disabled.*

Association for Education of the
    Visually Handicapped
919 Walnut Street
Philadelphia, PA   19107

Association for Educational
    Communications and
    Technology (AECT)
1126 16 Street, NW
Washington, DC   20036
    A professional association dedicated to improving instruction through technology. Publishes *Audiovisual Instruction.*

Association for Neurologically
    Impaired Brain Injured
    Children
217 Lark Street
Albany, NY   12210

Association for Parent Education
Public Information Office
170 Thompson Street
New York, NY   10012

Association for the Severely
   Handicapped
7010 Roosevelt Way N.E.
Seattle, WA   98115
   Serves professionals involved
with the education and care of
severely handicapped children. Organizes an annual conference; publishes research papers and curricular materials.

Asthma & Allergy Foundation of
   America
19 West 44th Street,
New York, NY   10036

Black Child Development Institute
1518 K Street, NW
Washington, DC   20005

Brooklyn Education Advisory
   Panel
Project ACE (Aiding Children's
   Education)
209 Joralemon St., Rm. 205
Brooklyn, NY   11201
   Publishes packet of pamphlets,
Being Me Is Great—building Self-
Concept, helping children prepare
for reading, accepting children's
feelings, learning from play, and
emphasizing everyone is special.
In five languages—English, French,
Italian, Spanish, Russian.

Carnegie Council on Children
1619 Broadway
New York, NY   10019
   Analyzes how children develop
in America. Provides writers and
producers of children's media with
ideas and leads to research materials.

Center for Parent Education
55 Chapel Street
Newton, MA   02160
   Assists professionals concerned
with the education of children
during the first three years of life.

Center for the Study of Multiple
   Birth
333 East Superior Street
Chicago, IL   60611

Childhood City
Center for Human Environments
Graduate Center - CUNY
33 West 42nd Street
New York, NY   10036

Children's Book Council
67 Irving Place
New York, NY   10003
   Concerned with bringing books
and children together.

Children's Defense Fund
1520 New Hampshire Avenue,
   NW
Washington, DC   20036
   Child advocate organization.

Child Welfare League of
   America, Inc.
67 Irving Place
New York, NY   10003

Citizens Committee for New York
   City, Inc.
3 West 29th Street
New York, NY   10001
   Organized to help with neigh-
borhood projects such as starting

block associations, crime prevention programs, clean-up programs, etc., programs for young children.

Clearinghouse on the
   Handicapped
U.S. Department of Health,
   Education & Welfare
Washington, DC   20202
   Publishes *Directory of National Information Sources on Handicapping Conditions and Related Services.*

Consumer Information Center
Department of Health &
   Human Services
General Services Administration,
Washington, DC   20201
   Provides information on health and nutrition.

Coordinating Council for
   Handicapped Children
407 South Dearborn Street
Chicago, IL   60605
   Publishes materials on handicapped children.

Council for Exceptional Children
1920 Association Drive
Reston, VA   22091
   Professional organization for those working with special children. Publications upon membership: *Exceptional Children* and *Teaching Exceptional Children*. Other books and pamphlets.

Council on Interracial Books for
   Children
1841 Broadway
New York, NY   10023
   A resource center for edu-

cators. Puts out teaching materials (both printed and audiovisual) newsletters, and guides for combatting racism and sexism.

Cystic Fibrosis Foundation
6000 Executive Boulevard
Rockville, MD   20852

Directory of Services for the
   Deaf in the United States
American Annals of the Deaf
Gallaudet College
Washington, D.C.   20002

Disability Rights Center
1346 Connecticut Ave., NW
Washington, DC   20036

Education Commission of
   the States
Early Childhood
1860 Lincoln Tower
Denver, CO   80203
   A clearing house for discussion of educational issues.

Educational Film Library
   Association (EFLA)
43 West 61 Street
New York, NY   10023
   An active library organization that serves as a national clearinghouse for information about 16mm film. Numerous publications and a reference service for members.

Emma Willard Task Force
   on Education
P.O. Box 14229
Minneapolis, MN   55414
   Publishes periodicals related to sexism.

ERIC Clearinghouse on
Elementary & Early Childhood
Education
University of Illinois
College of Education
Urbana, IL 61801

Prenatal factors, parental behavior; the physical, psychological,
social, educational, and cultural
development of children from birth
through the primary grades; educational theory, research, and practice related to the development of
young children, including teacher
preparation, educational programs
and curricula related community
services, groups and institutions,
administration, and physical settings as well as theoretical and
philosophical issues. Includes both
the early years of childhood (ages
0-7) and the "middle years" (ages
8-12).

ERIC Clearinghouse on
Handicapped and
Gifted Children
Council for Exceptional Children
1920 Association Drive
Reston, VA 22091

Aurally handicapped, visually
handicapped, mentally handicapped
developmentally disabled, abused/
neglected, autistic, multiply handicapped, severely handicapped,
physically handicapped, emotionally disturbed, speech handicapped,
learning disabled, and the gifted
and the talented; behavioral, psychomotor, and communication disorders, administration of special

education services; preparation
and continuing education of professional and paraprofessional personnel; preschool learning and development of the exceptional; general studies on creativity.

Family Service Association
of America
44 East 23rd Street
New York, NY 10010

Feminist Press
P.O. Box 334
SUNY/College at Old Westbury
Old Westbury, NY 11568

Publishes teaching resources,
books, and annotated bibliographies of children's books.

Food and Drug Administration
Consumer Communications
5600 Fishers Lane
Rockville, MD 20852

Publishes catalogues and lists
on nutrition, meal planning, and
related topics.

Foundation for Child Development
345 East 46th Street
New York, NY 10016

Good Nutrition Program
Patient Activity Department
Children's Hospital
Columbus, OH 43205

Human Growth, Inc.
307 Fifth Avenue
New York, NY 10016

Concerned with children with
growth problems such as dwarf-
ism, gigantism, and failure to
thrive.

Institute for Human Nutrition
Columbia University
College of Physicians & Surgeons
630 West 168th Street
New York, NY   10032

International Reading Association
800 Barksdale Road
Newark, DE   19711
    International organization for professionals and parents on reading and children.

The John Tracy Clinic
806 West Adams Boulevard
Los Angeles, CA   90007
    Distributes a free correspondence course for language and other development of deaf infants and preschoolers.

KNOW, Inc
P.O. Box 86031
Pittsburgh, PA   15221
    Distributes teaching materials and periodicals related to sexism and educational equity.

Lollipop Power, Inc.
P.O. Box 1171
Chapel Hill, NC   27514
    Offers readings and bibliographies related to educational equity.

Media Center for Children
43 West 61 Street
New York, NY   10023
    A nonprofit organization that researches film with children. Also screens and tests films for children. Publishes *Young Viewers*.

Migrant Child Development
    Program
Gettysburg Schools
    Administration Building
Route 34N
Gettysburg, PA   17325

Multicultural Resources
P.O. Box 2945
Stanford, CA   94305
    Distributes multicultural bibliographies for preschool through second grade; books and catalogues available.

Muscular Dystrophy Association
810 Seventh Avenue
New York, NY   10019

National Association of the Deaf
814 Thayer Avenue
Silver Spring, MD   20910

National Association for the
    Education of Young Children
1934 Connecticut Avenue, NW
Washington, DC   20009

National Association for
    Gifted Children
8080 Springvalley Drive
Cincinnati, OH   45236

The National Association of
    Parents and Professionals for
    Safe Alternatives in
    Childbirth (NAPSAC)
P.O. Box 267
Marble Hill, MO   63764

National Association for
    Retarded Children
420 Lexington Avenue
New York, NY   10017

National Association of
  Social Workers
1425 H Street NW
Washington, DC   20005

National Center on Child Abuse
  & Neglect
Office of Child Development
P.O. Box 1182
Washington, DC   20013
  Makes referrals to child-abuse
centers throughout the United
States.

National Center for Clinical
  Infant Programs
733 15th Street N.W.
Washington, DC   20005
  Ofers a forum for exchange of
information on clinical infant and
early childhood programs. Coor-
dinates research and training of
personnel.

National Center for Law &
  the Deaf
7th Street and Florida Avenue, NE
Washington, DC   20202

National Center for Law &
  the Handicapped
211 W. Washington St
Suite 1900
South Bend, IN   46601

National Center for the
  Prevention & Treatment of
  Child Abuse & Neglect
1205 Oneida Street
Denver, CO   80220
  Provides professionals with
current materials, conducts research, and provides help to both
abusive parents and abused children.

National Clearinghous for
  Bilingual Education
1300 Wilson Boulevard
Rosslyn, VA   22209
  Upon request, does a free search
for information on specific topics
in bicultural/bilingual education.

National Consortium for
  Children & Families
5 Westmoreland Place
Pasadena, CA   91103

National Council on
  Family Relations
Family Resource &
  Referral Center
1219 University Avenue, SE
Minneapolis, MN   55414

National Council of
  Organizations for
  Children & Youth
1910 K Street, NW
Washington, DC   20006

New York State Association for
  Retarded Children, Inc.
175 Fifth Avenue
New York, NY   10010
  Periodic publications on retarded children and their education as well as problems that parents face.

National Perinatal Association
52nd and F Streets
Sacramento, CA   95819

National Society for
     Autistic Children, Inc
169 Tampa Avenue
Albany, NY   12208

The National Society for
     Crippled Children and Adults
2023 West Ogden Avenue
Chicago, IL   60612

Office for Civil Rights
U.S. Department of Education
330 C Street, SW
Washington, DC   20202

Office of Cancer
     Communications
National Cancer Institute
9000 Rockville Pike
Bethesda, MD   20205

Office of Information and
     Resources for the
     Handicapped
U.S. Department of Education
330 C Street SW
Washington, DC   20202

Parenting Materials
     Information Center
Southwest Educational
     Development Laboratory
211 East 7th Street
Austin, TX   78701

Parents Without Partners, Inc.
7910 Woodmont Avenue
Washington, DC   20014

People to People Committee for
     the Handicapped
1522 K Street NW
Washington, DC   20005
     Distributes the *Directory of Or-
ganizations Interested in the Handicapped.*

Rehabilitation International
432 Park Avenue South
New York, NY   10016
     Has a contract with UNICEF to
develop services for the handicapped, especially children in underdeveloped countries.

Sex Information & Education
     Council of the U.S.
1855 Broadway
New York, NY   10023

SIECUS (Sex Information &
     Education Center of the U.S.)
New York University
51 West 4th Street
New York, NY   10003
     Provides inexpensive annotated
bibliographies and educational materials on topics in the field of
human sexuality.

Society for the Protection of the
     Unborn Through Nutrition
Suite 603
17 North Wabash
Chicago, Illinois   60602

Southern Association for
     Children Under Six
P.O. Box 5403, Brady Station
Little Rock, AR   72205

Southwest Educational
     Developmental Laboratory
211 East 7th Street
Austin, TX   78701
     Concerned with the needs of
special population—those with
physical, cultural, economic, or intellectual differences.

United Cerebral Palsy
Associations, Inc.
66 East 34 Street
New York, NY   10016

United Parents Associations
95 Madison Avenue
New York, NY   10016

The U.S. Committee for UNICEF
331 East 38th St.
N.Y. N.Y.   10016 (212) 686-5522.

This UNICEF support agency
produces excellent and interesting
educational materials about children who are mostly from developing countries. A free catalogue
is available upon request.

Women's Action Alliance, Inc.
370 Lexington Avenue
New York, NY   10017

Information and referral center for women's problems. Provides information and material related to educational equity.

World Organization for
Early Childhood Education
OMEP International
Headquarters
81 Irving Place
New York, NY   10003

Periodicals

Akwesasne Notes
Mohawk Nation
Roosevelt, NY   13683

Lists teaching resources and
periodicals related to native Americans and their community.

American Annals of the Deaf
(reference issue)
5034 Wisconsin Avenue, NW
Washington, DC   20016

Published annually in April,
supplies information on programs
and services for the deaf in the
United States, including educational, rehabilitational, social, and
recreational listings. Most information listed by state.

American Baby
575 Lexington Avenue
New York, NY   10022

Art Education
National Art Education
Association
1916 Association Drive
Reston, VA   22091

Arts & Activities
591 Camino de la Reina
San Diego, CA   92108

Birth and the Family Journal
International Childbirth
Education Association
110 El Camino Real
Berkeley, CA   94705

Black Child Journal
1426 East 49th Street
Chicago, IL   60615

Child Development
University of Chicago Press
5750 Ellis Avenue
Chicago, IL   60637

CDF Reports
Children's Defense Fund
P.O. Box 7584
Washington, DC   20044

Child Study Journal
State University College
1300 Elmwood Avenue
Buffalo, NY   14222

Child Welfare
Child Welfare League of America
67 Irving Place
New York, NY   10003

Childhood Education
Association for Childhood
    Education International
3615 Wisconsin Avenue, NW
Washington, DC   20016

Children Today
U.S. Superintendent of
    Documents
U.S. Government Printing Office
Washington, DC   20402

*Children's Health Care. Journal for the
    Association for the Care of Children
    in Hospitals*
Association for the Care of
    Children in Hospitals
6900 Grove Road
Thorofare, NJ   08086

Children's Legal Rights Journal
2008 Hillyer Place, NW
Washington, DC   20009

The Creative Child and Adult Quarterly
National Association for Creative
    Children and Adults
8080 Springvalley Drive
Cincinnati, OH   45236

*Day Care and Child Development
    Reports*
2814 Pennsylvania Avenue, N.W.
Washington, DC   20007

Day Care & Early Education
Day Care Council of America
711 14th Street, NW
Washington, DC   20005

Dimensions
SACUS
Box 5403, Brady Station
Little Rock, AR   72215
    Spotlights multicultural awareness.

Early Years
P.O. Box 912
Farmingdale, NY   11735
    For teachers of preschool and primary grades; how-to articles; a regular section on the exceptional child.

Educational Horizons
    official publication
Pi Lambda Theta—National
    Honor and Professional
    Association in Education
4101 East 3rd Street
Bloomington, IN   47401
    Promotes professional fellowship and cooperation.

Exceptional Children
Council for Exceptional Children
1920 Association Drive
Reston, VA   22091
    Articles outlining public policy and its impact on the education of handicapped and gifted children.

Exceptional Education Quarterly
Aspen Systems Corporation
P.O. Box 6018
Gaithersburg, MD   20760

Examines issues pertaining to the education of the disabled and gifted children.

Exceptional Parent Magazine
296 Boylston Street
Boston, MA   02116

First Teacher
P.O. Box 1308-T
Fort Lee, N.J.   07024

Getting It Together
Planned Parenthood of
    America Federation
810 Seventh Avenue
New York, NY   10019

Harvard Educational Review
Longfellow Hall
13 Appian Way
Cambridge, MA   02138

Instructor
P.O. Box 6099
Duluth, MN   55806

Journal of Family Issues
Sage Publications, Inc.
275 South Beverly Drive
Beverly Hills, CA   90212

Journal of Nurse-Midwifery
Elsevier-North Holland, Inc.
52 Vanderbilt Avenue
New York, NY   10017

Keys to Early Childhood Education
Capitol Publishers, Inc.
1300 North 17th Street
Arlington, VA   22209

Learning
1255 Portland Place
Boulder, CO   80321

*MCN: The American Journal of
    Maternal Child Nursing*
American Journal of Nursing Co.
555 West 57th Street
New York, NY   10019

Articles of interest to professionals working with infants and young children as well as families of child-bearing age.

Parent's Choice
P.O. Box 185
Walsan, MA   02168

A review of children's media—books, television, movies, music records, toys and games.

Parent's Resources
P.O. Box 107, Planetarium Station
New York, NY   10024

Partners in Parenting
Family Focus, Inc.
2300 Green Bay Road
Evanston, IL   60201

Perceptions
P.O. Box 142
Millburn, NJ   07041

An information source for parents of children with learning disabilities.

Psychology Today
P.O. Box 2990
Boulder, CO   80321

Report on Preschool Education
Capitol Publications, Inc.
1300 North 17th Street
Arlington, VA   22209

Resources in Education
Superintendent of Documents
U.S. Government Printing Office
Washington, DC   20402

School Arts
Davis Publication
50 Portland Street
Worcester, MA   01608

School Parent
United Parents Associations of
    New York City, Inc.
95 Madison Avenue
New York, NY   10016

Single Parent
Parents Without Partners, Inc.
7910 Woodmont Avenue
Washington, DC   20014

Teachers Guide to Television
145 East 69th Street
New York, NY   10021

Totline
Warren Publishing
P.O. Box 2253
Alderwood Manor, WA   98036
        Activity ideas for working with
preschool children.

Young Children
Association for Education of
    Young Children
1834 Connecticut Avenue, N.W.
Washington, DC   20009

Afterword

Bettye M. Caldwell

The individual chapters in *Resources for Early Childhood* provide an excellent overview to the broad field of Early Childhood Education. The book is being published at an exciting time in the evolution and development of the field of early childhood. As is true in perhaps all scientific and professional fields, the years since 1960 have witnessed more growth than has occurred throughout the history of the field. This spurt was occasioned by scientific evidence from a variety of fields of the importance of the early childhood period for optimal development of the individual (Caldwell, 1970; Hunt, 1962). It was then intensified by a widespread perception of the special need that children growing up in conditions of poverty and other types of social disadvantage have for habilitative experiences. The birth of Head Start in 1965 marked the official beginning of this growth spurt. To date, the spurt has yet to plateau, and one hopes it will not for a long time to come.

Major Advances of the Recent Past

A number of major advances that have occurred during this period could be cited. Five appear to be of particular importance.

1. *Expansion of Curriculum Research and Development.* In an earlier publication (Caldwell, 1967) I chided the field for being some-

what narrowminded about acceptable curricula for early childhood programs. That is, at the beginning of the 1960s only a fairly narrowly conceptualized and carefully standardized curriculum for early childhood programs was considered appropriate. It was characterized by a great deal of free play for the children with a minimum of direct instruction from the teachers. The curriculum was seen as more relevant for social and emotional growth than for cognitive growth. When innovators working in different parts of the country began to suggest that such an approach did not seem to work as well with children whose previous experiences did not allow them to capitalize on the learning opportunities present in such environments and suggested that the curriculum might need to be more carefully regulated or "structured," there was a strong resistance. It was not unlike the almost immediate rejection of the Montessori approach that had occurred a generation earlier when it was first introduced to this country.

Today resistance to new curriculum approaches appears to have weakened if not vanished altogether. New curricula have been developed and disseminated, with many having a substantial research base as evidence for their effectiveness. Furthermore, there is now general acceptance of the validity of modifying teaching approaches for children with different experiential backgrounds and with differing degrees of competence upon entering the programs. Particularly impressive is the fact that there have been programs developed that focus on learning processes rather than products. The importance of such a focus has long been recognized but only infrequently put into practice (see Bloom, 1981).

2. *Change of Attitudes Toward Evaluation.* For years the early childhood field had a subtle but powerful antievaluation bias. Assessment of young children is certainly more difficult than it is with older children who can read directions and possibly respond in groups. Furthermore, there are far more procedures available that purport to evaluate cognitive rather than socioemotional functioning. This has led to reliance on procedures that might have measured variables (such as IQ) in which the program administrators were not especially interested and neg-

lected variables that might have been more relevant for a meaningful evaluation. Competition for available funds has helped break down resistance to evaluation. Legislators who appropriate funds have become more sophisticated and ask for proof, not merely opinions, of the importance of different types of programs. Thus Early Childhood Education has been infinitely boosted by evidence such as that produced by the Consortium on Developmental Continuity (Lazar et al., 1977), which demonstrated that quality early childhood programs did indeed produce lasting effects—effects, furthermore, that made sense in terms of reducing the cost of subsequent educational efforts. Although evaluation is still not a standard part of every early childhood program, it is becoming a much more expected and accepted component. Information accrued in such efforts can only benefit the field in the long run.

3. *Redefinition of the "Early" in "Early Childhood."* Another important change of the past two decades involves the embracing of infancy as a legitimate phase of early education. Because of legitimate concerns that participation in group programs might possibly weaken infants' attachments to their primary caregivers, many people were reluctant to endorse any sort of early experience for infants outside their own homes. However, social realities—more maternal employment, rapidly changing family demographics, etc.—created something of an underground infancy movement. Certainly by the beginning of the 1970s there was a complex, poorly supervised network of programs available for infants throughout the country. The early childhood field essentially had to recognize the legitimate needs of many families for infant care or else let these services develop with no public or professional scrutiny. Today every state has some type of machinery for regulating, and at least intermittently assessing, quality in infant care. Furthermore, recent research summaries have shown that programs of good quality do not impair cognitive or social development and do not weaken the basic attachment of infants to their parents (Belsky & Steinberg, 1978; Caldwell & Freyer, in press; Rutter, 1981).

4. *Rapprochement Between Early Education and Day Care.* The de-

mands of parents for quality infant day care probably did more than anything else to bring together the previously separate fields of day care and early education. These two previously separate fields originated under different professional auspices and, for many years, operated under different sponsorships. Day care originated as a social service and was generally thought of as a service for families with some type of social pathology—like a working mother! Early education, on the other hand, was, at least in this country, an outgrowth of the mental health movement and was seen as a way of fostering independence and social skills in children likely to have insufficient opportunities to develop these in small, isolated family settings. One was for poor children, the other for the well-to-do, upper-middle-class children whose parents had the foresight to register them for "prestige" programs before or shortly after birth! Although some leaders of early childhood programs might deny the allegation, for years proponents of the field known as Early Childhood Education had a somewhat supercilious attitude toward persons involved in "day care." Now that the need for quality day care is greater than the desire for the short-session early childhood programs, this attitude has largely disappeared.

Although we still use both terms to describe early childhood programs, there is now a general recognition that educational programs must often be stretched to cover the "long" day (rather than the "half" day of previous years) and that day care cannot enhance the developmental potential of children without providing an educational component to the daily program.

5. *Orientation Toward Public Policy.* In many ways the field of early childhood has grown up during these two decades of which I have been writing. Once slightly patronized as a field for "little old ladies in tennis shoes," the sophistication of leaders in the field in shaping and influencing public policy for children and families has become widely acknowledged. The professional organization for young children with which I am most closely associated—the National Association for the Education of Young Children (see Chapter 16)—does an excellent job of keeping its members informed about national and local issues that could affect continuation of their programs. At local, state, and national meetings members are taught how to function as more

effective advocates for children and children's programs. This development of an informed and involved constituency should clearly benefit future designers and recipients of services.

Challenges of the Future

There are still many challenges ahead for the field. In spite of the gains in recognition of the importance of the early childhood period for subsequent development, there are people who view advances in this field with alarm. Some groups charge that the early childhood movement is "family-weakening." Often such persons are more vocal and persistent than those who either provide or utilize services, and their influence has occasionally blocked legislation designed to improve the quality of early childhood programs or to increase their scope. It is to be hoped that both providers and consumers—those most likely to appreciate the need for and value of early childhood services—will become more vocal and effective advocates in the future and help raise the consciousness of the general public about early childhood.

A legacy of the lack of social awareness of the importance of early childhood experiences is the fact that persons who work in the field cannot necessarily hope for financially remunerative work. Salaries tend to be low even for highly qualified professionals who work in the field, and for the less highly trained assistants whose contributions are essential to quality operations, salaries discourage entry into the field. Our services are also poorly articulated with other contemporary programs—health and social service—and often totally separated from the future educational experiences that the children will have. One of the brightest spots is that research in the field is clearly on the increase. As new data emerge to identify program components that can have specific effects, and as longitudinal followups of children who have participated in early childhood programs continue to produce new information about benefits to the children and their families—and to society at large—early childhood programs will cease to be thought of as "extras" to be provided if and when funding permits and instead will be seen as essential aspects of the developmental experiences that need to be made available to our children.

References

Belsky, J., and L. D., Steinberg. The effects of day care: a critical review. *Child Development, 49*, 929–949, 1978.

Bloom, Benjamin Samuel. *All Our Children Learning: A Primer for Parents, Teachers, and Other Educators.* New York: McGraw-Hill, 1981.

Caldwell, B. M. The rationale for early intervention. *Exceptional Children, 36*, 717–726, 1970.

Caldwell, B. M. On reformulating the concept of early childhood education—some whys needing wherefores. *Young Children, 22*, 348–356, 1967.

Caldwell, B. M., and M. Freyer. Day care and early education. In B. Spodek (ed.), *Handbook of Research in Early Childhood Education.* New York: Free Press, in press.

Hunt, Joseph McVicker. *Intelligence and Experience.* New York: Ronald Press, 1961.

Lazar, Irving, Virginia Ruth Hubbell, Harry Murray, et al. The Persistence of Preschool Effects: a long-term follow-up of fourteen infants and preschool experiments. DHEW Publication No. (OHDS) 78-130130, 1977.

Rutter, M. Social-emotional consequences of day care for preschool children. *American Journal of Orthopsychiatry, 51*, 4–28, 1981.

Author Index

Abrahams, Roger D., 413
Abt, Lawrence E., 103
Ackerman, Paul, 141
Adams, Barbara, 439
Adamson, Lauren, 35, 73
Adell, Judith, 487
Adoff, Arnold, 358
Akmakjian, Hiag, 178
Alcott, Bronson, 289
Alfano, Michael C., 178
Allen, J., 422
Allen, Janet, 380
Allessandra, Anthony J., 274
Alonso, Lou, 462
Alpern, Gerald, 465
Alvin, Juliette, 444
Amary, Issam B., 211
American Academy of Pediatrics, 178
American Association for Gifted Children, 469
American Association of University Women, 487
American Health Foundation, 179
American Library Association, Association for Library Service to Children, 344
American Medical Association, 178
American Speech-Language-Hearing Association, 413
Ames, Louise Bates, 54
Anastasi, Anne, 54, 295

Anderson, Elizabeth M., 439
Anderson, Frances E., 444
Anderson, Linnea, 218
Anderson, Scarvia B., 266, 295
Anderson, Valerie, 235
Andress, Barbara, 391
Applebee, Arthur, 345
Applegate, Kay, 211
Aquino-Mackles, Alexis, 413
Arbuthnot, May Hill, 358
Arenal, Jay M., 179
Aries, Phillipe, 54
Armstrong, David G., 295
Arnold, Eugene L., 123
Arnold, Joan H., 169–172
Aronoff, Frances W., 367–368, 369–370, 390
Arts, Education, and Americans Panel, 470
Association for Childhood Education International, 345
Association for Educational Communication and Technology, 503
Astin, Helen S., 487
Astor, Susan D., 236
Atheim, Daniel D., 439
Atlas, Stephen L., 89
Attanucci, Jane S., 163
Aubin, Neva, 390
Auerbach, Stevanne, 123, 266, 267
Austen, Jane, 336
Austin, Ethel, 211

Austin, Glenn, 179
Ayrault, Evelyn West, 440
Axline, Virginia M., 235, 468

Bader, Barbara, 345
Badger, Earladeen, 236
Badinter, Elisabeth, 123
Bailey, Rebecca Anne, 18
Baker, Augusta, 345
Baker, G. C., 417
Bakerzak, Edwin A., 276
Baldwin, Rahima, 18
Ball, S. J., 503
Ball, Samuel, 266, 295
Balter, Lawrence, 119–122
Bandura, Albert, 42, 54, 55
Banet, B., 273
Banfield, Beryle, 409–412, 414
Bangs, Tina, 444, 459
Banks, James A., 414
Baran, Annette, 102
Baranoff, Timy, 296
Barbe, Walter, 470
Barber, Virginia, 124
Barcus, F. Earle, 503
Barker, R. K., 503
Barkin, Carol, 124
Barkley, Russel A., 440
Barlin, Anne Lief, 390
Barnes, Joan, 236
Barr, Elinor, 299
Barrera, Rebeca, 414
Barrett, Kate R., 195
Barron, Cheryl, 124
Bartel, Nettie R., 453
Barton, Griselda, 355
Bartz, Wayne R., 124
Barzun, Jacques, 296
Baskin, Barbara, 346, 445, 470
Batchelder, Marjorie, 390
Bauer, Caroline Felder, 346
Bayless, Kathleen M., 391

Beall, Pamela Conn, 391
Beal, Virginia, 211
Bean, Reynold, 90, 130
Beck, Jo, 225
Becker, Wesley C., 125
Becking, Marjorie F., 377
Behrmann, Polly, 244
Behrstock, Barry, 179
Belsky, J., 529, 532
Belsky, Marwin, 180
Bemporad, Jules R., 55
Benjamin, Robert, 296
Bereiter, Carl, 235
Berends, Polly Berrien, 125
Berenstein, Jan, 125
Berenstein, Stan, 125
Berezin, Nancy, 18
Berger, Eugenia Hepworth, 125
Bergman, Anni, 30
Bergmann, Thesi, 445
Berko, Frances C., 440
Berko, Martin J., 440
Berlin, Irving Norman, 180
Berman, Claire, 89
Berman, Eleanor, 89
Bernard, Jessie, 89, 125
Bernheim, Kayla F., 468
Bernick, Deborah, 180
Berry, Mildred F., 459
Bershad, Carole, 180
Bettelheim, Bruno, 55, 296, 346, 469
Bing, Elizabeth, 18, 19
Bingham, Jane, 347
Birch, Herbert G., 128
Bissex, Glenda, 296
Blake, William, 342
Bland, Jane Cooper, 380
Blau, Rosalie, 267
Bloodstein, Oliver, 460
Bloom Benjamin Samuel, 528, 532
Bloom, Frances, 325

Blyton, Carey, 399
Boardman, Eunice, 391
Bobker, Lee, 503
Bode, Janet, 126
Boll, Thomas, 465
Bond, J. T., 275, 326
Bos, Bev, 380
Boston, Bruce O., 471
Boston Children's Medical
    Center, 181
Boston Women's Health Book
    Collective, Inc., 126
Bracken, Jeanne, 487
Bradley, Robert A., 19
Brady, Elizabeth H., 267
Braga, Joseph, 126
Braga, Laurie, 126
Bray, Helen, 489
Brazelton, T. Berry, 19, 20, 55, 90,
    181
Breckenridge, Kati, 132
Breitbart, Vicki, 255–257, 267, 299
Breslin, Deidre, 497
Brewer, Gail Sforza, 20
Brewer, Tom, 20
Brewster, Dorothy Patricia, 21
Briggs, Dorothy C., 126
Brittain, W. Lambert, 381
Broad, Laura Peabody, 237
Brodsky, Archie, 181
Brody, Jane E., 211
Broman, Betty L., 297
Bronfenbrenner, Urie, 56, 83, 236
Bronson, Margaret S., 413
Brooke, Leslie, 336
Brooks-Gunn, Jeanne, 65
Brown, Diana, 441
Brown, James W., 504
Brown, Les, 504
Brown, Marc, 359
Brown, Margaret Wise, 342
Brown, Sara, 441

Brown, Susan, 267
Brown, Virginia, 451
Bruner, Jerome, 268
Bryant, Bridget, 268
Bucher, Ida, 267
Burck, Frances Wells, 21
Burgess, Ann Wolbert, 90
Bursztajn, Harold, 181
Burton, Elsie Carter
Burtt, Kent Garland, 237
Buscaglia, Leo F., 127
Bush, Richard, 127
Bushnell, M. Margaret, 62
Bussis, Anne M., 297
Butler, Anne L., 237
Butler, Dorothy, 347
Buttenwieser, Elizabeth, 99
Butterworth, Nancy Towner, 237
Byram, Claudia A., 305

Cable, Mary, 56
Cahoon, Owen W., 127
Caldecott, Randolph, 336
Calderone, Mary S., 127
Cameron, Eleanor, 347
Caldwell, Betty M., 527–532
Cameron, Polly, 342
Campbell, Bertha, 511–512
Campbell, Donald Ross, 128
Caney, Steven, 237
Capaldi, Frederick P., 128
Caplan, Frank, 128, 212, 238
Caplan, Ronald M., 21
Caplan, Theresa, 38
Carlson, Bernice Wells, 347
Carmichael, Carrie, 488
Carnegie Council on Children, 95
Carter, Sylvia, 492
Carter, Thomas P., 415
Cartwright, Carol A., 322
Castle, Sue, 212
Cass, Joan E., 238

Cazden, Courtney, 56, 297
CBS Office of Social Research, 504
Cedeno, Lazar, 21
Cedeno, Olinda, 21
Cerf, Christopher, 128
Chall, Jeanne S., 283–285
Chalmers, Mary Ann, 99
Chambers, Aidan, 348
Champlin, Connie, 348
Champlin, John, 348
Charles, C. M., 297
Charles, Robert Henry, 334
Charren, Peggy, 504
Cherry, Clare, 238, 298, 381
Chess, Stella, 128, 161
Child, Irving L., 75
Children's Book Council, 348
Child Study Association of
    America, 129
Chinn, Peggy L., 182
Chittenden, Edward A., 297
Chodorow, Nancy, 129
Chomsky, Noam, 45
Chukovsky, Kornei, 56
Church, Helen Nichols, 220
Church, Joseph, 56, 57, 71, 129,
    130
Cianciolo, Patricia, 348
Cianciolo, Pauline, 506
Clark, Ann L., 182
Clark, Barbara, 470
Clay, Marie M., 298
Clemes, Harris, 90, 130
Clifford, Roy A., 263, 264, 265
Cline, Victor B., 130
Close, Sylvia, 130
Cobb, Vicki, 381
Cody, Thane R., 182
Cohen, Dorothy H., 57, 299
Cohen, Elaine P., 381
Cohen, Matthew M., 182
Cohen, Monroe D., 349
Cohen, Stewart, 58

Cohn, Sanford J., 472
Colangelo, Nicholas, 415
Cole, Ann, 238
Coleman, Madeleine, 415
Colen, B. D., 183
Coles, Jane Hallowell, 131
Coles, Robert, 131, 415, 416
Collins, Alice H., 269
Collipp, Platon J., 212
Colman, Arthur, 22, 131
Colman, Libby, 19, 22, 131
Comer, James P., 91, 300, 416
Comfort, Alex, 131
Comfort, Jane, 131
Conger, John J., 67
Connors, Frances P., 445
Copeland, Richard W., 300
Cordasco, Francesco, 416
Corrigan, Dean, 441–442
Cotera, Martha, 416
Council on Interracial Books for
    Children, 488, 489
Courtney, Rosalea, 297
Cowell, Catherine, 203–207
Cox, Barbara, 417
Cox, Vivian, 354
Crane, Paul, 335
Crews, Donald, 333
Croft, Doreen J., 306
Cromwell, Liz, 359
Crook, Elizabeth, 390
Cross, Delores E., 417
Crow, Gary A., 442
Cruickshank, William M., 442, 458
Cullinan, Bernice E., 331–333, 349
Cumming, Robert, 382
Cunningham, Cliff, 445, 465
Curry, Judith Bickley, 465
Curtis, Jean, 131

Dailey, Rebecca F., 455
Daley, Eliot, 132
Daniels, Pamela, 132

Danoff, Judith, 299
Darwin, Charles, 229
Davidson, Billee, 389
Davis, Enid, 489
Davis, Florence, 417
Davis, Malcolm D., 449
DeCaro, Matthew V., 183
Decker, Celia Anita, 269
Decker, John R., 269
DeFranco, Ellen B., 504
Delli Quadri, Lyn, 132
Delp, Jeanne L., 471
Dennis, Wayne, 58
Deppe, Philip R., 442
DeSalva, Nancy, 357
Despert, J. Louise, 91
DeVilliers, Jill G., 58, 300
DeVilliers, Peter A., 58, 300
DeVries, Rheta, 309
Dewey, John, 80, 230
DeWit, Dorothy, 349
Diagram Group, 183
Dibble, Marjorie, 218
Dickinson, Rita Mitton, 471
Dickman, Irving, 137
Diem, Lisellot, 183
Dillon, Diane, 333
Dillon, Leo, 333
Dimondstein, Geraldine, 382, 392
Dobzhansky, Theodosius, 58
Dodson, Fitzhugh, 91, 133
Doering, Susan G., 133
Dolan, Edward F., Jr., 91
Doman, Glenn, 300
Domanska, Janina, 333
Donovan, Bonnie, 22
Dopyera, John, 310
Dorian, Margery, 392
Doris, John, 468
Dorsey, Anne G., 277
Douglas, T., 139
Downer, Marion, 382
Dreikurs, Rudolph, 92, 133

Drouillard, Richard, 462, 464
Dunfee, Maxine, 418
Durkin, Dolores, 301, 350
Dustin, Dick, 415

Edel, Deborah, 449
Eden, Alvin N., 184
Edgar, Eugene, 321
Edgerton, Robert B., 466
Egger, Michael L., 467
Ehrlich, Virginia Z., 471
Eiden, L. J., 294
Eisenberg, Howard, 196
Eisenberg-Berg, Nancy, 67
Ekvall, Dhirlye, 219
Eliason, Claudia Fuhriman, 301
Elkind, David, 58, 59, 229–232
Elkins, Valmi Howe, 22
Ellis, Audrey, 212
Endres, Jeanette B., 213
Engler, Larry, 393
Entwisle, Doris R., 133
Environmental Programs, Inc., 23
Epstein, Anne S., 269
Erickson, Marion J., 466
Erickson, Erik H., 42, 48, 51, 52, 59, 301
Escobedo, Linda E., 448
Etkin, Ruth, 393
Evans, David, 393
Evans, Edmund, 350
Evans, Judith, 134
Ewy, Donna, 134
Ewy, Rodger, 134
Eyer, Dianne Widmeyer, 271

Faas, Larry A., 442
Fabe, Marilyn, 134
Faber, Adele, 135
Fahey, Thomas D., 184
Farber, B. A., 184
Fassler, Joan, 135, 184

Favat, F. Andrew, 350
Featherstone, Helen, 443
Feinbloom, Richard I., 181
Feingold, Ben, 213
Feingold, Helene, 213
Feldman, Philip, 97
Feldman, Silvia, 23
Feminists on Children's Media, 490
Fernandez, Happy Craven, 92
Ferreira, Nancy J., 213
Fiarotta, Noel, 383
Fiarotta, Phyllis, 382, 383
Fijan, Carol, 393
Finnie, Nancy R., 458
Fisher, Aileen, 333, 359
Fisher, Anne, 487
Fisher, Elaine Fory, 383
Fisher, Margery, 350
Fisher, Rhoda, 135
Fisher, Seymour, 135
Flavell, John, 59
Fleming, Bonnie Mack, 302
Fleming, Gladys, 394
Flores, Marina, 420
Fomon, Samuel J., 213
Forehand, Rex L., 443
Fortna, Richard, 471
Foster, Clifford D., 308
Fowler, William, 270, 302
Fox, Jane A., 169–173, 185
Foxley, Cecelia H., 415
Fraiberg, Selma, 23, 59, 85
Frank, Lawrence K., 240
Frank, Marjorie, 302
Franzell, Donna, 279
Freeman, Darlene, 472
Freud, Anna, 60, 271, 445
Freud, Sigmund, 42, 136
Freyer, M., 532
Friedland, Ronnie, 136
Friedlander, George, 466

Friedman, Delores L., 418
Friedman, Eugene B., 107–112
Friedman, Stanford, 185
Fries, James F., 193, 199
Frith, Greg H., 451
Froebel, Friedrich, 229
Frost, Joe L., 239
Furman, Erna, 136
Furth, Hans G., 60

Gable Liebowitz, Dorothy, 418
Gadow, Kenneth D., 185
Gaeld, Toni S., 302
Gainer, Ruth S., 381
Galdone, Paul, 335
Galinksy, Ellen, 136, 270
Gallagher, James J., 447, 472
Gallagher, Kathleen, 489
Galper, Miriam, 92
Gannon, Robert, 199
Gans, Roma, 302
Gardner, Howard, 383
Gardner, Richard, 92, 93
Garfield, Sydney, 185
Garland, Caroline, 270
Garritson, Jane S., 383
Garvey, Catherine, 239
Gaskin, Ina May, 24
Gates, Wende Devlin, 24
Gaughan, Janna, 155, 245
Gazella, Jacqueline Gibson, 24
Geismer, Barbara Peck, 359
Gellert, Elizabeth, 186
Gelles, Richard J., 102
George, William C., 472
Georgiou, Constantine, 351
Giese, James, 419
Gilbert, Anne G., 394
Gilbert, Christine B., 351
Gillespie, John T., 351
Gillis, Phyllis, 29
Ginglend, David R., 446

Ginott, Haim G., 137
Ginsberg, Gina, 472
Ginsburg, Herbert, 61, 303
Glasgow, Zela, 505
Glazer, Joan I., 351
Glazer, Susan Mandel, 303
Glazer, Tom, 394, 395
Glenn, J. A., 303
Glickman, Beatrice Marden, 271
Gliedman, John, 458
Glover, John A., 137
Goertzel, Mildred, 473
Goertzel, Victor, 473
Goffstein, M. B., 384
Gold, Milton J., 419
Gold, Ruth F., 450
Goldbeck, Nikki, 25
Goldenson, Robert M., 240
Goldfarb, Johanna, 25
Goldman, K. S., 276
Goldsen, Rose K., 505
Goldsmith, Robert, 214
Goldstein, Joseph, 93, 271
Gonzalez-Mena, Janet, 271, 419
Goodall, John, 333
Goode, Ruth, 93
Goodwin, Mary T., 214
Gordon, Ira J., 61
Gordon, Judith, 137
Gordon, Mary E., 462
Gordon, Sol, 137
Gordon, Thomas, 138
Gould, Bette Taylor, 309
Gould, Elaine, 446
Gould, Loren, 446
Gowan, John C., 473
Graedon, Joe, 186
Graedon, Teresa, 186
Graham,Richard M., 446
Graham, Terry Lynne, 142
Granger, Robert C., 419
Grant, Carl A., 419, 420

Grant, Gloria, 420
Grant, W. V., 294
Granzig, William, 154
Graselli, Rose N., 239
Greeley, Andrew M., 420
Green, Martin I., 186
Greenberg, Selma, 489
Greene, Ellin, 345, 351
Greene, Janice Presser, 20
Greenwood, Marion, 404
Gregg, Elizabeth, 138
Gregory, Hugo H., 460
Griffin, Al, 272
Griffore, Robert J., 303
Grollman, Earl A., 93, 138
Gropper, George L., 505
Grosett, Marjorie D., 272
Gross, Beatrice, 304
Gross, Dorothy W., 8–13
Gross, Leonard, 180
Gross, Ronald, 304
Grossman, Arnold H., 261–265, 272
Grotberg, Edith, 187
Groth, A. Nicholas, 90
Gruber, Ellen, 304, 352, 384
Gruber, Howard E., 61
Guerney, Louise F., 138
Guillaume, Paul, 61
Gulland, Frances, 392
Gullion, Elizabeth M., 153
Guttentag, Marcia, 489
Guttman, Dena, 385

Haber, Carol Chase, 54
Haessler, Herbert, 187
Haeussermann, Else, 459
Hagstrom, Julie, 239
Hakley, Abraham, 449
Hale, G. K., 62
Hale, Nathan Cabot, 139
Hall, Brenny, 356

Hall, Eleanor, 473
Hall, Francine S., 139
Halperin, Michael, 94
Halpern, Howard, 94
Hamilton, Caryl, 423
Hamilton, Darlene Softley, 304
Hamm, Robert M., 181
Hammill, Donald D., 451, 453
Hanes, Michael L., 420
Hanon, Sharron, 25
Hannum, Sara, 359
Hansen-Krening, Nancy, 304
Harclerood, Fred F., 504
Hardesty, Kay, 446
Harlan, Jean Durgin, 305
Harmonay, Maureen, 505, 506
Harrington, Charles H., 425
Harris, Karen, 346, 445, 470
Harris, Miriam, 268
Harris, Raymond, 187
Harrison, Charles H., 472
Harrison, Dorothy H., 187
Harrison-Ross, Phyllis, 421
Hartley, Ruth E., 240
Haskel, Lendall, 385
Hatoff, Sydelle H., 305
Haviland, Virginia, 352
Hawes, Bill, 395
Hayden, Erma, 390
Headley, Neith E., 240
Hearne, Betsy, 352
Heasley, C. Annette, 322
Heater, Sandra Harvey, 139
Hefferman, Helen, 324
Heffner, Elaine, 139
Hegeman, Kathryn T., 305
Hegner, Priscilla A., 239
Heinig, Ruth B., 395
Heins, Paul, 353
Heisler, Verda, 443
Hektoen, Faith, 357
Hendin, David, 26, 188

Hendrick, Joanne, 240, 306
Henley, Arthur, 151
Henry, George, 306
Henry, Jeannie, 158
Henson, Kenneth T., 295
Herberholz, Barbara, 385
Herbert-Jackson, Emily, 272
Hersh, Stephen P., 140
Herzig, Alison C., 26
Hess, Robert D., 306
Heslin, Jo-Ann, 214
Hewes, Dorothy, 273
Hibner, Dixie, 359
Hicks, JoAnne Deal, 302
Highlights Editors, 385, 386
Higley, Joan, 306
Hildebrand, Verna, 307
Hill, Dorothy M., 307
Hill, Robert B., 421
Hirsch, Elizabeth, 241
Hoberman, MaryAnn, 333, 360
Hodin, Jay, 222
Hoffman, Hubert A.,
Hofmann, Liesolotte, 214
Hohmann, Mary, 273, 307
Holdaway, Don, 308
Holkelman, Robert, 185
Hollingsworth, Paul M., 308
Holmes, Beth, 469
Holmstrom, Lynda Lytle, 90
Holt, Bess-Gene, 308
Honig, Alice S., 26, 140, 273
Hooks, William, 140, 270
Hoover, Kenneth H., 308
Hope, Karol, 94
Hopkins, Carol J., 315
Hopkins, Lee Bennett, 353, 360, 473
Hopper, Robert, 75
Horowitz, Alice M., 188
Horton, John, 396
Hotchner, Tracy, 26

Houston, John P., 313
Howard, Jane, 94
Howe, James, 188
Howell, Mary, 188
Howey, Kenneth, 441–442
Hubbel, Robert D., 460
Hubbell, Virginia Ruth, 532
Huck, Charlotte S., 353
Hufford, Larry, 416
Huggins, Hal A., 188
Hughes, Langston, 343
Hulme, Marylin, 488
Hunerberg, Catherine, 492
Hunsaker, Phillip L., 274
Hunt, J. McVicker, 35, 532
Hunter, Ilene, 396
Hunter, Marvin, 466
Hunter, Merrily, 224
Hurwitz, Abraham, 248
Hutchins, Pat, 333
Hymes, James L., 62
Hyson, Marion C., 305

Ilfield, Ellen, 134
Ilg, Frances L., 54
Ingram, David, 460
Ireson, Barbara, 360
Irwin, Ann, 461
Irwin, D. Michelle, 62
Irwin, John V., 463
Isaacs, Susan, 63

Jacklin, Carol N., 66, 490
Jackson, Brian, 274
Jackson, Sonia, 274
Jacobson, Ruth, 396
James, Elizabeth, 124
Janov, Arthur, 3
Jarolimek, John, 308
Jelliffe, Derrick, 215
Jelliffe, E. F., 215
Jenkins, Jeanne Kohn, 490

Jenkins, Loa Thomson, 301
Jenkins, Peggy D., 386, 397
Jensen, Julie M., 317
Jimenez, Sherry Lynn Mims, 27
Johnson, David W., 308
Johnson, Eric W., 127
Johnson, Ferne, 353
Johnson, G. Timothy, 189
Johnson, Roger T., 302
Johnson, Vicki M., 466
Jones, Genevieve, 397
Jones, Reginald L., 447
Jones, Sandy, 140
Jordan, June B., 455
Joyce, Mary, 397
Joyce, William W., 414
Judson, Marilyn, 396
Juhasz, Anne W., 316
Juliano, Rose A., 142
Justice, Blair, 95
Justice, Rita, 95

Kaban, Barbara T., 163, 241
Kagan, J., 67
Kahn, Alfred J., 95, 274
Kamen, Betty, 27
Kamen, Si, 27
Kamerman, Sheila B., 95, 274
Kamii, Constance, 309
Kamin, Leon J., 63
Kaniger, Herbert, 474
Kaplan, Jo Ann Butom, 309
Kaplan, Louise, 63, 141
Kaplan, Sandra Nina, 309
Kappelman, Murray, 141
Karl, Jean, 353
Karmel, Marjorie, 27
Karnes, Merle B., 386
Karrer, M. C., 349
Kastein, Shulamith, 463
Kaufmann, Felice, 474
Kay, Jane G., 447

Kaye, Evelyn, 506
Kaye, Marilyn, 352
Keats, Ezra Jack, 333
Keifer, Helen, 221
Keller, Jerry D., 463
Kellogg, Rhoda, 386, 387
Kelly, Joan Berlin, 103
Kelly, Marguerite, 141
Kempe, C. Henry, 95
Kempe, Ruth S., 95
Keniston, Kenneth, 95
Kennell, John, 5, 28
Khatena, Joe, 473
Kilmer, Sally, 275
Kinder, James S., 506
King, David C., 413
King, Edith, 421
Kirk, Samuel, 447
Kitzinger, Sheila, 27, 141, 215
Klaus, Marshall, 5, 28
Klein, Barry L., 239
Klein, Carole, 142
Klein, Hilary Dole, 487
Klein, Melanie, 241
Klesius, Stephen E., 395
Kliman, Gilbert W., 63, 142, 189
Kloss, Heinz, 422
Knight, Bryan M., 142
Knight, Jane, 249
Knight, Michael E., 142
Knotts, Judith, 138
Knox, Laura, 143
Kohl, Herbert, 143
Kohlberg, Lawrence, 64
Kokasha, Sharon Metz, 447
Konowitz, Bertram Lawrence,
    397
Korbin, Jill E., 96
Kornhaber, Arthur, 96
Kornhauser, Pat, 267
Kort, Carol, 136
Koste, Virginia Glasgow, 241

Koste, Virginia R., 398
Krause, Marie, 215
Krementz, Jill, 143
Krogman, Willard M., 64
Krone, Ann, 448
Kuskin, Karla, 333, 360, 405
Kuzma, Kay, 143
Kuznetz, Len, 310
Kwok, Irene, 422

Lagos, Jorge C., 455
LaLeche League International,
    28, 215
Lally, J. Ronald, 26, 273
Lamb, Michael E., 144
Lambert, Brittain W., 387
Lambie, Dolores Z., 275
Lamme, Linda, 144, 354
Lancy, David F., 242
Landau, Geneviere Millet, 246
Lanes, Selma, 354
Langer, Steven, 158
Languis, Martin, 310
Lansky, Vicki, 144, 216
Larenzen, Evelyn, 216
Larrick, Nancy, 310, 338-340,
    355
Lasky, Lila, 387
Laubenfels, Jean, 474
Lauffer, Armand, 191
Lawrence, Ruth, 28
Lay-Dopyera, Margaret, 310
Laybourne, K. T., 506
Lazar, Irving, 529, 532
Lazarre, Jane, 144
Leach, Penelope, 28, 145
Learning Technology, Inc., 145
Leboyer, Frederick, 5, 29
Lee, Doris M., 311
Lee, Patrick C., 481
Lefebvre, Claudette B., 233-234
Leichter, H. J., 79, 80

LeMaitre, George, 189
Lemlich, Johanna, 311
Lepman, Jella, 145
Lerman, Saf, 145
Lerner, Richard, 64
LeShan, Eda J., 113–118, 146, 147
Levine, James A., 147, 275
Levy, Janine, 148
Lewine, Richard R. J., 468
Lewis, Claudia, 312, 341–343
Lewis, David, 474
Lewis, Isabelle, 248
Lewis, M., 62, 276
Lewis, Michael, 29, 65, 66, 96, 148, 467
Lewis, Richard B., 504
Lichtendorf, Susan, 29
Lidstone, John, 405
Liedloff, Jean, 66
Lillard, Paula Polk, 312
Lillie, David L., 448
Lillywhite, Harold S., 461, 462
Lindberg, Lucille, 312, 500, 501, 502
Lindfors, Linda, 312
Lipe, Dewey, 226
Livingston, Carol, 97
Livingston, Myra Cohn, 333, 361
Lloyd, Janice, 244
Lobel, Anita, 333
Lobel, Arnold, 333
Logan, Ben, 506
Long, Kate, 448
Longstreet, Wilma S., 422
Lorimer, Anne, 97
Lorin, Martin I., 190
Lorton, Mary Baratta, 313
Love, Katherine, 361
Lowenberg, Miriam, 222
Lowenfeld, Margaret, 242

Lowenfeld, Viktor, 387
Lowndes, Marion, 148
Luke, Barbara, 30
Lynn, David L., 148

Macauley, Janet, 417
MacKeith, Ronald, 216
McBride, Angela Barron, 149
McCarthy, Melodie A., 313
McCaslin, Nellie, 313, 373–375, 398, 399
McClenathan, Day Ann K., 355
Maccoby, Eleanor E., 66, 490
McCollum, Audrey T., 190
McCord, David, 333, 361
McCoy, Elin, 242
McDermott, Gerald, 334
McDonald, Dorothy T., 399
Macdonald, Pam, 490
McElderry, Joanne S., 448
McElheny, Hugh, 404
McIntire, Matilda, 190
Mack, Alison, 149
Mack, Faite R-P, 313
McKeown, Joseph, 191
McLaughlin, Clara J., 30
McMahon, Robert J., 443
McNamara, Bernard, 452
McNamara, Joan, 452
McNeil, J. T., 326
McNeill, Earldene, 422, 424
McRae, Barbara, 128
McTwigan, Michael, 401
McWilliams, Margaret, 217
Maddox, Brenda, 97
Madsen, Sheila Kunishina, 309
Mahan, Kathleen L., 215
Mahler, Margaret S., 30
Maier, Henry W., 67
Makender, Bea, 251
Malehorn, Hal, 242

Mali, Jane L., 26
Malian, Ida M., 297
Malloy, Terry, 243
Manela, Roger, 191
Mankiewicz, Frank, 507
Manning, Judy, 154
Marge, Michael, 461
Margolin, Edythe, 314
Marilus, Esther, 30
Marion, Marian, 149, 314
Marks, Joan, 26, 188
Marks, Sema, 316
Markun, Patricia Maloney, 149, 243
Marsh, Frank N., 191
Marshall, Lyn, 191
Martin, Harold P., 97
Martin, J. P., 98
Martin, Robert J., 314
Martinel, Thomas J., 195, 327
Martinson, Ruth A., 471, 474
Marzollo, Jean, 31, 243
Maslow, Abraham, 414
Matanzo, Jane, 354
Maternity Center Association, 6
Mather, June, 244
Maxim, George W., 150
Maxwell, Marilyn, 423
May, Lawrence, 191
Mayer, Mercer, 333
Mayer, Morris Fritz, 276
Mayesky, M., 388
Mayle, Peter, 150
Maynard, Leslie-Jane, 217
Mays, Luberta, 497–502
Mazlish, Elaine, 135
Meadow, Kathryn P., 463
Meckel, Gail McFarland, 24
Meek, Margaret, 355
Meisels, Samuel J., 451
Melody, William, 507
Menolascino, Frank J., 467

Menyuk, Paula, 314
Mercer, Jane R., 467
Merritt, Doris, 217
Metz, Kathleen, 297
Meyer, Linda D., 31
Michalson, Linda, 148
Millar, Susanne, 244
Miller, Alice, 475
Miller, Allan, 465
Miller, Maureen, 98
Miller, Susan Mary, 150
Miller, William Hansford, 150
Miles, Betty, 491
Millman, Howard, 157
Millman, Joan, 244
Milne, A. A., 361
Mills, Gretchen C., 151
Minear, Ralph E., Jr., 195
Mintonye, Grace, 389
Minuchin, Salvador, 98
Missildine, W. Hugh, 151
Mitchell, Donald, 399
Mitchell, Grace, 276
Mitchell, Helen, 218
Moe, Alden J., 315
Moersch, Martha, 441
Moffet, Hugh L., 192
Monroe, Carole, 21
Monson, Dianne L., 355, 358
Montanari, A. J., 151
Montessori, Maria, 151, 315, 414
Montgomery, Chandler, 388
Moody, Kate, 507
Moor, M. Pauline, 462
Moore, Coralie, 452
Moore, Lilian, 361
Moore, Robert B., 409–412
Moore, Vardine, 355
Morris, Linda, 218
Morrison, George S., 315
Morrow, Lesley Mandel, 356

Morse, William C., 452
Morton, Kathryn Gorham, 452
Moser, Joy L., 371–372
Moss, Arthur, 192
Moss, Stephen J., 192
Mosse, Hilde L., 315, 461
Moustakas, Clark E., 245
Mueser, Anne Marie, 152
Mukerji, Rose, 387
Murphy, Lois B., 34
Murray, Harry, 534
Musick, Judith, 35
Mussen, Paul H., 67
Myklebust, Helmer R., 463

Napier, Y. Augustus, 98
Natalicio, Diana S., 75
National Cancer Institute, 218
National Multilingual Multicul-
    tural Material Development
    Center, 423
Natow, Annette B., 214
Nelson, Esther L., 400
Nelson, Keith, 67
Neser, Gwen, 152, 245
Neubauer, Peter, 68
Neuman, D., 388
Newson, Elizabeth, 245
Newson, John, 245
Newton, Dee, 268
Nicholson, Luree, 152
Nilsson, Lennart, 32
Noble, Elizabeth, 32
Noble, June, 98
Noble, William, 98
Non-Sexist Child Development
    Project, 490
North, A. Frederick, 33
Norwood, Christopher, 192
Noyes, Naomi, 334–337
Nye, Venice, 400

Oakley, Ann, 33, 152
O'Brien, Marion, 272
Oettinger, Anthony G., 316
Olin, Ferris, 489
Oliver, Julia Stone, 179
Ollila, Lloyd O., 316
Olson, James, 409, 412
Olson, Miken, 354
O'Neil, Onora, 99
Ong, Beale H., 193
Opie, Iona, 362
Opie, Peter, 362
Opper, Sylvia, 61
Ornstein, Allan C., 316
Osman, B. B., 453
Osofsky, Howard J., 153
Osofsky, Joy D., 153
Owen, Robert, 289

Pagano, A., 498, 502
Page, William D., 316
Paginkopf, Andrea L., 219
Painter, Marjorie, 278
Paley, Vivian Gussin, 317
Palinski, Christine O'Brien, 33
Palmer, Sushma, 219
Papert, Seymour, 317
Panabaker, Lucile
Pantell, Robert H., 193
Parelman, Allison, 487
Parent's Magazine, 193
Parfitt, Rebecca Rowe, 33
Parsons, Elia, 141
Passow, A. Harry, 475
Patterson, Gerald R., 153
Payne, Alma, 219
Peairs, Lillian, 153
Peairs, Richard H., 153
Pearce, Joseph Chilton, 154
Pearlman, Ruth, 219
Pearson, Gayle Angus, 222
Peavy, Linda S., 219

Peck, Ellen, 154
Peck, Judith, 401
Peery, Alice, 489
Pennington, Jean, 220
Peppe, Kathryn Kluss, 465
Perino, Joseph, 475
Perino, Sheila C., 475
Person, Ethel S., 160
Pestalozzi, Johann H., 229
Peterson, Carolyn Sue, 356
Petrillo, Madeline, 99, 193
Petty, Dorothy C., 317
Petty, Walter T., 317
Pflaum-Connor, S. 318
Phillips, John L., Jr., 68
Philpott, A. R., 401
Piaget, Jean, 42, 51, 68, 230,
    245, 414
Pialorsi, Frank, 423
Piazza, Robert, 449
Pickering, C. Thomas, 318
Piers, Maria W., 246
Pillar, A. M., 349
Pine, Fred, 30
Pinkwater, Jill, 220
Pinnell, Gay S., 316, 318
Pipes, Peggy, 220
Pisani, Joseph, 85
Pizer, Hank, 33
Pizzo, Peggy Daly, 154
Pogrebin, Letty C., 491
Polansky, Norman, 99
Polette, Nancy E., 356
Pollen, Gerry, 214
Pomerance, Herbert, 194
Pomeranz, Virginia E., 194
Pope, Lillie, 319, 449, 453, 454
Porcher, Mary Ann, 249
Porter, Judith D. R., 319
Porterfield, Jan, 272
Post, Henry, 401
Postman, Neil, 100, 319, 507

Potter, Beatrice, 336
Poussaint, Alvin F., 91, 416
Powers, Hugh, 220
Presley, James, 220
Presseisen, Barbara Z., 417
Price, Alvin, H., 127
Princeton Center for Infancy
    and Early Childhood, 34
Pringle, Sheila, 194
Provence, Sally, 277
Prudden, Suzy, 194
Pulaski, Mary Ann Spencer, 69

Radl, Shirley, 165
Rahn, Suzanne, 356
Rainey, Sarita R., 388
Ramirez, Manuel, III, 417
Ramsey, Brenda E., 194
Ramsey, Marjorie E., 391
Rank, Otto, 3
Rapoport, Rhonda, 154, 155
Rapoport, Robert N., 154, 155
Raven, Barbara C., 214
Raynor, Sherry, 462, 463, 464
Redl, Fritz, 69, 155
Reed, Gwendolyn, 359
Reger, Roger, 449
Reinisch, Edith H., 195
Renfro, Nancy, 401
Renzulli, Joseph, 470, 475
Reschly, B., 155
Resnick, Lauren B., 319
Reynolds, Maynard C., 449
Rice, F. Phillip, 156
Richards, John C., 179
Richards, Laura E., 362
Richardson, Elwyn S., 389
Richert, Barbara, 221
Richman, Leon H., 276
Rickman, John, 69
Riekehof, Lottie L., 464
Riessman, Frank, 320

Riggs, Maida L., 402
Riley, Marie, 195
Riley, Sue Spayth, 100
Rimstidt, Suzie, 195
Risely, Todd R., 272
Rivlin, Harry N., 419
Robertson, Mary Ann, 195
Robinson, Jerry W., Jr., 263, 264, 265
Roby, Pamela, 277
Rockwell, Anne, 362
Rockwell, Robert E., 213
Roedell, Wendy Conilin, 476
Rogovin, Anne, 320
Rojas, Mari, 414
Rollock, Barbara, 357
Romer, Nancy, 491
Rosario, Jose, 420
Rosenberg, B. G., 491
Rosenblum, Leonard, 29, 65, 66, 96, 467
Rosenfeld, Albert, 63
Rosner, Jerome, 454
Roson, Richard A., 124
Ross, Alan, 454, 455
Ross, Bette M., 456
Ross, E., 291, 294
Ross, Heather L., 100
Ross, Lee, 59
Roth, J., 221
Roth, Marian, 320
Roth, William, 458
Rothman, Roz, 449
Roussea, Jean Jacques, 229
Roy, Carolyn, 278
Rubin, Joseph B., 311
Rubin, Zick, 70
Rudolph, Marguerita, 156, 299
Rush, Timothy, 315
Russell, Helen Ross, 320
Russell, Joan, 402
Rutherford, Robert B., Jr., 321

Rutter, M., 529, 532
Ryan, James H., 195
Rynbergen, Henderika, 218

Sadker, David, 491
Sadker, Myra, 491
Safford, Phillip, 456
Safilios-Rothschild, Constantine, 492
Salk, Lee, 100
Salter, Michael, 246
Samuels, Shirley C., 70, 457
Sanders, Tobie, 310
Sandler, Martin, 504
Sanford, Linda Tschirhart, 101
Sanger, Sirgay, 99
Sarason, Seymour B., 468
Saul, Jane, 323
Saunders, Rubie, 156
Savage, Tom V., 295
Saville, Florence Rogers, 211
Saville, Muriel R., 424
    See also Saville-Troike
Saville-Troike, Muriel, 424
Sawhill, Isabel V., 100
Scarpa, Joannis, 221
Schachter, Francis Fuchs, 157
Schaefer, Charles, 157
Scharf, Battia, 463
Scharf, Peter, 70
Schenk de Regniers, Beatrice, 342
Scherze, Cathy, 124
Schick, Eleanor, 362
Schiff, Harriet Sarnoff, 157
Schmidt, Velma E., 422, 424
Schnert, Keith W., 196
Schoenfeld, Madalynne, 351
Scholt, Grayce, 347
Schorsch, Anita, 70
Schucman, Helen, 466
Schultz, Dodi, 194

Schuman, R. Baird, 321
Schwartz, Carol, 352
Schwartz, Judith G., 376–379
Schwartzman, Helen B., 247
Schwebel, Andrew I., 321
Schweinhart, L. J., 277
Sciarra, June, 277
Scoresby, A. Lynn, 127
Seaver, Judith W., 322
Sebesta, Sam L., 257
Seeger, Ruth Crawford, 402
Segal, Julius, 157
Segura, Roberto D., 415
Seidelman, James E.,
Self, Frank, 357
Sendak, Maurice, 333
Serbin, Lisa, 484, 485
Serebriakoff, Victor, 158
Sgroi, Suzanne M., 90
Shallcross, Doris J., 322, 476
Shanklin, Douglas, 222
Shapiro, Annette Frank, 473
Shapiro, June, 492
Shapiro, Lawrence E., 247, 322
Sharp, Evelyn, 247, 322
Sheeves, Rosamund, 403
Sheiman, Deborah Lovitky, 208–
210
Sherman, Judith, 443
Sherrill, Claudine, 450
Shigaki, Irene S., 14–17
Shiller, Jack G., 196
Short, Pat, 389
Short, Verl, 384
Sidel, Ruth, 71
Siegel, Ernest, 158, 450
Siegel, Paul, 158
Siegel, Rita, 158
Siepp, John M., 445
Siks, Geraldine, 403
Sills, Barbara, 158
Silver, George A., 196

Silver, Gerald A., 159
Silver, Myrna, 159
Sime, M., 323
Simkin, Diana, 34
Simms, Gloria C., 279
Simoes, Antonio, Jr., 425
Simon, Alvin C., 272
Sinberg, Janet, 101
Singer, Dorothy, 247, 507
Singer, Jerome, 247, 507
Sinquefield, Gail, 307
Sjolund, Arne, 278
Skaggs, Merrill Maguire, 124
Skinner, B. F., 42, 71
Skinner, Nancy, 473
Skolnick, Arlene, 101
Skolnick, Jerome, 101
Slattery, Jill, 222
Sloan, Sara, 222
Slonim, Maureen B., 176–177,
208–210
Sloper, Patricia, 445, 465
Smart, Laura S., 101
Smart, Mollie S., 101
Smith, Frank, 323
Smith, Henrietta T., 34
Smith, Lendon, 196, 197, 223
Smith, Sally L., 456
Smith, Theresa, 278
Smith, Vernon, 197
Snyder, Frederick, 173–175
Snyder, Martha, 323
Sorosky, Arthur D., 102
Spain, Bernie, 439
Sparling, Joseph, 248
Sparkman, Brandon, 323
Spaulding, Isabelle, 463
Spencer, Ruth Albert, 403
Spitzer, Dean R., 71
Spock, Benjamin, 71, 197, 222
Spodek, Bernard, 289–294, 324
Sponseller, Doris, 248

Spredemann, Sharon D. M.,
  457
Springer, Nesher Bass, 271
Sprung, Barbara, 481–486, 492
Stanley, Julian, 472
Stare, Frederick J., 224
Stecher, Miriam, 404
Stein, Lincoln David, 159
Stein, Morris, 476
Stein, Sara Bennett, 159
Steinberg, David, 160
Steinberg, L. D., 529, 532
Steinmetz, Suzanne K., 102
Stenson, Janet Sinberg, 102
Stern, Daniel, 160
Stern, Margaret B., 302
Stern, Virginia, 57
Sternlicht, Manny, 248
Stevens, George, 224
Stevens, Laura, 223, 224
Stewart, Nancie B., 272
Stewig, John Warren, 357
Stiles, L. J., 417
Stiles, Winifred E., 446
Stillwell, Lyda, 395
Stimpson, Catherine R., 160
Stoddard, Elizabeth, 475
Stommel-Fugeman, Margaret,
  223
Stone, Jeannette Galambos, 160
Stone, Lawrence, 72
Stone, L. Joseph, 34, 71
Stoner, Rosemary, 233, 224
Stoppard, Miriam, 197
Stout, Glenn R., Jr., 198
Straus, Murray A., 102
Streets, Donald T., 278
Strelitz, Ziona, 154, 155
Strickland, C., 290
Strickland, Dorothy S., 286–288,
  294, 358
Stuart, Irving R., 103

Stuart, Virginia, 472
Suitar, Carol, 224
Susman, Jeffrey, 194
Suter, Antoinette Brown, 359
Sutherland, Iris R., 425
Sutherland, Zena, 358
Sutton-Smith, Brian, 358, 491
Swedlow, R., 312, 500, 501,
  502
Swerdlow, Joel, 507
Sweeney, Edward A., 198
Sylva, Kathy, 278
Szasz, Suzanne, 72

Talmage, Harriet, 316
Tanner, John M., 72
Theroux, Rosemary T., 161
Thevenin, Tine, 161
Thomas, Alexander, 128, 161
Thomas, Linda, 224
Thompson, Stephanie C., 440–
  441
Tibbits, Edith, 25
Tiedt, Iris, 324
Tiedt, Sidney W., 324
Tindall, B. Allan, 242
Tingley, Josephine F., 161
Tipps, Steven, 310
Todd, Linda, 35
Todd, Vivian Edminston, 324
Torbert, Marianne, 404
Torbet, Laura, 152
Torrance, E. Paul, 473
Torre, Carolyn Talley, 222
Tosi, Umberto, 236
Traub, Nina, 325
Trohanis, Pascal L., 279
Troike, Rudolph C., 413, 424
Trojan, Judith, 508
Tronick, Edward, 35, 73
Trubo, Richard, 179

Tucker, Nicholas, 358
Tudor-Hart, Beatrix, 249

Updike, John, 363
U.S. Department of Health and
 Human Services/Public
 Health Service, 198, 249
Uzgiris, Ina C., 35

Vail, Priscilla, 476
Verrilli, George E., 152
Vickery, Donald M., 193, 199
Visher, Emily, 103
Visher, John, 103
Vonde, Dee, 225
Voneche, I. Jacques, 61
Vygotsky, Lev Semenovich, 73

Wagner, Marsden, 279
Wagner, Mary, 279
Walker, Hill M., 325
Wallerstein, Judith S., 103
Walsh, Huber M., 73
Wanamaker, Nancy, 225
Ward, Cecilia B., 322
Warlow, Aidan, 355
Warrell, Susan E., 161
Warren, David H., 464
Warren, Rita M., 74, 162
Watson, Clyde, 363
Watson, Eunice L., 269
Way, Brian, 404
Weaver, Phyllis A., 319
Weber, Evelyn, 325, 326
Webster, Elizabeth J., 457
Weeks, Thelma E., 74
Wei, Stephen H. Y., 199
Weihs, Thomas J., 458
Weikart, David P., 269, 273, 275,
 277, 307, 326, 420
Weinfeld, Nanci Regovin, 199

Weingarten, Kathy, 132
Weininger, Otto, 74
Weiss, Curtis E., 461, 462
Weiss, Joan Soloman, 162
Weiss, Robert S., 103
Weissbourd, Bernice, 35
Weitzman, Lenore J., 492
Welber, Delores, 258–260
Welber, Robert, 258–260
Wells, Hal M., 162
Wells, Melvin Wesley, 313
Werner, Emmy E., 425
Werner, Heinz, 42, 74
Werner, Roberta A., 466
Westin, Jeane, 162
Westland, Cor, 249
Whelan, Elizabeth M., 163, 224
Whitaker, Carl, 98
White, Barbara Notkin, 164
White, Burton L., 163
White, James D., 164
White, Karol, 36
White, Sheldon, 164
White, Stephanie, 270
Whitman, Walt, 341
Whitmore, Joanne Rand, 476
Whittaker, James K., 450
Wiederholt, J. Lee, 451
Wiener, Jack, 405
Wigutoff, Sharon, 487
Wikler, Norma, 134
Wilder, Rosilyn, 405
Wildsmith, Brian, 335
Williams, David P., 99
Williams, Frederick, 75
Williams, Leslie R., 425
Williams, Phyllis S., 36
Williamson, Gordon C., 445
Wills, A. Christine, 265
Wilson, Amos N., 426
Wilson, Geraldine L., 426

Wilson, Sue, 451
Wilt, Joy, 164
Wineman, David, 69, 155
Winick, Mariann Rezella, 508
Winick, Myron, 225, 226
Winn, Marie, 249, 405, 508
Winnicott, Donald W., 250
Winsor, Charlotte B., 326
Winter, Paula, 333
Wiseman, Ann, 389
Wishard, Laurie, 104
Wishard, William R., 104
Witkin, Kate, 406
Wlodkowski, R., 388
Wolff, Jurgen, 226
Wolfgang, Charles H., 250, 251
Wolfgang, Marie, 251
Worfsohn, Reeta Bochner, 164
Women on Words and Images, 493
Wood, Christopher, 216
Woodward, Kenneth, 96
Wordsworth, W., 341

Wright, David, 464
Wyden, Barbara, 421

Yahraes, Herbert, 157
Yamamoto, Kaoru, 326
Yarris, Steve, 367–368
Yeomans, Edward, 327
Yntema, Sharon, 226
Yocum, Jan C., 279
Young, James C., 419
Young, Jane, 395
Young, Leontine, 165
Young, Nancy, 94

Zaichkowsky, Leonard D., 327
Zaichkowsky, Linda B., 327
Zamm, Alfred V., 199
Zaslavsky, Claudia, 327
Zigler, Edward F., 75
Zimbardo, Philip G., 165
Zuckerman, Diane M., 507

Title Index

About Behaviorism, 71

Abused Child, The: A Multi-disciplinary Approach in Developmental Issues and Treatment, 97

Abusing Family, The, 95

ACT Guide to Children's Television: How to Treat TV with T.L.C., The, 506

Acting-Out Child, The, 325

Activities: For School-age Child Care, 267

Activities Deskbook for Teaching Reading Skills, 306

Administering Day Care and Preschool Programs, 278

Administration: Making Programs Work for Children and Families, 273

Adoption: The Grafted Tree, 104

Adoption Triangle, The: The Effects of the Sealed Record on Adoptees, Birth Parents, and Adoptive Parents, 102

Advances in Early Education and Day Care: A Research Annual, 275

Aesthetic Awareness and the Child, 383

Alerta—A Bilingual Multicultural Early Childhood Curriculum, 425

All Our Children: The American Family Under Pressure, 95

Amanecer, 414

American Bilingual Tradition, The, 422

American Family Life Films, 508

American Folk Songs for Children, 402

American Picturebooks from Noah's Ark to the Beast Within, 345

Analyzing Children's Art, 386

Annotated Bibliography of Children's Books, An: An Introduction to the Literature of Head Start's Children, 426

Answers for New Parents: Adjusting to Your New Role, 153

Art: Basic for Young Children, 387

Art: Another Language for Learning, 381

Art for All the Children, 444

Art for the Fun of It, 386

Art for Teachers of Children, 388

Artful Scribbles: The Significance of Children's Drawings, 383

Art Instruction for Handicapped Children, 448

Art in the Early Childhood Years, 385

Artist, An, 384

Art of Managing People, The, 274

Art of the Young Child, The, 380

Arts and Crafts for Physically and Mentally Disabled, 446

Arts and Crafts You Can Eat, 381

Aspects of Ethnicity: Understanding Differences in Pluralistic Classroom, 422

Assessment in Infancy: Ordinal Scales of Psychological Development, 35

*Astor Program for Gifted Children:
Prekindergarten Through Grade
Three, The,* 471
As You Eat, So Your Baby Grows, 25
*At Highest Risk: Environmental
Hazards to Young and Unborn
Children,* 192
Attention and Cognitive Development, 62
*Audience Participation Theatre for
Young People,* 404
*Audio-Visual Instruction: Technology,
Media and Method,* 504

*Babies as People: New Findings on Our
Social Beginnings,* 35, 73
Babies Need Books, 347
*Baby?, A . . . Maybe: A Guide to
Making the Most Fateful Decision
of Your Life,* 163
Baby and Child Care, 71, 197
*Baby Food Book, The: A Guide for
Preparing Fresh Nutritious Foods
for the Very Young,* 219
Baby Is Born, A, 31
*Baby Learning Through Baby Play: A
Parent's Guide for the First Two
Years,* 61
Babysense, 21
Barnes Book of Nursery Verse, The, 360
Becoming a Mother, 152
Becoming a Teacher of Young Children,
310
Before the Best Interests of the Child, 93
*Behavioral Pediatrics and Psychological
Aspects of Child Health Care,* 185
*Behind Closed Doors: Violence in the
American Family,* 102
Bereaved Parent, The, 157
*Best Books for Children: Preschool
Through Middle Grades,* 351
Best of Book Bonanza, The, 353
Better Health for Our Children: A

*National Strategy. The Report of the
Select Panel for the Promotion of
Child Health to States, Congress
and the Secretary of Health and
Human Services,* 198
*Better Homes & Garden's New Baby
Book,* 181
*Between Generations: The Six Stages of
Parenthood,* 136
*Between Parent and Child. New Solutions
to Old Problems,* 137
Beyond the Best Interests of the Child,
271
*Beyond the Medical Mystique: How to
Choose and Use Your Doctor,* 180
Bibliography of Books for Children, 345
*Bibliography of Child Psychiatry and
Child Mental Health,* 180
*Bibliography of Materials in Sexism and
Sex-Role Stereotyping in Children's
Books,* 489
*Bilingual Child, The: Research and
Analysis of Existing Educational
Themes,* 425
*Bilingual Schooling in the United States:
A Source Book for Educational
Personnel,* 416
*Birth of a Family: The New Role of the
Father in Childbirth,* 139
*Birth Primer, The: A Source Book of
Traditional and Alternative
Methods in Labor and Delivery,* 33
*Birth to Three: Developmental Learning
and the Handicapped Child,* 444
Birth Without Violence, 29
Black Child, 421
*Black Child, White Child: The
Development of Racial Attitudes,*
319
Black Child Care, 91, 416
*Black Children Just Keep on Growing:
Alternative Curriculum Models for*

Young Black Children, 415

*Black Experience in Children's Books,
The*, 357

Black Focus on Multicultural Education,
414

*Black Parent's Handbook: A Guide to
Healthy Pregnancy, Birth and
Child Care*, 30

*Blindness and Early Childhood
Development*, 464

Block Book, The, 241

*Body Workbook: Medical Tests You Can
Do In Your Home*, 187

*Bodyworks: The Children's Guide to Food
and Physical Fitness*, 180

*Bookfinder, The: A Guide to Children's
Literature About the Needs and
Problems of Youth Aged 2–15*, 457

Book for Grandmothers, A, 93

Books for the Gifted Child, 346, 470

*Books for Today's Children: An
Annotated Bibliography of
Non-Stereotyped Picture Books*, 487

*Book of Health, The: A Complete Guide
to Making Health Last a Lifetime*,
179

*Books, Puppets and the Mentally
Retarded Student*, 348

*Books with Options; An Annotated
Bibliography of Non-stereotyping
Books for Children and Young
People*, 487

Born at Risk, 183

Born to Talk, 74

*Bowes and Church's Food Values of
Portions Commonly Used*, 220

*Boys' and Girls' Book About Divorce,
The*, 92

*Brain and Learning: Directions in Early
Childhood Education*, 310

*Breast-Feeding: A Guide for the Medical
Profession*, 28, 216

*Breastfeeding Handbook: A Practical
Reference for Physicians, Nurses
and Other Health Professionals*
(Goldfarb and Tibbets), 25

*Bridging Two Cultures: Multi-
disciplinary Readings in Bilingual
Bicultural Education*, 416

*Bringing Learning Home: How Parents
Can Play A More Active and
Effective Role in Their Children's
Education*, 150

Broken Taboo, The: Sex in the Family, 95

*Careers with Young Children: Making
Your Decision*, 322

Care of Twin Children, The, 161

Caring: Supporting Children's Growth,
74, 162

*Caring About Kids: The Importance of
Play*, 249

*Caring and Cooking for the Allergic
Child*, 224

Caring for the Gifted, 471

Caring for Troubled Children, 450

*Celebrating Children's Books: Essays on
Children's Literature*, 352

*Centuries of Childhood: A Social History
of Family Life*, 54

*Cerebral Palsy: A Developmental
Disability*, 458

*Cesarean Birth Experience: A Practical,
Comprehensive, and Reassuring
Guide for Parents and Professionals,
The*, 22

*Cesarean (R) Evolution: A Handbook for
Parents and Childbirth Educators,
The*, 31

*Change for Children: Ideas and Activities
for Individualizing Learning*, 309

*Changing Perspectives in Nutrition and
Caries*, 178

Channeling Children: Sex Stereotyping on Prime Time, 491

Child Abuse, (Dolan), 91

Child Abuse (Kempe and Kempe), 95

Child Abuse and Neglect: Cross-Cultural Perspectives, 96

Child Advocacy Handbook, The, 92

Child and Its Family, The: The Genesis of Behavior, 96

Child and Society: Essays in Applied Child Development, The, 59

Child and Tale: The Origins of Interest, 350

Child and the Book, The: A Psychological and Literary Exploration, 358

Childarts: Integrating Curriculum Through the Arts, 383

Child Bearing: A Guide for Pregnant Parents, 27

Childbirth: A Source Book for Conception, Pregnancy, Birth and the First Weeks of Life, 25

Child Care, Family Benefits, and Working Parents, 274

Child Care, Who Cares? Foreign and Domestic Infant and Early Childhood Development, 277

Child Care and Preschool: Options for Federal Support, 268

Child Care and Public Policy: A Case Study, 276

Child Development and Personality, 67

Child Development in Normality and Psychopathology, 55

Child Growth, 64

Child Health: America's Future, 196

Child Health Encyclopedia. A Comprehensive Guide for Parents, 181

Child Health Maintenance: Concepts in Family-Centered Care, 182

Childhood: Pathways of Discovery, 164

Childhood and Adolescence, 42, 71

Childhood and Society, 59

Childhood Development: An Educational Perspective, 303

Childhood Illness and Childhood Injury, 196

Childhood Obesity, 212

Child Is Born, A, 32

Child Learning Through Child Play: Learning Activities for Two and Three-Year Olds, 61

Childminder: A Study in Action Research, 274

Children: The Challenge, 92

Children and Adolescents: Interpretive Essays on Jean Piaget, 58

Children and Adults: Activities for Growing Together, 126

Children and Books, 358

Children and Day Nurseries, 270

Children and Drama, 399

Children and Language, 311

Children and Literature, 357

Children and Literature: Views and Reviews, 352

Children and Minders, 268

Children and Their Literature, 351

Children and Youth in Action, 195

Children at Risk, 442

Children Cook Naturally, 222

Children Dance in the Classroom, 392

Children in Need of Special Care, 458

Children in the Hospital, 445

Children in the World's Art, 382

Children in Time and Space, 326

Children Learning: A Teacher's Classroom Diary, 312

Children Learn Physical Skills. Vol. 1, Birth to Three Years. Vol. 2, Four to Six Years, 183

Children of Crisis, Vol. 2. Migrants, Mountaineers, and Sharecroppers, 416

Children of Crisis, Vol. 4. Eskimos,
    Chicanos, Indians, 415
Children of Divorce, 91
Children of Separation and Divorce:
    Management and Treatment, 103
Children of the Crèche, 58
Children of the Dream, 55
Children on Medication: A Primer for
    School Personnel, 185
Children's Arithmetic: The Learning
    Process, 303
Children's Books: Awards and Prizes,
    348
Children's Choices for 1982, 348
Children's Doctor, The, 196
Children's Emotions and Moods, 148
Children's Faces Looking Up: Program
    Building for the Storyteller, 349
Children's Friendships, 70
Children's Language, 67
Children's Language and Learning,
    312
Children's Language Disorders: An
    Integrated Approach, 460
Children's Literature: An Annotated
    Bibliography of the History and
    Criticism, 356
Children's Literature in the Elementary
    School, 353
Children's Play and Playgrounds, 239
Children's Reading Begins at Home—
    How Parents Can Help Their
    Young Children, 310
Children's TV: The Economics of
    Exploitation, 507
Children Who Hate: The Disorganization
    and Breakdown of Behavior
    Controls, 69
Children Who Read Early: Two
    Longitudinal Studies, 350
Children with Learning Problems: A
    Handbook for Teachers, 442
Child Safety Is No Accident, 179

Child's Body: A Parent's Manual, 183
Child's Calendar, A, 363
The Child's Concept of Story, 345
Child's Eye View, A, 322
Child's Journey, A: Forces That Shape
    the Lives of Our Young, 157
Child's Parent Dies, A: Studies in
    Childhood Bereavement, 136
Child Under Six, The, 62
Childwatching at Playgroup and
    Nursery School, 278
Child with Spina Bifida, The, 439
Chinese Cultural Resource Book, 422
Choices in Childbirth, 23
Choosing Child Care: A Guide for
    Parents, 266
Choosing Toys for Children from Birth to
    Five, 241
Chronically Ill Child, The: A Guide for
    Parents and Professionals, 190
City Green, 362
Clay Play: Learning Games for Children,
    401
Clinical Management of Articulation
    Disorders, 462
Clinical Studies in Infant Mental Health:
    The First Year of Life, 23
Clumsy Child, The: A Program of Motor
    Therapy, 429
Cognitive Development, 59
Coming Parent Revolution, The, 162
Coming to Our Senses. The Significance
    of Arts for American Education.
    A Panel Report, 470
Commercial Children's Television on
    Weekends and Weekday Afternoons,
    503
Communicating with Children Through
    Television: Studies of Messages and
    Other Impressions Conveyed by Five
    Children's Programs, 504
Communicative Disorders: Prevention
    and Early Intervention, 461

Competency and Creativity in Language
    Arts: A Multiethnic Focus, 304
Competent Infant: Research and
    Commentary, The, 34
Complete Babysitters' Handbook, The,
    124
Complete Book of Children's Play, The,
    241
Complete Handbook of Children's Reading
    Disorders, The: A Critical
    Evaluation of their Clinical,
    Educational, and Social Dimensions,
    315, 461
Complete New Guide to Preparing Baby
    Foods at Home, The, 212
Complete Pregnancy Exercise Book, The,
    34
Concept Formation and Learning in Early
    Childhood, 71
Concepts and Theories of Human
    Development, 64
Concepts in Special Education, 442
Concepts to Guide the Education of
    Experienced Teachers with
    Implication for PL 94-142, 441
Conspiracy Against Childhood, The, 146
Continuum Concept, The, 66
Controversies About Stuttering Therapy,
    460
Cooking for Your Hyperactive Child,
    221
Cool Web, The: The Pattern of Children's
    Reading, 355
Coping with a Miscarriage: Why It
    Happens and How to Deal with Its
    Impact on You and Your Family, 33
Coping with Children's Misbehavior,
    133
Coping with Prolonged Health Impair-
    ment in Your Child, 190
Could I Speak to You About this Man,
    Piaget, a Second?, 304
Counseling with Parents of Handicapped

Children, 457
Cradles of Eminence, 473
Crafts for the Very Disabled and
    Handicapped, 447
Creative Activities for the Gifted Child,
    473
Creative Activities for Young Children,
    388
Creative and Mental Growth, 387
Creative Art for Learning, 386
Creative Art for the Developing Child:
    A Teacher's Handbook for Early
    Childhood Education, 298, 381
Creative Arts for the Severely
    Handicapped, 450
Creative Drama for the Classroom
    Teacher, 395
Creative Drama in the Classroom, 313,
    398
Creative Dance in the Primary School,
    402
Creative Food Experiences for Children,
    214
Creative Fun for Everyone: A Learning
    Center Approach to Creative
    Activities, 384
Creative Homes and Centers, 266
Creative Movement for Children: A
    Dance Program for the Classroom,
    405
Creative Movement for Special
    Education, 447
Creative Movement for Young Children,
    320
Creative Play for the Developing Child:
    Early Lifehood Education Through
    Play, 238
Creative Rhythmic Movement: Boys and
    Girls Dancing, 394
Creativity, Art and the Young Child, 381
Cricket in a Thicket, 359
Criteria for the Selection and Use of
    Visuals in Instruction, 505

Cross-Cultural Child Development: A View from the Planet Earth, 425

Crosscurrents of Criticism: Horn Book Essays, 1968–1977, 353

Cultural Awareness: A Resource Bibliography, 424

Cultural Awareness for Young Children, 422

Culture and Childrearing, 182

Curriculum and Assessment Guidelines for Infant and Child Care, 302

Cushla and her Books, 347

Cutting Loose: An Adult Guide to Coming to Terms with Your Parents, 94

Damaged Parents: An Anatomy of Child Neglect, 99

Danish National Child-Care System, The, 279

Day Care and the Public Schools: Profiles of Five Communities, 275

Day Care Book The, 276

Day Care Book, The: The Why, What and How of Community Day Care, 267

Daycare Institutions and Children's Development, 278

Deafness, 464

Deafness and Child Development, 463

Demythologizing the Inner City Child, 419

Developing Active Readers: Ideas for Parents, Teachers, and Librarians, 355

Developing and Administering a Child Care Center, 277

Developing Children's Language, 317

Developmental Handicaps in Babies and Young Children: A Guide for Parents, 441

Developmental Potential of Preschool Children, 459

Developmental Psychology of the Black Child, The, 426

Developmental Processes: Heinz Werner's Selected Writings, 74

Development of Affect: The Genesis of Behavior, The, 65

Development of Language and Reading in Young Children, The, 318

Development Screening Guide in Early Childhood: A Guide, 451

Development Through Drama, 404

Dibs: In Search of Self, 468

Dick and Jane as Victims: Sex Role Stereotyping in Children's Readers, 493

Dictionary of Puppetry, 401

Did the Sun Shine Before You Were Born?, 137

Dietary Guidelines, 216

Difference in the Family, A, 443

Difficult Child, The, 151

Disappearance of Childhood, The, 100, 507

Discovering Language with Children, 318

Discussing Death: A Guide to Death Education, 151

Disturbed Exceptional Children: An Integrated Approach, 457

Divorce Is a Grown-Up Problem, 101

Doctor and Child, 181

Dr. Miriam Stoppard's Book of Baby Care, 197

Dr. Montessori's Own Handbook, 151

Doing the Media: A Portfolio of Activities, Ideas, and Resources, 506

Don't Move the Muffin Tins, 380

Do Your Ears Hang Low? Fifty More Musical Fingerplays, 395

Down the Rabbit Hole; Adventures and Misadventures in the Realm of Children's Literature, 354

Dramatic Play in Childhood: Rehearsal
    for Life, 241, 398
Drama with Children, 403
Dynamic Self: Activities to Enhance
    Infant Development, The, 18

Early Childhood Art, 385
Early Childhood Education, 325
Early Childhood Education: A Guide
    for Observation and Participation,
    312
Early Childhood Education Today, 315
Early Childhood Experience: A
    Bibliography, 350
Early Childhood Music Kit—The First
    Year, 403
Early Education in Spanish-Speaking
    Communities, 279
Early Language, 300
Early Years in Childhood Education,
    The, 297
Earth Father Sky Father: The
    Changing Concept of Fathering,
    131
Educating Exceptional Children, 447
Educating the Ablest: A Book of
    Readings, 473
Educating the Gifted: Acceleration and
    Enrichment, 472
Educating the Learning Disabled, 450
Education: An Introduction, 295
Educational Handicap, Public Policy and
    Social History: A Broadened
    Perspective on Mental Retardation,
    468
Education and Care of Moderately and
    Severely Retarded Children, 465
Education and Physical Growth, 72
Education Handbook for Black Families,
    418
E is for Everybody: A Manual Intended
    for Bringing Fine Picture Books into

the Hands and Hearts of Children,
    256
Elementary Teacher's Complete Ideas
    Handbook, The, 324
Elements of Early Reading Instruction,
    321
Elements of Film, 503
Emerging Rights of Children in
    Treatment for Mental and
    Catastrophic Illnesses, The, 191
Emotional Care of Hospitalized Children,
    193
Emotional Care of Hospitalized Children:
    An Environmental Approach, 99
Emotional Experience of Motherhood
    After Freud and Feminism, 139
Empty Fortress, The: Infantile Autism
    and the Birth of Self, 469
Encourage Your Child to Read: A Parent
    Primer, 310
Encyclopedia of Baby and Child Care,
    The, 197
Energy Through Nutritive Basics, 213
Enhancing Self-Concept in Early
    Childhood, 70
Enjoying Single Parenthood, 142
Essential Exercises for the Childbearing
    Year: A Guide to Health and
    Comfort Before and After Your
    Baby Is Born, 32
Essential Piaget, The, 61
Essentials of Pediatrics, The, 192
Ethnic Modification of the Curriculum,
    418
Ethnic Stories for Children to Dance, 392
Everybody's Tooth Book, 191
Every Child's Birthright: In Defense of
    Mothering, 23
Every Child's Book of Nursery Songs,
    399
Everyday Enrichment for Gifted Children
    at Home and School, 474

Everyday Mother Talk to Toddlers: Early Intervention, 157

Excellent Paperbacks for Children, 349

Exceptional Children in the Regular Classroom, 449

Exciting Things To Do with Color, 380

Executive Parent, The, 140

Exercise Plus Pregnancy Program: Exercises for Before, During and After Pregnancy, The, 21

Experience of Breastfeeding, 215

Experiences in Language: Tools and Techniques for Language Arts Methods, 307

Exploring the Arts with Children, 382

Eye Winker, Tom Tinker, Chin Chopper: Fifty Musical Fingerplays, 394

Facts of Love, The: Living, Loving and Growing, 131

Fair Play: A Bibliography of Non-Stereotyped Materials, 488

Families, 94

Families: Developing Relationships, 101

Families and Family Therapy, 98

Family, Sex and Marriage in England 1500–1800, The, 72

Family, The, 86

Family as Educator, 81

Family Bed, The: An Age-Old Concept in Child Rearing, 161

Family Book About Sexuality, The, 127

Family Communication: Keeping Connected in a Time of Change, 98

Family Crucible, The, 98

Family Day Care: A Practical Guide for Parents, Caregivers, and Professionals, 296

Family Doctor's Answer Book, The: A Total Guide to Your Child's Health, 182

Family Games, 159

Family in Transition: Rethinking Marriage, Sexuality, and Childrearing and Family Organization, 101

Father, The: His Role in Child Development, 148

Father Feelings, 132

Father Fox's Pennyrhymes, 363

Fatherjournal: Five Years of Awakening to Fatherhood, 160

Fathers, Mothers and Society: Perspectives on Parenting, 154

Fathers, Mothers, and Society: Toward New Alliances, 155

Feeding Your Baby and Child, 222

Feeding Your Baby the Safe and Healthy Way, 219

Feed Me! I'm Yours, 216

Feed Your Kids Right, 223

Feelings and Friends, 423

Feingold Cookbook for Hyperactive Children and Others with Problems Associated with Food Additives and Other Salicylates, The, 213

Fifteen Centuries of Children's Literature: An Annotated Chronology of British and American Works in Historical Context, 347

Films for Childhood Educators, 508

Finger Frolics: Fingerplays for Young Children, 359

Finger Rhymes, 359

First Babyfood Cookbook, The, 218

First Birth, The: A Family Turning Point, 133

First Month of Life, The: A Parent's Guide to Care of the Newborn, 198

First Relationship, The: Infant and Mother, 160

First Steps in Teaching Creative Dance, 397

First Three Years of Life, The, 163
First Twelve Months of Life, The, 34
*First Year of Life: A Curriculum for
    Parenting Education, The,* 86
*530 Vital Questions Every Mother Asks
    About Her Child's Health: And a
    Noted Pediatrician's Quick,
    Authoritative Advice,* 193
Folkstories of Children, 358
*Follow Me: A Handbook of Movement
    Activities for Children,* 404
Food Adventures for Children, 225
Food Nutrition, and the Young Child,
    213
Food Nutrition and Diet Therapy, 215
*Food Power: Nutrition and Your Baby's
    Health,* 220
Foods for Healthy Kids, 223
*Food that Stays, The: An Update on
    Nutrition,* 198
*Foundation for Teaching English as a
    Second Language: Theory and
    Method for Multicultural
    Education,* 424
Foundations of Literacy, The, 308
*Franklin Watts Concise Guide to
    Baby-Sitting, The,* 156
*Friendship and Peer Relations: The
    Origins of Behavior,* 65
*From Childhood to Childhood: Children's
    Books and Their Creators,* 353
From Two to Five, 56
*Fundamentals of Early Childhood
    Education,* 313
Future of Motherhood, The, 125

*Games Children Play: Instructive and
    Creative Play Activities for the
    Mentally Retarded and Develop-
    mentally Disabled Child,* 248
*Games to Grow on: Activities to Help
    Children Learn Self-Control,* 247,
    322

*General Selections from the Works of
    Sigmund Freud,* 69
Genetic Connection, The, 26, 188
Genetic Diversity and Human Equality,
    58
Gentle Birth Book, The, 18
Get a Wiggle On, 464
*Getting Ready to Read: Creating Readers
    from Birth Through Six,* 303
Getting Started, 301
Getting the Most Out of Your Doctor,
    191
*Getting Your Kids to Eat Right: A Daily
    Program for Giving Your Children
    the Vitamins and Nutrients They
    Need in the Foods They Love,* 221
*Gifted and Talented, The: A Handbook
    for Parents,* 471
*Gifted and Talented Education in
    Perspective,* 475
*Gifted and Talented Young People,
    Studies in Excellence: An Annotated
    Bibliography and Guide,* 476
*Gifted and the Talented, The: Their
    Education and Development,* 475
*Gifted Children: A Guide for Parents
    and Teachers,* 471
*Gifted Children in the Regular Class-
    room: The Complete Guide for
    Teachers and Administrators,* 305
*Giftedness, Conflict, and Underachieve-
    ment,* 476
*Gifted Student, The: An Annotated
    Bibliography,* 474
Gifted Young Children, 476
Gift of Play, The, 246
*GNYS AT WRK: A Child Learns to
    Write and Read,* 296
*Going It Alone: The Family Life and
    Social Situation of the Single Parent,*
    103
*Good Beginnings: Parenting in the Early
    Years,* 134

Good Time Fitness for Kids: A Guide for Parents, Coaches and Counselors, 184

Grandparents-Grandchildren: The Vital Connection, 96

Gray Goose and Gander and Other Mother Goose Rhymes, 362

Gray's Anatomy Coloring Book, The, 183

Great American Nutrition Hassle, The, 214

Great Parties for Young Children, 124

Green and Burning Tree, The: On the Writing and Enjoyment of Children's Books, 347

Group Care of Children: Crossroads and Transitions, 276

Group Crafts for Teachers and Librarians on Limited Budgets, 388

Group Games in Early Education: Implications of Piaget's Theory, 309

Grow Healthy Kids!: A Parent's Guide to Sound Nutrition from Birth through Teens, 219

Growing and Learning through Play: Activities for Pre-School and Kindergarten Children: A Parent/ Caregiver Book, 251

Growing Up Equal: Activities and Resources for Parents and Teachers of Young Children, 490, 492

Growing Up Free: Raising Your Child in the 80's, 491

Growing Up Gifted, 470

Growing Up Handicapped: A Guide to Helping the Exceptional Child, 440

Growing Up on Television, 507

Growing Wisdom, Growing Wonder: Helping Your Child Learn from Birth Through Five Years, 138

Growing with Your Children, 143

Growth and Development: The Child and Physical Activity, 327

Growth and Development of Mothers, The, 149

Growth Standards in Children, 194

Guidance of Young Children, 149, 314

Guide for the Care of Infants in Groups, 277

Guidelines for Selecting Bias-Free Textbooks and Storybooks, 488

Guidelines for Teaching Students with Learning Problems, 453

Guidelines to Teaching Remedial Reading, 319

Guide to Culture in the Classroom, A, 424

Guide to Discipline, A, 160

Guide to Non-Sexist Children's Books, A, 487

Guide to Parenting: You and Your Newborn, 134

Guide to Subjects and Concepts in Picture Book Format, A, 352

Guiding Children's Reading Through Experience, 302

Gymboree: Giving Your Child Physical, Mental and Social Confidence Through Play, 236

Half-Parent, The: Living with Other People's Children, 97

Handbook for Elementary School Teachers, A, 308

Handbook for New Parents, 184

Handbook for Storytellers, 346

Handbook for Successful Urban Teaching, 311

Handbook of Bilingual Education, A, 424

Handbook of First Aid and Emergency Care, 178

Handbook on Accident Prevention: Injury Control for Children and Youth, 190

Handicapped Child in the Family: A
    Guide for Parents, A, 443
Handling the Young Cerebral Palsied
    Child at Home, 458
Having a Baby After Thirty, 19
Having Children: Philosophical and
    Legal Reflection on Parenthood, 99
Having Twins: A Parent's Guide to
    Pregnancy, Birth and Early
    Childhood, 32
Healing at Home: A Guide to Health
    Care for Children, 188
Health and Safety for Your Children:
    Child Involvement in Personal
    Health, 187
Health Needs of Children, 191
Health of the Preschool Child, 195
Help for the Lonely Child: Strengthening
    Social Perception, 158
Help for the Overweight Child, 226
Helpful Hints and Tricks for New Moms
    and Dads (And Not So New), 199
Helping Aggressive and Passive
    Preschoolers Through Play, 250
Helping Children Cope, 135, 184
Helping Children Grow Through Play,
    238
Helping Children Learn to Read: A
    Primer for Adults, 318
Helping Children Overcome Learning
    Difficulties, 454
Helping Maltreated Children: School and
    Community Involvement, 94
Helping Parents Help Their Children,
    123
Helping the Noncompliant Child, 443
Helping Your Children Grow: A
    Humanistic Approach to Parenting
    and Teaching, 161
Helping Your Exceptional Baby, 445
Helping Your Exceptional Baby: A
    Practical and Honest Approach to

Raising a Mentally Handicapped
    Child, 465
High-Risk Child, The: A Guide for
    Concerned Parents, 442
Home Teaching with Mothers and
    Infants: The Ypsilanti Carnegie
    Infant Education Project-An
    Experiment, 275
Hospital Book, The, 188
How Babies Learn to Talk, 154
How Children Learn Mathematics, 300
How Children See Our World, 145
How It Feels to Be a Child, 142
How It Feels When a Parent Dies, 143
How to Be a Gifted Parent, 474
How to Be Your Own Doctor
    (Sometimes), 196
How to Choose a Good Doctor, 189
How to Feed Your Hyperactive Child,
    224
How to Fight Fair with Your Kids . . .
    and Win!, 152
How to Generate Values in Young
    Children: Integrity, Honesty,
    Individuality, Self-Confidence, and
    Wisdom, 100
How to Grandparent, 91
How to Help Children with Common
    Problems, 157
How to Help Your Gifted Child-A
    Handbook for Parents and Teachers,
    472
How to Improve Your Child's Behavior
    Through Diet, 223
How to Live with Other People's
    Children, 98
How to Make Your Child a Winner:
    Ten Keys to Rearing Successful
    Children, 130
How to Parent, 133
How to Really Love Your Child, 128
How to Start a Day Care Center, 279

How to Start and Operate a Day Care Home, 272

How to Talk So Kids Will Listen, and Listen So Kids Will Talk, 135

How to Talk with Children About Sex, 145

How to Teach Your Child About Sex . . . Without Making a Perfect Fool of Yourself, 125

Human (and Anti-Human) Values in Children's Books: A Content Rating Instrument for Educators and Concerned Parents, 488

Humanistic Teaching for Exceptional Children, 452

Human Milk in the Modern World: Psychosocial Nutritional and Economic Significance, 215

Husband-Coached Childbirth, 19

Hyperactive Children: A Handbook for Diagnosis and Treatment, 440

I Can Do It! I Can Do It! Arts and Crafts for the Mentally Retarded, 451

I Can Make a Rainbow: Things to Create and Do . . . For Children and Their Grown-Up Friends, 302

Identification of the Gifted and Talented, The, 474

Identity and the Life Cycle, 301

Images of Childhood: An Illustrated Social History, 70

Imitation in Children, 61

Incredible Year-Round Playbook, The, 242

Infancy and Caregiving, 271

Infant and Child Care: A Guide to Education in Group Settings, 270

Infant Care, 33

Infant Caregiving: A Design for Training, 26, 263

Infant Center, The, 272

Infant Development Guide: You and Your Baby: The First Wondrous Year, 23

Infant Feeding and Feeding Difficulties, 216

Infant Nutrition (Fomon), 213

Infant Nutrition (Merritt), 217

Infantoddler Parenting: Activities for Child with Adult, 152, 245

Infants: Their Social Environments, 35

Infants and Mothers: Differences in Development, 19

Infant/Toddler: Introducing Your Child to the Joy of Learning, 236

Inner City Child, 320

In Praise of Diversity: A Resource Book for Multicultural Education, 419

In Praise of Diversity: Multicultural Classroom Applications, 420

In Search of Myself and Other Children, 146

Interracial Digest, 489

In the Early World: Discovering Art Through Crafts, 389

Introducing Books to Children, 348

Introducing the Young Child to the Social World, 73

Introduction to Early Childhood Education, 307

I Saw a Purple Cow and 100 Other Recipes for Learning, 238

I Think I Saw a Snail, 360

Jane Brody's Nutrition Book: A Lifetime Guide to Good Eating for Better Health and Weight Control, 211

"*Johnny's such a Bright Boy, What a Shame He's Retarded*": In Support of Mainstreaming in Public Schools, 448

Joint Custody and Co-Parenting
    Handbook, 92
Just Look: A Book about Paintings, 382

Kamen Plan for Nutrition During
    Pregnancy, The, 27
Kids Day In and Day Out: A Parents
    Manual, 128
Kids Having Kids: The Unwed Teenage
    Parent, 126
Kid-Slimming Book, The, 212
Kindergarten, The: Its Encounter with
    Educational thought in America,
    326
Kindergarten and Early Schooling, 299
Kindergarten Child and Reading, The,
    316
Kindergarten Minute by Minute, 296
Kits for Kids, 237
K-3 Teacher's Classroom Almanac: A
    Treasury of Learning Activities and
    Games, 242

Labeling the Mentally Retarded: Clinical
    and Social System Perspectives on
    Mental Retardation, 467
Labor and Birth: A Guide for You, 35
Language Acquisition, 58
Language and Cultural Diversity in
    American Education, 413
Language and Learning Disorders of the
    Pre-Academic Child: With
    Curriculum Guide, 459
Language and the Discovery of Reality,
    56
Language Development in a Bilingual
    Setting, 423
Language Disorders of Children: Bases
    and Diagnoses, 459
Language in Early Childhood Education,
    56, 297
Lean Out the Window: An Anthology of

Modern Poetry, 359
Leap To the Sun, 401
Learning Can Be Child's Play: How
    Parents Can Help Slower-than-
    Average Preschool Children Learn
    and Develop Through Play
    Experiences, 244
Learning Can Be Fun: A Learning Center
    Approach to Creative Activities,
    384
Learning Disabilities: A Family Affair,
    453
Learning Disabilities Glossary, 454
Learning Disability: The Unrealized
    Potential, 454
Learning Games: Through Games-
    Objective Based, 313
Learning Games for the First Three
    Years: A Guide to Parent-Child
    Play, 248
Learning Through Play, 243
Learning Together and Alone:
    Cooperation, Competition, and
    Individualization, 308
Learning to Love Literature (Preschool
    Through Grade 3), 354
Learning to Say Goodbye: When a Parent
    Dies, 146
Let Me Do It, 320
Let's Look at Children II: A Guide to
    Theory and Classroom Observation,
    297
Liberated Parents—Liberated Children,
    135
Liberty Cap, The: A Catalogue for Non-
    Sexist Materials for Children, 488
Life Among the Giants: A Child's-eye
    View of the Grown-up World, 165
Like It Is: Facts and Feelings About
    Handicaps from Kids Who Know,
    439
Listen! And Help Tell the Story, 347

Listen, Children, Listen: An Anthology of Poems for the Very Young, 361
Listen Children: An Anthology of Black Literature, 358
Literature and the Child, 349
Literature for Young Children, 351
Little Book of Baby Foods, The, 211
Little Book of Little Beasts, A, 360
Little Darlings, The, 56
Little Miss Muffet Fights Back, 490
Little Raccoon and Poems from the Woods, 361
Living with Children: New Methods for Parents and Teachers, 153
Longitudinal Follow-Up of the Ypsilanti-Carnegie Infant Education Project, 269
Lucile Panaboker's Song Book, 400

Magical Child, 154
Magic of Puppetry, The: A Guide for Those Working with Young Children, 397
Magic Years, The, 59
Mainstreaming and the Minority Child, 447
Mainstreaming Preschoolers: Children with Visual Handicaps, 462
Make a Circle, Keep Us In: Poems for a Good Day, 358
Making It as a Stepparent: New Roles, New Rules, 89
Making Puppets Come Alive: A Method of Learning and Teaching Hand Puppetry, 393
Making Schools Work: A Reporter's Journey Through Some of America's Most Remarkable Classrooms, 296
Making Things: The Hand Book of Creative Discovery, 389
Management of Brain-Damaged Children: A Parent's and Teacher's Guide, 440
Manual for Baby-sitters, A, 118
Maternal and Child Nutrition, 222
Maternal-Infant Bonding, 28
Maternal Nutrition, 30
Maternal Nutrition and Child Health, 222
Maximizing Young Children's Potential: A Non-sexist Manual for Early Childhood Trainers, 490
Mayo Clinic Diet Manual: A Handbook of Dietary Practices, 217
Meaningful Movement for Children: A Developmental Theme Approach to Physical Education, 395
Medical Choices, Medical Chances: How Patients, Families and Physicians Can Cope with Uncertainty, 181
Medical Dimensions of Mental Retardation, 467
Mental Retardation: Nursing Approaches to Care, 465
Mental Retardation: The Developing Child, 466
Mexican Americans in School: A Decade of Change, 415
Mexican Americans in School: A History of Educational Neglect, 415
Mind in Society: The Development of Higher Psychological Processes, 73
Mindstorms: Children, Computers and Powerful Ideas, 317
Momma, The Source Book for Single Mothers, 94
Montessori and Your Child: A Primer for Parents, 243
Montessori Method, The, 315
Moral Stages and the Idea of Justice: Essays on Moral Development, 64
More than Graham Crackers: Nutrition Education and Food Preparation with Young Children, 225

*Mother Care: Helping Yourself through
    the Emotional and Physical
    Transition of New Motherhood,* 132
Mother-Child Cookbook, The, 213
Mother Knot, The, 144
Mother Love: Myth and Reality, 123
Mother Person, The, 124
Mother's Almanac, The, 141
*Mother's and Father's Medical
    Encyclopedia, The,* 194
Mothers' Book, The: Shared Experiences,
    136
*Mother's Encyclopedia and Everyday
    Guide to Family Health,* 193
*Mother to Mother Baby Care Book,
    The,* 158
Move It!, 462
*Movement and Educational Dance for
    Children,* 403
*Movement Education for Preschool
    Children,* 402
*Move with the Music: Songs and
    Learning Strategies for Young
    Children,* 390
Moving Learning Action Pack, 400
Mud, Sand, and Water, 307
Multi-Cultural Cookbook, 426
*Multicultural Education: Commitments,
    Issues, and Applications,* 420
*Multicultural Education, A Functional
    Bibliography for Teachers,* 419
Multicultural Education for Practitioners,
    417
*Multicultural Nonsexist Education: A
    Human Relations Approach,* 415
*Multiethnic Education: Theory and
    Practice,* 414
*Multimedia Approach to Children's
    Literature, A: A Selective List of
    Films, Filmstrips, and Recordings
    Based on Children's Books,* 351
Music, 396
Music: A Way of Life for the Young

Child, 391
Music Activities for Retarded Children,
    446
Music and Movement, 396
Music and Movement Improvisation,
    404
*Music Book, The Kindergarten Teacher's
    Reference Book,* 391
Music for the Exceptional Child, 446
Music for the Handicapped Child, 444
Music for Young Children, 400
*Music Improvisation as a Classroom
    Method: A New Approach to
    Teaching Music,* 397
Music in Our Lives: The Early Years,
    399
Myself and Others, 413

Natural Childbirth the Swiss Way, 30
*Natural Parenthood: Raising Your Child
    Without a Script,* 146
*Natural Snack Cookbook, The: 151
    Good Things to Eat,* 220
*Natural Way to Raise a Healthy Child,
    The,* 178
*Near the Window Tree: Poems and
    Notes,* 360
Newborn Beauty, 24
*New Extended Family, The: Day Care
    That Works,* 86, 270
*New-Fashioned Parent: How to Make
    Your Family Style Work, The,* 89
*New Frontiers: A Bilingual Early
    Learning Program/Nuevas
    Fronteras: Un programa de
    aprendizaje bilingue para niños,*
    417
*New Pregnancy: The Active Woman's
    Guide to Work, Legal Rights,
    Health Care, Travel, Sports, Dress,
    Sex, and Emotional Well-Being,
    The,* 29
9 Months, 1 Day, 1 Year: A Guide to

Pregnancy, Birth, and Babycare, 31
*No Easy Answers: The Learning
    Disabled Child at Home and at
    School*, 456
*No-Nonsense Nutrition for Your Baby's
    First Year*, 214
Non-Sexist Childraising, 488
*Non-Sexist Education for Young
    Children: A Practical Guide*, 492
*Normality and Pathology in Childhood:
    Assessments of Development*, 60
*Not All Little Wagons Are Red: The
    Exceptional Child's Early Years*,
    455
*Notes from a Different Drummer: A
    Guide to Juvenile Fiction Portraying
    the Handicapped*, 346, 445
Not for the Poor Alone, 95
Nourishing Your Unborn Child, 36
*Now I Have a Stepparent and It's Kind
    of Confusing*, 102
*Now Upon a Time: A Contemporary
    View of Children's Literature*, 491
Now We Are Six, 361
*Nursery Years: The Mind of the Child
    from Birth to Six Years, The*, 63
Nutrition, 218
*Nutrition: Principles and Application in
    Health Promotion*, 224
Nutrition and Learning, 214
Nutrition Education for Young Children,
    225
Nutrition for the Childbearing Year, 24
Nutrition for the Growing Years, 217
*Nutrition Guide to Brand Name Baby
    Foods*, 223
Nutrition in Health and Disease, 218
Nutrition in Infancy and Childhood, 220

Observational Strategies for Child Study,
    62
*Observing and Recording the Behavior of
    Young Children*, 57

Oh, Boy! Babies!, 26
On Becoming a Family, 90
*On Becoming a Family: The Growth of
    Attachment*, 20
On Being Gifted, 469
One at a Time, 361
132 Gift Crafts Kids Can Make, 385
127 Anytime Crafts Kids Can Make,
    386
Oneness and Separateness, 63
*Oneness and Separateness, From Infant
    to Individual*, 141
On "How Do Your Children Grow?,"
    147
*On Learning to Read: The Child's
    Fascination with Meaning*, 296
*Open Family Series: For Parents and
    Children Together*, 159
*Open for Children: For Those Interested
    in Early Childhood Education*, 299
*Open Framework, An/Un Marco
    Abierto*, 420
*Opening Doors for Preschool Children
    and Their Parents*, 344
Origins of Behavior, The. Vol. 1, *The
    Effect of the Infant on Its Caregiver*,
    29
*Origins of Fear. The Origins of
    Behavior, The*, 66
*Origins of Human Competence, The: The
    Final Report of the Harvard
    Preschool Project*, 163
*Origins of Intelligence: Infancy and Early
    Childhood*, 65
Origins of Intelligence in Children, The,
    68
Ourselves and Our Children, 126
*Our Special Child: A Guide to Successful
    Parenting of Handicapped
    Children*, 456
*Out of the Minds of Babes: The Strength
    of Children's Feelings*, 74
Oxford Nursery Rhyme Book, The, 362

Pablum, Parents, and Pandemonium: Glimpses of a Pediatrician's World, 195

Paper Presented at the New York State Conference on Parenting, 1977, 86

Paraprofessional's Handbook, The: A Guide for the Teacher-Aide, 316

Parent Awareness Training: Positive Parenting for the 1980s, 145

Parent Effectiveness, 138

Parenting, 149

Parenting: A Skills Training Manual, 138

Parenting Advisor, The, 128, 212

Parenting in an Unresponsive Society. Managing Work and Family, 274

Parent Involvement in Early Childhood Education, 140

Parenting the Gifted: Developing the Promise, 475

Parents After Thirty: A Guide to Making the Right Decision, Having a Healthy Pregnancy and Normal Baby, and Raising a Well-Adjusted Child When you Are Over Thirty Years Old, 141

Parents and Preschool, 278

Parents and the Achieving Child, 127

Parents Are People, Too, 143

Parents Are Teachers: A Child Management Program, 125

Parents as Partners in Education: The School and Home Working Together, 125

Parents as Playmates, 244

Parents Book about Divorce, The, 93

Parent's Book of Physical Fitness for Children from Infancy Through Adolescence, The, 190

Parent's Guide to Children's Reading, A, 355

Parent's Guide to Child Therapy, A, 127

Parent's Guide to Good Nutrition, A: Growing Up Healthy, 225

Parent's Guide to Intelligence Testing, A: How to Help Your Children's Intellectual Development, 137

Parent's Guide to the First Three Years, A, 163

Parent's Guide to the Shy Child, A: Overcoming and Preventing Shyness from Infancy to Adulthood, 165

Parent's Medical Manual, The, 179

Parents on the Team, 441

Parent's When-Not-to-Worry Book, The: Straight Talk About All Those Myths You've Learned from Your Parents, Friends—and Even Doctors, 179

Parent Test, The: How to Measure and Develop Your Talent for Parenthood, 154

Partners in Language: A Guide for Parents/Companeros En El Idioma: Guia para Les Padres, 413

Partners in Play: A Step-by-Step Guide to Imaginative Play in Children, 247

Pediatric Basics, 199

Pediatric Infectious Diseases, 192

Pediatric Nutrition in Development Disorders, 219

Peoplemaking, 80, 81

People's Pharmacy-2, The, 186

Personnel Management in Recreation and Leisure Services, 272

Perspectives on Non-Sexist Early Childhood Education, 492

Phonological Disability in Children, 460

Physical Knowledge in Preschool Education: Implications of Piaget's

Theory, 309

Piaget, Children and Numbers, 309

Piaget for Teachers, 60

Piaget's Theory: A Primer, 68

Piaget's Theory of Intellectual Development, 61

Picture Books for Children, 348

Piggle, The: An Account of the Psychoanalytic Treatment of a Little Girl, 250

Planning and Administering Early Childhood Programs, 269

Play, 239

Play: Anthropological Perspectives, 246

Play: Children's Business, 240, 243

Play, Dreams, and Imitation in Childhood, 245

Play and Culture, 247

Play and Development: A Symposium, 246

Play as a Learning Medium, 248

Play as Development, 237

Playful Parenting: Games to Help Your Infants and Toddlers Grow Physically, 239

Playgroup Book, The, 249

Play in Childhood, 242

Playing, Living, Learning: A World-Wide Perspective on Children's Opportunities to Play, 249

Playing and Reality, 250

Play Therapy, 235

Pleasure of Their Company, The: How to Have More Fun with Your Children, 140

Plug-In Drug, The, 508

Pocketful of Rhymes, A, 361

Power of Play, The, 238

Practical Guide to Early Childhood Curriculum, A, 301

Pregnancy: the Psychological Experience, 22

Pregnancy and Childbirth: The Complete Guide for a New Life, 26

Pregnant Is Beautiful: The Complete Body Conditioning Program for Pregnant Women and New Mothers, 21

Preparing Young Children for Math: A Book of Games, 327

Preparing Your Preschooler for Reading: A Book of Games, 323

Pre-School Education for the Handicapped, 449

Preschool Programming of Children with Disabilities, 449

Pre-School Story Hour, The, 355

Preventing Tooth Decay: A Guide for Implementing Self-Applied Fluorides in School Settings, 188

Primary Health Care of the Young, 185

Principles of Childhood Language Disabilities, 461

Prisoners of Childhood, 475

Process of Child Development, The, 68

Profession and Practice of Program Evaluation, The, 268, 295

Program for English Experiences, 419

Program Guide for Infants and Toddlers with Neuromotor and Other Developmental Disabilities, 445

Programming for Very Young Children, 344

Promise and Performance: ACT's Guide to TV Programming for Children. Vol. 1, Children with Special Needs, 505

Promise and Performance: ACT's Guide to TV Programming for Children. Vol. 2, The Arts, 505

Promise and Performance: ACT's Guide to TV Programming for Children. Vol. 4, The Sciences, 506

Promoting the Health of Children: A Guide for Caretakers and Health Care Professionals, 194

Psychoanalysis of Children, The, 241

Psychological Aspects of Learning Disabilities and Reading Disorders, 455

Psychological Birth of the Human Infant: Symbiosis and Individuation, The, 30

Psychological Emergencies of Childhood, 142, 189

Psychological Modeling: Conflicting Theories, 54

Psychological Testing, 54

Psychology and Education of the Gifted, 470

Psychology of Children's Art, The, 387

Psychology of Deafness, The, 463

Psychology of Play, The, 244

Psychology of Sex Differences, The, 66, 490

Psychosocial Aspects of Pediatric Care, 186

Psychotherapy with Children: The Living Relationship, 245

Puppet Book, The, 395

Puppet Corner in Every Library, A, 401

Puppet Fun: Performance, Production and Plays, 398

Puppet Theatre Handbook, The, 390

Raising Readers: A Guide to Sharing Literature with Young Children, 144, 354

Raising the Young Blind Child: A Guide for Parents and Educators, 463

Reader's Guide for Parents of Children with Mental, Physical, or Emotional Disabilities, A, 452

Readings in Moral Education, 70

Reading Without Nonsense, 323

REAL Food for Your Baby, 221

Recipe for Reading: A Proven Program for Reading, Writing and Spelling, 325

Recreation Programming for Visually Impaired Children and Youth, 463

Re-Marriage: A Guide for Singles, Couples, and Families, 97

Reminiscences of Edmund Evans, The, 350

Remote Control: Television and the Manipulation of American Life, 507

Reproduction of Mothering, The Psychoanalysis and the Sociology of Gender, 129

Resource for Parents of Children with Cancer, A, 218

Resource List for Adults of Materials to Use with the Very Young Child (Up to Age Three), 357

Resources for Creative Teaching in Early Childhood, Education, 302, 304

Resources for Gifted Children in the New York Area, 472

Resource Teacher, The: A Guide to Effective Practices, 451

Responsible Parenthood: The Child's Psyche Through the Six-Year Pregnancy, 63

Retarded Child from Birth to Five, The: A Multidisciplinary Program for the Family and Child, 466

Rhythm Band Book, The, 393

Right Book for the Right Situation—for Parents, Teachers, Librarians, and Other People, The, 350

Right from the Start: A Guide to Nonsexist Child Rearing, 489

Right from the Start: Meeting the Challenges of Mothering Your Unborn and Newborn Baby, 20

Rights of the Pregnant Parent, The, 22

Ring a Ring o'Roses: Stories, Games and Fingerplays for Preschool Children, 362

Robert's Nutrition Work with Children, 211

Role of the Father in Child Development, The, 144

Role of the Special Education Paraprofessional, The, 451

Roots of Caring, Sharing and Helping: The Development of Presocial Behavior in Children, 67

Run, Computer, Run: The Methodology of Educational Innovation, 163

Schizophrenia: Symptoms, Causes, Treatment, 468

School Power: Implications of an Intervention Project, 300

Schools and Parents-Partners in Sex Education, 137

Science and Politics of IQ, The, 63

Science Experiences for the Early Childhood Years, 305

Science with Young Children, 308

Seeds of Movement: Philosophy of Movement with Techniques Applied to the Beginner, 397

See How They Run: Suzy Prudden's Running Book for Kids, 194

Seizures, Epilepsy, and Your Child: A Handbook for Parents, Teachers, and Epileptics of All Ages, 454

Selecting Material for Children with Special Needs, 344

Selecting Media for Learning: Readings from Audio Visual Instruction, 503

Self-Esteem: The Key to Your Child's Well-Being, 90, 130

Self-Portrait of a Family, 89

Sensuous Child, The: Your Child's Birthright to Healthy Sexual Development, 162

Sentences Children Use, 314

Sex and Identity, 491

Sex-role Cycle, The: Socialization from Infancy to Old Age, 491

Sex Roles: A Research Bibliography, 487

Sex Role Socialization and Sex Discrimination: A Synthesis and Critique of the Literature, 492

Sex-role Socialization in Picture Books for Preschool Children, 492

Sexual Assault of Children and Adolescents, 90

Sexual Enlightenment of Children, The, 136

Shady Hill School, The: The First Fifty Years, 327

Sharing Sounds: Musical Experiences with Young Children, 393

Shopping Cart Art, 389

Should the Children Know? Encounters with Death in the Lives of Children, 156

Show and Tell Machine, The, 505

Sigh of Relief, A: The First Aid Handbook for Childhood Emergencies, 186

Silent Children, The: A Parent's Guide to the Prevention of Child Sexual Abuse, 101

Silver Burdett Music: Teacher's Editions, Early Childhood, 390

Silver Burdett Music for Special Education, 446

Simple Folk Instruments to Make to Play, 396

Singing and Dancing Games for the Very Young, 400

Single Parenting: A Practical Resource Guide, 89

Six Practical Lessons for an Easier
Childbirth, 18

Smart Toys: For Babies from Birth to
Two, 237

Snips and Snails and Walnut Whales:
Nature Crafts for Children, 382

Social and Personality Development in
Childhood, 58

Social Cognition and the Acquisition of
Self, 65

Social Cognitive Development: Frontiers
and Possible Futures, 59

Social Development: Psychological
Growth and the Parent-Child
Relationship, 66

Social Development in Young Children,
63

Socialization and Personality
Development, 75

Social Learning Theory, 55

Society's Child: Nutrition in Children,
Diet, and Disorders, 226

Somewhere to Turn: Strategies for
Parents of the Gifted and Talented,
473

Sooner or Later: The Timing of Parenthood in Adult Lives, 132

Sounds of Children, The, 75

Sound/Symbol Activities: Kit A
Decoding Activities: Kit B, 302

Sourcebook on Food and Nutrition, 221

So You're Going to Run a Day Care
Service!, 272

Space Where Anything Can Happen, A,
405

Speak Up for Your Child's Health, 195

Special Child Handbook, The, 452

Special Delivery: The Complete Guide to
Informed Birth, 18

Special Needs: Special Answers, A
Resource of Reproductable Exercise
and Activities for Special Education

and Early Childhood Programs,
449

Special Needs and Services, 267

Special Student, The: Practical Help for
the Classroom Teacher, 297

Speech Pathology: An Introduction, 460

Spiritual Midwifery, 24

Start Early for an Early Start: You and
the Young Child, 353

Step-by-Step Guide for Retarded Infants
and Children, A, 466

Step-Families: A Cooperative Responsibility, 128

Step-Families: A Guide to Working with
Stepparents and Stepchildren, 103

Steven Caney's Play Book, 237

Story Programs: A Source Book of
Materials, 356

Storytelling: Art and Technique, 345

Strategies for Identifying Words, 301

Strengths of Black Families, The, 421

Stress and Burnout in the Human Service
Professions, 184

Student Teacher's Handbook, The: A
Step-by-Step Guide Through the
Term, 321

Study of Play: Problems and Prospects,
242

Success and Understanding, 68

Successful Children's Parties, 164

Successful Treatment of Stuttering, 461

Superkids: Creative Learning Activities
for Children 5–15, 243

Super Tips for Storytelling, 356

Supertot: Creative Learning Activities
for Children One to Three and
Sympathetic Advice for their
Parents, 243

Supporting the Changing Family: A
Guide To the Parent-to-Parent
Model, 155

Surviving the Breakup: How Children

and Parents Cope with Divorce, 103

Surviving with Kids: A Lifeline for Overwhelmed Parents, 124

Systematic Parent Training: Procedures, Cases, and Issues, 150

Talking About Death: A Dialogue Between Parent and Child, 138

Talking About Divorce and Separation: A Dialogue Between Parent and Child, 93

Talking with a Child, 164

Talk to the Deaf, 464

Take Care of Yourself: A Consumer's Guide To Medical Care, 199

Taking Care of Your Child: A Parent's Guide to Medical Care, 193

Taming of the C.A.N.D.Y. Monster, The, 216

Teacher in America, 296

Teachers and Parents: A Guide to Interaction and Cooperation, 321

Teacher's Arts and Crafts Almanack, 385

Teachers of Young Children, 306

Teacher's Practical Guide for Educating Young Children: A Growing Program, 305

Teaching and Learning in the Elementary School, 308

Teaching as a Conserving Activity, 319

Teaching Children to Love Themselves: A Handbook for Parents and Teachers of Young Children, 142

Teaching Children with Learning and Behavior Problems, 453

Teaching Creative Behavior, 476

Teaching Creative Behavior: How to Teach Creativity to Children of All Ages, 322

Teaching Ethnic Awareness: Methods and Materials for the Elementary School, 421

Teaching in a Multicultural Society: Perspectives and Professional Strategies, 417

Teaching in the Early Years, 324

Teaching Parents to Teach: Education for the Handicapped, 448

Teaching Practices: Reexamining Assumptions, 324

Teaching Preschool Reading, 139

Teaching Reading as Concept Development: Emphasis on Affecting Thinking, 306

Teaching Reading Comprehension, 316

Teaching Social Studies to Culturally Different Children, 414

Teaching Television: How to Use TV to Your Child's Advantage, 507

Teaching the Bilingual: New Methods and Old Traditions, 423

Teaching the Gifted Child, 472

Teaching the Retarded Child: A Developmental Approach, 466

Teaching the Three Rs Through Movement Experiences, 394

Teaching Through Encouragement: Techniques to Help Students Learn, 314

Teaching Under Pressure, 304

Teaching Young Children at School and Home, 314

Teaching Young Children with Special Needs, 456

Teaching Your Own Pre-School Children, 148

Teaching Your Wings to Fly: The Nonspecialist Guide to Movement Activities for Young Children, 390

Teach Your Baby Math, 300

Teeth, Teeth, Teeth, 185

Television: The Business Behind the Box, 504

Television's Awareness Training: The Viewer's Guide for Family and Community, 506

Telling Stories Through Movement, 392

Tell It Again: An Integrated Approach to Sharing Literature with Young Children, 352

Temperament and Development, 161

Ten-Minute Field Trips, 320

Testing the Gifted Child: An Interpretation in Lay Language, 471

Test Your Child's I.Q., 158

Thank You, Dr. Lamaze: A Mother's Experience in Painless Childbirth, 27

Theory and Practice of Early Reading, 319

Thinking Games 1, 235

Thinking Is Child's Play, 158, 232, 247

Think of Something Quiet, A Guide for Achieving Serenity in Early Childhood Classrooms, 298

Third R, The: Towards A Numerate Society, 303

Thought and Language, 73

Three Babies: Biographies of Cognitive Development, 57, 130

Three Theories of Child Development, 67

Time of Transition: The Growth of Families Headed by Women, 100

Tirra Lirra: Rhymes Old and New, 362

Toddler and the New Baby, The, 130

Toddlers and Parents: A Declaration of Independence, 55, 90

Toilet Learning, 149

To Love a Baby, 140

To Move to Learn, 406

Tools for Learning, Activities for Young Children with Special Needs, 448

Totalaction: Ideas and Activities for

Teaching Children Ages Five to Eight, 389

Total Learning for the Whole Child: Holistic Curriculum for Children Ages 2 to 5, 306

Toys, Play and Discipline in Childhood, 249

Toys and Playthings in Development and Remediation, 245

Traveling Games for Babies: A Handbook of Games for Infants to Five Years Old, 239

TV On/Off: Better Family Use of Television, 504

Two-Career Couple, 139

200 Years of Children, 187

Two Worlds of Childhood: U.S. and U.S.S.R., 56, 236

Uncommon Child, The: The Genesis of Behavior, 467

Uncomplicated Guide to Becoming a Super-Parent, An, 164

Under Five in Britain, 268

Understanding Children's Play, 240

Understanding Piaget, 69

Understanding Your Child From Birth to Three, 57, 129

Undoing Sex Stereotypes: Research and Resources for Educators, 489

Unexpected Minority: Handicapped Children in America, The, 458

Unspoken Language of Children, The, 72

Up Against the Clock: Career Women Speak on the Choice to Have Children, 134

Uses of Enchantment: The Meaning and Importance of Fairy Tales, The, 346

Using Instructional Media, 506

Using Literature in the English Classroom, 357

Vegetarian Baby, The: A Sensible Guide for Parents, 226

Very Young, The: Guiding Children from Infancy Through the Early Years, 150

Very Young Verses, 359

Vicki Lansky's Best Practical Parenting Tips, 144

Violence and the Family, 98

Violence and the Media, 503

Visual Handicaps in Children, 197

Vocabulary Builder, for Teaching Basic Second-Language Skills in Six Different Languages, The, 418

Vocabulary of First-Grade Children, The, 315

Watching Television: A Practical Guide for Practically Everybody, 504

Weaving Without a Loom, 388

Weekend Fathers: For Divorced Fathers, Second Wives and Grandparents—Solutions to the Problems of Child Custody, Child Support, Alimony and Property Settlements, 159

Wee Sing and Play: Children's Songs and Fingerplays, 391

Welcome Baby: A Guide to the First Six Weeks, 152

What Did I Write?, 298

What Every Child Needs, 153

What Every Child Would Like Parents to Know About Divorce, 100

What Every Pregnant Woman Should Know. The Truth About Diet and Drugs in Pregnancy, 20

What's Going to Happen to Me? When Parents Separate or Divorce, 147

What Shall We Do and Allee Galloo!, 405

What To Do When You Think You Can't Have a Baby. Based on the Clinical Experience of More than Thirty Infertility Specialists, 36

What to Tell Your Child About Sex, 129

What We REALLY Know about Child Rearing: Science in Support of Effective Parenting, 135

What You Should Know About Health Care Before You Call a Doctor, 189

When We Deal with Children: Selected Writings, 155

When Your Child Is Overweight, 217

Where Did I Come From?, 150

Whipping Boy, The, 469

White Teacher, 317

Who Cares for the Baby? Choices in Child Care, 271

Whole Child, The, 240

Whole Child, The: A Source Book, 123

Whole Child-Whole Parent, 125

Who's Who in Children's Books: A Treasure of the Familiar Characters of Childhood, 350

Who Will Raise the Children? New Options for Fathers (and Mothers), 147

Why Can't They Be Like Us? Facts and Fallacies About Ethnic Differences and Group Conflicts in America, 420

Why Raise Ugly Kids? Fulfill Your Child's Health and Happiness Potential, 189

"Why Was I Adopted?", 97

Why Your House May Endanger Your Health, 199

Womanly Art of Breastfeeding, The, 28, 215

Women: Sex and Sexuality, 160

Women and Child Care in China: A Firsthand Report, 71

Women as Mothers, 141

Women Confined: Toward a Sociology
    of Childbirth, 33
Women of Crisis: Lives of Struggle and
    Hope, 131
Working Mothers, 131
Working Mother's Guide to Child
    Development, A, 156
Working Parents: How to Be Happy with
    Your Children, 267
Workjobs: Activity-Centered Learning
    for Early Childhood Education, 313
World of Grown-Ups: Children's
    Conceptions of Society, The, 60
World of the Gifted Child, The, 476
World of Words, The: Writings by Bank
    Street College Faculty, 326
Writing for Young Children, 312

Years Before School, The: Guiding
    Preschool Children, 324
Yoga for Your Children, 191
You and Me Heritage Tree, The, 383
You and Your Pediatrician: Common
    Childhood Problems, 178
You and Your Toddler: Sharing The
    Developing Years, 148
You Can Breastfeed Your Baby . . .
    Even in Special Situations, 21
Young Child as Person, The: Toward the
    Development of a Healthy

Conscience, 323
Young Children Grow Up: The Effects of
    the Perry Preschool Program on
    Youths Through Age Fifteen, 277
Young Children in Action, 273
Young Children in Action: A Manual
    for Preschool Educators, 307
Your Baby and Child, From Birth to Age
    Five, 28, 145
Your Baby's Mind and How It Grows:
    Piaget's Theory for Parents, 69
Your Child Can Be a Super Reader, 310
Your Child Is a Person: A Psychological
    Approach to Parenthood Without
    Guilt, 128
Your Child's Ears, Nose and Throat: A
    Parent's Medical Guide, 182
Your Child's Self-Esteem, 126
Your Child's Teeth: A Parent's Guide to
    Making and Keeping Them Perfect,
    192
Your Gifted Child and You, 474
Your Inner Child of the Past, 151
Your One Year Old: The Fun-Loving
    Fussy 12-to-24 Month-Old, 54
Your Second Child, 162
Ypsilanti Perry Preschool Project, The:
    Preschool Years and Longitudinal
    Results Through Fourth Grade,
    326

Subject Index

Action for Children's Television
(ACT), 497
Amniocentesis, 4
Art(s), 367–406
children's drawings, 371
introducing children to, 367–368
materials for preschoolers, 372
music, 369–370
visual, and young children,
371–372
Attachment, of infants to parents,
48, 49
Autonomy vs. shame and doubt,
50
Baby. See Infant
Battered-child syndrome, 110
Behaviorism, 42
"Big Blue Marble, The," 498
Birthing rooms, 5
Bottle feeding, 203
Breast feeding, 203
Caesarean section
father in attendance at, 5
high incidence of, 4
Caretaker, attributes of good,
258–259
Child abuse, 87–88
efforts to protect against, 87
as parent-child dysfunction, 110
treatment of, 87
Childbirth, 3–7
alternatives to traditional
methods of, 5

and bonding, 5
and change in parents' lifestyle,
108
family-centered approach to, 5
father's role in, 5
at home, 6
Leboyer method of, 5, 6
natural, 4
and nurse midwives, 6
premature, 3
preparation for, 4
questionable medical procedures
in, 4
Child care, 255–279. See also Day
care centers
informal arrangement for, 256
issues in deciding upon type of,
259–260
management of programs for,
261–265
national commitment to,
256–257
solution to problems of, 256–257
Child development, 38–75
age five, 41
attachment of infant to parent
in, 48, 49
capacities of newborn, 39–41
Erikson's first stage of, 48
identification with family, 49
language, 44–48
nature vs. nurture in, 43
theories of, 42

Children's books
    history of, 336
    picture books, 334–337
    in public library, 335–337
Cognition, 42
Cognitive development
    Piaget's theories of, 51
    preoperational stage, 51
    symbolic thought, 51
Communication, between parent
        and child, 111
Cooking, with children, 206–207
Creative drama, 373–375
    criteria for successful, 374
    definition of, 373
    guidelines for, 374–375
    puppets in, 375
    values of, 373–374
Dance, children's, 376–379
    definition of, 376
    importance of, 377
    learning spatial concepts
        through, 377
    self expression through, 376
Day care centers
    limitations of, 85
    managing, 261–265
    quality of infant care in, 14–17
    and women's social equality,
        289–290
Death, dealing with, 115–116
Disabled children, dealing with
        special needs of, 432–435
Discipline, 117–118
    meaning of, 121–122
Displaced family, 110
Down's syndrome, 430
Drawings, meaning of children's,
        371
Drug abuse, dealing with, 109, 110
Early childhood education
    criteria for selecting, 292–294

effects of, on child, 293
history of, 290–291
Montessori method of, 291
nonsexist, 483–485
reading in, 286–288
selecting, program, 291–294
as social reform vehicle, 289
values communicated in,
    292–293
and women's roles, 289
Education for All Handicapped
        Children's Act (Public Law
        94–142), 176
"Electric Company, The," 283
Emotions
    communicating, between
        parent and child, 259
    and intellectual development, 43
Environment, in child develop-
        ment, 43
Erikson, Erik, developmental
        stages of
    autonomy *vs.* shame and doubt,
        49
    initiative, 52
    trust vs. mistrust, 48
Ethnocentrism, 50
Family, 82–104
    changes in structure of, 255
    child abuse in, 110
    and disabled or handicapped
        child, 435
    dealing with death in, 115–116
    displaced, 110
    drug abuse in, 110
    functions of, 83
    jealousy in, 116–117
    non-sexist education in, 482–483
    nuclear, 82
    preserving, 85–86
    problems in, 110
    sex education in, 111–112

sibling rivalry in, 116–117
single-parent, 81, 111
step, 111
working mothers in, 84, 111
Fears, in children, 113–114
Fetus
  monitoring of, 4
  stages of development of, 8–9
  stress testing of, 4
  surgery on, 3
Film
  evaluation of, with children,
    501
  as learning medium, 500–502
Finger foods, introduction of, 17
Fireside education, 290
Five year old, 41–42
  awareness of other's feelings
    by, 41–42
  social cognition in, 41
Gifted children, 436–438
  encouraging, 437
  optimum environment for, 436
Handicapped children, dealing
    with problems of, 432–435
Head start, 289
Health, 169–199
  advances in providing care, 173
  advocacy in promoting, 171
  care of infant, 170–171
  definition of, 169
    of American Academy of
      Pediatrics, 177
  delivery systems, 171
  improving care, 174
  new directions in child care,
    176–177
  preventive medicine, 176
  teaching child about, 169
  vaccinations, 170–171
  visiting health-care practitioner,
    171

of woman during pregnancy,
  8–9
Holophrases, 44
Homebirths, 6
Hyperactivity, 209–210
Immunizations, 170–171
Infants
  ability to differentiate self from
    others, 12
  feeding of, 203–206
    breast, 203
    bottle, 203–204
    solid foods, 204–205
  first smile of, 40
  health care for, 170–171
  newborn
    capacities of, 9, 39–41
    effective environment of,
      9–12
    hearing in, 39
    imitation of adults by, 40
    learning by, 40
    sight in, 39
  reading to, 332–333
  stranger anxiety in, 49–50
Infant care, 12–13
  affectionate emotional-social
    climate, 15
  consistency and variety in,
    15–16
  in Day Care, 14–17
  individualized, 14–17
  quality principles for, 14–17
  responsive environment in, 16
  routines, development of
    competencies through,
    16–17
Intellectual development, 43
Jealousy, in siblings, 116–117
Kindergarten
  history of programs in, 290–291
  reading in, 284

Language
  oral, as foundation for reading,
    340
  peak language-learning years,
    338
Language development, 44-48
  early childhood curriculum for,
    286-288
  modeling in, 46-47
  nativist's theories of, 45, 46
  symbolic realism in, 47
Leboyer childbirth method, 5, 6
Linguistic realism, 47
Literature, 331-363
  introducing at home, 338-340
  loving, 331-333
  picture books, 334-337
  poetry, 341-343
Lullabies, 332
Management
  of child care programs, 261-265
  humanistic approach to,
    259-261
  leadership in, 263
  and motivation, 263
  organizational style of, 262
  team approach to, 264-265
Masturbation, 122
Maternity Center Association
  (New York City), 6
Media, definition of, 497
Media Center for Children, The,
  501
Midwives, 6
"Mister Rogers' Neighborhood,"
  498
Modeling, in language develop-
  ment, 46-47
Montessori programs, 291
Motherhood, as career, 84. *See also*
  Working mothers
Mothers of Twins Clubs, 119

Movement
  and dance, 376-379
  in music education, 369-370
Multicultural education (EMC),
  410
  books and materials for, 411
  staffing of, 410
Music, 369-370
  and movement, 369-370
Natural childbirth, 4
Negativism, in toddler, 51-52
Networks, for parents, 119
Newborn. *See* Infant(s), newborn
New York Public Library
    Resource and Information
    Center, The, 119
Nightmares, 122
Nuclear family, 82
Nurse-midwives, 6
Nursery rhymes, 332
Nutrition, 203-226
  children in kitchen, 206-207
  and hyperactivity, 209-210
  for infants, 203-205
    bottle feeding, 203
    breast feeding, 203
    and contact with mother, 203
    formula, 203-204
    solid foods, 204-205
    water, 204
  information about, 208-210
  meal planning, 206
  and obesity, 209
  and sugar, 210
  for toddler, 205-206
  vitamins, 209
Obesity, 209
Oral language, 340
Parenting, 107-165
  as art, 108-109
  as career, 84
  concerns of, 119-122

consistency in, 108
difficulty in defining, 107
and disabled or handicapped
    child, 435
goals of, 120–121
help for, 122
and media, 497
networks for, 119
nonsexist, 482–483
and parent's childhood, effect
    on, 258
preparation for, 4, 120
self-sacrifice in, 121
by single parent, 111
and sex education, 111–112
training for, 85
by working mother, 111
Parenting issues
coping with child's fears, 113
death, dealing with, 115–116
discipline, 117–118, 121–122
punishment, physical, 118
spoiling, 117–118
temper tantrums, 117
time for self, 121
toilet training, 114–115, 122
Parents, abusing, treatment of, 87
Parents Without Partners, 119
Pediatrician, 172
views of, 173–175
Piaget's cognitive development
    theory, 51
Picture books, 333, 334–337
Play, children's, 229–251
according to Piaget, 230
as avenue of personal
    expression, 229
Darwinian viewpoint of, 229
historical perspective on, 229
and John Dewey's theory,
    229–230
nature and function of, 229–232

in Puritan period, 229
role in individual development,
    230
and stress, coping with
    through, 231–232
trivial theory of, 229–230
universal imperative of,
    233–234
Poetry
misconceptions of, 341–342
reading aloud, 343
reading to children, 333
Pregnancy, 3–7
high risk, 3, 4
mother's help during, 8–9
stages of fetal development in,
    8–9
Prenatal development, 8–9
Preschool programs. *See also* Early
    childhood education
art materials for, 372
choosing, 291–294
concerns in, 289
in libraries, 337
nonsexist education in, 483–485
reading in, 286–287
Quickening, 8
Race
child's awareness of, 409
parent's role in healthy
    education about, 411
Reading
aloud to children, 332, 335
difficulties with, 285
early childhood curriculum for,
    286–288
at home, 283–285, 338–340
in kindergarten, 284
learning over time, 283–285
in middle grades, 284
nursery rhymes and lullabies,
    332–333

Reading (*continued*)
  oral language as foundation
    for, 339
  picture books, 333
  poetry, 333, 341
  preschooler's experiences of,
    284
  in primary grades, 284
  printed language, early
    experiences with, 340
  progress in, 284–285
  "readiness" activities, 284
  skills for, acquired in early
    years, 338
  and television, 499–500
  work-related, 331
Rooming-in hospital facilities, 5
Schooling, 283–327
Security blankets, 122
"Self-righting" tendency of fetus,
  9
"Sesame Street," 283, 498
Sex education, 111–112
Sex-role education, 481, 482,
  484–485
Sibling rivalry, 116–117
Single-parent family, 82–83, 110,
  111
Social learning theory, 42–43
Solid foods, introducing to infant,
  204–205
Sonography, 4
Spoiling, 117–118
Step families, 110, 111
Stepparents, 110
Stranger anxiety, 49–50

Stress, coping with, through play,
  231–232
Stuttering, 122
Sugar, in diet, 210
Symbolic realism, 47
Television
  parents' responsibility
    regarding, 497
  positive use of, 498
  and reading, 499–500
  and social behavior, 498–499
Temper tantrums, 117
Test-tube babies, 3
Thumbsucking, 122
Toddlerhood
  autonomy in, 51
  feeding during, 205–206
  library programs for, 337
  negativism in, 51–52
Toilet training, 114–115, 122
Trust *vs.* mistrust (in Erikson's
  theories), 48, 50
Uncommonness, 429–431
  definition of, 429
  sources of, 429–431
Weaning, 122
"Well child care," 170–171
Word realism, 47
Working mothers, 110
  effect on children, 111
  increase of, 255–256
  reasons against, 85–86
  reasons for, 84
Vaccinations, 170–171
"Villa Allegre," 498
Vitamins, 209